Liberty, Wisdom, and Grace

APPLICATIONS OF POLITICAL THEORY

Series Editors: Harvey Mansfield, Harvard University, and Daniel J. Mahoney, Assumption College

This series encourages analysis of the applications of political theory to various domains of thought and action. Such analysis will include works on political thought and literature, statesmanship, American political thought, and contemporary political theory. The editors also anticipate and welcome examinations of the place of religion in public life and commentary on classic works of political philosophy.

Liberty, Wisdom, and Grace

Thomism and Democratic Political Theory

John P. Hittinger

LEXINGTON BOOKS
Lanham • Boulder • New York • Oxford

LEXINGTON BOOKS

Published in the United States of America
by Lexington Books
A Member of the Rowman & Littlefield Publishing Group
4720 Boston Way, Lanham, Maryland 20706

PO Box 317
Oxford
OX2 9RU, UK

British Library Cataloguing in Publication Information Available

Library of Congress Cataloging-in-Publication Data

Hittinger, John.
    Liberty, wisdom, and grace : Thomism and democratic political theory / John P.
Hittinger.
        p. cm. — (Applications of political theory)
    Includes bibliographical references and index.
    ISBN 0-7391-0411-X (cloth : alk. paper) — ISBN 0-7391-0412-8 (pbk. : alk.
paper)
        1. Democracy—Philosophy. 2. Religion and politics. 3. Liberalism. 4. Thomists.
I. Title. II. Series.

    JC423 .H66 2002
    320'.01—dc21   2002009875

Printed in the United States of America

♾ ™ The paper used in this publication meets the minimum requirements of
American National Standard for Information Sciences—Permanence of Paper for
Printed Library Materials, ANSI/NISO Z39.48-1992.

This Work is dedicated to the twelfth generation
Passing in the new world

Descended from Deacon Samuel Chapin (d. 1675)
Puritan and Founding Father of Springfield, Massachusetts
Philip Henry Pollard 1928–2001
Anne Pollard Hittinger 1927–1972
Willard Averell Pollard III, USN 1923–1954

"The mystic chords of memory, stretching from every battle-field,
and patriot grave, to every living heart and hearthstone,
all over this broad land, will yet swell the chorus of the Union,
when again touched, as surely they will be, by the better angels of
our nature"
—Abraham Lincoln, First Inaugural Address, 1861

Contents

Part III: Wisdom and Grace

~

Foreword: "The Very Graciousness of Being"

James V. Schall, S.J., Georgetown University

The phrase, "the very graciousness of being" (224) is taken from Marion Montgomery, a man who has been a quiet mentor and inspiration to many, including John Hittinger. In a fundamental sense, the phrase comes as close as anything to describe the purpose of this book. The phrase suggests that something more than a closed world exists—"the seemingly trivial acts of graciousness may do much to preserve the dignity of persons" (226). No deterministic theory either of natural or social science really accounts for such acts. In fact, it makes them impossible. And if there is more than a "closed" world, perhaps we can act in it. Yet, if we can act at all, we must be, indeed we would want to be, free and responsible. The world is not totally, or principally, defined by veils of ignorance, rights, or even duties, but by something beyond, call it sacrifice or love or generosity or, yes, graciousness. It is rooted in what Maritain, following Aquinas, once called the "superabundance" of being.[1] When Aquinas remarked that the world is created in mercy, not justice, we know something more is at work in our own world than our own world (I, 21, 4). "Et de plenitudine eius omnes accipimus, et gratiam pro gratia," as we read in the Prologue to John.

John Hittinger begins this book with an account of his family's own colonial background—"my ancestors came to this continent in the 17th century for religious liberty." Members of his family, several of whom are buried in Arlington Cemetery, fought in the Civil War; his father was killed in the Vietnam War. He recalls fondly his own teaching in various Catholic colleges, his professorship at the United States Air Force Academy. "It is my goal to receive and understand, engage and develop, and make available and pass along, the riches of these traditions" (xxi). This engaging, understanding, and passing along are precisely what goes on in this penetrating book.

This book is unique because Hittinger knows, almost as an underground occupation, that the best of classical and Catholic thought has not completely died out. It has continued, often vigorously, if not in the Catholic or secular universities, though sometimes there too, then at least by isolated individuals seeking the truth of things, often within groups like the American or Canadian or Italian Maritain Associations. If nothing else, this book is a guide to where that tradition is most alive. Hittinger affirms: "I consider myself ultimately a member of a tradition shaped by Thomas Aquinas. And it was through the reading of Jacques Maritain and Josef Pieper at Notre Dame that I first discovered the great adventure of liberal learning" (xxii). It is ever so, the preservation and growth of the deepest things usually commence with the unknown but attentive young student who chanced on the right book or teacher, whether it be at Notre Dame, Chicago, Oxford, Fordham, Dallas, Louisiana State, Christendom, or St. Mary's at Orchard Lake, where Hittinger himself is now located.

Hittinger ends the book with a chapter on Maritain's ideas on Church and State, with a special emphasis on the Vatican II document, *Gaudium et Spes* (*The Church in the Modern World*). This latter document, at the time intended in some sense symbolically to unite action and contemplation, intelligence and revelation, was presented to Pope Paul VI on December 8, 1965, by this same Jacques Maritain. Maritain was a French philosopher and diplomat, scholar and public intellectual. Though she only is mentioned in the last sentence of this vigorously argued book, Maritain's wife, Raïssa, and Maritain himself were among the most influential figures in intellectual life, not only in France and in the United States, but in the United Nations organization, in Germany, Latin America, Italy, Spain, and many other parts of the world.

We owe Maritain's coming to the United States to the fact that his wife was a Russian Jew. Though a convert, it was imperative that the Maritains leave France during its German occupation. The happy results of this exile are that Maritain taught in American universities and learned of the American way of life, which he praised in his *Reflections on America*, a book that the European left did not like. He ended his career at Princeton, before he finally returned to France after his wife's death. There in Toulouse, he became a member of the Brothers of Charles de Foucauld, among whom he died in 1973.

Fall of 1965 was the year I began to teach in Rome. I well recall being present in St. Peter's Square when the tall, white-haired figure of Jacques

Maritain came forward to be greeted affectionately by Paul VI, who had, earlier in his career, translated several of Maritain's works into Italian. It was a moving, touching moment. What strikes Hittinger in this book—he specifically mentions the episode in St. Peter's Square that I had witnessed at the time—is the irony of that scene. Just a few years later, Maritain published *The Peasant of the Garonne* in which, while not repudiating the work of the Council, he at least expressed considerable worry about the direction of these reforms in practice, a prophetic position that cost Maritain much popularity at the time and still does. This was the same Maritain who, in his earlier days, was considered a man "of the left" and perhaps, because of that, a remote cause of many of the confusions and problems that confronted the intellectual understanding of Christianity. One of the aims of this book is a proper understanding of Maritain. In this worthy endeavor, Hittinger is sympathetic but not uncritical.

The central figure of this book, then, is Jacques Maritain. He is central both because he discussed the issues of his day but also because he insisted on bringing up the issues that his day did not want to discuss. He is surrounded by a number of similar Catholic intellectuals, particularly Yves Simon and later Marion Montgomery, to both of whom Hittinger devotes an incisive chapter in this book. Beyond this purpose and in part because of it, Hittinger seeks to reestablish and deepen something that now seems obvious, namely, that Catholic philosophic thought was not, during the early and middle years of the twentieth century, in the disarray that many in recent decades had too easily assumed, often to justify later positions in fact at variance with the central core of Catholic inspiration. There is, no doubt, more intellectual disarray today than there ever was before 1970. Far fewer people proportionately read Plato and Augustine, Aristotle and Aquinas today than they did in Maritain's time. We are not better for it.

Indeed, Maritain, with Simon, Josef Pieper, Heinrich Rommen—Rommen's famous book *The Natural Law* was recently reissued by Liberty Fund with an Introduction by Hittinger's brother, Russell—and a number of other thinkers led a serious intellectual endeavor to reappropriate the Thomist tradition as Leo XIII had advocated, a movement that itself predated Leo XIII. This movement required, as men like Maritain's friend Etienne Gilson or Christopher Dawson understood, a rethinking of Patristic and Medieval thought in all its forms, especially that thought stemming from the great St. Augustine. Gilson's essay, "The Future of Augustinian Metaphysics," remains vital in our understanding that Catholic intellectual life includes both Augustine and Aquinas.[2]

This present book has three general purposes: (1) to recover and explain the central philosophic positions of Maritain, (2) to engage later philosophic

and political positions that arose after his time but in the light of his premises, and finally, (3) to take up several positions of Maritain himself, such as
human rights or his overly positive estimate of modern culture or world government, that do not themselves seem well founded. The work of Simon,
who was a student and friend of Maritain and a profound thinker in his own
right, often, as Hittinger shows, serves to clarify Maritain's own positions—
on the common good, on subsidiarity/autonomy, on authority.

One of the principal strengths of this book is Hittinger's own philosophical
acumen through which he is able to follow the wide-ranging Maritain in issues
of natural science, politics, art, theology, metaphysics, poetry, history, and
ethics. The chapter on Newman is of particular importance as it addresses the
whole problem of academic life, another area in which Maritain wrote exten-
sively. Hittinger has the welcome facility of seeing where ideas go and who in
the contemporary world embodies them. Following Gilson's guidance in *The
Unity of Philosophical Experience*, Hittinger is able to address himself in particular to problems of American culture and the serious deviations now appearing
within it at variance with basic classical or Christian positions.

In this regard, Hittinger devotes much attention to Locke, whom he sees
rightly to be at the origin of many of the more recent political and cultural
problems. Hittinger does not give much effort to Hobbes, but he is quite clear
that the Hobbesian notion of rights are also found in Locke. Hittinger's
polemic in this book with Rorty, Edward Wilson, and David Richards, not to
mention Hawking and a number of others in other areas, about the nature of
the American founding is one of the best treatments I know for seeing just
how perennial philosophical problems are related to movements in current
American public life.

Any reader of this book will quickly discover, something already present
in Maritain and the tradition out of which he comes, namely, that no single
discipline is adequate to understand the complexity and far reaches of the
human enterprise. This tradition is adamantly "anti-ideological," that is, it
must take each reality for *what it is*, not claiming to know what it does not
comprehend. It avoids imposing an idea on reality as if reality has no proper
being of itself. On the other hand, it does not deny some unifying and transcendent things within this same order of being. What strikes one again and
again throughout this book is that Hittinger and his tradition stand for philosophic openness. Oddly, it is the closed parameters of the modern mind that
most characterize it, in spite of its own claim that it is open to all things. It
is not.

The two core disciplines that come closest to grounding the whole human
world as an order and not a chaos are metaphysics and theology, the two

fields most shunted to the outskirts of modern academia. Chapter 12, "Maritain on the Intuition of Being" and chapter 14, "Newman, Theology, and the Crisis in Liberal Education," however, do serve to provide the order of intellectual and public things that is so characteristic of the Aristotelian and Thomist traditions. "The process of reasoning terminates in vision of what a thing is or the truth of some conclusion. Reasoning without some terminal insight, at least in aspiration, is nonintelligible in Thomas's scheme. All human knowledge, all human science, aspires to fruition in metaphysics" (207). This is well said.

In being also a defense of liberal education, this book, following Aristotle, Aquinas, and Maritain, has a deep appreciation of the contemplative order, that order in which we seek not to "do" something, but to know *what is*. In one sense, we can say that metaphysics points to action, for unless we understand the true nature of the world and the beings in it, we cannot act effectively. Yet, the end of action is not action, but knowing, beholding *all that is*, in its being and causes. It is this search in wonder that most awakens the potential philosophers, of whom Plato spoke, to devote their lives to knowing, and knowing the truth. Hittinger obviously understands this basic point.

But metaphysics, though noble, is not complete in itself. It leads to questions it cannot, by itself, answer. This failure to itself have the capacity to answer all questions may, at first sight, seem to be a defect in human nature, a sign that it is not well made in the first place. But rather the inability completely to account for the whole being of *all that is*, is the proper understanding possessed by the human intellect, while remaining truly an intellect. It is not a divine intellect, which latter causes what is not itself *to be* and *to be what it is* by its own power and purpose. And if metaphysics, as well as politics, leads us to understand that, however good things are, they are not themselves everything or the cause of themselves, it must mean that there is an expectant, intrinsic, reflexive openness to human being within the very structure of its own intelligence. This is the ultimate grounding of the excitement that philosophy, at its best, generates. It is also the grounding of its humility, its realization that, in the order of being itself, it is a receptive, not a creating, intellectual being.

It is precisely at this point that Hittinger brings in the figure, not of Aquinas, but of Newman, not that Aquinas would not have said the same thing. Newman is more immediately useful because he remains still the man who wrote the most incisive book ever written on what is a university. It does not take a genius to read Newman and compare his openness to all reality with the closed university curricula of more modern times. Hittinger delights in the blunt and carefully argued positions of Newman: "We should begin with Newman's simple beginning: 'Theology, I simply mean the Science of God, or the truths we know about God put into a system; just as we have a science of the stars and call it astronomy, or of the crust of the earth and call it geology' (3.7)" (239). Hittinger's point, with Newman, is simply that such a science exists with its own form and content, the denial of which is analogous to denying the existence of stars or the crust of the earth. Newman and the medieval thinkers called theology, not sociology or politics, "the queen of the sciences." As Leo Strauss, a man whose worth Hittinger recognizes, maintained, modern thought intimated that it has been an effort to depose this lovely queen, but the result is not only that we are not ruled by a queen, but that we wonder if there is any order or ruler at all.[3] Newman's case for theology as a necessary, indeed essential, part of the university was not based on some arcane desire to know obscure things from old books, but it was based on his understanding that theology did have something to say about the truth of things. The exclusion of theological considerations resulted not just in prejudice, but in an inability of the modern man to know as much as he could of the nature of the reality in which he finds himself.

This book often deals with matters that are called "practical," in Aristotle's sense (i.e., economics, politics, and poetry). It was held by many that this is where Christianity was most at loggerheads with the modern spirit. One of Maritain's life efforts, beginning at least with *Integral Humanism*, was to seek to reconcile modernity with Christianity. Maritain himself had something substantial to say in each of these areas of practical life. But there is an habitual awareness that behind worldly questions, important as they are, there lies prior questions of being and theology. The strength of the tradition within which Hittinger writes is that it takes metaphysics seriously and knows when a given author or school simply does not understand its meaning or importance, even to itself.

After a sympathetic effort to evaluate Wilson's famous "socio-biology," Hittinger finally concludes, forced by the evidence, that

> in fact, Wilson stumbles through many areas in his attempt to make these (intellectual) connections. He presents an appalling lack of liberal education, try as he might to read his way into the broader view. His book contains errors in history, poor metaphysics, ignorance of theology, faulty logic. One would appreciate some evidence that Wilson had read and seriously considered positions which challenge his own. (252)

These are strong words, even amusing ones, but they serve to emphasize how little capable the modern intellectual often is to understand a much broader philosophy than his own, which seeks to reduce reality to the dimensions of his own science.

Throughout this book, Hittinger refers to "the Philosopher Pope," to the thought of John Paul II. Both Maritain and the Pope were influenced by Thomas Aquinas and by certain strains in modern philosophy, Bergson, in the case of Maritain, and Scheler in the case of Karol Wojtyla. This background is important because of the project of both the Pope and Maritain of seeking to confront, treat fairly and sympathetically, the intellectual movements of modernity. At the same time, both are acutely aware of the longer philosophic tradition of the West. In *Fides et Ratio*, the Holy Father explains that modern philosophy is often untrue to philosophy itself. Maritain's long reflection particularly on Descartes, the founder of specifically "modern" philosophy, show his awareness that something in modernity has broken with the basic realist foundations of classic and Thomist thought.

Hittinger devotes several chapters to Maritain's social thought—not merely church and state, but also to liberal democracy, to equality, liberty, and rights. Hittinger is quite aware that the fault line of modern social thought runs through our theory of rights and hence our understanding of natural law and its foundations. Maritain is optimistic that the modern notion of rights and the classic notion of natural law or right can be harmonized. As a Frenchman, Maritain was quite aware of the French Catholic struggle with a kind of absolutist democracy stemming from the French Revolution. Many, not merely Burke, think that a good deal of modern ideology and totalitarianism, arises out of a faulty understanding, first brought forth in the revolution, of "human rights." Hittinger, to his credit, is very much aware of the problems arising from any rights theory. This problem as left by Maritain is still found in the works of the Holy Father and many Catholic apologists.

The modern school of "rights" stemming from Hobbes, but going back to Gerson and nominalism, as Hittinger points out, is grounded in will, not in any being. Rights come to mean whatever it is that we enforce, no matter what it is. The classic notion of natural law or right, in so far as that was a classical or medieval term, was always related to duty, which in turn was related to the being of something in reality. The rhetorical problem, at least, of a vigorous defense of "human rights," leads to the dubious position of having to approve, on the grounds of mutually agreed upon "rights," of things that are quite contrary to the Christian or classical positions. Thus the "right to life," as Hittinger points out, for all its nobility is countered by the "right to abortion." As we cannot have it both ways, it seems clear that something is clearly amiss in the widespread use of "rights talk," as Mary Ann Glendon called it.[4] Hittinger does not think Maritain adequately solved this problem.

This book is not a biography of Maritain, nor is it a complete excursus on his general thought. What it is, I think, is a very perceptive and indeed critical reading of the leading Thomist thinker of half a century and more ago. I say "reading" because Hittinger is likewise aware that Maritain takes us back to Thomas, who takes us back to both the Bible and Aristotle. There are those who have constantly held that Maritain (or a number of other scholastic writers) were not "pure" Thomists, that it was better to go directly to the text of Aquinas. And while I have no difficulty with going directly to the text of Aquinas, I think that this Hittinger book shows us the value of also seeing the philosophic tradition of Aquinas as it engaged itself, through Maritain and his friends, in an actual period of time much closer to our own. It will ever be true that a direct reading of Aquinas will give us insights that not even a Maritain may have noticed. We may even find that Maritain's understanding of, say, the analogy of being or the proofs for the existence of God or the nature of modern psychology and psychiatry was faulty.

The fact remains that Maritain will have a lot to say that is true on each of these subjects and that he can lead us back to a reading and a tradition that, when done properly, can correct even itself, indeed correct Aquinas if need be. In other words, philosophy remains itself, even when we read the philosophers, however great. This was the meaning of the Pope's point in *Fides et Ratio* that, while there is no Christian philosophy, as such, there is a genuine philosophy and there are philosophers who have pursued it better than others. Not every philosophy can support revelation, something that becomes itself a major stimulation of philosophy itself in its own order. It is not an accident that those who pursue philosophy best are those, like Hittinger, who have read their Plato and Aristotle, Augustine and Aquinas, yes, Maritain, Pieper, Gilson, Marion Montgomery, and Yves Simon.

We are now passing a quarter of a century from the death of Maritain. The Philosopher Pope is a very old man. As this book proves, the legacy of Maritain has been passed on to another generation, who, in turn, is engaged in passing it on to yet another generation. It is now argued by those who have reached intellectual maturity decades after Maritain himself flourished. Maritain's own work on education would ask about its being passed on again, this time in an intellectual and cultural world much more hostile to Thomism, Christianity, and to the classics themselves.

What a reading of this book suggests is the importance of keeping alive this tradition, in its integrity, even when the culture either refuses to consider it or rejects it implicitly by the way they live. Eric Voegelin, another major figure of the time during which Maritain lived, once remarked that "no one is required to participate in the crisis of his time. He can do something else."[5] It is within the spirit of this Voegelinian comment that this book of John Hittinger exists. That is, he is doing something else, something other than what the main line of the intellectual culture is doing. But since this book also falls within the tradition of St. Thomas, it will necessarily include a careful and sage consideration of the "adversaries," of what they hold and how they argue. This book does both of these things. It continues the tradition of the *philosophia perennis* and within that tradition it accounts for what alternatives are presented as explications of the reality in which we all live.

The special feature of this book is "the political philosophy" of Jacques Maritain, as the title of the first chapter indicates. As I suggested earlier, Hittinger quite clearly understands that political philosophy does not stand wholly by itself. On the other hand, as Strauss indicated, political philosophy has a certain priority over philosophy. Why is this? Because in order to philosophize, there is at least some need of a polity that does not claim the whole of the human soul.

Maritain wrote in the heady days of the early formation of the United Nations. Indeed, Maritain was on the French delegation to UNESCO in which the first drafts of the Declaration of Human Rights were proposed. Maritain valiantly sought a way to achieve some sort of "practical"agreement whereby men could officially and legally agree to respect the possibility to worship, marry, form a family, speak, participate in public life, teach, learn, basically live in peace.

Even though during Maritain's lifetime, the Communist threat was the main political ideology that concerned him, after the defeat of the Nazis, we would be hard pressed today not to acknowledge the lack of these human capacities in many cultures and countries, not excluding our own. Maritain was not naive. He did not think that "practical" arrangements would last long if there were no valid theoretical basis behind their existence. He was fully aware of the need of prudence and compromise in the practical political order. The general notions of secular modernity maintain that more democracy and more freedom, less fanaticism and less cult, will lead to a more peaceful world. But as the Holy Father has frequently pointed out, there is such a thing as a "totalitarian democracy" that is every bit as dangerous as any other kind of totalitarianism.

And freedom oriented to nothing but itself has come to undermine any sense of a life of virtue or order based on nature. It seems that the notions of equality, democracy, rights, and freedom to which Maritain devoted so much attention have become rooted in unexpectedly dangerous intellectual flaws and notions. It is these latter ideas that are now being lived out in the political realm. What this book points to is the inadequacy of many of Maritain's noble initiatives.

Something else seems to have been at work within the culture that, with intellectual bases of its own, has managed not to turn to the ideals that Maritain, with many others, thought mankind would accept after the experience of the wars of the twentieth century. Maritain lived in an era in which the civil governments of Europe and America still retained some connection with the classic western heritage. They also lived in a time when armies and military force could protect Christians. The working of democratic theory, for better or worse, has now made it impossible for any connection between armies and religion, something that has not happened in Muslim lands or for that matter in China or even India.

The Catholic alternative to the Maritain proposal that theoretic questions are still vital to work out has been taken up by John Paul II who has initiated, wherever he could, various commissions, colloquia, papers, and studies to try to resolve or mitigate, theoretically, the intellectual origins of political and cultural differences. This vital work of contemplation must bear fruit if the disorders of our time have any hope of moderate resolution.

The problem of political philosophy is twofold, as Hittinger recognizes. First is a question of the most workable form of the state, the problem of the "best regime," either, as Aristotle said, for this particular people, say, Athens or Sparta, or in general, granted the way most people in fact are. In modern times, the word "democracy" has come, however dubiously, to be a vague word intended to mean what the classics meant by "the best regime." The Aristotelian cycle of regimes, from best to least best, from worst to least worst, always was a sober reminder that any effort to change bad or tolerable regimes might produce a better regime, but often it produced a worse one. Regimes change when the population, customs, or principles of a people change. Europe and the United States are now flooded with new peoples as well as with philosophic ideas that seem far more dangerous than anything we had previously in our society. This, too, is a problem of political philosophy.

The second side of political philosophy is theoretic. It is not merely that of finding and founding or re-founding a regime in which what it is to be a human being can flourish, but one in which the very idea of what this flourishing can be will be discussed without excluding in principle the revelational responses to the perplexities of philosophy and the failures of virtue that appear in any existing society.

The strength of this book, to repeat, is its very existence within the contemplative order that made its writing possible. In publishing this book, John

Hittinger presents his argument to the world. If it is true that no one need to participate in the "crisis of his time," as Voegelin said, it is likewise true that no one, though at some cost, "need" to pay any attention to either reason or revelation, argument or metaphysics. Philosophy, Strauss remarked, seeks a "knowledge of the whole."[6] It is the peculiar virtue of this book of John Hittinger that his own philosophy is not closed to that whole that includes, as Newman said, the orderly understanding of what is revealed, not just as a curiosity, but as a furthering of philosophy itself when philosophy is most itself, that is, when it asks the right questions and honestly admits both that it does not itself create all answers and that it can recognize real answers when they are given, even by revelation.

Again, let me conclude with the notion of "the graciousness of being." In Maritain's *Notebooks* for May 6, 1911, is found this entry: "Saw (Georges) Rouault at the Moreau Museum. This man has a gift of which none of the others possess, a frankness before reality and *an immediate awareness* of things which nothing can replace."[7] In his philosophy of art, Maritain paid much attention to the work of Rouault. The phrase "an immediate awareness" was in italics in the text.

With this phrase, I return to chapter 12 on the "Intuition of Being" in this book. Here John Hittinger writes, referring to Marion Montgomery's book, *Why Hawthorne Was Melancholy*, a book "I commend to you very highly," that "Hawthorne was quite aware of the issue of being and the tragic presumption of men who elevate their mind to a point of denying the givenness of things and the common plight of humanity." This book is, in fact, a commendation of "being" and knows of "the tragic presumption of men who elevate their mind to a point of denying the givenness of things and the common plight of humanity." To understand these notions within the tradition of political philosophy, we also need metaphysics and revelation, and indeed all else that belongs to that practical consideration Aristotle called, not the queen of the sciences, but the "highest of the practical sciences," to politics and how we ought to live that we may be free to know the truth and acknowledge freely of *what is*, that it is.

Notes

1. See James V. Schall, "The Law of Superabundance," (Maritain), *Gregorianun* (Rome) 72, no. 3 (1991), 515–42.

2. Etienne Gilson, *A Gilson Reader* (Garden City, N.Y.: Doubleday Image, 1957), 82–104.

3. Leo Strauss, *The City and Man* (Chicago: University of Chicago Press, 1964), 1.

4. Mary Ann Glendon, *Rights Talk* (New York: The Free Press, 1991).

5. *Conversations with Eric Voegelin*, ed. R. Eric O'Connor (Montreal: Thomas More Institute Papers, 1980), 33.

6. Leo Strauss, "On Classical Political Philosophy," *What Is Political Philosophy and Other Studies* (Glencoe, Ill.: The Free Press, 1959), 92. See also, Josef Pieper, *In Defense of Philosophy*, trans. L. Krauth (San Francisco: Ignatius Press, 1992).

7. Jacques Maritain, *Notebooks*, trans. J. Evans (Albany: Magi Books, 1984), 71.

~

Preface

I had to fly with the swift wings of desire, behind the guide who gave me
hope and was my light

—Dante, *Purgatorio* IV.28

I am the beneficiary of various traditions—political, philosophical, and
religious—which have served to shape my understanding of the city, the
academy, and the church. I view my reading and writing as an exercise in
what J. Pelikan calls the "discovery" and "vindication" of tradition.[1] It is
my goal to receive and understand, engage and develop, and make available and pass along, the riches of these traditions.

Thus I write as an American citizen whose history and form of government has provided great liberty and opportunity; it has provided example of
open debate and conversation, compromise and innovation, courage and discipline, as well as examples of majority opinion, suppression of debate, lack
of resolve, and frivolity. I am fully conscious of a great heritage that has been
sustained by many acts of sacrifice and devotion to liberty; my ancestors
came to this continent in the seventeeth century for religious liberty; they
founded cities and churches and moved across the land; they fought for liberty in the civil war, pioneered out West, fought in two world wars, and of
late my own father was killed in action during the Vietnam War. I worked for
seven years with the U.S. Air Force in the education and formation of future
military officers. A number of my students, as well as former colleagues, are
now actively serving the country and the cause of freedom in places as far

flung as Alaska, Florida, Bosnia, Saudi Arabia, and Afghanistan. In short, I have a deep love and respect for political freedom and the structures and culture that make it possible.

I also write as a philosophy professor who has spent over thirty years in the academia—eight years as a student, twenty-three years as a professor, and one year as an academic dean. I studied with a number of outstanding teachers and philosophers (Joseph Evans, Stanley Hauerwas, Ralph McInerny, Richard Kennington, John Wippel, William Wallace, Jude Dougherty, Thomas Prufer, Thomas West, Leo Paul de Alvarez, Glen Thurow). I have taught college students in Kansas, Illinois, Colorado, and Michigan. I have taught adult students who ventured to college after years in the work force, and I have taught seminary students and military cadets. It is one of my core convictions that the "unexamined life is not worth living," and that liberal education by way of great books and great ideas is one of the most precious gifts I have received and am able to share. As I have taken on more teaching assignments I find myself increasingly drawn to interdisciplinary study and teaching in the humanities learning ever more about music and art, history and literature, and theology—in addition to philosophy. I have developed a deep appreciation for the medieval roots of liberal learning and the university system. I have an abiding sense of gratitude for the contribution of ancient Greek philosophy and literature. I consider myself ultimately a member of a tradition shaped by Thomas Aquinas. And it was through the reading of Jacques Maritain and Josef Pieper at Notre Dame that I first discovered the great adventure of liberal learning. The love of wisdom so colored their lives and writings that any of their disciples cannot but feel that attraction too. It is a living quest, not a mere academic exercise. Their quest points back to the great masters Thomas Aquinas and behind him St. Augustine and Aristotle. In sum then I have sought to receive and understand the thought of Aquinas, Aristotle, and Augustine; and to engage it and develop it. It is humbling to place oneself in the position of a lifelong student and devotee of such great thinkers. First of all of course because of the sheer scope and extent of their writings; it would be a lifelong goal to read through and begin to comprehend any one of them, let alone such three. Their antiquity and their strange tongue present yet another barrier to reception and understanding. And finally their own disagreements, tensions, and subtleties of style pose but yet a third obstacle to learning. The goal to receive and understand this tradition is steep. It is tempting to abandon the task. From afar I can appreciate Emerson's "American newness" and his call to abandon the book and take on nature afresh.

Without indulging in personal reminiscence, I can only say that I tried briefly in the late 1960s to engage in such a way; but adolescent impatience and bad experiences marred it. My fate was cast when I chose between An-tioch College, Ohio, and Notre Dame, Indiana, unknowing but forever leav-ing behind radical innovation and embracing the burden of tradition. But this is to digress. The very real obstacles posed by these mentors—Aristotle, Augustine, Aquinas—are quickly mounted by the living organism of the tra-dition. That is, it is thanks to my teachers, and the authors I celebrate in these articles, that the great minds and teachers become available across the great divide. There is a staying power to the authors of the great traditions here. I have seen it in my life and the lives of my students, young and old, cadet or seminarian, Christian or not. There is a richness, a wisdom, a power to enlighten and order the soul. I do strive now to make available and pass along the tradition. This at least constitutes the value of these essays and my reason for publication. I wish to bring to the attention of the reader the great riches of Aristotle, Augustine, and Aquinas and the tremendous achieve-ment of a few of their twentieth-century disciples. Perhaps in some small way I may too develop and apply it. But I must honestly say that the great work of development and application was done in such a significant and profound way by the "greatest generation" of this century writing in the midst of the most earth shaking historical events, primarily World War II and its after-math—Maritain, Simon, Strauss, Pieper, Kolnai—that I but light my small candle flame from their large and furious torches. I take to heart the words of Newman: "I have a part in this great work. I am a link in a chain, a bond of connection between persons."

Finally, I must say a word about the third tradition, the religious one, Ro-man Catholicism. How has it shaped these essays and why would these essays be of interest to those outside of that tradition? First of all, it is my experi-ence and conviction that political and academic traditions inevitably cross paths with religious ones. From the ancient city to the modern state, and our own American founding, the question of gods and God, prophets and priests, oracles and scriptures, have played decisive roles in forming the city and stak-ing the destiny of a historic people. Michael Platt has shown me that a study of our own founding document, the Declaration of Independence, finds four references to God (as creator, legislator, judge, and executive). The city of man echoes in some way the city of God (and vice versa). The quest for wis-dom must entertain the question, *quid sit deus?* Surely in our academia, a ban on God would lead to the pitching of Socrates and Plato, Aristotle and Lu-cretius, Cicero, as well as Aquinas, Descartes, Leibniz, the "God intoxicated" Spinoza, and even Nietzsche himself. It is a more recent type of phobia to be-come instantly nervous when the topic of God is broached. Perhaps then it is salutary to have the question raised. I suppose as a minor premise I must add that one must begin from somewhere; that is, it is precisely here that a tradition provides for some discipline and grammar to begin such discourse. Many generations of my American ancestors (Congregationalists) came as Protestants and fanned out over the country; but in the great melting pot and according to the ironies of American history my Grandmother (Quaker) converted to Catholicism, raised my father as a devout Catholic, and subsequently my mother and uncle (Lutherans) converted also. It is the tradition I inherit; *fides quarens intellectus*. As an additional reason for making the theological dimension a part of this quest and tradition—the historic fact is that Roman Catholicism has deeply influenced the course of Western history. It must be acknowledged and studied. It seeks to be a friend of liberty and an ally with all seekers of God and seekers of truth. And for both friends and critics, its contemporary presence in this country and throughout the world makes it an important tradition to understand. The historic drama of the church in the twentieth century alone makes these particular thinkers of chief importance. The Council of Vatican II may well stand as one of the great religious events of history, comparable to Constantine's conversion or the Protestant Reformation and Catholic Reformation of the sixteenth and seventeenth centuries.

Thus I write as an American citizen, a professor of philosophy, a Roman Catholic, who has a deep love of liberty, a great passion for learning and wisdom, and a pervasive sense of God's gracious presence. It is my hope that these essays convey something of each and brings you, the reader, to the sources that nourish them.

This book is a collection of essays compiled from more than twenty years of reading, speaking, and writing. There will inevitably be some overlap, some repetition, and some gaps in the material. It is a topical collection, not a systematic presentation of the thinkers and the themes. It is my hope that the collection, with such limitations, will prove useful for the retrieval and appreciation of the traditions of which I speak.

Note

1. Jaroslav Pelikan, *The Vindication of Tradition: The 1983 Jefferson Lectures in the Humanities* (New Haven, Ct.: Yale University Press, 1984).

~

Acknowledgments

I wish to acknowledge first of all the teacher who led me to the study of Maritain, Simon, and Pieper—Joseph W. Evans (d. 1976), Professor of Philosophy at the University of Notre Dame and Founder and Director of the Jacques Maritain Center. He was revered by students at Notre Dame for his humor and his dedication to student learning: his course on Basic Concepts of Political Philosophy was filled each semester as a new class learned of the great philosophers, from Plato to Maritain. Joe Evans was a witness to the "graciousness of being." Walking across campus, with cigar in hand, he would gesture toward a tree and, with a nod, acknowledge indeed that "being is a glory waiting to be recognized." The likes of Joe Evans and his colleague Frank O'Malley are gone forever from the Notre Dame campus; it appears, sadly, that Notre Dame has no more room for their projects or progeny.

I also wish to acknowledge the people who kindly extended invitations to me to speak and write on Maritain and Simon and other topics in political philosophy—Jude Dougherty, Ralph McInerny, Mary T. Clark, Peter Redpath, Christopher Wolfe, Ken Grasso, Don Mahoney, Thomas Levergood, and my friends abroad, Joseph Dunne in Dublin and James Conroy and Bob Davis in Glasgow. Next, I must thank those colleagues who have been ever ready to discuss Maritain, Aquinas, Locke, and the like. My brother Russell, although at times many miles and worlds away since we left Notre Dame as students in 1974, keeps a discussion going always with fresh insights and fresh leads. In addition, I mention Tim Fuller at Colorado College, whose catholic tastes were always ready to be indulged. At the United States Air Force

Academy, I must mention Bill Gibson, Tony Aretz, Bruce Linster, Anne Reagan, Rich Lemp, Jim Cook, and Paul Carrese; at Saint John Vienney Seminary in Denver—Sister Prudence Allen, Rev. Phil Larrey; at St. Francis University in Joliet—Dan Hauser, Marcia Marzec; at Benedictine College in Achinson, Kansas—John and Sheri Lange, Rev. Linus McManaman, Don Scholz, William Frank, and Katherine Delaney.

The many seminars that I attended at the Ramsey Colloquium sponsored by Father Neuhaus, Liberty Fund seminars, and the American Maritain Association have provided me with many discussions, ideas, and friendly colleagues for which I am grateful.

I wish to thank Lynn Layton, my administrative assistant, for helping me pull together many tasks to get this manuscript ready; Peter Greenman for his index work.

I thank Tony Simon for his many years of support for my projects and for his great work in keeping the works of his father Yves R. Simon and his godfather Jacques Maritain available for use and for facilitating conversations about them.

I have learned so much from Father Ernie Fortin and Father Jim Schall, who have achieved with infinitely greater scope and success the project of reading Aquinas and Augustine, Maritain, and Strauss.

I express my love and thanks to my wife Molly and children Jack, Ellie, Jim, and Joe for their support and understanding of the odd schedule, interests, and friends of an academic.

Finally, I express my esteem and gratitude to the President of Saint Mary's College of Ave Maria University, Thaddeus Radzilowski, and the faculty and staff for allowing me the privilege of developing with them a new Catholic integrated core curriculum based in large measure upon Jacques Maritain's *Education at the Crossroads* and Pope John Paul II's *Fides et ratio*.

PART I

~

JACQUES MARITAIN AND YVES R. SIMON: RESPONDING TO THE POLITICAL CRISIS OF THE TWENTIETH CENTURY

Maritain is admired even by those who may be of very different philosophical and religious convictions. He is admired not only for his life-long zeal for Truth and impassioned commitment to Freedom, but also for his exceptional qualities as a person—his humility, his charity, his fraternal attitude toward all that is. Increasingly he is being recognized as one of the great spirituals of his time.

—Joseph W. Evans

One is struck by one quality that distinguishes the whole of Simon's work: the combination of a profound understanding of the basic insights of Western philosophy with a vivid experience of the philosophical problems of the contemporary world. It is the interaction of these two factors which is at the root of Simon's originality and importance for contemporary philosophy.

—Hans J. Morganthau

~

CHAPTER ONE

The Political Philosophy
of Jacques Maritain

Jacques Maritain's *Man and the State*, is one volume in the remarkable series of lectures sponsored by the Charles Walgreen Foundation at the University of Chicago in the mid-twentieth century. The Walgreen Lectures prompted a set of books that set the agenda for political philosophy for fifty years, having guided now three generations of students of political philosophy. *Man and the State* finds its place alongside Leo Strauss's *Natural Right and History*, Eric Voegelin's *New Science of Politics*, and Yves R. Simon's *Philosophy of Democratic Government*, among others.[1] Ex-patriots from war-torn Europe, these seminal thinkers combined European scholarship with deep admiration for the American constitution, aiming to show, through the recovery of classical and medieval thought, the true foundation of modern liberal democracy.[2] In order to do this, they had to outline a classically grounded political science adequate to understand the prospects and perils of the modern achievement of liberal democracy in a century that had crushed the easier optimism of the Enlightenment tradition. Especially they sought to refute the prevalent modes of political science, especially those fostered by positivism and Marxism.

What seems more obvious to us today about the shortcomings of such reductionist modes of thought is so because of what these thinkers accomplished fifty years ago when it was by no means obvious. Nevertheless, all were influenced by, and took seriously, contemporary philosophy (for Maritain it was Bergson) and sought to make the case for the ancient wisdom in the deepest issues of philosophy and politics in awareness of what had been

.

said against the ancient wisdom. They had to make sense of the incessant experience of war, the onset of the Cold War, and to chart a future for the defenders of liberty against the totalitarianism of left and right. Neither the positivism nor the historicism of the day could provide the tools for the job. These thinkers, in attempting to recover the ancient wisdom, did not necessarily agree with each other at the level of speculation. But they came to a profound convergence on what ought to be opposed in thought and action.

For Maritain, the principal inspiration was Thomas Aquinas.[3] Thus Maritain's work bears a double mission of enlightening American citizens as to a deeper, sounder philosophy of government, but also of representing modern liberal democracy to the church, whose conflicts with, and suspicions of the modern liberal, democratic state (the suspicions were, of course, reciprocal) date back centuries at least to the English and French revolutions as well as to numerous other skirmishes in both political and philosophic matters.[4] *Man and the State* is a double achievement, for both the city of man and the city of God, for both its political philosophy and its theology. Sadly this double achievement has waned in its proper recognition. His achievement does not set the debate in the sphere of political thinking, in part, because the exponents of natural law philosophy, with claims about a stable nature and natural ends, continue to focus on the reductionism of social science and the deconstruction of postmodern philosophy. Maritain has, of course, in other works, launched a defense of natural foundations and an elaborate critique of the positivist mentality and the shortcomings of existentialist and historicist approaches. These achievements may wax again since they are, in principle, compatible with the revival of interest in natural law. What may be surprising is the neglect with which Maritain is treated in his own historic tradition. Applauded before Vatican II as a source of renewal, yet disdained by some as too liberal, Maritain saw his reputation and influence slip after the Council, even though he was chosen by Paul VI to receive the conciliar "Message to Men of Thought and Science."[5] A postconciliar work entitled *The Peasant of the Garonne*, subtitled, "an old laymen questions himself abut the present time," was received with much disappointment and rejection.[6]

The great enthusiasm and readiness for experimentation was not yet ready for the words of caution and criticism. Many seemed to embrace change for the sake of change. But perhaps a passage from Burke's *Reflections* would help to indicate Maritain's attitude about the "revolution" —the experience of change and liberation is likened to a "wild gas" and Burke cautions that we "suspend our judgment until the first effervescence is a little subsided, and until we see something deeper than the agitation of a troubled and frothy surface."[7] But Maritain's caution was not heeded. Many reviewers focused on the tone, which they found bitter, or on its occasional *ad hominem* arguments.[8] Some declared that he had lost his wit as an old man who fearfully returned to a conservative position. Few seemed to appreciate the significance of the work as a completion of a lifetime project of engaging modernity as a twentieth-century disciple of Thomas Aquinas. Maritain's project attempted to unite Thomistic and Aristotelian traditions with the human rights thrust of modern political philosophy. Maritain wished to reassess the liberal state in light of ancient and medieval political traditions, seeking to find what is true, enduring, and practical in the modern liberal state, while criticizing its excesses and reconceptualizing its philosophical foundations. This great project, whose trajectory begins with the criticism of the French right wing, runs through *Integral Humanism* and *Man and the State*. *The Peasant of the Garonne* displays the spiritual and intellectual center of Maritain's work and reveals many of the ideas that shaped Vatican II.

There is a great myth concerning the intellectual life of the church prior to Vatican II—specifically that it was impoverished by a lack of imagination, narrowly focused on scholastic hair-splitting, rigidly enclosed by dogma and irrelevant to the contemporary world. Many clerics and religious, educated by scholastic textbooks, were very susceptible to this view, and they found it liberating to read more progressive writers such as Karl Rahner, Teilhard de Chardin, and Hans Kung. And while Rahner and Chardin may have kept faith, many of their enthusiasts followed the new methods and sources into dissent and often out of the church and beyond Christianity itself. The attempt to reconcile the Tradition with the intellectual trends of the day is risky business. More often than not, the new element (be it Heidegger, Wittgenstein, or now Kolhberg and Derrida) comes to predominate and the Tradition is transformed beyond recognition or rejected outright. This is not always the case. John Paul II is a case in point; thoroughly steeped in phenomenology, John Paul is faithful and has successfully combined the old and the new. He was deeply influenced by prior generations of faithful scholars such as Garrigou-Lagrange and Jacques Maritain. Thus, while it is the case that textbook Thomism often ruled the day with a formulaic approach to the big questions, the deep intellectual germination of Leo XIII's encyclical *Aeterni Patris* (1890) came to bear extraordinary fruit during the 1930s and 1940s in the works of a number of French Thomists, including Father Garrigou LaGrange, Jacques Maritain, and Yves R. Simon.[9] The fruits of their scholarship, along with many other initiatives in liturgy, education, and politics gave rise to the great renewal of Vatican Council II. Maritain's books remain to give a sound interpretation in a time of a wildly swinging pendulum from one extreme to another, from an outright rejection of Vatican II by the traditionalists to the strained interpretation of the progressive wings of liberation theology and biblical deconstruction. In *The Peasant of the Garonne* Maritain humorously refers to these extremes as "the ruminators of the holy alliance" and the "sheep of the panurge."[10] But this is yet the "frothy surface" after a great council. Maritain refers to the need for "a great and patient work of revitalizing in the order of intelligence and the order of spirituality."[11] Such a revitalization or renewal has tremendous political significance. It may be perhaps claiming too much to be reminded of Augustine's reference to his own work, *The City of God*, as a "great and arduous task."[12] But Maritain's scope and ambition, his inspiration and method, are no less. In *The Peasant of the Garonne* Maritain describes the post–Vatican II political and theological scene as follows: "In truth, every vestige of the Holy Empire is today liquidated; we have definitely emerged from the sacral age and the baroque age. After sixteen centuries which it would be shameful to slander or repudiate, but which have completed their death agony and whose grave defects were incontestable, a new age begins."[13]

The collapse of the Roman Empire and the emergence of the post–Constantinian era are of decisive historical weight. Perhaps the mid-twentieth century, after a second world war, a surprising ecumenical council, and the collapse of the Marxist empire prove the need of a new Augustinian effort. Maritain certainly thought so, as does John Paul II. We should not allow the contemporary lull and drift of world events at the beginning of a new century, or the sordidness of recent American public life, to discourage us from seeing the new possibilities for thought and action on behalf of liberty and human fulfillment and the new risks and challenges that loom on the horizon. It is at just such a time that Maritain's freshness and purity of vision provides such charm and attraction. In the preface to the new edition of *Man and the State*,[14] Ralph McInerny challenges us to ask why we have lost the optimism of Maritain. It strikes us, upon rereading *Man and the State*, how much the climate has changed in this country since these lectures were initially given. Then there was a bold openness about the theological questions. In the 1940s and 1950s, it was part of common public philosophy to acknowledge the importance of religion for the democratic polity.

All the Walgreen Lecturers were fully conversant with the theological/political question as it had emerged over the centuries of modern European history. It is a historic fact that religion has played no less a role than science or modern philosophy in the conception and founding of liberal democracy. The theological/political question is part of a broader, fuller political analysis, as Alexis de Tocqueville, with characteristic perception, noted long ago.

We should find it is an ever-present predicament—under the rubric of separation of church and state—that must realistically be resolved in a pluralistic society. It is a complex issue requiring legal and constitutional, as well as sociological, philosophical, and theological approaches for a comprehensive solution. It is unremarkable, then, that Maritain chose as a central theme of *Man and the State* the importance of the religious and the theological to the health and vitality of liberal democracy. But no longer is the theological/political question even seriously considered. Religion and irreligion have been reduced to the narrow confines of partisanship. Mainstream accounts of public philosophy now seek to exclude religion from the public square, formulating criteria by which religion can have no place in public reason. Our jurisprudence looks with suspicion upon religious expression, often declaring it hostile to the rights of citizens. Our education seeks to neutralize religious expression or even attacks it as politically incorrect. The very situation against which Maritain warned us fifty years ago has come to pass: the isolating antagonism of church and state. But his is a voice that should continue to be heard; he demonstrates the possibility of a public philosophy that is religious in its deepest inspiration and yet rational in its presentation, maintaining the possibility of dialogue in truly pluralistic conditions. He is an example of a noble and magnanimous soul who loves what is best in liberal democracy and who provides for its defense in speech and deed. He provides a historical and metaphysical perspective on the nature and prospects for liberal democracy, and at the same time points the way to a higher source of heroism and good citizenship so necessary for the vitality of liberal democracy. And this all centers on a constructive engagement between church and state, liberal democracy and the kingdom of God.

Reading *Man and the State*

There are many paths into Maritain's account of, and defense of, liberal democracy, we shall first consider the structure of *Man and the State*. Chapter one reflects on the notion of the people and the body politic. The very notion of the common good, Aristotelian in form, evidences the source of politics in the experience of polity. So, too, the notion of a pluralist conception of society with various forms of community, prepolitical as well as intermediate groupings, grounds the limit on state power in a naturally multifaceted human situation and allows us to see afresh alternatives to monistic accounts of the state and its power. Maritain sharply distinguishes the "state" as the "topmost" administrative function from the "body politic" which is steeped in heritage and characterized by "structural pluralism." Maritain achieves in this chapter a fresh application of Aristotle's account of the political regime to the complexities of modern political life. In chapter two, Maritain criticizes the notion of sovereignty insofar as it excludes accountability to the people, and reminds us of the limits to power exercised under God. In chapter three, Maritain offers a profound critique of Machiavelli as the ingenious advocate of technical artistry, to which he counters with a notion of the moral rationality of politics, by which he means that a regime must draw upon the vital energies and generosity of its citizens. Freedom and conscience will prove to be more politically enduring than the Machiavellian mode of manipulation and hypocrisy. Writing in 1950 Maritain serenely anticipates the demise of such "gigantic Machiavellian robots" as the Soviet Union, which must become "more perfect and ruthless in techniques of oppression, universal mutual spying, forced labor, mass deportation and mass destruction."[15] He says that "they do not possess lasting inner force; their huge machinery of violence is a token of their inner human weakness." He asks "how long can the power of the state endure which becomes more and more of a giant as regards the external or technical forces, and more and more of a dwarf as regards the internal human actually vital forces?" He confidently concludes, circa 1950, "I doubt that it can take root in the historic duration of nations."

By way of contrast, Maritain proposes the "moral rationalization" of political life—recognition of the human ends of political life and at the same time the use of human means—the use of "human energies as energies of free men." Maritain cites his mentor, Henri Bergson, who suggested that the gospel is the deepest root for democratic feeling and philosophy. "Democracy can only live on Gospel inspiration."[16] Without that inspiration, we would deprive democracy of its lifeblood, of faith in supra-material, supra-mathematical, and supra-sensory realities. In the central and key chapter, chapter four, we encounter the orienting idea in Maritain's account of liberal democracy: the natural law foundation for human rights. It is well known that Maritain helped to draft the UN Charter on Human Rights. He explores this theme in various works.[17] Here we find a listing of basic rights and an explanation of human rights in light of natural law. He explains how human rights presuppose some notion of a stable human nature and an order of human goods. Again he proposes the thesis that the gospel leads to the greatest clarity concerning natural law, human rights, and the dignity of the person.[18] Now Maritain does not claim that this account is the only account; indeed he says that a secularist or a rationalist may give another account. But this leads to the next chapter on the democratic charter, expounding a key element of Maritain's philosophy of the pluralist state. No longer will there be a religious belief that gives unity to the political society. In fact, the society will be pluralist and have many diverse spiritual families, institutions, and bodies. But they must share a common "secular faith" concerning the essentials of liberal democracy. Basic tenets at the core of our life together include the dignity of the human person, involving the enjoyment of basic rights but also the acceptance of civic responsibility individually, in the family and in our voluntary associations. We must adhere to the rule of law, to human equality, ideals of justice and fraternity, religious freedom, and mutual tolerance. These are practical tenets, points of practical convergence. In our common subscription to these we will, nevertheless, both have and confront varying theoretical justifications, given the diverse groups that must appear in political society. We can agree on the temporal or secular order of things to a substantial degree, and yet be divided on the theological issues or philosophic justifications for them. By the same token, Maritain doubts that a purely rational or scientific creed will be able to justify the practical convergence sufficiently. He urges that "religion and metaphysics are an essential part of human culture, primary and indispensable incentives in the very life of society;" the individualist and neutral approach to rights he thinks (incorrectly) is a thing of the past, although he correctly notes the weakness of such an approach. The polity can defend itself and its creed through democratic means—censorship, he says, is the worst way to seek unity. Inner energies, reason and conscience, are best. Education is key because it is the primary means to foster a "common secular faith." But the state's competency is severely limited. The "creed" must be "intrinsically established in truth."[19] Hence the state cannot help but resort to "philosophical and religious traditions and schools of thought that are spontaneously at work in the consciousness of the nation."

It is an illusion to think our convictions can be taught effectively if abstracted from their metaphysical root. Do we not wish to allow for full understanding and personal inspiration in teaching? Jacques Maritain is perhaps the finest example of such a teacher: a defender of democracy using the full range of philosophical and theological arguments, a dialectical partner whose aim is not victory but discovery of the common truths of our lives together. In the chapter on the church and state, Maritain outlines the significance of the "post-Constantinian" approach that came to characterize official church teaching at Vatican II. Maritain explains the enduring principles of the roles of church and state and yet provides a very effective argument concerning the different historical context in which they are to be applied. No longer is religion the basis for civil unity. But religion has a tremendous role to play in the field of education, morality, and culture. One must read this chapter and then look at Paul VI's "Message to Guardians of Temporal Power,"[20] to fully appreciate the influence of Maritain. The closing chapter is perhaps the most controversial. As we noted above, Maritain was instrumental in drafting the United Nations Declaration on Human Rights. In chapter seven Maritain makes a case for world government. As an associate of the Adler and Hutchins group, Maritain was deeply attracted to the idea of world government. I believe the reader will find a careful analysis of the problems and promises; he does not expect an overnight solution. He rejects a "super state" notion and he would undoubtedly deplore the centralized bureaucratic approach to world problems which has emerged of late from the United Nations. But he meditates deeply upon the problem of war and the exaggerated claims for state sovereignty. He argues for a "political" approach to world unity. Such an approach will undoubtedly take much time and generations of effort. But Maritain referred to himself as "a kind of spring finder pressing his ear to the ground in order to hear the sound of hidden springs, and of invisible germinations."[21] *Man and the State*, for all of its flaws and shortcomings, has indeed discovered some hidden springs for democratic politics and contains yet more invisible germinations for the city of God and the city of man.

On Christianity, Democracy, and Rights

Although lacking the historical scale of *Integral Humanism* or the technical analysis of *Man and the State*, Maritain's *Christianity and Democracy* and *The Rights of Man and Natural Law* are his most accessible works in political philosophy. These two books contain most of the great themes of Maritain's political philosophy.

Maritain's political philosophy is animated by the conviction that political reality is inextricably linked with the hidden spiritual life and movement of men's souls. He is much like Solzhenitsyn in this respect. It lends to his thought a sense of grandeur and exigency, even an apocalyptic tone. In the midst of World War II he says that "freedom, honor, and the possibility of living as a man" will die for centuries if Nazism triumphs. Maritain sees the unresolved tensions of Western civilization that continue to live well beyond the war itself. The nihilism that created a climate for Nazism continues apace, domesticated in form but still virulent in its effects. A commitment to truth, a cultivation of virtue, and a love of God are the ever present origins for political order in Maritain's account. He is convinced that the West needs Christianity as much as it repudiates it.

Maritain sets himself to an important task, the harmonizing of Christianity and the democratic ideal. The tragedy of the modern age finds "the motivating forces in modern democracies repudiating the Gospel and Christianity in the name of human liberty, while motivating forces in the

Christian social strata were combating the democratic aspirations in the name of religion." It is the burden of *Christianity and democracy* to have "Christian inspiration and the democratic inspiration recognize each other and become reconciled." It is a problem and task that require a mind as worthy as that other French thinker, Alexis de Tocqueville, against whom Maritain ought to be compared. Although both men see connections between Christianity and democracy, Maritain seems less aware of the moral and political problems endemic to democratic regimes. Maritain believes that modern democracy transcends aristocracy and monarchy, somehow preserving the best of both. Tocqueville was close enough to the old order to see them as exclusive alternatives. I am not sure that Maritain envisioned the degree to which "democratic inspiration" would far outstrip "evangelical inspiration," thereby creating forms of conflict. Consumerism and gay rights can both claim "democratic inspiration," whereas their "evangelical inspiration" is dubious. Still, Maritain's praise of democracy is always qualified and critical as he wishes Christianity to serve as a check on the base tendencies of the democratic impulse which culminate in "bourgeois liberalism," a form of regime brought under judgment by the world war and its aftermath.

The major thesis of the work is that modern democracy owes its vitality to Christianity: "the democratic impulse has arisen in human history as a temporal manifestation of the inspiration of the Gospel." The full historical adequacy of this claim is surely questionable; yet for its part it is a great and salutary truth. Human dignity, the value of labor, the rights of conscience, the relativity of earthly authority are but a few of the truths elaborated by Maritain as due to Christian inspiration. The problem is that "democratic impulse" is not a single force. As Maritain knows, its origins also lie in ancient republicanism and in the modern turn to mastery of nature and worldly satisfaction. Both movements bear some antagonism toward Christianity, even if the latter movement often masks itself in Christian phraseology. Maritain hopes to purge the democratic movement of its errors, and rest it on a Christian footing. But perhaps the modern project is now at long last purging itself of its Christian trappings. Maritain's "true democracy" would now appear as countercultural and perhaps antidemocratic. For example, he equates the "pursuit of happiness" with the cultivation of the mind and self-sacrificial love. More generally, Maritain identifies freedom with moral mastery and virtue. Maritain is thus truly premodern in outlook. Those democratic theories proposing a "thin theory of the good" would not find in Maritain the true essence of democracy. Although the Christian theorist may appropriate the terms of democracy, and even show origins in Christianity, the fact that those terms have developed a life of their own make the prospects for reconciling Christianity and contemporary democratic ethos problematic in the extreme. Maritain has high hopes that Christians may be on the vanguard of democratic reform; but we cannot now fail to see that Christians may be called to resist its destructive excesses, risking the epithet of reaction. In this situation we may take comfort from the words of T.S. Eliot: "when a man takes politics and social affairs seriously the difference between revolution and reaction may be the breadth of a hair."

While *Christianity and Democracy* outlines the spirit of Maritain's task, *Rights of Man and Natural Law* outlines the basic concepts of his political philosophy. Maritain gives a masterful and lucid account of human rights, beginning with the philosophical notion of person as a being with intellect and will in virtue of which he is oriented toward the realm of being, truth, and goodness. Therein resides human dignity: the person possesses some measure of wholeness and independence, and cannot live as a mere part or in servility. Moreover, the person is social by nature in function of both his needs and perfections. The personalist basis for politics demands a communal correlate; the good of persons is a communion in the good life. Maritain uses the dignity of the person to resist all forms of totalitarianism; man is more than a part of a temporal society. The person as such aspires to a supra-temporal good. Maritain often cites the words of Thomas Aquinas, "man is not ordered to political society by reason of himself as a whole and by reason of all that is in him." Maritain's idea of the common good expounded here involved him in a dispute with Charles DeKonninck.

Similarly, Maritain's derivation of rights from natural law is the source of some controversy. Human rights flow from the divine order reflected in human nature; it is the "right possessed by God to see the order of His Wisdom in beings respected, obeyed and loved by every intelligence." He does not give a Kantian-type account based upon human autonomy. From a definite conception of the good life does Maritain derive the rights of man. He defines the key modern notion of freedom in terms of virtue, which he calls liberty of expansion: it is "the flowering of moral and rational life, and of those interior activities which are the intellectual and moral virtues." The political task, therefore, is "essentially a task of civilization and culture." The rights of man follow from this goal—they represent the conditions necessary for the full flowering of human perfection in the multitude. Maritain expounds upon personal, civic, and economic rights in light of this concrete human good. The material and legal conditions for human perfection must be met. For the precise enumeration one may consult the work. Suffice it to say that Maritain expects the slow but steady emancipation of man from the conditions that thwart his aspirations to truth and virtue. Liberation is for the sake of human perfection, not an end in itself, nor a freedom without ter-minus or measure. This account of freedom would appear to preserve what is best in a theory of rights by joining it to a notion of virtue.

Maritain is daring in plan and often exquisite in execution. His political philosophy, informed by the wisdom of the ancients, aims at the highest in man and challenges contemporary aspirations for justice. Lacking his bal-ance, some of his readers have readily exploited latent ambiguities for radical and illiberal causes. These books serve a purpose no less vital than when they were originally issued in 1942–1943: in the face of a corrupt liberalism and the menace of totalitarianism they make palpable the cause of "freedom, honor, and the possibility of living as a man"

Maritain's Influence

Jacques Maritain's great influence on Catholic intellectuals from 1920 to 1970 is due first of all to his fresh interpretations of St. Thomas Aquinas and his ap-plication of Thomistic principles to problems of the day. On this matter, Mar-itain's books speak for themselves. A second factor contributing to his great in-fluence is his outstanding character, acclaimed by many to be saintly. One can get a feel for this side of his influence in such books as Julie Kernan's *Our Friend, Jacques Maritain* and Brooke W. Smith's *Jacques Maritain*. Bernard F. Doering's *Jacques Maritain and the French Catholic Intellectuals* brings to our at-tention a third factor in Maritain's influence—his engagement in the affairs of his day through the medium of intellectual journals such as *La Revue Univer-salle, Esprit, Sept*, and *Temps Present*. For some twenty to thirty years Maritain's presence was a constant point of reference, whether for acclaim or disdain. He did much to define the issues for a generation of French Catholics. To this same factor, Doering attributes Maritain's decline. When Maritain came to the United States in the forties he took himself out of the mainstream of French intellectual life and thus the younger generation lost "the habit of his pres-ence." Doering thus says that the later generation did not understand the basis for his judgments; even if they corresponded in judgment, it was often for dif-ferent reasons. But Maritain lost his influence not only because of his absence, but also because of the intellectual positions that he worked out through decades of involvement and reflection, as this book gives ample testimony.

Maritain became unacceptable to Catholic intellectuals, French or other-wise, because they took positions further to the left and their political philoso-phy transformed their theology and metaphysics. Maritain insisted throughout his career on the "primacy of the spiritual," a metaphysical and theological po-sition which preserved the transcendence of God and integrity of the church's supernatural mission. Politically, Maritain came to defend a certain ideal of liberal democracy, and he showed great sympathy for American democracy. Thus it is ironic that positions which Maritain formulated in his opposition to the European right came to be the stumbling block for the new Catholic left. Professor Doering's book thrusts us directly into the controversies.

The *Action Francaise* was a French political movement that sought the restoration of the monarchy and traditional social order. Its leader was Charles Maurras. Maurras was not a Catholic but he gladly accepted and used traditional Catholic sentiment for his cause. In 1926 the Vatican forbade Catholics from participating in the movement because of its violence and its implicit irreligious character. Doering's account of Maritain's involvement is very instructive. First of all, Maritain never directly embraced the cause and he always felt uneasy about Maurras' use of Catholic sentiment. For this very reason he agreed to serve as an editor of its journal, *La Revue Universal/c*. He might have been able to give it theological and philosophical guidance. Maritain was a recent convert to Catholicism. Many of the priests and theologians with whom Maritain associated were sympathetic to the cause of monarchy because it seemed to include the cause of the church against the French Revolution and the French Republic. It was assumed that religious conversion entailed a change in political allegiance. Further, his spiritual director encouraged him to become involved with the movement. Maritain took it as a matter of obedience. Professor Doering's judgment here is pointed and instructive: "With naive and imprudent docility, he failed to distinguish between what constituted, for a Catholic, the supreme teaching authority of the church and what was merely the expression of personal opinion by individual clergymen." Further, Doering quotes approvingly the judgment made by Thomas Molnar concerning the involvement of Maritain's friend George Bernanos with the same *Action Francaise*:

> With the usual idealism of generous men, Bernanos had attributed the values he believed in and the qualities which he possessed to the Action Francaise (in a way like the left-wing idealist who lent the Communist Party their own good intentions until some eye-opening experience).

The lessons learned here about the attraction of religious-minded individuals to political causes are still important ones, as Molnar is quick to point out. Even more important is the formulation of principle to which Maritain never ceased to appeal. There was in Maurras, Maritain said, "a dangerous agnosticism that gave no consideration to the supernatural end of man." Thus his political movement simply used the church and obscured its "essential end, function and dignity, which is to dispense to men supernatural truth and the means to eternal life." In response to the Vatican's condemnation he wrote a book entitled *The Things That Are not Caesar's* or *The Primacy of the Spiritual*. These alternate titles may serve as mottos for Maritain's political philosophy.

Ten years later, Maritain applied the same principle to the problem of the Spanish Civil War. The church took an official position of neutrality; but with special vehemence she protested the atrocities committed by the Loyalists against Catholic personnel and property. Thus many Catholics came to take up the cause of Franco as a "Holy War" and a "White Crusade" against the communists. Maritain wrote very little directly on the Spanish Civil War, yet he was a virtual lightning rod for protest and fury. In one article, he objected to the idea of a "Holy War." War is a matter for the temporal or secular sphere of action and thus it should not be deemed holy. Let them invoke the justice of war, Maritain said, but not its sanctity: "Let them not kill in the name of Christ the King, who is not a military leader, but a King of grace and charity, who died for all men, whose kingdom is not of this world." It is blasphemy to identify the cause of politics with the cause of religion. In another article, Maritain objected to the use of unjust means whereby innocent civilians are indiscriminately slaughtered. He had in mind, of course, the Guernica bombing and other massacres. These objections to the war are quite reasonable and orthodox. Maritain did not directly criticize the Franco cause. Thus it is hard to understand the storm of indignation against his articles and his presence. Partly, it must have been due to the blind and excessive support of some Catholics. But partly, it might have been due to some ambiguity latent in Maritain's position. Maritain called for mediation between the two sides. This call, coupled with Maritain's criticism of the holy war and the unjust means, gave support to the anti-Franco and the pro-Republican forces. There are rhetorical problems associated with the stance of neutrality.

Political action often requires choosing between the lesser of two evils. Many Catholics judged that Franco and fascism were the lesser evils compared to communism and Soviet domination. Maritain's call for mediation could have appeared to have been evasive. Further, the criticism of means often gets viewed as a criticism of ends. Doering's account does not make it clear how Maritain stood on the question of the lesser evil, nor if he approved of the way that his remarks could be used to support the other side. Maritain proclaimed himself to be a man of the left when it came to "the things of Caesar." Maritain's connection with the Catholic left goes back to his association with Emmanuel Mounier and the founding of *Esprit* and extends to his association with Dorothy Day and the *Catholic Worker*. Maritain's relation to Mounier has been described in two books, Joseph Amato's *Mounier and Maritain: A French Catholic Understanding of the Modern World*, and John Hellman's *Emmanuel Mounier and the New Catholic Left, 1930–1950*. Doering adds to these studies a helpful chapter entitled "The Decade of Manifestos," in which he shows Maritain's uneasy alliance with the left. Maritain joined their cause in protesting the same injustices and inequities which abounded during the thirties. Both Mounier and Maritain were attacked as "Red Christians." But the constant tension and eventual divergence were inevitable. Maritain's involvement parallels his previous involvement with the *Action Francaise*. He worked with *Esprit* in order to give it spiritual and philosophical guidance. He insisted that political action be grounded in the proper principles. Maritain feared that the linking of a political cause with religion would jeopardize once again the primacy and freedom of the spiritual. Maritain was often quite harsh with Mounier on these points. One article in the journal advocated a two-stage revolution—a collectivist stage followed by a "personalist" stage. Maritain called such a proposal "Kerenskyist foolishness." The principles of the solution are already contained in the principles of the critique; thus he was wary of Marxist analysis being used at all. Doering believes that Maritain would have had the same type of criticism for the Catholic left, "Mounier's progeny," some thirty years later.

In formulating the editorial policy of another journal, *Sept*, Maritain spoke of a need to find a center above politics. He made a distinction between three spheres of action. On the first level is "Catholic Action" properly speaking. It is an extension of the apostolic work of church to bring men supernatural truth and eternal life. At a second level, the church may intervene in temporal affairs when the interests of religion are at stake. At a third level, Christians engaged in political action as citizens engage in political action as citizens for a temporal good. They act as Christians only insofar as Christianity may inspire their work; but their goals and ideals pertain to the temporal order. The Christian acts as a leaven in society. In light of this distinction Maritain hoped to separate and distinguish the work of the church proper from political action. Thus he said that "It is quite evident that the reforms and revolutions of temporal forms of government are not the affair of the church, whose ends are not temporal, but eternal and spiritual, essentially above and beyond political and social concerns, and who jealously guards against becoming the vassal of any regime, class, or party." Maritain's distinction precludes development within the Catholic left toward forms of liberation theology, with identification of social revolution and the cause of the church.

Maritain's distinction does not give solace to the conservative either. Maritain insisted quite strongly that Christians should take up the cause of social justice in the temporal order. Writing in the 1930s, he was very much afraid of a capitalist oligarchy in which a few rich would dominate and abuse the poor majority. He was concerned about the widespread unemployment and poverty. Thus "Christian inspired politics" include a concern for improving the condition of the working class and the downtrodden. To this extent Maritain is a man of the left. He is of course repeating the great papal social encyclicals. But what is the extent of the problem and what is its solution? As Maritain thought through this question he began to diverge from the Catholic left.

The French periodical *Le Figaro* contained a very interesting exchange between Maritain and Paul Claudel. Professor Doering spends a couple of pages on this exchange, for it gets to the heart of the problem of the Catholic left and Maritain's relationship to it. Claudel came across a passage from Maritain's *Integral Humanism* which reads: "As long as modern society secretes poverty as the product of its normal functioning, there can be no rest for Christians." Claudel objected that modern society does not aim at creating a poverty-stricken class; poverty is an imperfection which must be improved upon and which requires from Christian works of charity. Further, revolutionary action will not serve the cause of justice. Claudel feared that fanatical action would expose the Christian to folly, ridicule, and positive evil insofar as the Christian's desire exceeds his capability and competence. Thus Claudel urged caution. Maritain responded by pointing to the crisis of unemployment as a sign that capitalism entails destitution for a great number of men. He further cited papal encyclicals to back up his judgment that the condition is a scandal and grave injustice. Christians should be "mobilized" to remedy the situation. The exchange went back and forth, although it did seem to progress much beyond Claudel's and Maritain's initial disagreement.

Professor Doering accuses Claudel of begging the question. But it seems to me that both men fail to meet each other head to head. Maritain's statements are ambiguous; the context of *Integral Humanism* does not fully resolve the ambiguity. Claudel does not beg the question; he insists that Maritain spell out more exactly the nature of the defect and the remedy. Maritain did define capitalism in terms of a structural or organic defect leaving a large class of exploited workers; a defect which calls for extreme measures to remedy the situation. But Maritain later changed or modified his views after his trip to the United States. He then came to say that the United States is not capitalist or bourgeois as narrowly defined. In fact, he found it the "living reality of democracy." Furthermore, liberal democracy is open to reform and its institutions are necessary for the preservation of personal rights and true freedom. This would seem to qualify very much his statement in *Integral Humanism*, and it would move him closer to Claudel, I would surmise, than to Mounier. Unfortunately, Professor Doering's book is incomplete on the question of capitalism and the French Catholic intellectuals. The chapter on Maritain and America is far too short and does not probe the period when Maritain solidified his views on democracy and wrote reflections on America and *Man and the State*. One wonders how the French Catholic intellectuals received these books. Mounier became increasingly hostile to American democracy and more sympathetic to Marxism or at least to "real socialism." Could the Catholic left claim the Maritain of this period? It would seem not, if their hostile reception to *The Peasant of the Garonne*, documented by Doering, gives any indication. The primacy of the spiritual and the defense of liberal democracy led to a parting of the ways.

Jacques Maritain bequeathed a rich heritage to Christian thinkers. He sought above all else the things of God in distinction from the things of Caesar. His true center of gravity was the life of the spirit. This gave Maritain a certain freedom from political causes. At the same time it gave him the true source for criticism and challenge. Although he appeared on the left, Maritain was much like Solzhenitsyn. He was a great-souled man who discerned the spiritual crisis of the West. Although above the partisan fray, he embodied the tensions in liberal democracy. He took up the cause of social justice. As a man of compassion he encouraged Christians to live with the poor and to carry their burdens. But he also took up the cause of democratic institutions. As a man of prudence he recognized the need for checking the power of the state and for encouraging the initiative of private individuals and groups.

Notes

This chapter is derived from articles previously published as "Maritain and the Reassessment of the Liberal State," with Timothy Fuller. In *Reassessing the Liberal State: Reading Maritain's Man and the State*, ed. John P Hittinger and Timothy Fuller. (Washington, D.C.: Catholic University of America. 2001); "Review of Maritain's Natural Law and the Rights of Man." *Crisis* (Fall 1987); "Discussion/Review of Jacques Maritain and the French Catholic Intellectuals by Bernard Doering." *This World* V (Spring 1983) 164–68.

1. Eric Voegelin, *The New Science of Politics* (Chicago: University of Chicago Press, 1952); Leo Strauss, *Natural Right and History* (Chicago: University of Chicago Press, 1953); Yves R. Simon, *Philosophy of Democratic Government* (Chicago: University of Chicago Press, 1951).

2. Timothy Fuller, "Reflections on Leo Strauss and American Education," in *Hannah Arendt and Leo Strauss: German Emigres and American Political Thought after World War II*, ed. Peter Graf Kielmansegg, Horst Mewes, and Elisabeth Glaser-Schmidt (New York: Cambridge University Press, 1995), 61–80.

3. See Jacques Maritain, "The Apostle of Modern Times," in *St. Thomas Aquinas*, trans. Peter O'Reilly (New York: Meridian Books, 1958), 88–118.

4. See John P. Hittinger, "Jacques Maritain and Yves R. Simon's Use of Thomas Aquinas in Their Defense of Liberal Democracy," in *Thomas Aquinas and His Legacy*, ed. David M. Gallagher (Washington, D.C.: Catholic University of America Press, 1994), 149–72. On Maritain's critique of the origins of modernity see his *Three Reformers: Luther, Descartes, Rousseau* (New York: Charles Scribner's Sons, 1929) and *Antimoderne* (Paris: Editions de la Revue des Jeunes, 1922).

5. See new translation, "To Seekers of Truth: Message to Men of Thought and Science," in *Reassessing the Liberal State: Reading Maritain's Man and the State*, ed. Timothy Fuller and John P. Hittinger (Washington, D.C.: Catholic University of America Press, 2001), 245.

6. Jacques Maritain, *The Peasant of the Garonne: An Old Layman Questions Himself about the Present Time*, trans. Michael Cuddihy and Elizabeth Hughes (New York: Holt, Rinehart and Winston, 1968).

7. Edmund Burke, *Reflections on the Revolution in France*, ed. Conor Cruise O'Brien (New York: Penguin, 1969), 90.

8. See Brooke W. Smith, *Maritain: Antimodern or Ultramodern?* (New York: Elsevier Scientific Publishing, 1976) and Bernard Doering, *Jacques Maritain and the French Catholic Intellectuals* (Notre Dame, Ind.: University of Notre Dame Press, 1983).

9. See Leo XIII, "On Christian Philosophy," in *The Church Speaks to the Modern World: The Social Teachings of Leo XIII*, ed. Étienne Gilson (Garden City, N.Y.: Image, 1954), 29–54, and Victor B. Brezik, ed., *One Hundred Years of Thomism: Aeterni Patris and Afterwards—A Symposium* (Houston, Tex.: Center for Thomistic Studies, 1981).

10. Maritain, *Peasant of the Garonne*, 25.

11. Maritain, *Peasant of the Garonne*, 53.

12. "*Magnum opus et arduum, sed Deus adiutur noster est.*" Augustine, *The City of God against the Pagans*, trans. George E. McCracken, 7 vols. (Cambridge: Harvard University Press, 1957), vol. 1, 10. See Peter Brown, *Augustine of Hippo* (Berkeley: University of California Press, 1969), 299–312.

13. Maritain, *Peasant of the Garonne*, 4.

14. Jacques Maritain, *Man and the State* (Washington, D.C.: The Catholic University of America Press: 1998).

15. Maritain, *Man and the State*, 58. For recent comments on Maritain's refutation of Machiavelli, see James V. Schall, *Jacques Maritain: The Philosopher in Society* (Lanham, Md.: Rowman & Littlefield, 1998) and his article "Was Maritain a Crypto-Machiavellian?" in *The Failure of Modernism: The Cartesian Legacy and Contemporary*

Pluralism, ed. Brendan Sweetman (Washington, D.C.: American Maritain Association and Catholic University of America Press, 1999), 87–100; see also Markus Fischer, *Well-Ordered License: On the Unity of Machiavelli's Thought* (Lanham, Md.: Lexington Books, 2000), 199–205.

16. Maritain, *Man and the State*, 61. For an elaboration see Jacques Maritain, *Christianity and Democracy*, trans. Doris C. Anson (New York: Charles Scribner's Sons, 1950) and *On the Use of Philosophy* (Princeton, N.J.: Princeton University Press, 1961), chapter three.

17. See in particular, *The Rights of Man and Natural Law*, trans. Doris C. Anson (New York: Charles Scribner's Sons, 1943).

18. Maritain, *Man and the State*, 90. See John P. Hittinger, "Three Philosophies of Human Rights," in *In Search of a National Morality*, ed. William Bentley Ball (Grand Rapids, Mich.: Baker Book House, 1992), 246–58.

19. See Ralph McInerny, *Art and Prudence: Studies in the Thought of Jacques Maritain* (Notre Dame, Ind.: University of Notre Dame Press, 1988), chapter nine.

20. For the content of the message see *Reassessing the Liberal State: Reading Maritain's Man and the State*, ed. Timothy Fuller and John P. Hittinger (Washington, D.C.: Catholic University of America Press, 2001), 246.

21. Jacques Maritain, *Notebooks*, trans. Joseph W. Evans (Albany, N.Y.: Magi Books, 1984), 3.

~

CHAPTER TWO

On Virtue with Genius: The Achievement of Yves R. Simon

And have men always dwelt in a world in which nothing is connected?
Where virtue is without genius, and genius without honor?

—Alexis de Tocqueville, *Democracy in America*

Philosophy Before the Council

Yves R. Simon (1903–1961) is an outstanding example of that tradition which refers to itself as the "perennial philosophy." Like flowers in spring, the concepts of virtue and natural law, God and being, nature and causality, weather many winters of discontent and return again in full bloom throughout the centuries. Although rooted in the ancient philosophy of Aristotle, and developed by medieval masters like Thomas Aquinas, of course the concepts must be reappropriated in light of new knowledge and social conditions and be applied appropriately to contemporary challenges. In a day when especially virtue has become in vogue and subject to superficiality, Simon exhibits a genius to bring forth the solid and profound teaching of Aristotle and makes it available for contemporary appropriation (see, for example, his *Definition of Moral Virtue*). In politics, he has shown connections between liberty and order and the claims of excellence with the claims of the people in ways that protect and purify the achievements of modern liberal democracy. In the fields of epistemology and metaphysics he has worked through modern science and returned to the concepts of purposeful nature and realistic understanding of things. Thus the perennial themes and accomplishments of Aristotelian philosophy are richly proffered for contemporary readers.

Yves R. Simon studied and wrote and taught during a challenging era prior to and after World War II. "One of the brightest in the history of philosophy"— so Yves R. Simon described the period between the wars, referring in particular to his mentor Jacques Maritain and also Etienne Gilson.

> Having understood that philosophy needs the light of faith, the Christian philosopher is saved from entertaining two kinds of truths and risking the divorce of his intellectual from his spiritual life. In my opinion it is this union of philosophical intelligence and Christian faith, brought about by the labor of a few great minds, that makes this period one of the brightest in the history of philosophy.[1]

Maritain, Gilson, and Simon, of course, came to North America during World War II and all three established themselves as outstanding scholars and philosophers in American academia and beyond. Thus it could equally be said that the bright period extended beyond World War II into the 1960s and that Simon himself made up part of its splendor. It is important to get the story of Catholic intellectual life straight. There is a great myth concerning the intellectual life of the church prior to Vatican II; specifically that it was impoverished by a lack of imagination, narrowly focused on scholastic hair-splitting, rigidly enclosed by dogma, irrelevant to the contemporary world, and the like. Many clerics and religious, educated by scholastic textbooks, are very susceptible to this view. While it is the case that textbook Thomism often ruled the day with a formulaic approach to the big questions, two things must be kept in mind. First, the formulas were true; second, a deep intellectual germination of Leo XIII encyclical *Aeterni Patris* (1890) came to bear extraordinary fruit during the 1930s and 1940s in the works of a number of Thomists, including Garrigou LaGrange, Josef Pieper, Jacques Maritain, and Yves R. Simon. They herald and embody the great truths and authentic renewals of Vatican II, and thus it may be rightly said that the preconciliar era was the brightest in quite some time.

Their work is premised on a rejection of the notion that a "firewall" separates philosophy and faith. Simon found too many scholars accept some version of the "two truth theory" according to which one may compartmentalize science and scholarship isolating it from faith, holding in effect "two truths" and never bothering to verify "whether there was any agreement." It is a theory that winds all the way back to Plato and ancient forms of civic and poetic religion as popular forms of belief which only approximate the real truth of reason. Simon clearly understood that various trends of thought contradict the faith. He encountered "university conformism"—authors were to be read or not read, journals consulted or not consulted, questions raised or not raised—in short the whole style of research, thought, and expression was preset. Then it was Descartes and French rationalism; today it is deconstruction, existentialism, or linguistic analysis. The penchant for fads and trends affects academia no less than Fifth Avenue, only philosophers call their trends "paradigms" and dress themselves out accordingly. The fortunes of the perennial philosophy are not now or always great in academia. But the solidity and scope of its wisdom are apparent to numerous readers beyond academia; and the stability of faith seems to offer it place and shelter. Being subject to intellectual trends, often not lasting, evinces a failure to establish a unity of life, allowing the light and grace of faith to make a difference in how one thinks and acts.

According to Vatican II, *Church in the Modern World*, "this split between the faith which many profess and their daily lives deserves to be counted among the most serious errors of the age." Virtually every Catholic university and college in the United States, save those conspicuous few, are under the sway of this error, ironically in the name of renewal and Vatican II! Of course, temporal matters have their own proper autonomy because "all things are endowed with their own stability, truth, goodness, proper laws, and order. Man must respect these as he isolates them by the appropriate methods of the individual sciences or arts" (#36). So too, believers must "keep the laws proper to each discipline, and labor to equip themselves with a genuine expertise in their various fields" (#43). But the autonomy of temporal affairs does "not mean that created things do not depend on God or that they can be used without reference to their creator" (#36). Moreover grace is needed to cling to what is good and achieve integrity even within the natural order (#37). All human activity must be purified and perfected by grace. The life and work of Yves R. Simon is a testimony to the unity of life, in this case rigorous academic and intellectual work with devout faith, envisioned by Vatican II.

Life and Works

Yves R. Simon was born in Cherbourg, France in 1903. His father was the technical director of a manufacturing plant. He went to Paris in 1920 for higher education; in 1921 he attended philosophy courses at the Sorbonne and at Institute Catholique; there he came to know Jacques Maritain. Although interested in the study of philosophy he also studied science, economics, and medicine. He prepared a doctoral dissertation on the philosophy of Proudhon. He obtained degrees from the University of Paris in 1923 and 1926 and from the Institute Catholique in 1929 and 1934. Simon taught at the University Catholique in Lille in 1930. Although Simon was deeply influenced by Maritain and devoted himself to the philosophy of Thomas Aquinas, he was not impressed by the Action Française, a Royalist group to which most Catholic intellectuals were attracted. In fact he saw Thomists being compromised by its association with this group. A series of books on these matters help one to appreciate the political passion of Simon: *The Road to Vichy* and *Community of the Free*. He was a strong supporter of De Gaulle in France and the Democratic Party in the United States. In 1938 he came to the United States and he taught at the University of Notre Dame from 1938 to 1948. In 1948 he was appointed to the Committee of Social Thought, a prestigious interdisciplinary group that included Leo Strauss, David Grene, F. A. Hayek, Edward Shills, and M. Elide. In a distinguished University of Chicago series that includes *Natural Right, Road to Serfdom, Man and the State*, Simon published his famous book *Philosophy of Democratic Government*. In his lectures at the University of Chicago one can find careful analysis and distinctions, a breadth of sources including literary and political, and most of all a remarkable use of the language with a careful ear for idiomatic expression, concrete examples, and analogies. Yves R. Simon, who struggled with the effects of polio since childhood, died of cancer in 1961. Maritain later wrote about the tremendous burdens he suffered for his handicap and pain: "The dreadful and unceasing physical sufferings with which he was visited by God's unfathomable love prepared him to approach the shores of eternal life with an admirably purified soul." Many of his lectures and articles have been published posthumously, being carefully translated and edited by his many devoted students.

Perhaps the best way into the thought of Yves R. Simon is *The Definition of Moral Virtue*, a delightful and instructive work about real virtue in contrast to contemporary substitutes for it; *Practical Knowledge* is a good follow up to many of its themes. Of course the classic work which must be read is *Philosophy of Democratic Government*, a difficult but powerful explanation and defense of democracy using the principles of Aristotle and Thomas; to appreciate his exploration of themes about science and nature one should read *The Great Dialogue of Nature and Space*; to understand the political context of Simon's passion for democracy his critique of French politics is explained in *The Road to Vichy*; for advanced reading one should get *The Tradition of Natural Law; Freedom of Choice;* and *An Introduction to the Metaphysics of Knowledge*.

Freedom and Democratic Government

Since the French Revolution, with its extreme ideological and political agenda, many Catholics believe that the democratic or republican movement was in principle opposed to Catholic truth and practice. Tocqueville's lament could well be that of Simon's:

> Men of religion fight against freedom, and lovers of liberty attack religions; noble and generous spirits praise slavery, while low servile minds preach independence; honest and enlightened citizens are the enemies of all progress, while men without patriotism or morals make themselves apostles of enlightenment. Have all ages been like ours? And have men always dwelt in a world in which nothing is connected? Where virtue is without genius and genius without honor? Where love of order is confused with a tyrants' taste and the sacred cult of freedom is taken as a scorn of law? Where nothing seems forbidden or permitted, honorable or dishonorable, true or false?

In fact, Simon is a contemporary Tocqueville; a thoughtful and passionate defender of liberty and the democratic regime, pointing out its superiority to the alternatives, clearly articulating the conditions for its flourishing, and yet chastising its internal weaknesses and contradictions. Simon, as Maritain, sought to work out the implications of the renewal of Leo XIII, especially the recognition of the importance of liberty and justice as animating ideals of political order. Both men could watch history unfold before their eyes as one form of socialism transformed into another, and liberty be snuffed out in the process. In an article entitled "The Doctrinal Issue between the Church and Democracy" Simon argued that the problem lay partly in understanding the nature of political authority. Many church documents condemned the new democratic movement insofar as it seemed to exalt human freedom and power over divine and moral law. The theory of consent of the people as a source of power was understood to mean that authority emanates from the people and nothing can brook its will; and similarly it could support an individualistic anarchy in which no man need obey or submit to a law to which he did not give his consent. The church was thus a defender of authority and order. And many Catholics understood this to mean a negative position toward democratic regimes; a Catholic must be a royalist, an aristocrat, or even a "corporatist," but certainly not a republican or a socialist. Thus, Simon's first great intellectual accomplishment is his careful analysis of authority; he explains the various functions and types of authority.

Authority is derived not simply or primarily from defects in human nature, but from plenitude; it is needed for united action and what he calls the material volition of the common good. Authority in principle frees up the energies of particular people and particular groups to see to the flourishing of their own realm of activity. Ultimately he shows the vital interconnection of autonomy with authority. Thus he proves that the lover of liberty need not despise authority; and that authority properly understood must draw upon the vital energies of the people under its sway. And this indeed is essential to the "liberal attitude": the belief that the social whole is best served by the spontaneous operation of the elementary energies. This is one part of the great Catholic social principle of subsidiarity. In addition he works through various kinds of authority to show (as did Aristotle and Thomas before him) that political authority, rule over free men, is different in kind from paternal and despotic authority. Democracy is to be defended today because it is best able to achieve political life itself—rule over free men and to avoid the great dangers of tyranny.

Thus, Simon's case for democratic government does not consists of elaborate justifications of the ends of the liberal democratic state—maximum freedom or equal regard for every plan of life. Such justifications in the contemporary context rely very heavily on moral relativism and have become codified in the push for multiculturalism, right to choose, and the politically correct. Simon avoids what John Paul II refers to as an alliance between democracy and relativism, which opens the way to totalitarian manipulation. Rather he argues that universal suffrage ultimately guards against the indifference or tyranny of the few. In our day this would take the form of an intellectual or scientific elite. The advantage of democracy lies in universal suffrage as a check on excessive power, especially power of scientific elites. Simon examines a democratic "postulate of equal ability." He has one imagine a physicist, a genius to boot, making a speech at a political meeting; to a workman it may be said "He knows more physics than you, but in politics you are his equal." On the one hand, this postulate may be interpreted to mean that politics requires no special excellence or that we are all of equal virtue; in fact, Simon claims that good government requires "unusual virtue, intelligence and many other qualifications that cannot be expected to be possessed by any great number of men." Further he says that "the definition of the good man is frightfully exacting, for goodness implies achievement, accomplishment, completeness, totality, integrality, plenitude," and is therefore not in great supply. Why then democracy and universal suffrage? The postulate of equal ability reminds us that "political wisdom is not a specialty an expertness, not art or craft but a human quality on account of which intellect and will are righteously disposed with regards to the goods of man." Democracy returns us to the question of the human good and good life. Unfortunately technology, an en-

gine for democratic reform and democratic achievement, may well undermine its very promise.

The Challenges of Technology

The changes brought about by technology are complex and ambivalent;
Simon describes six categories of significant change concerning time, nature, life, reason, labor, and leadership. First, technology has speeded the
time frame in which projects can be accomplished, thereby weakening
"our sense of dependence upon the past and future of society" and increasing a sense of loneliness; second, there is an increased ratio of artificial things over natural things; third, an increased ratio of the nonliving
to the living things in our environment. By changing these ratios "technology threatens to impair the communion of man with universal nature."
Fourth, a technological society raises the expectation of a "greater amount
of rationality in the arrangement of things." The ratios of danger and security are altered; great confidence is placed in human power to control
chance; fifth, there develops in technological society as substitution of
technical education for humanistic education. Sixth, there is a rise to
prominence of technical experts and instrumental reason, often displacing
authentic leaders, "men of virtue and human experience." The cumulative
effects, the end of such a society, without an ethical compass, is a lust for
power and alienation from nature and from others. The pursuit of happiness all but loses its substantive meaning. Specific challenges are twofold:
first, a "hedonistic philosophy" combined with the loss of traditional or
customary discipline; and second, the creation of expert elite with its
dream of social engineering.

Simon observes that "by increasing the amount of goods available, technology gives to many men their first chance to look beyond satisfaction of
elementary needs." Some seek literature and music; others wild pleasures,
and others power. Simon says that the ratio is indeterminate in itself; but
he combines this with the fact that democracy overturns paternalistic customs and irrational customs, thereby lessening the hold of traditional discipline. "Politicians and theorists spread the belief that democracy expects
little and lessens pain and exertion." The end of paternalism "requires new
and costly forms of heroism." "The promise of an easy life is but a seduction
into decadence." In addition Simon finds spontaneity of feeling and desire
as a substitute for virtue. Or a "psycho-technology" which seeks to secure
universal happiness through techniques of ordering and releasing emotion
and passion.

But the great challenge is surely the rise of an expert elite with the dream of social engineering. A technological society raises the expectation of a "greater amount of rationality in the arrangement of things." But as a result the world of man becomes "irritatingly unintelligible." The "untrustworthiness of man" is a scandal as we come to "trust physical processes controlled by techniques." As Simon puts it, technology is not only a material cause of modern society, but also its exemplary cause—a model for how life is to be approached. The experts focus on new techniques and knowledge to control behavior, but must come to grief against human freedom and the contingency of human affairs; and the "rationalism born of technological pride hates human liberty both on account of its excellence and its wretchedness." This is the least reconcilable enemy of democracy and liberty. Schemes for controlling teenage pregnancy are perhaps the greatest example of this; there is a belief that the right technology and the right knowledge will lead to virtuous outcomes or dependable behavior. But only virtue and the disposition of character can provide the modicum of stability or dependability in human affairs.

Simon's prophetic voice rings true again when he said that humanity will not be saved by educational reforms: "it would be exceedingly naive to believe that with good courses in history, literature, the classics, etc., we can expect a young surgeon to live up to his ethical and social obligations." To put the matter simply—right use is a matter for prudence not science. Knowledge and art can be ignored at the time of action. But there is a form of knowledge that would be prove most beneficial to a human use of technology. Technical energy should be devoted toward a genuine human good; hence there is a need for a "sound knowledge of human finalities." This knowledge is difficult to obtain, but with it men would be willing to serve nobler ways of life. This is the key issue of an ethics of technology. The older view of *techne* as articulated by Aristotle was that art imitates and cooperates with nature; it was enfolded within the finalities of nature. Simon is very much aware of the character of modern science as nonteleological and its subsequent technology would in some way be oblivious to finality.

The Meaning of Nature

The core problem with technological basis for modern democracy is the loss of the sense of nature. Given the permanence of technology and its connection to the realization of democratic ideals he counsels men to avoid "antisocial dreams" and simplistic condemnations of technological society. So Simon holds out agrarian life as a counterpoint to urban technology; and he drives deeper to find an ethics of technology within the very notion and vocation of technology itself; this leads finally to a deepened understanding of the meaning and viability of teleological nature.

At first glance, the advocacy of a rural ideal seems even further out of date than when it was first proposed in 1950. He did not suggest that we leave the city and all return to rural life; but he believed that the witness and opportunity of such a life would have a leavening effect upon society and perhaps serve as an analogous ideal: "the enthusiastic few needed to maintain the family farm as a pole of attraction acting upon the whole of society." In rural life one could find a more human scope for work, greater solidarity, greater appreciation for the cycles of nature. Such a life would promote "things that can never become indifferent to men—communion with universal nature, the conquest of time through everlasting faithfulness, temperance, dignity in poverty, holy leisure, contemplation." Perhaps the family farm can no longer serve much of a sociological base for these great things. But it is our challenge to find ways to make them a reality in human life. Just raising a whole family in the contemporary society would accomplish much, excepting for holy leisure.

The deeper quest for nature may also arise out our very use of technology; Simon stresses the fact that the tool itself can be used for good or for ill. The importance ethical concern lies in the right use. Indeed ethics itself is a matter of "good human use both of things and of one's powers in relation to oneself as well as other people." Good use requires application of human finalities—respect for and nurturing of an integral human good. One needs a knowledge of human nature and human perfection, in short a basis for natural law This requires a knowledge of nature. It is a great axiom of Simon's work, as it must be for any authentic Thomism, that "a sound philosophy of man without a minimum of soundness in the philosophical interpretation of nature is inconceivable." This is very demanding. It takes a knowledge of modern science, historical origins, and philosophy of nature. Perhaps the greatest achievement of the intellectual renewal is that work of Stanley Jaki, Charles DeKonninck, and Yves R. Simon all of whom have combined these fields of scholarship. Suffice it to say that Simon devoted much attention to the problem of purpose in nature (teleology) and especially the ways in which mathematical models of nature exclude purpose from the start. It is also due to mechanistic notions of deterministic causality that the social engineers draw their ideal for human science as well. The philosophy of mechanism may be useful as a methodological tool, but problematic as a comprehensive philosophy of nature.

Simon draws upon human experience and plays of Shakespeare to convey the teleological concept of nature. His most sophisticated scholarly studies of human knowledge outline the grounds for an authentic and scientific knowledge of natural purpose.

Natural Law and Virtue

Once we can attain a proper understanding of nature (derived from Aristotelian philosophy and doctrine of creation) the contours of natural law ethics can be discerned. Simon uses the classic Thomistic text concerning the three levels of human good and finality—first, the good of life and preservation of being, shared with all things; second, the good of marriage, procreation, and family life shared to some degree with other forms of animal life; and third the distinctively human quest for friendly association, truth, and ultimately God himself. In light of philosophy nature these goods are clear. But in the present condition we may need the stabilizing influence and light of revelation.

But natural law, as a law or rule for behavior, is still on the level of universal precept; human action requires attention to particularities; in short it requires prudence and virtue. At long last we arrive at the core of Simon's philosophy—the notion of human prudence and virtue. The dependability that the social engineers so long for, the happiness of psychotechnology, and the freedom that cult of spontaneity admire are actually to be found in the achievement of human virtue—and there is no short cut to virtue. The core idea revolves around "*habitus*" or "*hexis*" translated as character. He has an excellent description of this notion clearing away modern confusions. In the ancient meaning habit is not an involuntary, thoughtless, mechanical conformity; rather it designates what is vital and creative and a necessity which is objective and firm. Maritain calls them titles to metaphysical nobility.

The virtuous man is in a state of existential readiness to act; this is the result of years of education and formation, but it is a readiness to know what to do and a facility to do what is good. It requires a disposition of the soul; an ordering of its parts—moderation of appetites, striving for what is a noble good. In final analysis it takes a range of virtues, all of which are interdependent. All are guided by the ancient virtue of prudence. Prudence does not mean selfish or calculating regard; it means a reasoned and true capacity to act for human goods. No axioms, rules, or formulas can substitute for prudence.

Conclusion

Yves R. Simon is an intellectual of the highest caliber; that he is also a man of devout faith is not unrelated to his achievement. The tremendous courage and perseverance that lie behind his work are obvious. For one of the clearest and instructive teachers of the perennial philosophy, the works of Yves R. Simon should head the top of our list. His genius served virtue and we can proudly honor his genius. Because of his work, we can once again dwell in a connected world. The heritage of Catholic philosophy, germinating from the last century and culminating in the works of the generation of scholars prior to Vatican II, is splendid indeed.

Notes

This chapter first published as "The Achievement of Yves R. Simon," *Crisis* (January 1996), 36–39.

1. Yves R. Simon, "Philosophy and Faith: Extracts from the Memoirs of a French Philosopher," *Notes et Documents de l'Institut International Jacques Maritain* XIV (January–March 1979), 5–8

~

PART II

Thomism, Liberty, and Democracy

Freedom is for them not only a right, but an obligation, a duty for which they must render to God an account.

—George Bernanos, *Plea for Liberty*

The American body politic is the only one which was fully and explicitly born of freedom, of the free determination of men to live together and work together at a common task. And in this new political creation, men who belonged to various national stocks and spiritual lineages and religious creeds—and whose ancestors had fought the bitterest battles against one another—have freely willed to live together in peace, as free men under God, pursuing the same temporal and terrestrial common good. Lincoln's phrase about the government of the people, by the people, and for the people is the best definition of political democracy, and was but an expression of the concrete, existing reality he dealt with. Furthermore, as regards the aim of American democracy, they cannot be better defined, I think, than by another statement of Abraham Lincoln's—when he spoke, in his First Message, of "the struggle for maintaining in the world that form and substance of government whose leading object is to elevate the condition of men; to lift artificial weights from all shoulders; to clear the paths of laudable pursuit for all; to afford all an unfettered start and a fair chance in the race of life."

—Jacques Maritain

Jacques Maritain and Yves R. Simon's Use of Thomas Aquinas in Their Defense of Liberal Democracy

Although his writings on the topic are sparse, St. Thomas left a rich legacy for political philosophy.[1] Some of the great themes of Aristotelian political philosophy were transmitted and developed by Aquinas, such as the social and political nature of man, the importance of the common good, and the role of virtue. In addition, Thomas developed the classic formulations of natural law philosophy by which human reason could appeal to a standard higher than positive human law. Finally, mention must be made of the development of Catholic social teaching that owes much to the theology of Aquinas.[2] This rich legacy has been appropriated and transformed by two of the chief Thomist philosophers of the twentieth century, Jacques Maritain (1882–1973) and Yves R. Simon (1903–1961). These two French philosophers, who spent much time in the United States, developed a very persuasive and influential philosophy of democratic government. Their work helped to shift the axis of Catholic social and political thought away from tradition and monarchy to support for liberal democratic regimes.[3] Because the development and exposition of the political thought of Thomas Aquinas has been virtually identified with the work of these two authors, it is important to examine the use that they make of Aquinas in their justification of democracy. We propose in this chapter therefore to outline the case that Maritain and Simon make for liberal democracy and the warrants they claim for it in the legacy of St. Thomas. The validity of their claim is examined in light of the texts and philosophy of Aquinas. We hope to draw some conclusions about the continued relevance of the political legacy of St. Thomas.

The great achievement of Maritain and Simon was to provide a Thomistic defense of liberal democracy in the face of a crisis rooted in the mutual antagonism of the Catholic Church and western liberal democracy dating back to the French Revolution and conditioned by the dramatic rise of totalitarian states of the right and left. As French ex-patriots living in the United States, both men were deeply disturbed by the trauma and treachery of Vichy. They came to believe that western liberal democracy contained the principles of right order and that it must be defended against the onslaught of totalitarian regimes. Both were devout Catholics and committed to the philosophy of St. Thomas; yet both were sharply criticized by conservatives and fellow Catholics.

The regime they sought to defend includes popular elections; commitment to freedom, i.e., civic rights and structural pluralism; a commitment to social justice—that is, the equal dignity of all and respect for the working class. In addition, they had to come to terms with the modern technological and economic infrastructures. And yet both were not simple apologists for western liberal democracy. They sought that elusive goal of much contemporary religious political thought, the third way between liberal individualism and totalitarianism. Their defense of liberal democracy is a qualified one; it is qualified by their roots in the philosophy of St. Thomas and the ideal of a new Christendom. Their philosophy of democratic government combines freedom and authority, natural law and natural rights, and equality and excellence.[4]

The Maritain/Simon Case for Democracy

The case for liberal democracy made by Maritain and Simon relies on four clusters of themes and texts. These are: (1) Political rule and the problem of universal suffrage; (2) the transmission theory and the problem of consent; (3) subsidiarity and the problem of liberty; and (4) equality and human rights. We must examine these four themes and the texts of St. Thomas, and attempt to determine whether the legacy of Aquinas does indeed warrant an endorsement of liberal democracy.

Political Rule and the Problem of Universal Suffrage

Universal suffrage is an essential element of the western liberal democratic regimes that Maritain and Simon sought to defend. On what basis can this feature of democracy be justified from within the legacy of St. Thomas? Simon makes a very interesting case for universal suffrage on the basis of a classic distinction between despotic and political rule; it is a distinction that Thomas derives from Aristotle's *Politics*.[5] In his treatment of the sensual powers of human beings, Thomas queries whether the appetites obey reason (ST, Ia, q. 81, a. 3, ad. 2). It is objected that the appetites resist reason, and therefore they are not subject to reason. Thomas replies to the objection as follows:

> For a power is called despotic whereby a man rules his slaves, who have not the right to resist in any way the orders of the one that commands them, since they have nothing of their own. But that power is called political or royal by which a man rules over free subjects, who, though subject to the government of the ruler, have nevertheless something of their own, by reason of which they can resist the orders of him who commands.[6]

Thomas concludes that reason rules the body despotically, but that reason rules the appetites with a royal or political rule because the appetites can resist the rule of reason. In a similar text, Thomas queries whether in the state of innocence man would have been master over man (ST, Ia, q. 96, a. 4).[7] Thomas explains a two-fold meaning of the term master: the first meaning entails mastery of slaves, the second, entails rule over free men. The essential difference, Thomas points out, between a slave and a free man, is that a free man has "disposal of himself" whereas "a slave is ordered to another." Thomas concludes that in a state of innocence there would be no rule of master over slave; however there would be rule of one over others on the basis of acting for the unity of the common good and on the basis of superior knowledge and virtue.

Now Simon understands that political rule, and the presence of resistance, does not warrant democracy alone; democracy is one form of political rule, exercising its peculiar form of resistance to unjust rule, but there are other means available to other types of regimes. Democracy, therefore, insofar as it helps to establish conditions of political rule, and avoids tyranny, is a regime justified by the Thomistic text. However, Simon seeks to go beyond this legitimation to a recommendation of democracy as the best regime available. What is the feature that goes beyond political rule and what is its warrant? Simon defines that feature as follows:

> When the political idea assumes the democratic form, the people asserts, over and above its freedom from abusive power, its freedom to govern itself. Keeping the government confined within a definite field is no longer held sufficient; the government has been taken over by the people. Such is democratic freedom, the defining feature of democracy.[8]

In order to justify this feature of democratic government Simon recapitulates the partisan dialogue of Aristotle's *Politics*, Book III, chapters 9–13.

Simon weighs very carefully the arguments for and against the practice of universal suffrage. He classifies these arguments into three types, (1) the statistical; (2) the sociological; and (3) the romantic. Thus, the objections to universal suffrage (the many) and in favor of aristocracy (the few) are first, the statistical fact that the qualifications for good government cannot be expected by a very great number of people: "good government is the work of excellent wisdom; it demands unusual virtue, intelligence, some education, a great deal of experience, and many other qualifications which cannot be expected to be possessed by any great number of men."[9] Second, the rule of the few is preferred because of the sociological fact that the upper class of society produces a "comparatively high rate of excellence." Third, an argument is sometimes made based upon the romantic conception that the upper class is capable of lofty pursuits and disinterested service of society. On the other hand, Simon makes a case for what he calls democratic "optimism." First, from a statistical perspective there is less evil in a large group: "evil may have a selective affinity for this minority and saturate it, while remaining infrequent in mankind at large." Similar arguments are made in favor of rule by a larger group rather than a smaller group by Aristotle and Madison.[10] A second reason for democratic optimism is the sociological consideration that the many people can produce an aggregate virtue and wisdom through the pooling of their many talents and perspectives. Aristotle again makes a similar argument in the *Politics* III.11 with respect to the feast and the drama critic; in addition he mentions the judgment of the patient over the physician. Finally, the romantic conception of the many deems the poor as intrinsically good. Surprisingly, Simon finally recommends none of the three arguments for democratic optimism. Universal suffrage he says is rooted in pessimism and the requirement in the present age for political rule. Simply put, the common man "will be crushed unless the constitution of society attaches some power to the only distinction that he certainly possesses, *viz.*, that of having numbers on his side." It is protection of the people from despotism then that finally justifies universal suffrage; it is the Thomistic distinction between despotic and political rule that provides Simon's warrant for democracy. But what is it about the present conditions that does so? At this point in his argument Simon does not elaborate other than to say that an elite cannot be trusted with rule: "there was a time when it was possible to believe that the destiny of the common man was safely entrusted to the wisdom of the upper class. That time is apparently gone forever."[11] It is the conditions of contemporary society, at least in the menace posed by elites, which justify democracy, not the intrinsic claims of the many to rule.

Maritain, on the other hand, sets out to justify universal suffrage from an axiom of the authority of the people. That is, Maritain merely asserts the sociological argument in favor of the rule of the many.[12] He does not engage the dialectical argument as to who should rule. It is an axiom of Maritain's thought that the people should rule. That axiom is given some defense by Maritain and Simon through another cluster of texts and themes entitled the transmission theory of authority. To that theme and text we now turn.

The Transmission Theory and the Problem of Consent

The problem of universal suffrage points to a more original problem, that of the origin of the right to rule and the role of popular consent. As we have seen, Maritain bypasses the question of limited government as a means to justify universal suffrage and proceeds directly to the transmission theory of authority. This somewhat arcane debate about a theory which developed around issues pertaining to the temporal and spiritual powers of the supreme pontiff and the divine right of kings is developed by Maritain and Simon into a centerpiece of their Thomistic justification of liberal democracy.[13] In an important article entitled "The Doctrinal Issues between the Church and Democracy," Yves R. Simon outlines three issues of major significance: the general relation between the state and religion; freedom of belief and expression; and the origin and ultimate meaning of temporal power.[14] The third issue is the most important because it is most specific to democracy; and further, church leaders had singled out an interpretation of democracy as inconsistent with church doctrine and sound political principles. Both Leo XIII and Pius X condemned a theory that asserts men are bound only by laws to which they consent. Simon believes that democracy does not in fact rest upon such a view; but the problem is real in terms of giving an interpretation of the fact of obedience and the role of consent in the political order. To get at this issue Simon constructs his famous typology of theories of authority: the "coach driver" theory, the "divine right" theory, and the "transmission" theory of authority.

The coach driver theory accords no authority to the statesman or officials of government. The rulers are but "pure instruments" of prior decisions of the people. This theory seems to justify the democratic practices whereby representatives are seen as hired servants, public opinion and lobby groups form decisions of these representatives, and it honors the autonomy of the individual. Simon argues that this theory is a "masked anarchy." His proof is that a majority must rule the minority lest there be chaos and inability to act. Real authority is required by the need for united action. The coach driver theory mistakes the final cause (for the good of the whole) and the efficient cause (by the whole). This is the doctrine condemned.

In reaction to the coach driver theory, some have resorted to the divine right theory; God gives authority to the ruler. In part, this theory arose as a seventeenth-century problematic concerning the Christian prince. The disturbing implications of the theory are that the ruler holds a power with no accountability. Maritain describes the same position as the theory of absolute sovereignty, which he rightly rejects. It places the ruler as separate from the political body and without limit or accountability.[15]

As a solution to the extremes, Maritain and Simon propose to develop the "transmission theory" of authority. According to this theory authority resides in the people, in the civil community as a whole, and not in distinct persons. The civil community designates its rulers and thereby transmits power to the ruler. There are many ways in which such power is transmitted, but the clearest form is universal suffrage. It is argued that there is a genuine transmission, and therefore real authority and integrity of rule in the governing officials. The ruler must be granted the power of judgment and decision.

The Thomistic warrant for this theory is quite slim; there is an intriguing but ambiguous passage in the *Treatise on Law*. In response to the query "whether the reason of any man is competent to make laws," St. Thomas states that:

A law properly speaking, regards first and foremost the order to the common good. Now to order anything to the common good, belongs either to the whole people, or to someone who is the vice-regent of the whole people. And therefore the making of a law belongs either to the whole people or to a public personage who has care of the whole people: since in all other matters the directing of anything to the end concerns him to whom the end belongs.[16]

This text is construed to mean that authority resides in the civil community and not in distinct persons; and that the governing person would rule as a substitute or representative of the people. Simon and Maritain both compare the spiritual authority of the Pope as the Vicar of Christ and the temporal authorities who serve as vicars of the people. The temporal ruler is said by Maritain to be the "image and deputy of the people." He represents the "majesty of the people" in their collective life. Simon and Maritain are following the lead of the great Thomistic commentators Cajetan, Bellarmine, and Suarez all of whom use this text to solve disputes surrounding temporal and spiritual power. For example Cajetan argues that while the Pope cannot be deposed by the people, the king may be so deposed. Similarly, Bellarmine argues that authority is given to no particular man, it belongs to the multitude; it may be added that Sir Robert Filmer makes Bellarmine's democratic thesis his first object of attack in *De Patriarchia*. Finally Suarez claims that democracy is the most natural form of government because it requires no institution, whereas all other forms require a conventional institution. It is in this tradition of interpretation which Maritain and Simon follow. Now Simon admits that the text itself warrants nothing like a full justification of democracy; at most it points out the role of consent in political order and perhaps does grant a power to depose in extreme circumstances. It is a development from the text of Thomas to make it serve the purpose of democratic theory.

Accordingly as part of democratic theory Simon continues in this vein: the power of rule may not be transmitted and then we have direct democracy; when the power is transmitted this is done through periodic exercise of consent through election; power is never completely transmitted, thus in some way every democracy is a direct democracy or a deliberative assembly. Elections, referenda, and public opinion are the means whereby such authority is exercised and transmitted. As mentioned above Simon insists that the transmission is genuine, which vouchsafes the integrity and judgment of the designated personnel in command.

Thus from the debate on temporal and spiritual powers that gave rise to the transmission theory of temporal authority Simon develops a very rich analysis of the various meanings of the phrase "consent of the governed." He carefully distinguishes and elaborates on seven meanings; this passage provides a nice summary of the issue and its significance for political philosophy.[17] For example, the consent of the people reflects the fact that politics should be an act of reason and will and not instinct or blind force; or that persuasion is a better instrument of rule than is coercion. These are propositions pertaining to political order in general. The phrase may mean that the rulers are not self-appointed nor do they receive their power directly from God; rather, the people designate their rulers at least through popular approval and thereby "transmit" the authority to the rulers. This is the "transmission theory": on this reading of consent, a regime need not be democratic as such; but the rulers must acknowledge their limited claim to rule and the proper end of rule. The transmission theory demands at least a properly political regime, but it is surely implicitly democratic. The other meanings of "consent of the governed" are explicitly democratic. It may "imply a demand for periodic exercise of popular consent" such as through elections of representatives. Even more specifically, democratic meaning Simon calls the "incomplete transmission" of authority, which is proper to democracy: the people retain the character of a deliberative body. The final meaning of "consent of the governed," which Simon emphatically rejects as the real error of some democratic theories, is that the people are bound only by laws to which they give their consent. With this analysis, Simon hopes to have settled the doctrinal dispute between the church and democracy and to develop Thomas' implicit concern with the role and consent of the people into an explicit defense of democratic principles.

Maritain, for his part, follows a more axiomatic approach to the issue and arrives at a pithier conclusion. He declares that the people have a right to rule by essence, and the ruler a right only by participation in the people's original right.[18] Authority derives from the will or consensus of the people and their "basic right of self-governance." This right he says is inherent and permanent. The recognition of this right, he says, is a "basic verity" and a "conquest of democratic philosophy." Therefore, "whatever the political regime may be, monarchical, aristocratic, or democratic, democratic philosophy appears as the only true political philosophy." As a warrant for this claim, Maritain refers the reader to text of Thomas cited above and the medieval developments by Suarez and Bellarmine. From the Thomistic reference to the whole multitude as a lawmaker and the ruler as its "vice-regent," Maritain and Simon derive a full-blown justification of liberal democracy.

Subsidiarity and the Problem of Liberty
One of the key elements in their social-political philosophy is the principle of subsidiarity or autonomy. They formulate this principle in slightly different ways. Simon formulates the "principle of autonomy" which he states as follows:

> no task which can be satisfactorily fulfilled by the smaller unit should ever be assumed by the larger unit. . . . It is perfectly obvious that there is more life and unqualifiedly greater perfection in a community whose parts are full of initiative than in a community whose parts act merely as instruments transmitting the initiative as the whole.[19]

Maritain, who cites Simon's work on this principle, formulates the "principle of pluralism" which he states as follows:

> everything in the body politic which can be brought about by particular organs or societies inferior in degree to the state and born out of the free initiative of the people should be brought about by those particular organs or society.[20]

The Thomistic warrants for this principle of subsidiarity are found in unlikely places. The texts are from the *Summa Theologiae* in which Thomas queries "whether it be necessary for the human will in order to be good to be conformed to the Divine will as regards the thing willed?" and again "whether all things are governed immediately by God?"[21] In the former text,

Thomas argues that the wife of a thief condemned to death rightly wills that he be spared, whereas the judge rightly wills that he be punished. The wife wills a private good, the judge wills a good for the whole, a common good. Thomas explains that not everyone must will the common good, or even the divine will, in a material way; they must will the divine good formally, but they do not always perceive the universal good to be willed materially.[22] In the latter text Thomas explains that "As to the design of government, God governs all things immediately; whereas in its execution, He governs some things by means of others. . . . God so governs things that He makes some of them to be causes of others in government; as a master, who not only imparts knowledge to his pupils, but gives also the faculty of teaching others."[23]

The first text is said by Yves R. Simon to be "the most profound thing ever written on the foundation of authority" and "the most precise exposition ever made of the principle commanding the theory of government."[24] With these texts Simon builds a very intricate theory of authority. Authority is required, as we have seen, for unity of action, but also for the direction of the community to the common good materially willed. And the same argument for authority establishes the principle of autonomy; that is, insofar as the authorities will the material good of the common good, it is up to particular people and particular groups to will the material good of the particular person or group. Simon states "that particular goods be properly defended by particular persons matters greatly for the common good." Simon sees himself making common cause with Aristotle against the excessive unity of the state posited by Plato in The Republic. Accordingly, it is the modern democratic state that protects and encourages particular groups as opposed to the totalitarian attempts to control all sectors and activities of the citizens.

The principle of autonomy is also invoked to justify those institutions and practices which check the power of the state. Simon says that it is our duty to keep the state confined within its function and hold in check its threatening tendency to trespass.[25] Therefore he says that the salvation of society depends upon an array of institutions provided with "the power of resistance"—private property, churches, press, private schools, labor unions, and free economic enterprise. In effect then Simon now combines the principle of political rule with the principle of autonomy to defend the structural pluralism of modern democracy.[26]

Maritain similarly applies his principle of pluralism to defend the existence of intermediate groups: the body politic must include a "multiplicity of particular societies which proceed from the free initiative of citizens and they should be as autonomous as possible" and be granted institutional recognition.[27] The state, he observes, is "inevitably dull and awkward—and as a result, easily oppressive and injudicious" in the fields of industry, culture, science, and the like. He concludes that the pluralist principle is even more vital to democracy than is universal suffrage: "vital energy should unendingly rise from the people within the body politic. In other words the program of the people should not be offered from above to the people . . . it should be the work of the people." Maritain bases his argument more in the second text cited above, concerning God's governance through intermediates or secondary causes. The pluralist principle demands a democratic regime if the people are to be free to exercise initiative.

Equality and Human Rights

Universal suffrage, popular consent, and private initiative are formal and material conditions for democracy. But it is the goal or end that most properly shows the nature of the regime. Democracy is classically defined by liberty; but liberty is traceable to the principle of equality against the claims to superiority made by aristocrats or monarchs. It is the ideal of equality that arguably animates contemporary democratic convictions. From the ideal of equality, democracy finds its goal of social justice and the defense of human rights. Indeed, one may well argue that the development of a natural rights doctrine is the distinguishing characteristic of modern political philosophy as distinguished from the ancient and medieval traditions. Maritain and Simon develop a notion of equality in which they combine the modern concern for rights with the natural law tradition. It also provides a ready defense of liberal democracy. Their notion of equality is derived from Thomas' metaphysics and epistemology.[28] Equality is founded on the real unity in nature of the essence of the human. By sharing the same nature all human beings are accorded the same fundamental rights.

The basic text upon which both ground the democratic ideal of equality is from *Being and Essence*.[29] Thomas explains that a nature or essence may be considered in two ways: one in individual things and one in the mind. In the former case it exists in an individual; in the later as a universal. The essence abstracts from individual differences but it is open to such individual determination; the nature considered absolutely is truly predicated of each individual. This nature includes all features that are essential to that nature; it abstracts from individual differences. Accordingly, there is a single human essence that is the same. Simon concludes therefore "It is highly proper that they should be described as created equal for in each of them the same system of intelligible features supplies individual reality with ability to exist."[30] Further, this metaphysical explanation allows one, he says, to make sense of the notions of brotherhood, natural rights, and rights belonging to all men. Simon cites Maritain's treatment of the notion of equality in which he explains the realistic interpretation of equality as opposed to the nominalist and the idealistic interpretations. Nominalism is blamed for the racist and fascist totalitarian ideologies; for on sheer empirical grounds it is possible to deny the equality of individuals or races. There exists no real foundation for unity in essence or nature. Both men claim that is a quirk of history that natural rights doctrines arose within a climate of nominalist thought and they see nominalist tending toward denial of equality. They believe that the modern notion of rights can be purged of its nominalist trappings and put on the proper grounding of natural law and a realistic metaphysics. Thus, by the same token, Maritain rejects an idealist denial of factual inequality and their role in social order. Rather, the idea of equality as unity in nature establishes the social solidarity to include all within the good of the civic community. It is not as such a justification for democracy; it imposes an obligation upon all to respect the fundamental dignity and good of each human being. Here is the link to natural law:

> There is no right unless a certain order is inviolably required by what things are in their intelligible type of essence, or by what the nature of man is, and is cut out for: an order by virtue of which certain things like life, work, freedom are due to the human person . . . such an order . . . imposes itself upon our minds to the point of binding us in conscience, exists in things in a certain way, as a requirement of their essence.[31]

Thus Maritain's grounding of rights is different from the modern nominalist and self-interested grounding; and it is not simply a theological grounding in the brotherhood of men, God's workmanship in all men, and so on. Rights on their account are demands to establish the legal recognition of and the promotion of the good human life; it is telic, communal, and conditional. Maritain claims that all human beings possess certain rights; a minimum array of rights must be respected absolutely; but most rights are conditioned by the social and political conditions. That is, he says their exercise depends upon social conditions. He opposes the tendency to inflate and make "absolute and limitless" individual rights. Yet on the other hand, he sets a dynamic goal for human society which is properly democratic; that is, the failure to realize and have all men exercise their rights is a sign of an "inhuman element that remains in the social structure of each period."[32] Thus the metaphysical doctrine as a shared nature justifies the goal of liberal democracy. Modern democracy is the most progressive attempt to realize the latent rights of all human beings, which rights are implicit in the shared unity of human nature.

Simon adopts a similar dynamic, but with his usual greater precision and political sobriety. He distinguishes the strict equality accorded to all by the minimum precepts, such as do not kill and fairness in exchange. But he says that many social goods are capable of a dynamic egalitarian tendency to be realized in time. Education, health, and welfare are goods that society must aim at establishing in greater equality. The true notion of equality demands social progress. But then Simon says that the egalitarian dynamic is legitimately delayed when its claim would infringe upon real human goods and in particular when it destroys subsidiarity and the autonomy of persons and institutions like family: he says that equal opportunity is a first class wrecker of institutions. It is this reading of equality in nature as establishing a dynamic or tendency toward greater and greater social progress that leads to the eventual transformation of the political philosophy of St. Thomas.

St. Thomas, Democracy, and the Best Regime

Do these texts indeed establish a justification of democracy? There are a number of possibilities. They may prove that democracy is a legitimate political regime consistent with fundamental principles of St. Thomas or they may be construed as recommending democracy as the best regime. The best regime may be qualified or absolute; qualified as a limited achievement and best under certain conditions; absolute if best under any conditions or best as the model in ideal conditions. It is clear that Maritain and Simon have developed a justification for liberal democracy that goes beyond the first option. Neither do they argue that democracy is the best regime under any conditions, Simon for one is adamant in avoiding this excess of "democratic faith." They are recommending democracy as the best regime; in what sense do they do so? And how does it fit with the political philosophy of Thomas Aquinas? An examination of the texts of St. Thomas will help us to answer these questions.

Thomistic Warrants for Democracy

The first cluster of texts draws the distinction between the political and the despotic regime. These texts certainly permit the justification of democracy as a means to resist tyranny and unjust rule. Specifically, the practice of universal suffrage is indeed an effective means to resist despotic rule. Democracy is therefore consistent with the Thomistic texts. But as Simon points out democracy is not the only "political" regime. Other forms of regimes have effective means to resisting despotic rule; and indeed, he says that democracy may well consider some of these as well. Hence the texts do not recommend democracy as the absolutely best regime or even the ideal regime. However, given the circumstances of the contemporary world, such as the tendency toward centralization, technical control, and new elites, democracy may be judged the best available regime to resist tyranny.

The second cluster of texts, the basis for the transmission theory of authority, again seems to legitimate democracy as one form of decent government. The power to depose in extreme circumstances and the role of consent in normal circumstances lend weight to the claims of popular authority. But again, it is not clear that the texts are exclusively democratic in nature. Simon again acknowledges that the transmission theory was never meant to be an unqualified endorsement of democracy, nor does the text in the *Summa* warrant this.[33] A further criticism of the transmission theory pertains to the interpretation of the key text. Thomas says that either the people or the representative may make laws. This is not a strict exclusive alternative. The representative may legitimately make laws; the text does not imply that he must consult with the people through election, referendum, or that he derives power through transmission. He is said to represent and to care for the whole community. Thomas Gilbey provides some interesting commentary on this text. First, he points out that the term "vice gerent" derives from "*gerere vicem*," to act on behalf of: hence the term designates "the public personage, the figure who personifies the community, and is its guardian and, in the fullest sense, its caretaker, '*qui curam habet*'."[34] This description or explication does not point to a hypothesis about the origin of temporal power; the implications for the meaning of temporal power are simply that it must serve the common good. Again it does not exclusively endorse one or the other (multitude or ruler), or derive one from the other, but affirms both as legitimate when commensurate to the common good.[35]

This problem of interpretation points to an ambiguity and possible equivocation in the Maritain/Simon case for liberal democracy. Maritain speaks of the "democratic philosophy" being the only true philosophy and that this philosophy can then legitimate any form of regime, aristocratic, monarchical, and the like.[36] We seem to have two meanings of democracy. Democracy$_1$ means a political regime, as opposed to a despotic regime, which is aimed at the common good, and gives due consideration to popular consent and custom; Democracy$_2$ means a regime which includes popular elections, referenda, and the like. Of course Democracy$_1$ does not automatically entail Democracy$_2$. The Thomistic texts establish Democracy$_1$ and not Democracy$_2$. How do the authors make the transition from Democracy$_1$ to Democracy$_2$? There are additional elements in their account. This is in part due to the historical conditions which make Democracy$_2$ the best approximation or embodiment of Democracy$_1$; but there is also a partisan argument for Democracy$_1$ that may well put them at odds with the spirit and text of their mentor. Further, it begs the question to make the claim that there is a properly democratic body prior the establishment of a regime, which is the fundamental political phenomenon according to the Aristotlean political science followed by Thomas Aquinas. We shall elaborate on this below.

But the ambiguity is further compounded in the text at hand. What does Thomas mean by the "*multitudo*." Gilbey explains that "this does not mean the multitude, the masses, the populace, but the entire people, the whole body of citizens."[37] Similarly, Strauss points out that multitude does not necessarily designate a "democratically ordered multitude."[38] Indeed, Thomas at other times indicates that a multitude, by definition, must have an order of rule, and that rule must be by the best element in the whole.[39] His idea of the ordered multitude is more inclined to monarchy or aristocracy, as we shall see below, and not democracy, which is the rule of a part over the whole. The ambiguity of the "multitude" repeats that of "democracy" insofar as multitude could mean an ordered whole (Democracy$_1$), or the majoritarian part of the whole (Democracy$_2$). These texts do not endorse the latter.

The third cluster of texts used to justify democracy pertain to the principle of subsidiarity, called pluralism or autonomy, derived from the metaphysics of divine governance. Maritain and Simon show the importance of freedom and particularity in the Thomistic metaphysics. Again, it does not as such justify democracy; the principle calls for the political power to respect the integrity and prerogatives of the prepolitical associations such a family, business, and the like. This respect for the less perfect society may be found in any number of regime forms. Modern liberal democracy is one such form; and perhaps it is an especially suitable form to allow for individual initiative. Perhaps it is the best regime available today to guarantee the integrity of intermediate groups; the problem of centralization is best resisted by the granting of political freedom. Tocqueville argues this case for political freedom as the buttress of intermediate groups. But this reading and justification of democracy runs into conflict with the reading of the fourth justification for democracy, the tendency toward greater equality. That is, the principle of subsisidiary, pluralism, or autonomy sets up a principled resistance to monarchical or oligarchical arrangements, but also to the encroachment of the state for liberal goals.

The basis for equality in the metaphysics of St. Thomas, the shared unity of human nature, provides an interpretation of rights as correlated with duties of natural law. These rights, as the moral foundation for liberal democracy, are the heart of the justification for liberal democracy. The Thomistic account of these rights, however, allows for a minimum of natural precepts to be turned into the formulation of rights. But not only are other possible regimes consistent with the respect for fundamental human rights, i.e., fundamental precepts of natural law, there are serious doubts as to whether the Thomistic account is consistent with the interpretation given them by the jurisprudence of liberal democratic regimes. The Thomistic account is communally based and aimed at a substantive notion of the good life; the contemporary democratic one is individually based and neutral toward questions of the good; it is a procedural notion of rights. The contemporary notion is a development of that proffered by the founders of the modern political philosophy, Hobbes and Locke. There are equivocations in identifying the right language of a Maritain with that of a Nozick, Rawls, or Dworkin. Simon and Maritain both admit that the theory of rights emerged in a climate of philosophical nominalism, but they consider this accidental and in some way a distortion of true rights theory. To what degree rights theory depends essentially on nominalist and voluntarist interpretations of natural law is a historical philosophical question of great import.[40] It is a question barely treated by Maritain and Simon. Further, the identification and endorsement of the goal of liberal democracy as the tendency to a greater realization of equality requires a theory of progress. And this conflicts with the principle of autonomy as Simon himself admits.[41] Therefore, their justification of liberal democracy is not fully consistent within itself and it is not fully warranted by the texts of St. Thomas.

The texts cited by Simon and Maritain warrant democracy as a good regime to the extent that democracy embodies the conditions of a good regime—that it offers means of resistance to tyranny, serves the common good, protects intermediate groups, and protects the rights of its citizens in accord with the minimalist precepts of natural law. The texts may even warrant a justification of democracy as the best available under contemporary circumstances of centralized power, and modern economic and educational conditions. This a qualified acceptance of democracy. However, Maritain and Simon go beyond these claims in their justification and philosophy of democratic government; they endorse what Simon calls the "democratic spirit" and what Maritain calls the "democratic faith." After a brief review of Thomas' explanation of the problems with democracy and his recommendations for the best regime, we shall return to this question of the democratic spirit as a way to account for the gap between Thomas and these two Thomists on important issues in political philosophy.

Democracy and the Best Regime in St. Thomas

As classically defined, rule by the many, democracy is not the best regime according to St. Thomas. In his treatise, *On Kingship*, Thomas outlines the major problems with democracy. As the rule of a part over the whole, it is an unjust regime, i.e., "an unjust government exercised by the many is called a democracy, that is, 'rule by the people,' which occurs when the common people use the force of numbers to oppress the rich. In this case, the whole people acts like a tyrant."[42] Second, government by one person is better than government by many because one can better promote "unity in peace." From experience he argues we may learn that "provinces and cities that are not rule by one person are torn by dissension." Continual dissension leads to civil war, as was evident in the Roman Republic. In addition, Thomas believes, following Aristotle, that the majority are not capable of a high or perfect virtue; accordingly law must seek a moderate goal.[43] If virtue is the major qualification for rule, then it would follow that democracy is not the best form of government.

The argument for the best regime follow along these lines. Monarchy is best from the standpoint of unity in peace. This is an empirical fact, Thomas believes. Further, as seen above, Thomas argues that a multitude is not a flat multitude, an egalitarian sameness; there is diversity of achievement, virtue, and function. The best should rule; and such a principle could justify monarchy, aristocracy, or polity defined as rule by the warriors. Virtue and character are mentioned as a basis for kingly rule. Thomas also sees the need for some limit on the power of the king lest it become tyrannical. He recommends legal constraints, and therefore something like constitutional monarchy.

One of the most succinct and comprehensive statements of political philosophy may be found in the *Treatise on Law* in conjunction with his analysis of the judicial precepts of the old law. "Whether the Old Law Enjoined Fitting Precepts Concerning Rulers?" is the query of ST, IaIIae, q. 105, a. 1.[44] Thomas here argues that divine law provided for a mixed regime, combining monarchy, aristocracy, and democracy. Combining unity, rarity of virtue, and popular consent is the great challenge of political form. The mixed regime does it best, not democracy.

Thomas' legacy in political philosophy therefore does not provide an unqualified endorsement of democracy . It actually provides grounds for a strong case against democracy and in favor of monarchy. The best regime is a mixture of the various regimes. Maritain's remarks about regimes and the mixture of regime will help us to see whether and why he and Simon go well beyond the texts and spirit of their mentor St. Thomas in their justification of liberal democracy.

Conclusion

As a conclusion I should like to account for the gap between the spirit and letter of St. Thomas and the twentieth-century Thomists Jacques Maritain and Yves R. Simon. I believe that it is to be found in their sense of the historical situation and the possibility of progress such that the regimes of a liberal democratic character are hailed as the best regimes. Their perspective raises some serious questions of the substance, as well as the rhetoric and method, of contemporary Thomistic political philosophy.

In order to appreciate the depth of commitment to the democratic ideal found in Maritain and Simon we have to look at some of the passages which preface and intertwine the actual deployment of texts and which reveal the convictions which animate their works. For example, Maritain claims that democracy is "the highest terrestrial achievement of which the rational animal is capable here below."[45] He believes that humanity is progressing to a definitive moral rationalization of political life and that we are at the early stages of that process; democracy is now "the only way through which the progressive energies in human history do pass." This is due in great part to the need for the "human energies of free men," thus reflecting his use of the principle of subsidiarity. But also this is due to the fact that democracy is the true "gospel regime"—democracy relies upon the inspiration of the gospel for its origins and true success and it best reflects the terrestrial hope of the gospel.[46] In a very important passage in his *Rights of Man and Natural Law* Maritain explains his interpretation of Aristotle's typology of regimes. Monarchy produces unity and strength, aristocracy produces a differentiation of value and cultivates the highest and rarest virtues, and the democratic or republican regime tends toward freedom.[47] Furthermore, the best regime is a mixed regime combining all three values. But then he goes on to say that monarchy and aristocracy are stages on the road to the mixed republican regime which assimilates the values of unity and excellence and it thereby transcends them. In order to develop the progressive tendency of mankind Maritain is wont to praise what he calls "prophetic shock minorities," self-appointed elites who will awaken the people and lead them to the deeper realization of democracy. In particular he praises John Brown, Thomas Paine, and French Revolutionaries.[48] This surplus of democratic conviction goes well beyond the philosophy of Thomas Aquinas and may lead one to suspect that it may run counter to some fundamental principles of his philosophy.

Similarly Simon exhibits the deeper convictions in favor of democracy in a number of significant passages in *Philosophy of Democratic Government*.[49] In a sarcastic tone uncharacteristic of the book as a whole, Simon accuses the conservatives of advocating paternal authority of the few over the many because they view the many on par with an inferior race or no better than children, criminals, and the feeble-minded. He says that an elite of "leaders trained and educated by men of rare knowledge and superior virtue" may not be "a perverse ideal," but it is not democratic. Further, he admits that some conditions tending toward anarchy or tyranny may rule out democracy in favor of nondemocratic measures. What characterizes the democratic spirit is an "audacity" and a willingness to take risks in granting full autonomy to individuals. The risks, he says, require "new forms of discipline" and "new and costly forms of heroism" if democracy is to maintain itself. In the argument for universal suffrage he makes the case on the basis of checks and balances; then he concludes by saying the belief that the destiny of the common man could be entrusted to the wisdom of the upper classes is gone forever. He makes the argument more pointed in a lengthy discussion and critique of the upper class as unable to be in communion with the people and therefore apt to seek their own advantage. Tocqueville makes a similar argument for the justice of the democratic claim against aristocracy.[50] Social conservation in the face of egalitarian progress he describes as "maintenance of advantages traditionally enjoyed by small minorities." Although he gives very serious consideration to the claim of excellence and virtue put forward by nondemocrats, Simon advocates a democratic spirit, a liberal attitude, as opposed to the a conservative one historically characterized at best by paternalism and at worst by selfishness, indifference, or exploitation. Simon acknowledges many problems of democracy posed by Aristotle, Thomas, and contemporary writers, he scrutinizes many very closely, but others are left virtually untouched.

The advocacy of the democratic spirit and the sense of historical progress take Simon and Maritain well beyond the political philosophy of St. Thomas. The justification of democracy and the differences from Thomas raise some important substantive, as well as methodological and rhetorical, issues.

The substantive issues are at least two. First, have Maritain and Simon done an adequate analysis of political regimes? Second, can the liberal notion of rights be so readily assimilated to traditional natural law? We have seen how Maritain speaks of a democratic philosophy which precedes the form of regime; in addition, he speaks of democracy as the term of progress incorporating the values of monarchy and aristocracy. Although he speaks of the analogous realization of the values of unity and excellence in a democracy, it is not clear that he admits the trade off and possible loss of the strong or definitive sense of those values within democracy. This makes him either too blind to its shortcomings, or too expectant in the prospects for progress.[51] In the final analysis, Maritain makes appeal to Christian inspiration as means to realize the heights of democracy. Simon makes a much more careful attempt to weigh the various claims to rule; indeed, his chapter on "Democratic Freedom," in which he recapitulates the partisan dialogue of *Politics* III, is a truly masterful account. His account relies more on the classical notion of the mixed regime as way to ensure its success and excellence. Part of the difference between Thomas and Simon is simply due to the change in historical conditions. Many have pointed out that Aristotle's critique of democracy is premised upon the lack of education and development in the many due to primitive economic and technological conditions. With a majority who are educated, the prospects and claims for democracy takes on a persuasive validity. But in Simon's case the problem is that he has not quite successfully merged the democratic spirit and the goods which he seeks to preserve from his Thomistic position, such as virtue and family. Why new forms of discipline or new forms of heroism are so hard to maintain in the contemporary situation are in part due to the very democratic spirit and conditions of democratic regime which he ardently advocates. Strauss has pointed out that Simon assumes the conditions are modern technology, and therefore of modern democracy, are the normal or natural conditions; Strauss indicates that there is a certain audacity and lack of moderation in the technology which conditions modern democracy.[52] Is it a feature of the democratic spirit to push its audacity to immoderate measures?

The second substantive issue deals with the problem of human rights. We cannot begin to treat this very important issue of the relation of natural law and natural rights.[53] It is curious that both Maritain and Simon minimize the historical origins of the doctrine of rights. Maritain considers the nominalistic philosophy as an accidental error which preys upon the truth, and Simon believes that it was accidental that the doctrine arose in a nominalistic climate. Their account of human rights, based on natural law, is telic and communal. Rights are conditions which insure and promote human excellence and flourishing. Maritain would distinguish his "personalist" account from the "individualist" account given by the modern philosophy.[54] But the doctrine of human rights as it unfolds in western theory and practice of democracy is increasingly neutral with respect to the good and individualistic in orientation. Are Maritain and Simon now in a situation of a serious equivocation in their advocacy of rights? Ironically, the two authors are now classified as natural law theorists and conservatives, despite their best effort, as we have seen, to be positioned on the left and in the progressive spirit of democracy.

This in turn raises an issue about the rhetoric of their political philosophy. What are the possibilities of a common democratic faith and cooperation in a divided world given the development of the liberal notion of rights found in Dworkin or Rawls? We find attempts to free the public from any demand for virtue, pushed to extremes of decriminalization of the most serious vices and practices, all in the name of natural rights. Maritain and Simon would of course denounce such accounts as perversions of the true idea of natural rights. But they can do this to the extent that they cling to the natural law account of morality and politics, which the modern account explicitly rejects. Perhaps Thomistic political philosophy must reverse the fields of rhetorical emphasis. Rather than highlight the promise of democracy and progress and then bring out the conservative constraints of pluralism and virtue, perhaps their account now must be presented with an emphasis upon the promise and prospects of the good life as traditionally understood and then praise the democratic approximations to this standard.

This brings us finally the question as to the method for appropriating the legacy of Thomas Aquinas. Maritain and Simon are concerned lest Thomism become paleo-Thomism by an excessive attention to historical and textual study. Of course they strive to be faithful to the texts and spirit of Thomas. But as Simon state in the opening of an article entitled "Thomism and Democracy":

> A discussion of Thomism and democracy might have the character of an historical investigation; the question would be to disentangle, from many texts scattered in the works of St. Thomas, what he actually thought about the democratic regime such as he knew it. Now, if Thomism enjoys, as we believe it does, a vitality which is not by any means confined within the limits of St. Thomas's short life, it should be possible to give a Thomistic treatment of the problem of democracy such as it appears to us. The latter point of view will prevail in this study.[55]

Accordingly Simon does two things; he places a focus on the metaphysical texts and not the political texts of Thomas; and he takes his bearings by the dispute between democracy and totalitarianism. The problematic for Simon and Maritain is the struggle between democracy and totalitarianism: this struggle, they claim, will lead us to better appreciate the true essence of democracy and the importance of the common good.[56] This methodological decision helps to explain the rhetorical and substantive issues mentioned above. Rhetorically, there was the fear that a critique of liberalism would feed into the nihilism of the right wing in Europe.[57] Today of course the problem of nihilism is posed from the left, not the right. Any attempt to put forward standards of natural justice and virtue are decried as impositions on the freedom of individuals. Substantively, it tends to obscure other sets of problems that may give a better analysis of the political regimes. For example one may make thematic the problem of ancients versus moderns in the method of Leo Strauss; this yields a very different reading of the problem of regime both in terms of emphasis and in terms of analysis.[58] As an example, the problem of consent and universal suffrage takes on a different light when removed from the awkward problematic of the transmission theory; the tension of wisdom versus consent is actually a more directly political perspective on the problem of rule and the right to rule. Simon may have set up a methodological division between historical reading and the contemporary problematic. Closer attention to text and intention in light of the challenge of modern philosophy may actually yield more insight than approaching the text from the contemporary problematic prior defined. One might also consider the problematic of traditions or communities of discourse and the breakdown of contemporary moral language as does Alasdair MacIntyre. Again, this would allow one to approach Thomas on terms closer to his own and perhaps allow a more natural unfolding of political themes; for example, the natural law and virtue ethics of St. Thomas would not be rushed up so quickly into the terms of modern natural rights. This may actually offer much-needed alternatives to the stalemate of contemporary moral and political philosophy.

In conclusion I would offer this summary evaluation of the legacy of St. Thomas and that of his disciples, Jacques Maritain and Yves R. Simon. The legacy of St. Thomas is rich and diverse; it is found throughout his writings; in particular the explicit writings on political philosophy, but also in his metaphysics of liberty and order which and Simon so well developed. They developed a very significant and timely defense of liberal democracy and it is of deep Thomistic inspiration and influence. The success of their justification requires further development and broadening. The basis for natural rights and the prospects for virtue in democracy are important areas for a sharpened analysis. Simon's own account of the various claims to rule is a very important contribution and an item to be developed; so too is Maritain's critique of modern individualist democracy. The legacy of St. Thomas is the legacy of political philosophy itself: how to mix freedom (democracy) with unity (kingship) and virtue (aristocracy). One needs a perspective outside of modern liberal democracy to assess its strengths and weakness. Tocqueville had this, as did Maritain and Simon. How St. Thomas, a premodern, a theologian, and an advocate of monarchy could inspire a modern, secular account of democracy is testimony to his rich legacy. Such is the fruitful tension we find in Maritain and Simon in their use of Aquinas in the justification of democracy.

Notes

Extract from a paper presented at Catholic University of America, Machette Lecture Series on "The Legacy of Aquinas," Fall 1990. Published in *The Legacy of Aquinas*, ed. David Gallagher (Washington, D.C.: Catholic University of America Press, 1992).

1. The chief writings are the unfinished *Commentary on Aristotle's Politics*, the treatise *On Kingship*, portions of theological writings pertaining explicitly to politics and law, and remarks scattered throughout works related to matters of metaphysics, ethics, and so on. For judicious selections of key texts see Saint Thomas Aquinas, *On Law, Morality and Politics*, ed. with introduction by William P. Baumgarth and Richard J. Regan (Indianapolis: Hackett, 1988); Saint Thomas Aquinas, *On Politics and Ethics*, ed. with introduction by Paul E. Sigmund (New York: Norton, 1988).

2. See Janko Zagar, "Aquinas and the Social Teaching of the Catholic Church," *Thomist* 38 (October 1974): 826–55.

3. See Paul Sigmund, "Maritain on Politics," *Understanding Maritain*, ed. Deal Hudson and Mancini (Macon, Ga.: Mercer University Press, 1987): 153–55; Idem, *Natural Law in Political Thought* (Cambridge, Mass: Winthrop Press, 1971); Heinrich Rommen, *The State in Catholic Thought* (St. Louis: Herder, 1947).

4. The success of this achievement I have evaluated in the following articles and reviews: "Approaches to Democratic Equality" in *Freedom in the Modern World*, ed. Michael Torre, (Notre Dame, Ind.: American Maritain/Notre Dame Press, 1989), 237–52; review of *Natural Law and the Rights of Man* by Jacques Maritain, *Crisis* 5 (July/August 1987): 51–52; review of *Theology of Freedom* by John Cooper, *Crisis* 4 (December 1986): 32–33; "Maritain and the Intellectuals," *This World* 5 (Spring 1983): 164–68; and "Maritain and America," *This World* 3 (Fall 1982): 113–23. I have taken leads from Leo Strauss, review of *Philosophy of Democratic Government* by Yves Simon in *What Is Political Philosophy?* (New York: Free Press, 1959), 306–11, and Ernest Fortin, "The New Rights Theory and the Natural Law," *Review of Politics* 44 (October 1982): 590–612. See also Brian Benested, "Rights, Virtue and the Common Good," *Crisis* 1 (December 1983): 28–32.

5. Aristotle, *Politics*, I.2.

6. "*Dicitur enim despoticus principatus, quo aliquis principatur servis, qui non habent facultatem in aliquo resistendo imperio praecipientis, quia nihil sui habent. Principatus autem politicus et regalis dicitur, quo aliquis principatur liberis, qui, etsi subdantur regimioni praesidentis, tamen habent aliquid proprium, ex quo possunt reniti praecipientis imperio.*" See James M. Blythe, "The Mixed Constitution and the Distinction between Regal and Political Power in the Work of Thomas Aquinas," *Journal of the History of Ideas* 47 (October/December 1986): 547–65.

7. "*Utrum homo in statu innocentiae homini dominabatur?*" Thomas says "*Cuius ratio est, quia servus in hoc differt a libero, quod liber est causa sui . . . servus autem ordinatur ad alium.*"

8. Simon, *Philosophy of Democratic Government*, 76.

9. Simon, *Philosophy of Democratic Government*, 78, 81; for the following citations, 94, 93, 79.

10. Aristotle, *Politics* III.15 1286a30ff—a large volume dilutes poison; James Madison, *Federalist No. 10*—a large republic is more likely to frustrate evil schemes; see Alexis de Tocqueville, *Democracy in America*, "Corruption and Vices of the Rulers in a Democracy and Consequent Effect on Public Morality."

11. Simon, *Philosophy of Democratic Government*, 98–99.

12. Maritain, *Man and the State* 53, 65.

13. On the transmission theory, see Rommen, *The State in Catholic Thought* (St. Louis: Herder, 1947), chapters 19–20.

14. Yves R. Simon, "The Doctrinal Issue between the Church and Democracy," in *The Catholic Church in World Affairs*, ed. Waldemar Gurian and M. A. Fitzsimons (Notre Dame: University of Notre Dame Press, 1954), 87–114.

15. Maritain, 1951, 28–53.

16. ST, IaIIae, q. 90, a. 3: "*Dicendum quod lex proprie primo et principaliter respicit ordinem ad bonum commune. Ordinare autem aliquid in bonum commune est vel totius multitudinis vel alicjus gerentis vicem totius multitudinis.*"

17. Simon, *Philosophy of Democratic Government*, 190–94.

18. Maritain, *Man and the State*, 35, 127.

19. *Philosophy of Democratic Government*: 129–30; cf "Thomism and Democracy": 264

20. Maritain, *Man and the State*, 67.

21. "*Utrum necessarium sit voluntatem humanam conformari voluntati divinae in volito ad hoc quod sit bona.*" ST IaIIae. q.19, a.10. "*Utrum omnia immediate gubernentur a Deo.*" ST Ia. q.103, a.6.

22. "*Voluntas igitur humana tenetur conformari divinae voluntati in volito formaliter (tenetur enim velle bonum divinum et commune), sed non materialiter.*" ST IaIIae., q.19, a.10.

23. "*Quantum autem pertinet ad executionem gubernationis, Deus gubernat quaedam mediantibus aliis. . . Et ideo sic Deus gubernat res ut quasdam aliarum in gubernando causas instituat; sicut si aliquis magister discipulos suos non solum scientes faceret, sed etiam aliorum doctores.*" ST Ia, q.103, a.6.

24. Simon, "The Doctrinal Issue," 104; Simon, *Philosophy of Democratic Government*, 40.

25. Simon, *Philosophy of Democratic Government* 134.

26. See David T. Koyzis, "Yves R. Simon's Contribution to a Structural Political Pluralism," in *Freedom in the Modern World*, 131–40.

27. Maritain, *Man and the State* 11, 23. See Joseph W. Evans, "Jacques Maritain and the Problem of Pluralism in Political Life" in *Jacques Maritain: The Man and His Achievement*, ed. Joseph W. Evans (New York, Sheed and Ward: 1963), 215–36.

28. See Jacques Maritain, "Human Equality," in *Ransoming the Time*, trans. Harry Lorin Binesse (New York: Scribner's, 1941), 1–31; Yves R. Simon, "Democratic Equality," in *Philosophy of Democratic Government*, 195–259. See my "Approaches to Democratic Equality," in *Freedom in the Modern World*.

29. "*Natura autem vel essentia sic accepta potest dupliciter considerari. Uno modo, se-cundum rationem propriam, et haec est absoluta consideratio ipsius . . . alio modo consid-eratur, secundum esse quod habet in hoc vel in illo. . . . Patet ergo quod natura hominis ab-solute considerata abstrahit a quolibet esse, ita tamen quod non fiat praecisio alicuius eorum. Et haec natura sic considerata est quae praedicatur de individuis omnibus.*" *De ente et es-sentia* III.17–18. For the translation see Simon, *Philosophy of Democratic Government*, note 2, 198; *On Being and Essence*, trans. A. A. Maurer (Toronto: PIMS, 1949), 38–39.

30. Simon, *Philosophy of Democratic Government*, 201.

31. Maritain, *Man and the State*, 96–97.

32. Maritain, *Man and the State*, 102–03.

33. Simon, "The Doctrinal Issue," 112; Simon, *Philosophy of Democratic Govern-ment*, 177. See Wilfrid Parsons, "Saint Thomas Aquinas and Popular Sovereignty," *Thought* 16 (Spring 1941): 473–92.

34. Saint Thomas Aquinas, *Summa Theologiae, Law and Political Theory*, (IaIIae. 90–97), ed. and trans. Thomas Gilby, *Blackfriars* vol. 28, (New York: McGraw-Hill, 1966), 13, note c.

35. "He does not touch on the hypothesis of a legal act by the people transferring the power of governing and legislating to the ruler, but leaves the matter as a general principle, that the people or their guardian are the only power under God commen-surate with the common good." Gilbey, vol. 28, 175.

36. See Maritain, *Man and the State*, 129.

37. Gilbey, *Summa Theologiae*, 14.

38. Strauss, *What Is Political Philosophy?* 308.

39. "Wherefore also in all things that are ordained toward one end, one thing is found to rule the rest. Thus in the corporeal universe, by the first body—the ce-lestial body—the other bodies are regulated according to the order of divine prov-idence; and all bodies are ruled by a rational creature. So, too, in the individual man, the soul rules the body; and among the parts of the soul, the irascible and the concupiscible are ruled by reason. Likewise among the members of a body, one such as the heart or the head, is the principal and moves all the others. Therefore, in every multitude there must be some governing power." St. Thomas Aquinas, *On Kingship*, trans. Gerald B. Phelan (Toronto: PIMS, 1949), 6. "*Oportet igitur, praeter id quod movet ad proprium bonum uniuscuiusque, esse aliquid quod movet ad bonum commune multorum. Propter quod et in omnibus quae in unum ordinatur, aliq-uid invenitur alterius regitivum. In universitate enim corporum per primum corpus, scil-icet caeleste, alia corpora ordine quodam divinae Providentiae reguntur, omniaque cor-pora per creaturam rationalem. In uno etiam homine anima regit corpus, atque inter animae partes irascibilis et concupiscibilis ratione reguntur. Itemque inter mebra corporis unum est principale, quod omnia movet, ut cor, aut caput. Oportet igitur esse in omni multitudine aliquod regitivum.*"

40. See Richard Tuck, *Natural Rights Theories: Their Origin and Development* (Cambridge: Cambridge University Press, 1979).

41. Simon, *Philosophy of Democratic Government*, 226–29. I treat this problematic in "Approaches to Democratic Equality."

42. This argument and the following three are from Aquinas, *On Kingship*, 11–13.

43. *"Lex autem humana ponitur multitudini hominum, in qua major pars est hominum non perfectorum virtute. Et ideo lege humana non prohibentur omnia vitia a quibus virtuosi abstinet, sed solum graviora a quibus possibile est majorem partem multitudinis abstinere, et praecipue quae sunt in nocumentum aliorum, sine quorum prohibitione societas humana conservari non posset: sicut prohibentur lege humana homicidia, furta, et hujusmodi."* ST, IaIIae, q. 96, a. 2.

44. *"Unde optima ordinatio principum est in aliqua civitate vel regno, in qua unus praeficitur secundum virtutem qui omnibus praesit; et sub ipso sunt aliqui principantes secundum virtutem; et tamen talis principatus ad omnes pertinet, tum quia ex omnibus eligi possunt, tum quia etiam ab omnibus eliguntur. Talis enim est optima polita, bene commixta ex regno, inquantum unus praeest; et aristocratia, inquantum multi principantur secudnum virtutem; et ex democratia, idest potestate populi, inquantum ex popularibus possunt eligi principes, et ad populum pertinet electio principum."* See John R. Kayser, "Aquinas's 'Regimen Bene Commixtum' and the Medieval Critique of Classical Republicanism," *Thomist* 46 (April 1982): 195–220.

45. Maritain, *Man and the State*, 59.

46. Maritain, *Man and the State*, 61ff; See also *Christianity and Democracy*, passim.

47. Maritain, *Rights of Man and Natural Law*, 131–33.

48. Maritain, *Man and the State*, 139–40.

49. Simon, *Philosophy of Democratic Government* on paternalism, 13–18; on universal suffrage, 98–99; on progress toward greater equality, 207; on the blindness of the upper class, 215–22; on unequal exchange, 234.

50. "The Real Advantages derived by American society from democratic government" in Tocqueville, *Democracy in America*, 231–35.

51. See my article "Maritain and America."

52. Strauss, *What Is Political Philosophy?* 310–11.

53. John Finnis, *Natural Law and Natural Rights* (New York: Oxford Press, 1978); Henry Veatch, *Human Rights: Fact or Fancy* (Baton Rouge, La.: LSU Press, 1985); *Swimming against the Current in Contemporary Philosophy Studies in Philosophy and the History of Philosophy*, vol. 20 (Washington D.C.: Catholic University of America Press, 1990); Alasdair MacIntyre, *After Virtue* (Notre Dame, Ind.: University of Notre Dame Press, 1984).

54. Jacques Maritain, "The Human Person and Society," in *Scholasticism and Politics*, ed. and trans. Mortimer J. Adler (New York: Doubleday, 1940), 61–90.

55. Yves R. Simon, "Thomism and Democracy," in *Science, Philosophy and Religion*, ed. Louis Finkelstein and Lyman Bryson (New York: The Conference on Science, Philosophy and Religion in Their Relation to the Democratic Way of Life, Inc., 1942), 258.

56. Simon, "Thomism and Democracy," 260. See Yves R. Simon, *The Road to Vichy: 1918–1938*, rev. ed., introduction by John Hellman (Lanham, Md.: University Press of America, 1988).

57. See Yves R. Simon, "Beyond the Crisis of Liberalism," in *Essays in Thomism*, ed. Robert E. Brennan (New York: Sheed and Ward, 1942), 265.

58. See Charles N. R. McCoy, *The Structure of Political Thought* (New York: McGraw-Hill, 1963); James V. Schall, "Metaphysics, Theology, and Political Theory," *Political Science Reviewer* 11 (Fall 1981): 1–26; Ernest Fortin, "Thomas Aquinas," in *History of Political Philosophy*, ed. Leo Strauss and Joseph Cropsey, 3rd ed., (Chicago: University of Chicago Press, 1987), 248–75.

~

CHAPTER FOUR

Maritain's Evaluation
of Bourgeois Liberalism

Few, if any, occupy so prominent a place in the development of twentieth-century theology—and especially Catholic political thought—as Jacques Maritain does. He was a student of the social encyclicals, with their articulation of a "third way" between liberalism and communism, as well as the teacher of Pope Paul VI. Radical theologians, such as Gustav Gutierrez, see in Maritain a forerunner of their own "liberation theology." Yet some American political thinkers consider Maritain an important step in the appreciation of American democracy. "Bourgeois liberalism" is a key term in Maritain's political philosophy. Maritain develops his philosophy by way of comparison and contrast; bourgeois liberalism and totalitarianism (fascist and Communist) are the two antipodes. The best political regime is a mean between those extremes. In the realm of practice and historical assessment, bourgeois liberalism is Maritain's main point of reference. The once-dominant bourgeois or capitalist world has been in decline; its exaggerations called forth socialism and fascism; its conflicts and deficiencies gave rise to world wars. The movement of history, Maritain wrote, had passed beyond bourgeois civilization to one that is neither capitalist nor Communist. In order to understand Maritain's political philosophy we must grasp his concept of bourgeois liberalism. His analysis is complex, and the sometimes-enigmatic quality of Maritain's thought faces us most directly in his evaluation of bourgeois liberalism. From his writings in the 1930s to *The Peasant of the Garonne*, written in 1966, Maritain proclaimed himself a "man of the left" with respect to "the things of Caesar." He expressed sympathy with Dorothy Day, Saul Alinsky, and Emmanuel Mounier. Disdain for bourgeois life is apparent in much of his writing.[1] Yet Maritain also expressed great love for the American regime, in an offhand way in early writings, and with open praise in *Reflections on America*. How, one may ask, is this possible? Is America not the arch-bourgeois, arch-capitalist re-regime? Maritain answers, no; to the contrary, America represents the best example of the new way between bourgeois liberalism and socialism. But if America is not bourgeois, then what does Maritain mean by the term?

Maritain's Critique of Bourgeois Liberalism

Bourgeois liberalism is marked first of all by its individualism. The end or purpose of political society is taken to be nothing more than a collection of private, individual goods. There is no common good, no common work, and no room for public spiritedness. Public life is reduced to the competition of private interest. Taken to an extreme, the anarchy of bourgeois liberalism undermines any social organism. Thus individualism also distorts human nature. Maritain draws on his distinction between the "individual" and the "person" in order to press this claim. "Democracy of the individual" acknowledges and encourages only the "narrow grasping" and selfish ego of the "material individual." This is contrary to the true life of the person, who is social by nature and tends toward the "super-existence" of knowledge and love. Political society should encourage and draw on the person's aspirations to communion with others. As a second mark, bourgeois liberalism has a defective understanding of freedom, which we may call "libertarianism." It makes "freedom of choice" an end in itself. No restriction is placed on the freedom of the individual, save that which would interfere with the freedom of another. But this is an exaggerated sense of human autonomy that distorts the idea of freedom and right. It makes the claim of human freedom, Maritain wrote in 1943, "infinite, escaping every objective measure, denying every limitation imposed upon the claim of the ego, and ultimately expressing the absolute independence of the human subject and a so-called right . . . to unfold one's cherished possibilities at the expense of all other beings." But liberty must be ordered to a good, a good to be embodied in action and character. Freedom of choice is not an end in itself; it is ordered to what Maritain calls "freedom of expansion," by which he means the freedom of self-mastery and ultimately virtue. The tragedy of modern man, Maritain says, is that he believes in liberty without mastery of self and moral responsibility.

Third, the individualism and freedom result in oppression of the working class. Bourgeois liberty, Maritain says, amounts to the liberty of the strong to oppress the weak. This oppression is most apparent in economics. Writing in the 1930s, Maritain embraced a common charge made by the old left: the capitalist world is a dead failure simply in terms of economics. Economic spasms convulse the society. The working class becomes impoverished. It is the very nature of bourgeois society to introduce class conflict and to maintain it. There is, he says, an irreducible antagonism between the bourgeoisie and the proletariat which prevents capitalist societies from ever realizing the ideal of democracy. Thus Maritain's concept of the bourgeoisie entails a rigid class set in opposition to the proletariat or working class. Their relationship is that of exploiter to exploited. The bourgeoisie treat the labor of the working class as merchandise and thereby dehumanize it. The very idea of wage labor reflects this exploitation. In fact, any servitude or instrumentality of the worker is an "offense" to his dignity and an affliction of the person's aspiration to independence. Bourgeois liberalism falls so far short of the ideal of democracy and the dignity of the person that revolution is often inevitable.

The fourth characteristic of bourgeois liberalism is "anthropocentric humanism," or what we now call "secular humanism." This is a humanism which defines man by excluding all reference to the transcendent and divine. Human happiness is to be found in this world alone. Anthropocentric humanism grounds the modern project to master nature; its aim is "to be lord of exterior nature and to reign over it by means of technological procedures [and] . . . to create. . . a material world where man will find, following Descartes' promises, a perfect felicity." Bourgeois life is a "cult of earthly enrichment"; economic life absorbs every other field of activity. Thus it debases human nature. Maritain often cited Werner Sombart, who said that the bourgeois man is neither ontological nor erotic because he lives by external signs such as money and honor, and he loves things more than persons. False humanism is the source of the other characteristics of bourgeois liberalism. By excluding the eternal and spiritual values, the bourgeoisie have only material goods for private consumption and no basis for a common good. By excluding a transcendent measure for human action, libertarianism and mere mutually agreed to restrictions on liberty obtain. And the cult of earthly enrichment, the lust for profit, leads to exploitation of the worker. The problem of bourgeois liberalism is spiritual at heart. Thus the best regime, the new Christendom, would commence with a new, integral humanism that reestablishes man's relationship to God and to the transcendent values required by that relationship.

Maritain's Best Regime

According to Maritain's principle of "the double movement of history" all historical progress is ambivalent, containing both good and creative forces and evil destructive ones. Bourgeois liberalism as a historical force contains within it true aspirations of the human person but deformed by the false philosophy of modernity. The central hope is the "conquest of freedom." This aspiration must be purified and corrected, in both theory and practice. "Personalism" is the true good and creative force that must be freed from the false philosophy of bourgeois liberalism. Personalism is the keynote for Maritain's sketch of the best regime. The best regime will be based on the respect for the dignity of the human person and it will encourage the development of persons. Thus personalism will correct the individualism and libertarianism of bourgeois liberalism, without being totalitarian. Personalism is the basis for a "concrete historical ideal" called a "new Christendom."

Maritain identifies the purpose of this regime with the natural end or purpose of the temporal world. The ultimate end of human history is the kingdom of God and a new heaven and new earth. But there is a relatively final end within the order of nature. The temporal world has enough autonomy to set a purpose for earthly regimes. This end is the "conquest of freedom." Human history progresses toward a conquest of freedom. This natural terminus will not be perfectly realized; also, it brings with it many new dangers and evils. But Maritain does note a definite trend in historical progress. What is this term of history which earthly regimes must now approximate ever more closely? The primary meaning of "conquest of freedom" is virtue. It is "the flowering of moral and rational life and of those (immanent) interior activity which are the intellectual and moral virtue." Human freedom must be achieved or won, hence the "conquest of freedom." It is primarily a work of education, whose very aim Maritain says, in *Education at the Crossroads*, is the liberation of the human person through knowledge and wisdom, good will and love.[2] Thus the progressive goal of the best earthly regime is "the maximum development of persons so that the concrete person gains in the greatest possible measure, compatible with the whole, real independence from the servitude of nature. The servitudes of nature include physical necessity and the instrumentality of work, or the subjection of one man to another. Thus, the best regime will incorporate the highest aspirations of modern science to conquer nature's physical necessities. The best regime will incorporate the rights of man, in economic and civic terms, so as to overcome servitude and to guarantee the aspiration of the person to achieve real independence and virtue.

The personalism of the best regime entails that it be also communal. That is, it would aim for the good of the multitude and their communion in good living.

In Maritain's phrasing, the good of the whole must flow back to the parts. The political good must be a sharable good. So as well as public services and commodities, the common good includes civic conscience and symbols, and moral and political virtues, all of which are communicable and which perfect the very life and liberty of persons. Uniting the personalist and communal characteristics of the best regime is the principle of structural pluralism and subsidiarity. Maritain was fond of quoting Yves Simon's formulation of the principle: "There is more perfection in a whole, all of whose parts are full of life and initiative than in a whole whose parts are but instruments conveying the initiative of the supreme organs of the community." Maritain had such a keen appreciation of this principle that he never failed to cite the danger of totalitarianism and the suppression of intermediate groups. The state, he says, is dull, awkward, oppressive, and injudicious in matters of business, art, culture, and industry. A just pluralism is the most normal remedy for the abuse of authority and for the difficulties inherent in democracy.

Such, in brief, is Maritain's idea of the best regime. It is, he says, a "concrete historical ideal." It may take centuries to realize, but it is not a utopian hope. The ideal is concrete enough to summon forth human initiative and energy and to guide human action. The advent of the new regime points to some critical aspects of Maritain's political philosophy. First, the advent of the new regime requires the complete dissolution and passing away of bourgeois-capitalist regimes. In *Integral Humanism* Maritain is perhaps overly zealous on this score. But the basic idea is constant throughout his thought: a radical change is required, a complete transformation, a dissolution of capitalism must transpire. The errors of bourgeois liberalism are not to be simply weakened or modified. The working class will be the origin of the new regime. The working class has a mission to lead humanity to the next phase of human development. Their consciousness of humiliation and dignity will supply the energy for instituting a new order of society. The liberating mission of the working class has a "Christian resonance." So, also, the new regime will be the result of Christian inspiration. The new ideal of society holds "the hope of men in the terrestrial efficacy of the gospel" and it is a "refraction of gospel truths in temporal history." This Christian inspiration of the temporal order is ambiguous in Maritain's account. Sometimes he seems to mean that a true notion of human dignity and natural rights depends on a vision of man as a creature made in the image of God. Or further, that the temporal order requires the stabilizing influence of religion strengthening natural and civic virtue. But Maritain seems to go beyond this to mean that Christian inspiration will be a major source of activity supplementing if not supplanting political virtue. He talks of the "passing of something divine into the human"; "a victorious outpouring of brotherly love from above"; a brotherly city where man is free from misery and bondage. From this perspective Maritain can say that humanity is in a "prehistoric age" with respect to realizing the social-temporal possibilities of the gospel. Let me clarify at once that Maritain does not expect the kingdom of God on earth. Nor does he believe that socialist revolutions and tyrannical schemes will further the cause of the best regime. But still his notion of the best regime does seem to require some new human developments and even a special outpouring of grace. The discontinuity between present-day liberal democracy and the full scope of the new Christendom seems very great indeed.

Maritain and the American Regime

Maritain's encounter with the American regime led him to qualify his view of the radical discontinuity between present-day liberal democracy and the new Christendom. America points to the new regime and might be a good soil for it to grow in. In America Maritain saw hints of the personalist, communal, and pluralist marks of the best regime. Maritain's encounter with America is best brought out in his puzzling remark that America is not a bourgeois regime. There are three reasons why he makes this claim. First, compared to those in Europe, America is a classless society. In his mind, class entails a fixed and permanent position; whereas in America social status is comparatively flexible and mobile. His concept of the bourgeoisie was of a closed, antagonistic class set in opposition to proletariat. Second, the "spirit" of the American people runs counter to the "logic" of the system of profit. The economic structure of free enterprise and profit-making is external and imposed; the people keep themselves free of it to a certain extent. Thus, for example, the people are compassionate and not materialistic, while the economic system demands materialism and self-interest. Finally, he claims, America is not a bourgeois regime because the economic system itself has passed beyond capitalism and socialism. Labor unions and social legislation protect and preserve the dignity of the worker. The corporations realize that they must take into account the welfare of the workers and society at large. There is a cooperative tension between the owners and the workers that enables free enterprise to operate in a social context.

Maritain's *Reflections on America* leads us then to deal with some possible equivocations and difficulties in his political philosophy as a whole. America is not a bourgeois regime as he defined it. Yet for all the transformations in the American way of life, and they are many, the American regime still finds its form in the constitution of 1787. That is, the present American regime continues the liberal tradition of John Locke, Thomas Jefferson, James Madison, and Alexander Hamilton. Individualism, libertarianism, and self-interest all have their continuing influence. The transformation of the regime arose from "intelligent self-interest" on the part of workers and management. And self-interest is far from the Christian ideal, Maritain insists. The discontinuity between present-day liberal democracy and the new Christendom is great. In order to arrive at a new Christendom more than "transformation" or "evolution" is required. Essential features of bourgeois liberal democracy must be left behind. New foundings and new constitutions would be in order.

The Problem of Political Regimes
Maritain had a wide involvement in and appreciation of political things. He came from a leading political family, once favored a return to monarchy in France, and later became a partisan of democracy and a friend of the United Nations. In one very interesting passage from *The Rights of Man and Natural Law*, Maritain notes well Aristotle's concepts of regimes. Monarchy has strength and unity; aristocracy has a differentiation and hierarchy of values. Yet a mixed regime is usually most favorable. He goes on to say that monarchy and aristocracy are stages on the way to democracy and that the perfections of the former can be preserved in the latter. Here we arrive at a deep difficulty in Maritain's political philosophy. Was he sufficiently aware of the problem of democracy as such? There is an inherent difficulty in making virtue widespread, and in preserving unity in a democracy. Let us explore this problem as it pertains to Maritain's evaluation of bourgeois liberalism and his idea of the new Christendom.

In the perspective of ancient political thought, virtue is difficult to attain in the democratic majority for a number of reasons. The first is that of physical necessity; most people do not have the leisure or equipment to develop their powers. Second, there is some mysterious dispensation of talent and ability that renders some souls less capable. And third, the democratic principle of justice stands in the way. Democratic thought tends to measure all things by the principle of equality, thus making it most difficult to preserve differentiation and hierarchy of values. But for Maritain the natural term of history seems nothing less than a "universal aristocracy," where the great majority has attained a high degree of virtue and perfection. Two factors come between the distant past of ancient political philosophy and the present day: Christianity and technology. Technology frees men from the burden of physical necessity; Christianity disposes all souls to virtue. So we have the formula—technology plus Christianity yields the possibility of a universal aristocracy. But it is not so clear that these two factors will readily solve the problem of democracy and virtue. The very conditions required for technological progress undermine some conditions necessary for virtue. Freedom of thought undermines the steady opinion that guides virtue, and the openness to constant innovation upsets habit and character. Technological progress rejects any moral restraint to innovation and development. Also, to what extent is Christian virtue political? Granted, Maritain speaks of the Christian inspiration strengthening natural virtues "within their own order." Grace presupposes and perfects nature; the problem still remains of developing excellence within democratic regimes. Christianity has its role to play, but it is not sufficient politically.

In most political regimes a less than perfect virtue is found in the phenomenon Aristotle called "citizen virtue." Except for a rare instance, the "good citizen" will not be the same as, nor exhaust the possibilities of, the "good man." Citizen virtue may approximate and imitate perfect virtue to one degree or another. Almost always it depends on such external signs as honor and profit. Citizen virtue succeeds if it makes men "less base," or moderate. Not the same as virtue, it provides a soil in which true virtue may grow. Finally, citizen virtue springs from the middle part of the soul between reason, with its universality, and passion, with its grasping individuality. Myth, story, and a disciplined imagination form and moderate the necessary attachment to one's own. There is a kind of citizen virtue in bourgeois regimes: it is "enlightened self-interest" and commercial success. Maritain is only partly right to say that the American people see the system of profit-making as something external and imposed. They understand and live it all too well. It is not alien, but integral, to the American regime. America is a republic founded squarely on democratic principle and commercial activity. As long as modern democracy separates church and state it cannot be the purpose of political regimes to directly encourage high virtue. Political measures can be taken to moderate men. Self-interest properly understood is one such device. As Tocqueville points out, it is not the same as noble virtue; but its discipline may make men moderate, orderly, and cooperative with others.[3] The doctrine of natural rights might also moderate character. It is up to intermediate groups to sustain high virtue, but the political and economic systems will always create some drag. The tension between the good man and the good citizen cannot be eliminated. Maritain's ideal of the new Christendom seems to posit an identification between the good man and the good citizen. The lesser types of character formed by the externals of honor and profit are rendered superfluous. Perhaps Maritain's distinction between individuality and personality hid from his view the importance of citizen virtue and the middle part of the soul. In any case, his critique of bourgeois liberalism and his idea of a new Christendom seem to expect too much from politics.

A Critique of Bourgeois Capitalism

Let me conclude, if I may, with a prolegomena to any future critique of bourgeois liberalism. First, what part of the criticism pertains to the limits of political life as such and what part simply to the bourgeois way of life? The deficient type of virtue in bourgeois society is a case in point. Virtue is indeed the norm for political analysis. But political life must reckon with a great many necessities. Bourgeois liberalism can make a claim to deal with political necessities in an adequate, if not a decent, fashion. Political regimes are to be commended if they secure relative freedom and stability. Many political regimes, past and present, are ravaged by civil war and tyranny. Thus, it is no small achievement to secure stability and freedom. Bourgeois regimes are designed to achieve civil concord and peace. Locke makes a very persuasive case for majority rule and limited government in order to thwart civic discord and tyranny. All the stratagems of the *Federalist* are likewise aimed at this goal. For example, in *Federalist* numbers 10 and 51 James Madison faces squarely the problem of self-interest and faction. To remove the cause of faction requires taking away liberty or imposing uniformity of opinion, passion, and interest. This would be to war on human nature itself. Thus competing interest should be tempered, enlightened, and regulated, but by no means eliminated.

The attempt to arrive directly at virtue and complete public spiritedness is utopian. Noble impulse can breed extremism. If Maritain looks too high in placing demands on bourgeois liberalism, he also looks too low in understanding its concrete reality. So, second, a critique of bourgeois liberalism must not be allowed to simply assume a Marxian-type reductionism. The very terms "bourgeois" and "capitalist" are terms of contempt which imply that western democracy is nothing but an economic system and that politics, religion, and morality are "super-structure" and a mere mask for economic and selfish interest. This is simply not true. Bourgeois regimes are multifaceted, comprising political and moral–cultural bases as well as economic. This is the fact that so surprised Maritain about the American regime. The political and moral dimensions are not absorbed by the economic life, whatever pressures there may be. The bourgeois regime is constituted as a true body politic committed to a commendable principle of justice—the equal rights to life, liberty, and the pursuit of happiness. In many ways bourgeois regimes resemble an Aristotelean-type "mixed regime," combining democratic and oligarchic elements in a fresh and successful way. Further, in their founding they stand on an appeal to a natural and higher law and thus they stand against that slide into historical

consciousness and the ultimate groundlessness of right initiated by
Rousseau and culminated by Nietzsche. Of course, the crucial role of economics should not be downplayed. As mentioned above, bourgeois regimes
are commercial; but the economic system helps to preserve the democratic
ideal. Freedom and opportunity are linked to private ownership and a dynamic economy. The third and last item of my prolegomena concerns the
rhetoric of political philosophy. Is the idea of a "third way" between liberalism and communism really valid in practice? Even-handed criticism is
neither possible nor desirable. Professor Hellman notes in his book *Emmanuel Mounier and the New Catholic Left* that the quest of Catholic social
thought for a "third way" is "a philosophical enterprise at once vague in
what exactly it would like to set up in practice and precise in what it did
not want to occur." But political thought should not forget its "ruling question": who should rule? This question focuses the mind and will. Should it
be the few rich, the majority, the clerics, the generals, the workers, or the
worker's party? Critics of bourgeois regimes must be precise in terms of this
question. If they desire the democratic principle and majority rule can they
find a better heritage than bourgeois liberalism? The alternatives seem to
be rule by party elites and the totalitarian principle. The idea of a third
way, specifically Maritain's idea of a new Christendom, stresses a great discontinuity between the heroic ideal and the present-day liberal regimes. It
is an ideal too tenuous: as we wait for the great transformation and the
emergence of the new we are led to neglect or even scorn the concrete demands of the present regimes. The radical critique cannot but encourage
forms of totalitarianism, which are antithetical to the inner spirit and freedom of the church.

How then should we formulate a critique of bourgeois liberalism? It should
be primarily on the plane of the moral life. Catholic social thought is right
to criticize the bourgeois way of life and to challenge its moral laxity and social conscience. The moral–cultural life of bourgeois regimes is most vulnerable to economic and political pressure. Its people come to view morality as
a free-market system according to which values are arbitrary and the result of
personal preference and popular demand. Or the political ideal of equality
paralyzes the ability to make judgments of better and worse, of noble and
base. Anyone who teaches ethics in an American college can witness to this
sad tendency. It is the role of the church, and philosophy, to challenge the
citizens to virtue and the life of the spirit. Socrates exhorted his fellow Athe-
nians: "Wealth does not bring about virtue, but virtue brings about wealth
and all other public and private blessings for men" (*Apology* 30b). The political influence of this challenge should be indirect. At most, it would encour-

age the good and ameliorate the evil consequences of liberal democracy. But its main contribution, I think, should be in the field of education. Here Maritain is at his best. Education is still "at the crossroads," and Maritain's thought is of vital importance.

The supra-political activities of religion and liberal arts education contribute to the well being of a liberal democracy, even as they go against the grain of the economic and political demands of vocationalism and pragmatism. The church and the educators are duty-bound to use their freedom to challenge the typical bourgeois way of life by reminding people, in Maritain's words, that:

> Men do not live by bread, vitamins, and technological discoveries. They live by values and realities which are above time, and are worth being known for their own sake; they feed on that invisible food which sustains the life of the spirit.

Being, truth, goodness, beauty—the transcendentals—elevate human life and make it worth living. Maritain traces the root of human sociability and the very possibility of a common good to the participation of the human soul in the transcendentals.[4] Further, it is through liberal arts education that democracy may in some way approach a "universal aristocracy." By education shall we achieve that conquest of freedom which Maritain takes to be the hope of our day.

In Maritain's evaluation of bourgeois liberalism we find both a radical critique and a friendly challenge. The radical critique *seems to appeal most* to present-day Christian thinkers. But this does not come to grips with the problem of political regimes, in theory or in practice. The friendly challenge, I think, is truer to Maritain's own life and thought. Just as Maritain once rose to the defense of bourgeois France in the face of Nazi totalitarianism, so now in the face of Communist totalitarianism would he not have us defend those regimes that attempt to secure the blessings of liberty.

Notes

This chapter was excerpted from "Maritain and America," *This World*, no. 3 (Fall 1982).

1. The European intellectual tradition generally holds the bourgeois class in disdain. For a good description of the intellectual and cultural milieu of Maritain's time, see Joseph Amato, *Mounier and Maritain: A French Catholic Understanding of the Modern World* (Tuscaloosa, Ala.: University of Alabama Press, 1975), especially pp. 4–7, 78, 129, 185 n. 18. John Hellman, *Emmanuel Mounier and the New Catholic Left 1930–1950* (Toronto: University of Toronto Press, 1981). (This book is now republished by Ave Maria Communications, Inc., Ypsilanti, Michigan.)

2. *Education at the Crossroads* (New Haven, Ct.: Yale Univ. Press, 1943), 10–11. Maritain says here that "the chief aspirations of the person are to freedom—I do not mean that freedom which is free will and which is a gift of nature in each of us; I mean that freedom which is spontaneity, expansion or autonomy and which we have to gain through constant effort and struggle."

3. "By itself it cannot make a man virtuous, but its discipline shapes a lot of orderly, temperate, moderate, careful, and self-controlled citizens. If it does not lead the will directly to virtue, it establishes habits which unconsciously turn it that way." Written by Tocqueville in *Democracy in America*, "How Americans Combat Individualism by a Doctrine of Self-Interest Properly Understood."

4. "The moment one touches a transcendental, one touches being itself, a likeness of God, an absolute, that which ennobles and delights our lives; one enters into the domain of spirit. It is remarkable that men really communicate with one another only through being or one of its properties. Only in this way do they escape the individuality in which matter encloses them." *Art and Scholasticism and the Frontiers of Poetry* (New York: Scribner's, 1962), 32.

CHAPTER FIVE

~

Three Philosophies of Human Rights: Locke, Richards, and Maritain

The moral and political landscape of America today is dominated by a single feature: the discourse of rights. What began as a matter of carefully delimited political prerogatives and protections in Anglo-American jurisprudence has become a wild free for all of personal and collective claims and counter-claims. Serious matters involving, for example, questions of life and death or fair participation in the political order as well as frivolous matters such as the legitimation of any felt need—all moral and political questions—have been enveloped in a disputation concerning rights. The proliferation of rights' claims is a concern not simply because of the sheer number of things to which people now claim rights, but especially because of the unmanageable conflicts between those claims. As is known too well, the right to life of the unborn is in conflict with the right to choose of the woman; the right to hire and fire is in conflict with the right to equal opportunity for minorities; the right of citizens to safety in a drug-free environment is in conflict with the right to privacy of workers; and so forth. In the United States the courts are swamped with conflicts which they must adjudicate. And in personal life, the claims of rights are frequently used to justify any course of action that an individual has chosen, at least if accompanied with the provisio that it does not harm anyone. A subjectivist situation ethic has taken to itself the discourse of rights to conceal its confusion and disorder.

All citizens, including those who are Christian, cannot help but be perplexed by this state of affairs. There is the obvious benefit of employing rights language. It is needed to protect the claims of religion from unwarranted state intrusion, to protect vulnerable members of society, and in general to influence public policy. On the other hand, the rights discourse carries with it many assumptions about human nature and the moral order which run contrary to the very things to be protected; assumptions involving unbounded freedom or an individualist conception of political order.[1]

In light of this confusion in theory and practice in politics and ethics today, there is a pressing need for a sound philosophy of human rights. In addition to the careful work of jurisprudence and political science in analysis of rights' claims and the strategic planning for political action, there is the need for an ultimate rationale or account of the nature of and foundation for rights. This would provide us with a point of reference or orientation for assessing the spirit and in some way the letter of rights' claims. It is my intention in this essay to discuss three philosophies of human rights in order to explore the question whether a doctrine of rights should be derived from a thesis concerning the autonomy of the human being from any constraint such as a divine or natural order, or whether human rights are to be construed precisely as an element or part of an objective moral order.

The three philosophies I intend to examine are: first, the modern liberal philosophy of John Locke; second, the contemporary jurisprudence of David A. Richards; and third, the project of Jacques Maritain, the French Catholic philosopher who was active in the development of a Thomistic philosophy of rights.

Hobbes, Locke, and the Origin of Modern Philosophies of Human Rights

There is scholarly dispute over the historical origin of moral and political discourse involving rights. Richard Tuck, for example, traces the origin back to the late medieval ages and the theology of Jean Gerson, who in a work published in 1402 first assimilated the term "*ius*," that is justice or right, to the term "*libertas*" or freedom.[2] As Tuck explains, this is one of the first appearances of the idea of an active right, a right that does not have a strict correlative duty, thereby implying that right is a dominion over something to use as one pleases. Human freedom becomes the fundamental moral fact, not virtue, or divine command. The development of such a notion wound its way through late medieval nominalism and became the main theme of Hugo Grotius, John Seldon, and finally to Thomas Hobbes. Hobbes' work, especially *Leviathan*, is usually marked as the turning point from the ancient natural right or natural law to the modern account of natural rights.[3] Hobbes most articulately challenged the fundamental presuppositions of the Thomistic synthesis of biblical theology and Aristotelian philosophy such as the sociability of man and the possibility of a common good, the existence of a highest good in virtue and contemplation, and the natural law derived from such human teleology. Hobbes, rather, began with a state of nature as a state of war, the futility of seeking a good higher than the pleasant preservation of the individual—that is, comfortable self-preservation, and a natural law clearly derivative from more fundamental rights of nature such as the right to self-preservation. Following the early lead of Gerson, Hobbes defines "right of nature" (*jus naturale*) as "the liberty each man hath, to use his own power, as he will himselfe, for the preservation of his own nature."[4] Hobbes clearly distinguishes right (*ius*) from law (*lex*)—"right, consisteth in liberty to do, or forbeare; whereas Law, determineth, and bindeth to one them; so that Law, and Right, differ as much, as Obligation, and Liberty." For Hobbes, right (liberty) clearly takes precedent over law (obligation). The fundamental right or liberty of the self is unbounded or unlimited by anything; by the fundamental right of preservation, each man has a right to everything and anything done in the pursuit of preservation is without blame. The intolerable conflicts between individuals, however, amounts to a state of war. It is reasonable, therefore, to limit ones claim to things for the sake of self-protection. Morality exists by way of contract. Morality is a rational deduction of moral rules from the right of self-preservation.[5] Hobbes's defense of individual rights required the existence of an absolute power in society to keep all potential wrongdoers in a state of awe such that they would obey the law. Hobbes' account was shocking in so many ways, not the least of which was its implicit antitheistic philosophy, that it was frequently decried and banned. The direct contrast between Hobbes and the biblical and philosophical accounts of moral and political order would in many ways be the easiest approach to take to the philosophical questions about rights.

However, the philosophy of John Locke presents a more instructive case. Locke transformed the Hobbesian philosophy into a more palatable and balanced philosophy of natural rights. It is in the Lockean form that many Americans came to know about rights. And Locke's philosophy contains a fundamental ambiguity that pertains to the alternatives mentioned above. That is, the very tension over the autonomy of the person and the workmanship of God is played out in the writing and interpretation of Locke.

Locke sought to find a solution to the problem of politics that would restore peace to a country divided by wars of religion. The tolerance of religious belief required, in his mind, the lowering of the goal and mission of the temporal order, away from the inculcation of virtue and the defense of the faith to the protection of the temporal welfare of its citizens, that is to the protection of the rights to life, liberty, and property of its citizens.[6] By removing the matter of religious contention from the civil sphere Locke hoped to quell the disturbances inflicted upon Europe because of intolerance. Hobbes, however, removed contentious matters by making the sovereign absolute over the determination of the beliefs of its citizens. It was Locke who overcame the inconsistencies in this account, and sought to place structural and formal limits upon the sovereign political power and to bind the sovereign to the respect of rights to life, liberty, and property. The division of powers, taxation with representation, and limited prerogatives of the state power balanced by a "right to revolution" are all part of the Lockean system. For Hobbes, rights are fundamental moral claims against others; Locke adds to this the claim of the individual against the state, at least when a "long train abuses" are perceived by a majority and rouse it to act. Locke's more moderate and reasonable account of human rights has appealed to generations of political statesmen and thinkers. John C. Murray, in discussing the First Amendment of the U. S. Constitution, calls the "articles of peace" reasonable devices, learned through experience, to limit government. He rejects certain "theologies of the First amendment," which posit, for example, the ultimate subjectivity of religious truth.[7] Locke has been interpreted along both lines. However, the same seed of radical autonomy as the basis for human rights remains in Locke.

Like Hobbes, Locke derives the principles of limited government from a hypothetical state of nature.[8] This original state of nature is said to be a state of "perfect freedom." By freedom Locke here means no more than an absence of restraint. Locke mentions in the same passage with the perfect freedom, the bounds of a natural law. This is to distinguish "liberty" from "license." The natural law which initially guides men in the state of nature is to refrain from harm: "The State of Nature has a Law of Nature to govern it, which obliges every one; And Reason, which is that Law, teaches all Mankind, who will but consult it, that being all equal and independent, no one ought to harm another in his Life, Health, Liberty, or Possessions." The restraint demanded by natural law derives from an additional characteristic of the state of nature: in the state of nature men are equal in addition to being free.[9] Locke makes clear that equality means equal jurisdiction, or the absence of subordination and subjection. The basis for this mutual respect and recognition is the fundamental problem, since it is the basis for natural law.

The key difficulty in interpreting the philosophy of John Locke pertains to the foundation of natural rights and the rationale for mutual restraint. Locke in fact gives a twofold rationale and foundation. On the one hand, he speaks of man as God's workmanship, and from this axiom derives the right to life, liberty, and property as essential to the divine moral order; on other occasions he simply appeals to the primacy of self-preservation and unfolds from radical autonomy the list of rights and the self-interested basis for mutual respect.

In the first model, the basis for equal respect is divine workmanship and the order of creation. Locke argues that all creatures are equal under God and occupy the same rank or status as "creature."[10] Thus, no one can assume to take the position of God and rule over others. This argument from the order of creation reflects a premodern understanding of equality. Men are neither beasts nor gods, but occupy equally a ground midway between.[11] It is neither appropriate to act as a god nor to treat others as beasts or inferior creatures. Locke explicitly uses this premodern image. In light of this order of creation, man can make no claim to absolute dominion over his fellow creature. Mutual respect depends upon the recognition of one's status as creature, along with others, before the Creator. That is, man cannot claim the type of superiority that would authorize the destruction or arbitrary use of another, and rights protect this status.

But Locke says that the grasp of "natural law" does not depend on divine revelation nor does it depend on knowledge of God's promulgated law and sanctions. This content can be appreciated independently of the workmanship model. For to deny the mutuality of equal right is to propel oneself into a state of war with others. And by such a declaration one has "exposed his Life to the others Power to be taken away by him" (2.16). To put oneself in such an insecure state is most unreasonable and dangerous. One is open to being treated like a noxious beast.[12] It is more safe, more reasonable to acknowledge the equality of rights. Thus, mere self-interest would counsel mutuality and restraint. Locke refers to the law of nature as simply the law of reason and common equity: the law of nature is the reasonable restraint of common equity that will establish mutual security (2.8). It is discovered through the person's own desire for safety and security. The basis for restraint is fear of harm and self-interest. According to this model of rights, selfish interest, comfortable preservation, is the basis for my claims. Enlightened self-interest leads me to recognize the equal right of others to their life, liberty, and property.[13]

The legacy of Locke is therefore ambivalent. The advocate of limited government, and an apparent friend of the theistic tradition, Locke nevertheless underwrote a model of radical human autonomy in which freedom dominates the moral order. Locke's philosophy of human rights is derived from a subjectivist account of the good; it lowers the goal of the state to a supposedly neutral position; it imposes a minimal obligation of nonharm; and ultimately does encourage self-interest. The minimal obligations embodied in civil law become the extent of morality; the wide sphere of private life must come to occupy the bulk of human energies. With Locke, such freedom was aimed at unlimited acquisition of property and the self found its affirmation in labor and the "work ethic," or what Leo Strauss called "the joyless quest for joy." But such terms as equal freedom and mutual respect came to be transformed under the inspiration of Rousseau and Kant to mean much more than civic liberty and protection of private property. In contemporary American jurisprudence they have come to promote the existence of what University of Illinois Law Professor Gerard Bradley has recently referred to as the "erotic self."[14]

Contemporary Developments by David A. Richards

David A. J. Richards is Professor of Law at New York University and Director of New York University's Program for the Study of Law, Philosophy and Social Theory. His publications cover constitutional and criminal law, political philosophy, and ethics. One of his works is entitled *Sex, Drugs, Death and the Law*.[15] It is a treatise which follows the logic of the right to privacy to the point of the decriminalization of all consensual sex acts including prostitution, as well as drug use, and euthanasia. Richards stresses the radical departure in ethics and politics characteristic of the modern theory of rights elaborated by Locke.[16] He seeks to purge American thought and culture of its religious influence; this includes what Richards calls its Calvinistic public morality and also natural law principles derived from Catholic morality and tradition.[17] Richards' work is animated by a grand democratic vision of a "national community of principle," based upon human autonomy and human rights; such a vision demands the radical critique and elimination of premodern communities and traditions which have practiced "majoritarian tyranny" and "degradation of persons."[18] Richards accuses the premoderns of being defined by an externally imposed system of appropriate roles; such a system is "contemptuous of the just liberties of a free person because it denies in principle the place or weight of such capacities of persons for rational freedom."[19] Such degradation lies at the heart of alternatives to liberalism, he supposes, whether it be ancient Greek, medieval Christian, or contemporary conservatives. Indeed, the Bible or Thomistic natural law must be considered degrading because they attempt to guide or otherwise restrict the creative freedom of individual persons.

Richards adopts a Lockean view on the legitimate scope of governmental interference with human freedom. The only grounds for interference are the protection of "general goods" such as life, liberty, health, and property. He describes the general goods as those goods "that rational and reasonable people would want protected as conditions of whatever else they want."[20] This has been called a "thin theory of the good," because of its minimal elaboration of what constitutes a good human life.[21] The government cannot impose a substantive way of life upon the citizens nor act in behalf of such a vision; the government must be properly "neutral among diverse ways people may interpretively weight the pursuit of those goods in their vision of a good and decent life."[22] Autonomy is precisely the ability to form a plan of life; for the government to act on behalf of a distinctive conception of the good life would be to violate the equal respect for persons, many of whom choose diverse ways of life: "fundamental political morality rests upon a neutral theory of the good for persons, which is compatible with broadly pluralistic life styles and forms, and the most fundamental right of persons is their right to equal concern and respect, compatible with a like respect for all, in defining their own visions of the good life."[23]

Richards thus construes the First Amendment as an attempt to "guarantee and secure to a person the greatest equal respect for the rational and reasonable capacities of the persons themselves to originate, exercise and express and change theories of life and how to live it well."[24] The deepest value protection therefore is not religion per se, but the higher powers of the person, the capacity for critical reflection as a rational and reasonable person and creative expression of oneself.

The right of conscience is the primary right and the paradigm for all others; expanded to include any conscientious belief or actions derived therefrom, so too other rights are similarly expanded and developed in light of the principle of autonomy and respect for persons. The scheme is applied to free speech, with some interesting results such as the defense of a right to pornography; indeed pornography is extolled as the higher option against the repressed Catholic and Puritan public morality.[25] The abstract background right concerns intimate personal relationships, "through which we express and realize a wholeness of emotion, intellect and self image guided by the just play of the self-determining powers of a free person."[26] As a good liberal he wishes to demonstrate the constitutional legitimacy of the right to privacy, its rightful application in such cases involving contraceptive use in marriage, nonmarital contraceptive use, pornography in the home, and abortion services; in addition he criticizes the court for its failure to apply privacy rights to consensual homosexual acts.[27] Homosexuals ought to be afforded the same rights to privacy, family, adoption, and so on as heterosexuals.[28] Such would forward the "great work of collective democratic decency that is the Constitution of the United States."[29] Such would enhance the rational dignity of women who are freed from prejudice and traditional duties of the procreative function. Abortion, pornography, and homosexual acts are liberated from false moral condemnation and individuals freed from the oppressive weight of tradition and convention.

In the work of David Richards the seed of radical autonomy planted by Hobbes and Locke, for the sake of acquisition of property and comfortable self-preservation, has matured to become the fruit of a full moral subjectivism and the clear abandonment of and attack upon any shred of classical natural law and virtue. How can a Christian philosopher or theologian meet the challenge of this philosophy of human rights?

Jacques Maritain and a Thomistic Philosophy of Rights

The philosophy of Jacques Maritain is very important in the development of Thomistic social and political philosophy. Maritain's work has influenced the writings of both Pope Paul VI and John Paul II. Maritain was a man of the world, who actively participated in the United Nations drafting of a Charter of Human Rights. He was very interested in incorporating a sound philosophy of human rights into Christian social doctrine. Maritain insisted that we must face the difference between two philosophies of rights that must be traced back to fundamental differences in philosophy of God. He distinguishes the underlying philosophies as anthropocentric humanism and theocentric humanism: "the first kind of humanism recognizes that God is the center of man; it implies the Christian conception of man, sinner and redeemed, and the Christian conception of grace and freedom. The second kind of humanism believes that man himself is the center of man and implies a naturalistic conception of man and of freedom."[30] According to the philosophy of theocentric humanism, human rights rest upon a natural and divine order, according to which human beings possess a dignity in virtue of their nature and destiny as creatures before God. The rights are limited in scope and are designed to assist the person in attaining their full stature as human beings. According to anthropocentric humanism, rights are based upon "the claim that man is subject to no law other than that of his will and freedom" and as a result have become "infinite, escaping every objective measure, denying every limitation imposed upon the claims of the ego."[31] In his philosophy, Maritain sought to rescue the notion of human rights from the philosophical errors in which it has been put forward.

Maritain sets himself to the larger task of harmonizing Christianity and the democratic ideal, such as that of human rights. The tragedy of the modern age finds "the motivating forces in modern democracies repudiating the Gospel and Christianity in the name of human liberty, while motivating forces in the Christian social strata were combating the democratic aspirations in the name of religion." It is the burden of Christianity and democracy to have "Christian inspiration and the democratic inspiration recognize each other and become reconciled." Maritain believes that modern democracy transcends aristocracy and monarchy, somehow preserving the best of both. Maritain did not envision the degree to which "democratic inspiration" would far outstrip "evangelical inspiration," thereby creating forms of conflict. Consumerism and gay rights can both claim "democratic inspiration," whereas their "evangelical inspiration" is dubious. Still, Maritain's praise of democracy is always qualified and critical as he wishes Christianity to serve as a check on the base tendencies of the democratic impulse which culminate in "bourgeois liberalism," a form of regime brought under judgment by the world war and its aftermath.

Maritain believes that Christianity is actually the historical condition necessary for the emergence of a philosophy of human rights. The full historical adequacy of this claim is surely questionable; yet for its part it is a great and salutary truth. Human dignity, the value of labor, the rights of conscience, the relativity of earthly authority are but a few of the truths elaborated by Maritain as due to Christian inspiration. The problem is that "democratic impulse" is not a single force. As Maritain knows, its origins also lie in ancient republicanism and in the modern turn to mastery of nature and worldly satisfaction. Both movements bear some antagonism toward Christianity, even if the latter movement often masks itself in Christian phraseology. Maritain hopes to purge the democratic movement of its errors, and rest it on a Christian footing. But perhaps the modern project is now at long last purging itself of its Christian trappings. Maritain's "true democracy" would now appear as countercultural and perhaps antidemocratic. For example, he equates the "pursuit of happiness" with the cultivation of the mind and self-sacrificial love. More generally, Maritain identifies freedom with moral mastery and virtue. Maritain is thus truly premodern in outlook. Those democratic theories proposing a "thin theory of the good" would not find in Maritain the true essence of democracy. Although the Christian theorist may appropriate the terms of democracy, and even show origins in Christianity, the fact that those terms have developed a life of their own make the prospects for reconciling Christianity and contemporary democratic ethos problematic in the extreme. Maritain has high hopes that Christians may be on the vanguard of democratic reform; but we cannot now fail to see that Christians may be called to resist its destructive excesses, as represented by a Dworkin or a Richards.

Christianity and Democracy outlines the spirit of Maritain's task, *Rights of Man and Natural Law* outlines the basic concepts of his political philosophy. Maritain gives a masterful and lucid account of human rights, beginning with the philosophical notion of person as a being with intellect and will in virtue of which he or she is oriented toward the realm of being, truth, and goodness. Therein resides human dignity: the person possesses some measure of wholeness and independence, and cannot live as a mere part or in servility. The freedom of human beings is intimately connected to truth and objective moral good.[32] Moreover, the person is social by nature in function of both his or her needs and perfections, that is, in virtue of human indigence and human generosity. The personalist basis for politics demands a communal correlate; the good of persons is a communion in the good life. The individualism of modern philosophies of human rights must be challenged by a more adequate appreciation of the social nature of the person. Maritain uses the dignity of the person to resist all forms of totalitarianism; man is more than a part of a temporal society. The person as such aspires to a supra-temporal good. Maritain often cites the words of Thomas Aquinas, "man is not ordered to political society by reason of himself as a whole and by reason of all that is in him." Human rights protect this human dignity against the onslaught of totalitarian power. But the liberal interpretation of rights also is premised upon the denial of transcendence; thus we are faced with the question whether a project such as Professor Richards' is leading to the enhancement or the ultimate degradation of the human person.

The philosophy of human rights must address the issue of the human good and human perfection. According to Maritain human rights flow from the divine order reflected in human nature; it is the "right possessed by God to see the order of His Wisdom in beings respected, obeyed and loved by every intelligence." He does not give a Kantian type account based upon human autonomy. From a definite conception of the good life Maritain derives human rights. He defines the key modern notion of freedom in terms of virtue, which he calls liberty of expansion: it is "the flowering of moral and rational life, and of those interior activities that are the intellectual and moral virtues." But the modern philosophy of human rights "believes in liberty without mastery of self or moral responsibility."[33] For Maritain, therefore, the essential political task is "a task of civilization and culture." The rights of man follow from this goal—they represent the conditions necessary for the full flowering of human perfection in the multitude. Maritain expounds upon personal, civic, and economic rights in light of this concrete human good. For the precise enumeration one may consult *The Rights of Man and Natural Law*, including a resume of rights provided at its end.[34] They protect and provide the material and legal conditions for human perfection. Suffice it to say that Maritain expects the slow but steady emancipation of man from the conditions that thwart his aspirations to truth and virtue. Liberation is for the sake of human perfection, not an end in itself, nor a freedom without terminus or measure. This account of freedom would appear to preserve what is best in a theory of rights by joining it to a notion of virtue. Rights are not a claim of subjectivity or a liberty free of obligation, but conditions for human excellence challenging political prudence in its task to achieve a common good and a decent human life for all.

Conclusion: The Challenge of Rights Discourse

There is an obvious need for the understanding of and the use of rights discourse today. It is necessary for the very protection of the claims of religion and religious activity in a secular state. The original impetus of Locke, freedom for and toleration of religious belief. Rights language helps to explain the advocacy for the vulnerable members of society which Christian conscience demands. Thus to influence pubic policy in a salutary way, rights discourse is inevitable. But the basis for and purpose of human rights discourse must be clearly understand if we are to avoid the confusion and equivocations of the present day. We must engage in a serious reading of modern philosophers such as Hobbes and Locke; in addition, the contemporary developments of Rawls, Dworkin, and Richards must be squarely faced; finally, Christian thinkers like Maritain and John Paul II have opened up horizons for a sound philosophy of human rights.[35]

The use of rights discourse is fraught with difficulties, not the least of which is sheer equivocation when engaged in discourse with the dominant liberal culture. The philosophy of human rights underlying such accounts, the radical autonomy of the human person, must be challenged and redefined. A sound philosophy of rights must make it clear that freedom is not an absolute, that rights are imbedded in an objective moral order which is accessible by reason (natural law) and revelation (divine law) and finally that rights are correlated with duties to the community, to others, and ultimately to God.

Notes

This chapter extracted from "Three Philosophies of Human Rights," in *In Search of a National Morality*, ed. William Bentley Ball (Grand Rapids, Mich.: Baker Book House, 1992), 246–58.

1. See Stanley Hauerwas, "The Church and Liberal Democracy: The Moral Limits of a Secular Polity," in *A Community of Character* (Notre Dame, Ind.: University of Notre Dame Press, 1981), 72–88.

2. Richard Tuck, *Natural Rights Theories: Their Origin and Development* (Cambridge: Cambridge University Press, 1979), 24–31.

3. See Leo Strauss, *Natural Right and History* (Chicago: University of Chicago Press, 1953) and *What Is Political Philosophy?* (New York: Free Press, 1959); Richard Tuck, *Hobbes* (New York: Oxford, 1989); C. B. MacPherson, *The Political Theory of Possessive Individualism* (New York: Oxford University Press, 1962); David Johnson, *The Rhetoric of Leviathan* (Princeton: Princeton University Press, 1986); Ian Shapiro, *The Evolution of Rights in Liberal Theory* (Cambridge: Cambridge University Press, 1986).

4. Thomas Hobbes, *Leviathan*, chapter 14. In the Penguin edition edited by C. B. MacPherson (New York: Penguin Books, 1968), 189.

5. See Hobbes, *Leviathan*; see also Richard Tuck, Hobbes, and Leo Strauss, *Natural Right and History*.

6. John Locke, *Letter Concerning Toleration*.

7. John Courtney Murray, *We Hold These Truths* (New York: Sheed and Ward, 1960), 48–56.

8. "To understand Political Power right, and derived it from its Original, we must consider what state all Men are naturally in, and that is a state of perfect Freedom to order their Actions, and dispose of their Possessions, and Persons, as they think fit, within the bounds of the Law of Nature, without asking leave or depending on the Will of any other Man." John Locke, *Two Treatises of Government*, ed. Peter Laslett, (Cambridge: Cambridge University Press, 1968), (2.4).

9. "A State also of Equality, wherein all Power and Jurisdiction is reciprocal, no one having more than another: there being nothing more evident, than that Creatures of the same species and rank promiscuously born to all the same advantages of Nature, and the use of the same faculties, should also be equal one amongst another without Subordination or Subjection, unless the Lord and Master of them all, should by any manifest declaration of his Will set one above another, and confer on him by an evident and clear appointment an undoubted Right to Dominion and Sovereignty." Locke, *Two Treatises of Government*, (2.4).

10. "For Men being all the Workmanship of one Omnipotent, and infinitely wise Maker; All the Servants of one Sovereign Master, sent into the World by his order and about his business, they are his Property, whose Workmanship they are, made to last during his, not another's Pleasure. And being furnished with like Faculties, sharing all in one Community of Nature, there cannot be supposed any such Subordina-

tion among us, that may authorize us to destroy one another, as if we were made for one another's uses, as the inferior ranks of Creatures are for ours." Locke, *Two Treatises of Government*, (2.6).

11. See Harry Jaffa, "Equality as a Conservative Principle," in *How to Think about the American Revolution*, (Durham, N.C.: Carolina Academic Press, 1978), 13–48.

12. "One may destroy a Man who makes War upon him, or has discovered an Enmity to his being, for the same Reason, that he may kill a Wolf or a Lyon; because such men are not under the ties of the Common Law of Reason, have no other Rule, but that of Force and Violence, and so may be treated as Beasts of Prey, those dangerous and noxious Creatures, that will be sure to destroy him, whenever he falls into their Power." Locke, *Two Treatises of Government*, (2.16).

13. See also Locke's *Essay Concerning Human Understanding*, ed. Peter Niditch (Oxford: Clarendon Press, 1975), I.3.6: "It is no wonder, that every one should, not only allow, but recommend, and magnifie those Rules to others, from whose observance of them, he is sure to reap Advantage to himself. He may, out of Interest, as well as Conviction, cry up that for Sacred; which if once trampled on, and prophaned, he himself cannot be safe nor secure."

14. Gerard V. Bradley, "The Constitution & the Erotic Self," *First Things*, no. 16 (October 1991): 28–32.

15. David A. J. Richards, *Toleration and the Constitution*, (New York: Oxford University Press, 1986); *Sex, Drugs, Death and the Law*, (Totowa, N.J.: Rowman & Littlefield, 1982); *Foundations of American Constitutionalism*, (New York: Oxford University Press, 1989); "Human Rights and Moral Ideals: An Essay on the Moral Theory of Liberalism," 5 *Social Theory and Practice*, 461 (1980); "Rights and Autonomy," 92 *Ethics*, 3 (1981).

16. Richards, *Sex, Drugs, Death and the Law*, 1; "Rights and Autonomy," 3.

17. On Calvinism see Richards, *Sex, Drugs, Death and the Law*, 2, 14, 90, 126, 194; *Foundations of American Constitutionalism*, 25, 54; *Toleration and the Constitution*, 235, 240. On Catholicism see Richards, *Sex, Drugs, Death and the Law*, 52; *Foundations of American Constitutionalism*, 217; *Toleration and the Constitution*, 207, 259–60, 277–78.

18. On the community of principle, see Richards, *Foundations of American Constitutionalism*, 295–99. On the degradation of traditional communities, see *Foundations of American Constitutionalism*, 277; "Human Rights and Moral Ideals," 485–86: "The detailed casuistry of one's personal life, typical of older moral traditions, imposes unreal and factitious constraints which deny and disfigure the moral freedom that we, as persons, possess. To deny such freedom is to impose a false passivity and resignation, a slavery of the spirit which is neither natural nor humane."

19. *Toleration and the Constitution*, 81–82.

20. *Toleration and the Constitution*, 245. See *Sex, Drugs, Death and the Law*, 12–13.

21. See Michael Sandel, *Liberalism and the Limits of Justice* (Cambridge: Cambridge University Press, 1982), pp. 25–28; see also John Finnis, *Fundamentals of Ethics* (Washington, D.C.: Georgetown University Press, 1983), 48–53.

22. Finnis, *Fundamentals of Ethics*, 246.

23. Richards, "Human Rights and Moral Ideals," 461.

24. Richards, *Toleration and the Constitution*, 136.

25. Richards, *Toleration and the Constitution*, 206–10.

26. Richards, *Toleration and the Constitution*, 255–58.

27. Richards, *Sex, Drugs, Death and the Law*, 63. "Certain of the traditional moral condemnations of homosexuals, appear, on analysis, to be vicious forms of social and legal persecution." "Human Rights and Moral Ideals," 479.

28. See Richards, *Foundations of American Constitutionalism*, 246–47.

29. Richards, *Foundations of American Constitutionalism*, 246–47.

30. Jacques Maritain, *Integral Humanism* (Notre Dame, Ind.: University of Notre Dame Press, 1973), 27–30; *The Range of Reason* (New York: Charles Scribner's Press, 1952), chapters 7, 8, 14.

31. Jacques Maritain, *Christianity and Democracy* and *Rights of Man and Natural Law*, tran. Doris C. Anson; introduction by Donald Arthur Gallagher. (San Francisco: Ignatius Press, 1986), 145–47.

32. See also, John Paul II, "Rediscover the Relationship of Truth, Goodness and Freedom," *L'Osservatore Romano* 28 April 1986, 12. *Redemptor Hominis*, section 12.

33. Maritain, *Range of Reason*, 187; see also Maritain, *Freedom in the Modern World* (New York: Charles Scribner's Press, 1936); and a collection of essays on Maritain, Simon, and Adler, *Freedom in the Modern World*, ed. Michael D. Torre (Notre Dame, Ind.: University of Notre Dame Press, 1989).

34. See pp. 152–89; this list may also be found in *The Social and Political of Jacques Maritain*, ed. Joseph Evans and Leo R. Ward, recently reissued by Notre Dame Press.

35. See James V. Schall, *The Church, the State and Society in the Thought of John Paul II* (Chicago: Franciscan Herald Press, 1982).

~

CHAPTER SIX

Why Locke Rejected an Ethics of Virtue and Turned to Utility

Locke's pivotal role in the development of political philosophy is acknowledged by all; still there is a controversy as to whether he stands out more as a thinker rooted in the traditional natural law teaching or as one clearing the way for a new teaching of rights alone. In the field of ethics Locke is not as fully recognized as a pivotal figure; yet in the *Essay Concerning Human Understanding* we find a clear rejection of an ethics of virtue and a turning to an ethics of utility. Because Locke continues to use the rubric of natural law to put forward this ethics of utility the scholars continue to debate the significance of his turn. The clear rejection of an ethics of virtue and the grounds for his utilitarianism, however, should say something about his role as the founder of a new moral and political order.

Conceptual Analysis

In terms of Locke's classification of ideas, the moral good is a relation.[1] The relation of an action to a law constitutes it as morally good or bad, or indifferent (2.28.15). The action must be "denominated" and subsumed under a type. Thus the same positive idea of an action, such a dueling, can be a virtue, a sin, or crime. An action is neutral if it is not contained in the given law. Locke says that lying is as much a positive idea as is the "speaking of a parrot" (2.28.15). It takes on moral value (Locke uses the term, 2.28.14) only insofar as the action is related to a rule. So the speaking of a parrot does not usually have moral value; but neither does lying if it is not contained in a law; the action as such is morally neutral unless prohibited or enjoined by a lawmaker.

Thus, Locke insists that the positive idea of the action be distinguished from the idea of its relation to a rule. His doctrine anticipates after a fashion the contemporary distinction of fact and value.[2] The positive idea is the fact of the action, its "end, object, manner and circumstances." These constitute the positive idea of the action. As such it is neutral. But moral names such as stealing "intimate" sin and the like are understood to signify the "pravity" of the action. But there is confusion, here Locke says, because "two distinct considerations" are contained in one term. The idea of the action is one consideration; the relation to a rule or norm is another (2.28.16). The latter consideration constitutes its "value." It seems to be separable from the factual description of the action itself. Thus, in his discussion of mixed modes in Book III, Locke treats ideas of productive activities such as drilling or distilling and moral actions such as patricide or incest as if they were similar.

Because a relation to law constitutes the moral good, Locke accordingly approaches the problem of morality in terms of various laws that govern human action. Law in general is the command of a superior with the power of enforcement. So the law is divided into three kinds, depending on the lawgiver and the sanctions. Locke distinguishes three moral norms or laws, the divine law, the civil law, and the law of reputation—"By the relation they bear to the first of these, Men judge whether their Actions are Sins, or Duties; by the second, whether they be Criminal or Innocent; and by the third, whether they be Vertues or Vices" (2.28.7).

Virtue as the Law of Opinion or Fashion

The third of these categories Locke names variously as the law of fashion or private censure, the law of opinion or reputation, and even the law of philosophers in the first edition of the *Essay*; whatever the name, this law designates actions as virtue or vice. Virtue is simply "that which is praised" and vice, "that which is blamed" (2.28.10,11). Certain actions are held by a group in reputation or discredit; the former is termed virtue, the latter is termed vice. The lawgiver in this case is nebulous; it appears to be a social group about which Locke does not inquire further. For example, poets, statesmen, priests, or even philosophers could in some way be responsible for shaping the opinions of men.[3] But in a way it is irrelevant just how the opinion is formed; the point being that a group must come to hold an action in esteem, then it is called virtue; or they hold an action in discredit, then it is called vice.

By the same token, opinion and reputation are also the sanction of the law. The group bestows or withholds its esteem on individuals as much as on actions. Hence people acquire a "reputation" among a group. Praise and blame are the positive and negative sanctions of the law of reputation. Through praise and blame the common opinions acquire the force of law. Locke is aware of the novelty in his designation of reputation as a major part of his division of law; yet he insists that the dynamic of praise and blame fits exactly his notion of law. The essence of law is the power to declare and enforce its will; "commendation and disgrace" have a great power to enforce opinion. The greatest part of mankind, Locke says, govern themselves "chiefly if not solely by this Law of Fashion."[4] In fact, Locke considers the law of fashion to be the most effective of all the three laws. People may ignore the divine law or believe that they can avoid the civil law; but, he says, "No Man scapes the Punishment of their Censure and Dislike, who offends against the Fashion and Opinion of the Company he keeps, and would recommend himself to" (2.28.12). The law of fashion is effective because of man's social nature—that is, human beings obviously take pleasure in the company of others, and therefore they seek to be held in esteem by them. The bestowal of praise and blame is a tremendous power residing almost unreflectively in society at large.

Book I of the *Essay* gives ample testimony to the diversity of common opinion. Locke uses the fact of moral diversity as an argument against innate practical principles. In fact, Locke uses a similar terminology throughout the discussion of diversity, making clear its connection with the law of fashion and opinion. He asks the reader to look at the "several tribes of men" to see that any given principle of morality is "somewhere or other, slighted and condemned by the general Fashion of whole Societies of Men, governed by practical Opinions, and Rules of living quite opposite to others" (1.3.10). The same point is made in Book II: "That this [praise and blame] is the common measure of Vertue and Vice, will appear to any one, who considers, that though that passes for Vice in one Country, which is counted a Vertue, or at least not Vice, in another" (2.28.11). Virtue and vice are as various as the customs of different peoples at different times and places.[5] As Locke uses the term, virtue is what is thought praiseworthy; it is no more than the judgment of common opinion. As a moral norm, virtue therefore is too shifting and arbitrary. Although it is an effective law, perhaps too effective for Locke's taste, it is not grounded in reason. It is not philosophically precise nor is it universal. Therefore it will not serve as the foundation for morality or make up the content of natural law.

The "Sociological" Approach to Virtue

Locke's approach to virtue is novel, not in its the connection between virtue and praise, but in its peculiar division of the law and in its approach to the normative issues involved. These novel positions begin a "sociological" approach to virtue. It should be apparent now why this term may be appropriate.

For Locke lays down certain fundamental themes of sociology. First, he stresses the importance of social groups, as a prepolitical phenomenon, in the formation of opinion and behavior. Second, he adopts a methodological neutrality on the normative issue. That is, virtue is approached from a detached or value-free point of view.

The methodological neutrality is clear from the outset of Locke's treatment of virtue and vice. He says that "Vertue and Vice are Names pretended, and supposed every where to stand for actions in their own nature right and wrong" (2.28.11). For his inquiry Locke suspends the supposition of correctness by nature. His only methodological rule is that which is called virtue is praised, and that which is called vice is blamed. This connection is found in all societies. Now since different societies call different things virtue and vice, then one or the other must be in error. Contraries cannot both be correct. The question then arises, which one is correct? True natural law inquiry begins at this point—moral diversity is the rationale for beginning a quest for what is good by nature, not a skeptical reason for abandoning virtue altogether.

Locke knows something of this ancient tradition. In the first edition of the *Essay* he calls the law of fashion the "philosophical law," rather than the law of opinion or reputation.[6] The philosophers always talked about virtue; but they did not call into question radically enough the pretension to or the supposition of correctness. Locke's approach is new because it does so and thereby explains how it comes to have its authority. In the subsequent editions Locke retained the following reference to the ancient philosophers: "This is the language of the Heathen Philosophers, who well understood wherein their Notions of Vertue and Vice consisted" (2.28.11). What does Locke mean by this remark? The ancient philosophers took their bearings by common opinion, that is, by what people praise and blame. Indeed, some of the ancient philosophers, especially Aristotle, conduct their inquiry from a standpoint within the "citizen's perspective," and the gentleman's assessment of noble and base. This opinion was subjected to a dialectical examination with the aim of ascending to a higher philosophical perspective, and insight into what is good by nature. But the mooring in common opinion is neither abandoned nor rejected.

Locke on the other hand begins with a complete break with common opinion by a bracketing or suspension of judgment as to the correctness of the opinion. He reports the fact alone. The issue of correctness is another inquiry. What type is the inquiry about correctness? He gives two indications of what it may be. He makes pious remarks about the divine law as the true ground. Although he rejects the citizen's perspective, he leaves open the possibility of a divine perspective as a norm for moral action. He says at the outset that virtue and vice are supposed as right and wrong; they are really so if they are "coincident with the divine law" (2.28.10). In the note he refers the reader to such remarks in order to make clear his belief in "an eternal and unalterable nature of right and wrong."[7] I call these remarks "pious" not in order to suggest that Locke made them insincerely; but to suggests that they are made in the mode of faith and not reason. That is, they are but bare assertions. They are given in faith, and should be taken as such. Knowledge of the divine law requires knowledge of God's existence and attributes as well as knowledge of his positive commands. It is a norm placed too high for human reason to comprehend, at least by the canons of reason established by the *Essay* itself.

Axiological Considerations

The deepest novelty and departure of Locke's ethics can be traced to its metaphysical and axiological foundation. At this level we discover the reason why moral diversity is taken as a ground for neutrality and relativism. The traditional doctrine of natural law uses nature as a norm. Within the context of a teleological understanding of nature, the good is defined in terms of human perfection. Virtue as human excellence is the fulfillment of nature. At its peak the notion of good represents an ontological perfection which is diffusive of itself and attracts the human agent by its fullness and beauty. In more mundane terms, the good man performs his functions well and perfects his human faculties of reason and will. Locke constructs a science of ethics that is metaphysically neutral. It does not depend on a notion of nature with purpose and fulfillment, nor does is depend on any notion of spiritual faculties to be perfected. Locke cuts ethics off from metaphysics. His analysis of the self is neutral—it does not matter if man is material, spiritual, or a mixture. The question of substance does not directly affect the ethical analysis. A notion of person, as a conscious self, replaces the traditional notion of soul. For this reason Locke cannot prove the immortality of soul, an argument which depends on a spiritual substance. The quest for a divine law, as Locke sets it up, falters from the very beginning. Similarly, the artificial construct of "person" does not require a narrative for its self-identity—this is precisely the arbitrary stuff of the law of reputation.

Accordingly, the axiological foundation for ethics shifts radically in Locke's account. The good is not a perfection of a nature. The good is defined exclusively in terms of pleasure and pain. The very idea of a good and noble deed and a good and noble man disappears from the terminology. The notion of a noble or honest good is crucial for the traditional account of ethics, in both the Greek and medieval traditions. It is apportioned to the law of fashion and is deemed parochial and irrational. For this reason Locke rejects an ethics of virtue. But the abandonment of a full axiology opens the way to a relativism and irrationality of its own. Happiness is variable with individual preference. Happiness is not the idea of doing well or human flourishing. Happiness is a matter of satisfaction of desire and is subjective. Locke says that the ancient philosophers "in vain" raised the question of the highest good.[8] The notion of happiness serves no normative role as its does for Aristotle or Thomas Aquinas. Their ethics of virtue requires some metaphysical and axiological commitments.

The New Morality

How does Locke get himself out of the pit of moral relativism that he dug by the sociological approach to virtue and the axiological nihilism? He provides two lines of approach to the "eternal standards of right of wrong." The first way requires proof for God's existence, the immortality of the soul to bolster a "divine law." This is exactly how Locke sets up the problem in the *Essay*. We cannot comment further on the success of this line of approach except to say that Locke knows that it is doomed to failure given his empiricist outlook. But he weaves into the language of divine law a form of utilitarianism that springs out of his very sociological approach to virtue and bears deep kinship with his axiological nihilism.

Even though the law of fashion is so diverse, there is an important exception to made for certain types of actions that have to do with "the general good of mankind" and self-interest. Despite the diversity of customs and manners, virtue and vice are "for the most part kept the same everywhere" (2.28.11). Locke's thesis is simple: men praise what is useful, that is, they praise what is to their own advantage. It is advantageous for others to be courageous and just; the courageous man may offer his assistance and the just man will not deprive one of his goods. Self-interest has a rationality that goes deeper than wayward fashion. On its basis a unity or universality of the law of fashion is found. Because men are "constantly true" to their interests, the "true boundaries of the Law of Nature" are preserved. The advantages of the true morality accrue to both individuals and the society at large. For Locke says that there is a visible connection between the "general good" and true morality. Again, rationality (the ability to perceive connections) is deeply embedded in the practical pursuits of life. Even the corrupt and depraved will give lip service to virtue because of the advantage that accrues to its observance by others.

After going through the litany of enormities practiced by men at different times and places, and playing up moral diversity, Locke makes a short aside: an exception must be made for those principles "that are absolutely necessary to hold society together" (1.3.10). In this case, the advantage to society is stressed. These principles are easily discovered because of a "visible connection" between public happiness and virtue.[9] The same account of the praise accorded virtue is given here as well: the virtuous man is useful to others and for this reason he is praised. Similarly rules for the good order of society are useful and make one "safe and secure." No other basis is need for the knowledge of these rules than the reasonable pursuit of self-interest. Locke says that the divine basis for the laws need not be known explicitly as such.

This line of approach to ethics sounds a lot like Hobbes. Has Locke then baptized Hobbes and made him more palatable? Early in the *Essay* Locke outlines three possible grounds for moral precepts: the Christian, the Heathen, and the Hobbist (1.3.5).[10] Each corresponds to one of three moral laws. The Christian appeals to the eternal sanctions of the divine law; the heathen appeals to virtue, which is the law of fashion; the Hobbist appeals to the requirements of public order and the power of the magistrate. As the *Essay* unfolds, Locke rejects the law of fashion as a stable or rational ground for morality. The divine law is too high and remote. Does Locke not embrace a form of Hobbesian natural law through the elimination of the other alternatives? Reason can only discover rules of social order that derive from self-interest. Indeed, in the following section Locke says that without them one cannot be "safe or secure" (1.3.6). This formula clearly echoes the "Leviathan" to which Locke had previously made reference.

The content of moral precepts must be pared down to a minimum. It must be made to focus on the civil goods of life, liberty, and property; a "thin theory" of good. The rules that protect civil goods can be universally appreciated and acknowledged as right even if not followed in action. Without these rules one can be neither safe nor secure. So despite the variability of fashion and the subjectivity of happiness, the precepts of this restricted morality are universal. Everybody requires the protection of their life, liberty, and property whatever their notion of happiness. By lowering the aim of ethics, restricting it scope, Locke can assure its effectiveness. By reorienting ethics to the demands of self-conscious concern and rational liberty he can assure its certainty.

Theological ethics also shares in the new orientation and scope. It is the supreme irony of the *Essay* that the divine law is reconstrued in the very attempt to reassure the Christian believer. The rational part of the divine law is utility. The nonrational part of the divine law is subject to enthusiasm and sectarian quarrels. So it is fitting to restrict the divine law to its rational portion— to utility. Locke does not deny the integrity of faith, or the existence of a life beyond this world. But he has little to say about the content of faith and the way to the next world. He sometimes mentions a twofold practical aim of human understanding—"comfortable provision for this life and the way that leads to a better" (1.1.5). The two aims come to be identified through the rational law, now appropriated through faith. Thus Hans Aarsleff comments that "the wisdom of creation is such that the steady pursuit of happiness under the guidance of reason, disengaged from any immediate and contrary passions will in fact constitute virtuous conduct."[11] By following a rational pursuit of happiness, however variously happiness may be defined, is virtuous conduct. It is really an astounding remark, incorporating as it does, such moral relativism and concern for temporal convenience. The appropriation of the rational laws of utility by faith reorients that faith to the things of this world. The irony is that the concern for the better world, an afterlife, is superfluous. For if by following the rules for happiness on earth one is de facto virtuous, no other special "religious" concern is called for.

In some other passages in the *Essay* Locke drops out the aid of finding the way to a better life after this one and speaks only of the aim of using knowledge to increase the stock of conveniences for the advantages of ease and health (4.12.10). And when the two aims are put into juxtaposition, the greatest praise by far goes to the inventor as the "greatest benefactor." It does not go to the works of mercy and charity.[12] Nor does it go to contemplation, philosophic or religious. He praises the discovery of iron and deems him the "Father of Arts and Author of Plenty" (4.12.11). At the very least, this judgment entails an elevation of human power and places God in the background. Technological "know-how" is to be esteemed above the quality of mercy. Technology saves men from the grave, Locke says. But works of mercy may secure men's "eternal estate." Whatever Locke's interest in Christianity, it surely differs from the traditional Christianity in which works of mercy and charity are the stuff of sanctity, and not technological discovery and entrepreneurial ambition. Despite the acknowledgement of God and religious duty, the temporal focus of Locke's practical aim is manifest. Locke has constructed a purely secular ethic.

If faith is superfluous, then why is it even retained? We know that Locke wished to communicate his new ethic to various audiences, including Christian believers. The use of a familiar terminology is retained so that the new ideas are made "easy and intelligible to all sorts of readers," as Locke admits in his "Epistle to the Reader." John Yolton quotes approvingly a statement that "Locke secured for posterity advances made by radical and progressive forces." Those who openly professed themselves "antithetical to revealed religion" found in Locke "tools to be exploited." Yolton notes that others of more moderate temperament, aligned to orthodoxy, effected more gradual and long lasting modifications:

> It was in the hands of these men, even more than in those of the Deists who appealed to Locke's epistemology, that the new tendencies within religion were most aided and abetted by the theoretical structure of the *Essay*. The application by the Deists was flashy and superficial; that of the traditionalist much more penetrating, perceptive, and positive.[13]

Locke found a way to enter into the most sacred and guarded of domains—theology and morality—and leave his philosophic mark. Whereas
Bacon, Descartes, and especially Hobbes and Spinoza, stirred up great resistance, Locke was able to introduce modern rationalism and the conquest of
nature into the theological heart of the moral and political order.

Locke's legacy in ethics has been too long neglected, overshadowed by his
epistemological and political contributions to philosophy. F. J. E. Wood-
bridge observed in 1932 that "Locke himself was more of a moralist than a
logician or psychologist."[14] And we may add that his politics follows from his
ethics. So we need to reconsider the questions posed by Locke—must the
awareness of moral diversity seem to undermine an ethics of virtue? do we
need a more robust and normative conception of human nature to sustain an
ethics of virtue? should a religious ethic allow itself to be so easily subsumed
into some secular counterpart?

Notes

This chapter extracted from "Why Locke Rejected an Ethics of Virtue and Turned to
an Ethic of Utility." *American Catholic Philosophical Quarterly* 64 (1990): 267–76.

1. "There is another sort of Relation, which is the Conformity or Disagreement, Men's voluntary Actions have to a Rule, to which they are referred, and by
which they are judged of: which I think, may be called Moral Relation" (2.28.4).
John Locke, *An Essay Concerning Human Understanding*, edited by Peter H. Nidditch, The Clarendon Edition of the Works of John Locke (Oxford: Oxford University Press, 1975). The citation refers to book, chapter, and section numbers, respectively.

2. He says that moral judgments are not propositions but commands; therefore
they are neither true nor false. See Locke, *An Essay Concerning Human Understanding*, 1.3.12.

3. On the power of the "law of fashion" see Locke's journal entry of December 12,
1678 in Lord Peter King, *The Life and Letters of John Locke: With Extracts from His
Journals and Commonplace Books* (London: Henry G. Bohn, 1888), 110.

4. See Locke, *An Essay Concerning Human Understanding*, 2.28.12; also the journal, King, *The Life and Letters of John Locke*. On the feared danger of combining the
law of fashion and civil law, the law of the sword, see Locke's early work, *Two Tracts
of Government*, ed. Philip Abrams (Cambridge: Cambridge University Press, 1967),
161, 216–17.

5. Locke continues: "by the different temper, Education, Fashion, Maxims, or Interest of different sorts of Men it fell out, that what was thought praiseworthy in one
Place, escaped not censure in another; and so in different Societies, Vertues and Vice
were changed."

6. Locke, *An Essay Concerning Human Understanding*, 2.28.7; see note by Nidditch, 353.

7. He refers the reader to 1.3.18: "The true and only measure of virtue," and in "its own nature right and good" is an action which conforms to God's will.

8. See the full statement: "The Mind has a different relish, as well as the palate; and you will as fruitlessly endeavor to delight all Men with Riches or Glory, (which yet some Men place their Happiness in,) as you would satisfy all Men's Hunger with Cheese or Lobsters; which though very agreeable and delicious fare to some, are to others extremely nauseous and offensive: And many People would Reason preferr the griping of a hungry Belly, to those Dishes, which are a feast to others. Hence, it was, I think, that the Philosophers of old did in vain enquire, whether Summum bonum consisted in riches, or bodily Delights, or Virtue, or Contemplation: and they might have as reasonably disputed, whether the best Relish were to be found in Apples, Plumbs, or Nuts; and have divided themselves into Sects upon it. For as pleasant Tastes depend not upon the things themselves, but their agreeableness to this or that particular Palate, wherein there is great variety." Locke, *An Essay Concerning Human Understanding*, 2.21.55.

9. "For God, having, by an inseparable connexion, joined Virtue and publick Happiness together; and made the practice thereof, necessary to the preservation of Society, and visibly beneficial to all, with whom the Virtuous Man has to do; it is no wonder, that every one should, not only allow, but recommend, and magnifie those Rules to others, from whose observance of them, he is sure to reap Advantage to himself. He may, out of Interest, as well as Conviction, cry up that for Sacred; which if once trampled on, and prophaned, he himself cannot be safe nor secure." Locke, *An Essay Concerning Human Understanding*, 1.3.6.

10. "That Men should keep their Compacts, is certainly a great and undeniable Rule in Morality: But yet if a Christian, who has the view of Happiness and Misery in another Life, be asked why a Man must keep his Word, he will give this as a Reason: Because God, who has the Power of eternal Life and Death, requires it if us. But if an Hobbist be asked why; he will answer: Because the Publick requires it, and the Leviathan will punish you, if you do not. And if one of the old Heathen Philosophers had been asked, he would have answer'd: Because it was dishonest, below the Dignity of a Man, and opposite to Vertue, the highest Perfection of humane Nature, to do otherwise." Locke, *An Essay Concerning Human Understanding*, 1.3.5.

11. Hans Aarsleff, "The State of Nature," in *John Locke: Problems and Perspectives*, John Yolton, ed. (Cambridge: Cambridge University Press, 1969), 114; see Michael Zuckert, "The Recent Literature on Locke's Political Philosophy," *The Political Science Reviewer* 5 (Fall 1975): 276–78.

12. See St. Augustine, *The City of God*, Book 9, chapters 20, 22.

13. John Yolton, *John Locke and the Way of Ideas* (Oxford University Press, 1956), 203–206.

14. "Locke's Essay," *Studies in the History of Ideas* 3 (1935): 243.

~

CHAPTER SEVEN

The Two Lockes: On the Foundation of Liberty in Locke

It is more important to recognize the dependence of secular liberalism for its moral bite upon the strength of Protestantism in English-speaking societies. Most of our history is written by secularists who see the significant happening as the development of secular liberalism. They are therefore likely to interpret the Protestants as passing if useful allies in the realization of our modern regimes. This allows them to patronize Protestant superstitions in a friendly manner, as historically helpful in the development of secularism. To put the ethical relation clearly: if avoidance of death is our highest end (albeit negative), why should anyone make sacrifices for the common good which entail that possibility? Why should anyone choose to be a soldier or a policeman, if Lockean contractualism is the truth about justice? Yet such professions are necessary if any approximation to justice are to be maintained. Within a contractualist belief, why should anyone care about the reign of justice more than their life? The believing Protestants provided the necessary moral cement which could not be present for those who consistently directed by contractualism or utilitarianism or a combination of both. . . . As Protestants accepted the liberalism of autonomous will, they became unable to provide their societies with the public sustenance of uncalculated justice which the contractual account of justice could not provide from itself. . . . Most intellectuals in our societies scorned the fundamental beliefs of the public religion, and yet counted on the continuance of its moral affirmations to serve as the convenient public basis of justice. Clever people generally believed that the foundational principles of justice were chosen conveniences, because of what they had learnt from modern science; nevertheless they could not turn away from a noble content to that justice, because they were enfolded more than they knew in long memories and hopes.

—George Parkin Grant, *English-Speaking Justice*[1]

Introduction

For such a prosaic and bland writer, John Locke has bequeathed an astonishing legacy; there are more papers and books on John Locke than stars in the sky. And speaking of Locke, there are quite a diverse number of Lockes. There is first of all the popular Locke and the philosophic Locke, or the Locke of the statesmen and the Locke of the scholars; and these of course can all be further subdivided; my friend Marion Montgomery writes of "Locke North" and "Locke South" in discussing American sensibility prior to the civil war.[2] And then there are the various Lockes that emerge from his various writings, most of which he did not attach his own name to, the Locke of the *Treatises*, and the Locke of the *Reasonableness*, or the Locke of the *Essay*, all interpretations of which are to be further scrambled by the Locke of the notebooks and private correspondence. And then we must add to our Locke pile, the old Locke and the new Locke of scholarly interpretation, without forgetting that the old Locke was the new Locke of forty years hence. All of which brings me to the point of this chapter; on the occasion of the recent publication of a splendid volume from the University of Kansas, *John Locke's Two Treatises of Government: New Interpretations*, edited by Edward J. Harpham, which provides a good summary and prospectus of this "new Locke," I wish to examine the significance of the Locke for our understanding of liberal democracy and to criticize the "new Locke" from the perspective of reading one specific text of Locke (the *Essay*) and by making the case for the old new Locke (of Strauss and Macpherson).

Who Is the New Locke?
The last thirty years has witnessed an explosion of scholarly books and articles on Locke which, claims Harpham, has "recast our most basic understanding of Locke as a historical actor and political theorist, the *Two Treatises* as a document, and liberalism as a coherent tradition of political discourse."[3] The seven articles in this volume attempt to assess this "new scholarship," self-described as revisionist and historicist. This volume is now probably the best introduction to the "new scholarship." The introduction by Edward Harpham, "Locke's Two Treatises in Perspective" and the bibliogra-

phy provide a nice summary of key ideas, books, and articles. If there is any single point of agreement among the mainstream scholars today it is the view of Locke as a Christian thinker who developed a natural law teaching to meet the challenges of political transformation in the English polity during those turbulent years surrounding the Glorious Revolution. The essence of the new perspective is best stated by Richard Ascraft in "The Politics of Locke's Two Treatises of Government": "Locke's thought is thus both philosophically more conservative and politically more radical than we have hitherto supposed. In short, Locke is at once closer to Aristotle and Hooker and to the levelers and Sidney than the prevailing interpretations of his political thought maintain."[4] Most scholars now accept something like this assessment of Ashcraft's; although disagreement is still found about the particular spin that this claim must take. The precise nature of his religious or conservative belief is not agreed upon; and while agreeing upon the nature of the *Two Treatises* as a political document calling for resistance to the king, there is still disagreement about the full extent of its meaning in terms of property rights. And of course, the relevance or irrelevance of Locke's political philosophy to present-day liberalism and American regime is a point of contention. The core to the new Locke scholarship remains constant— Locke is a religious thinker, whose active Christianity is essential to his political philosophy.

The new scholarship, however, continues to look back over its shoulder at the counter views of C. B. MacPherson and Leo Strauss.[5] Although their work is declared otiose, blind, and fundamentally in error, these two mavericks continue to haunt the scene. Their work stands as a point of reference for explicating the newness of the new scholarship on Locke, and they serve as convenient whipping posts for the historicist scholars propounding the new Locke. Although Strauss and MacPherson differ greatly in method, perspective, and interpretation, the two are rightly linked together as propounding the older "new" view of Locke, which portrays him as a philosophical radical who makes a decisive break with the older natural law tradition, abandoning both its philosophical and religious principles, and who remolds an essentially Hobbesian principle into a more consistent and prudent form of political regime dedicated to the unlimited acquisition of property. Ashcraft attempts to separate Locke from the philosophy of Hobbes on issues such as resistance, toleration, justice and natural law, and obligation; he directs his argument against Macpherson and Strauss. Yet although many of the particulars of Macpherson's interpretation are addressed, there is a curious silence about the particular claims of Strauss. Ashcraft actually makes the erroneous claim that Strauss never reconsidered his position on

Locke stated in the *Natural Right* in light of von Leyden's edition of Locke's *Essays on the Law of Nature*, while in fact Strauss' most seminal essay on Locke is an analysis of just that work.[6] And unfortunately many of the works produced in this vein are neglected by the new scholarship.[7]

In this chapter I should like to outline the central case against the reading of Locke as a teacher of Christian natural law on the basis of his *Essay Concerning Human Understanding*. The central problem to interpreting Locke involves his theology and the basis for natural law. James Tully et al. invoke the divine workmanship model as the "framework" for interpreting Locke.[8] But I would like to discuss one of the central problems of interpretation that persists with this reading of Locke and that leads in the direction back to something like a Straussian reading of Locke. First, I shall outline the central conflict in Locke's account of natural law as found in the "Second Treatise;" then I shall show what the *Essay* may have to say about this conflict; I shall conclude with some remarks about the continual relevance of Locke for understanding liberal democracy on the issue of religion and justice.

Divine Workmanship or Radical Autonomy?

The "Workmanship Model" for Natural Rights and Natural Law

Locke uses the term natural law throughout the *Two Treatises of Government* with confident assertion. In chapter two of the "Second Treatise" alone the term appears fourteen times. In many instances, passages from the Bible and the great natural law theorist Richard Hooker are intertwined with Locke's own assertions. Locke employs what is now called the "workmanship model" of natural law. Natural law is first mentioned as a limit upon natural freedom. Chapter two, entitled "of the State of Nature," opens with the following paragraph:

> To understand Political Power right, and derive it from its Original, we must consider what state all Men are naturally in, and that is a state of perfect Freedom to order their Actions, and dispose of their Possessions, and Persons, as they think fit, within the bounds of the Law of Nature, without asking leave or depending on the Will of any other Man. (2.4) [9]

This original state of nature is said to be a state of "perfect freedom." By freedom Locke here means no more than an absence of restraint. Thus later in his defense of law as the preserve of freedom, Locke says that "liberty is to be free from restraint and violence" (2.57). Law protects men from the arbitrary will of another; thus without law, freedom cannot be. Natural freedom, therefore, does not as such entail any special moral development or virtue. It does require the use of "reason." Locke mentions in the same passage with the perfect freedom, the bounds of a natural law. This is to distinguish "liberty" from "license." The content of this law is specified in section six. The natural law which initially guides men in the state of nature is to refrain from harm: "The State of Nature has a Law of Nature to govern it, which obliges every one; And Reason, which is that Law, teaches all Mankind, who will but consult it, that being all equal and independent, no one ought to harm another in his Life, Health, Liberty, or Possessions." The restraint demanded by natural law derives from an additional characteristic of the state of nature: in the state of nature men are equal in addition to being free. In section four, the passage cited above continues as follows:

> A State also of Equality, wherein all Power and Jurisdiction is reciprocal, no one having more than another: there being nothing more evident, than that Creatures of the same species and rank promiscuously born to all the same advantages of Nature, and the use of the same faculties, should also be equal one amongst another without Subordination or Subjection, unless the Lord and Master of them all, should by any manifest declaration of his Will set one above another, and confer on him by an evident and clear appointment an undoubted Right to Dominion and Sovereignty. (2.4)

Locke makes clear that equality means equal jurisdiction, or the absence of subordination and subjection. In effect, equality simply reiterates the notion of natural freedom. As Tocqueville later pointed out, in the most extreme form, equality and freedom merge into one.[10] In Locke's account, natural freedom is the determining characteristic of the state of nature. Equality of jurisdiction preserves the freedom. Thus, later Locke states that he does not endorse the notion of equality of parts, and that the equality of jurisdiction is consistent with inequality in age, virtue, birth, or merit (2.54). The nature of equality intended in sections four and six, he says, is "an equal Right that every Man hath, to his Natural Freedom, without being subjected to the Will or Authority of any other Man" (2.54). The notion of equality holds together both the idea of freedom as the absence of restraint and the idea that liberty is not license. In the former case, equality nullifies any subordination or subjection of one to another. Subjection contradicts freedom. In the latter case, equality entails a mutual respect or mutual recognition of the equal freedom of others. The basis for this mutual respect and recognition is the fundamental problem, since it is the basis for natural law.

What is the nature and basis for this equality? In the passage cited above from section four, the basis for equality is the order of creation. That is, Locke argues that all creatures are equal under God and occupy the same rank or status as "creature." Thus, no one can assume to take the position of God and rule over others. This argument from the order of creation reflects a premodern understanding of equality. Men are neither beasts nor gods, but occupy equally a ground midway between. It is neither appropriate to act as a god nor to treat others as beasts or inferior creatures. Locke explicitly uses this premodern image. The major text reads as follows:

> For Men being all the Workmanship of one Omnipotent, and infinitely wise Maker; All the Servants of one Sovereign Master, sent into the World by his order and about his business, they are his Property, whose Workmanship they are, made to last during his, not anothers Pleasure. And being furnished with like Faculties, sharing all in one Community of Nature, there cannot be supposed any such Subordination among us, that may authorize us to destroy one another, as if we were made for one anothers uses, as the inferior ranks of Creatures are for ours. (2.6)

In light of this order of creation, man can make no claim to absolute dominion over his fellow creature. That is, man cannot claim the type of superiority that would authorize the destruction or arbitrary use of another. Mutual respect depends upon the recognition of one's status as creature, along with others, before the Creator.

Locke's first account of natural law depends on a religious basis. The workmanship model simply assumes the notion of creation; further, it ascribes to God the attributes of omnipotence and infinite wisdom. The model describes human existence in terms of God's order and the fulfillment of God's "business." Thus, the first problem to emerge with the doctrine of natural law in the "Second Treatise" is its dependence upon religious presuppositions. For some readers this presents no special problem at all, and they view it as part of the historical context of Locke's work. In light of the *Essay*, the religious assumptions are quite troubling indeed. The attributes required of God for the workmanship model are problematic to the extreme. But leaving aside the *Essay*, we can find indications of Locke's own problem with the workmanship model in the *Two Treatises of Government* itself. To allow the doctrine of natural law and the account of government to depend wholly on revelation violates Locke's declared intention in writing the *Two Treatises of Government*.

In the "First Treatise" Locke continually upbraids Filmer for failing to provide argument for his position. Locke says that we should expect clear and evident reasons for his position, especially for the fundamental idea that all men are naturally subordinated to the king (1.50). Filmer proceeds by way of simple assertion or "bare supposition" (1.11). No reason or proof is provided

for his major judgments; a "mighty structure" is raised upon "bare suppositions." The style of Filmer's treatise matches its content: "Had he been an
Absolute Monarch this way of talking might have suited well enough; *pro ratione voluntas*, might have been of force in his mouth, but in the way of proof
or argument is very unbecoming" (1.51). Filmer, like an absolute monarch,
denies any maturity or rationality in the part of his people or audience. Discourse itself would be destroyed in the regime proposed by Filmer: will, or
whim, alone rules. Philosophy, as well as liberty, is threatened by Filmer's
method. Similarly, Locke accuses Filmer of using repetition as a rhetorical
device in the place of argument. Among some men, Locke says, repetition
goes for argument (1.13). Filmer plays upon this weakness: he strings together his assertions to look like arguments.[11]

Locke's positive account of government in the "Second Treatise" is no
mere counter assertion, as if Locke replaces *"pro ratione voluntas"* with *"vox
populi, vox dei."* Since Locke demands that one's main supposition be "proved
and established with all the evidence of arguments" (1.11), the reader should
expect no less of Locke. Of course, the "Second Treatise" is not one pure argument, an Euclidean, systematic unfolding of the origin and extent of government. It too contains its share of bare assertions, unproved suppositions,
and repetitions. For example, Locke's own "great foundation" for limited government, the natural state of perfect freedom, appears first as a bare assertion.
Similarly, the idea of natural law often appears as a bare assertion and is repeated again and again. But Locke warns the reader not to take repetition for
argument. The proof must be found as the "Second Treatise" develops. The
workmanship model, however, contains problems of its own, not the least of
which is its suppositional nature. It is hard to believe that Locke would rest
his case on a mere supposition after excoriating Filmer for doing so. In fact,
there is another line of argument for natural freedom and equality in the
"Second Treatise." It is an argument that does not depend upon the supposition of creation or special revelation. It is a sense of equality as mutual restraint based upon a reasonable or realistic self-interest. That is, from the
strongest passion of self-preservation the entire argument for natural freedom, mutual jurisdiction and the derivation of the civil society can be obtained. The means of coming to know the law of restraint, the scope of the
law, and the execution of law operate entirely independently of the supposition of creation and divine workmanship.

The Model of Radical Autonomy
The workmanship model may stand as a nice supposition that convinces
many readers. But Locke indicates that the grasp of natural law does not

depend on divine revelation nor does it depend on knowledge of God's promulgated law and sanctions. Locke refers to revelation and reason as sources for the natural law. The natural law is said to be reason itself.[12] That is, reason is the measure itself, not simply the power which grasps an independent or transcendent law issued by God. What is the rule of reason? The rule of reason is mutuality and nonharm to others. This content can be appreciated independently of the workmanship model. For to deny the mutuality of equal right is to be oneself into a state of war with another. And to do so, opens oneself to destruction as a noxious beast. Mere self-preservation would counsel mutuality and restraint. Another indication of Locke's intention to find a basis for government independent of divine revelation is the doctrine of individual execution. By placing the execution into the hands of each individual Locke assures the effectiveness of the law in this world:

> And that all Men may be restrained from invading others Rights, and from doing hurt to one another, and the Law of Nature be observed, which willeth the Peace and preservation of all Mankind, the Execution of the Law of Nature is in that State, put into every Mans hands, whereby every one has a right to punish the transgressors of that Law to such a degree, as may hinder its Violation. For the Law of Nature would, as all other Laws that concern Men in this World, be in vain, if there were no body that in the State of Nature, had a power to Execute that Law, and thereby preserve the innocent and restrain offenders, and if any one in the State of Nature may punish another, for any evil he has done, every one may do so. For in that State of perfect Equality, where naturally there is no superiority or jurisdiction of one, over another, what any may do in Prosecution of that Law, every one must needs have a Right to do. (2.7)

But to demand effective sanctions in this life is to remove the natural law from the domain of divine law and the eternal sanctions. Further, Locke says that the individual comes by the right to execute the law of nature because he must do it. An early indication that Locke's notion of right means that one acts without doing wrong in the rational pursuit of preservation.

The problematic status of the workmanship model is also indicated by the ambiguity of the general precept of natural law. The precept is first stated as follows:

> Every one as he bound to preserve himself, and not to quit his station wilfully; so by like reason when his own Preservation comes not into competition, ought he, as he can, to preserve the rest of Mankind, and may not unless it be

to do Justice on an Offender, take away, or impair the life, or what tends to the Preservation of the Life, the Liberty, Health, Limb, or Goods of another. (2.6)

As mentioned above, the fundamental law of nature is often stated in this ambiguous fashion. The precepts commands the preservation of self and others, or it commands the preservation of as many as possible, or it commands the preservation of the innocent. But in conjunction with the individual execution of the natural law, there will often be a dispute as to who is innocent. So the possibility of conflict arises. And in this simple first statement of the precept of the natural law, Locke makes the command to refrain from harm and the preservation of others depend upon the qualification that one's own preservation not be in conflict. Presumably, in conflict self-preservation takes priority. Of course, Locke does not push the conflict and relishes the ambiguity.[13]

A more radical case for Locke's questioning of the workmanship model arises from the chapter on property. In addition to asserting that man is God's property, Locke also says that "every man has property in his own person" (2.27,44). Indeed, on this basis Locke constructs his account of private possession against the common claim by all mankind. The absolute dominion over his own property and person effectively excludes God or other human beings from having a meaningful claim over the human agent. The contradiction between this statement on property and the workmanship model seems patent. But the significance of the contradiction has been a source of controversy.[14]

The problems with the natural law doctrine in the "Second Treatise" are resolved in light of the primacy of self-preservation. The knowability of the law, the effectiveness of the law, and the content of the law, are all traced back to the right of the individual to self-preservation. The strange doctrine of the individual execution of the law of nature confirms this approach, as we shall see in the subsequent section. The reduction of natural law to one general precept, that of preservation, and the individual right of execution of that law, constitute a major change in doctrine from the premodern tradition of natural law. It is part of Locke's genius to play on the ambiguity of the general precept so as to hide or partially conceal the primacy of self-preservation. But with careful reading, the primacy of self-preservation must be acknowledged as the centerpiece of Locke's account of government, and of moral obligation itself. The doctrine is first outlined in a very important section of the "First Treatise."[15] It is apparent in the "Second Treatise" that the rights to life, liberty, and property are analytically ordered to the primacy of self-preservation.

Locke ends the chapter on inheritance in the "First Treatise" with a short precise of the "Second Treatise."

Property, whose Original is from the Right a Man has to use any of the inferior Creatures, for the Subsistence and Comfort of his Life, is for the benefit and sole advantage of the Proprietor, so that he may even destroy the thing, that he has Property in by use of it, where need requires: but Government being for the Preservation of every Mans Right and Property, by preserving him from the Violence or Injury of others, is for the good of the Governed. For the Magistrates Sword being for a Terror to Evil Doers, and Society made conformable to the Laws of Nature, for the public good. (1.92)

Property is based on the strongest desire for self-preservation; as it turns out, the right to liberty also derives from the sole inclination of self-preservation. The so-called laws of nature all derive from the single inclination of self-preservation.

Locke's "great position" in the "Second Treatise" is that all men are by nature free. How does he establish this position? The chapter on slavery provides the most direct answer to that question. Locke says that "freedom from absolute, arbitrary power, is so necessary to, and closely joined with, a man's preservation, that he cannot part with it, but by what forfeits his preservation and life together" (2.23). Freedom is a necessary condition for preservation; the argument follows the Lockean idea of demonstration put forward in the *Essay*. Locke shows the connection or the agreement and disagreement of ideas. Self-preservation entails freedom; and the absence of freedom disagrees with the idea of self-preservation. And indeed freedom is treated throughout the chapter on the state of war as the correlate of self-preservation. Consider the situation in which freedom is denied; in such a situation one's preservation is jeopardized. To assume absolute power over another amounts to a "declaration of war." Locke says, "to be from such force is the only security of my Preservation: and reason bids me look on him, as an Enemy to my Preservation, who would take away freedom, which is the Fence to it: so that he who makes an attempt to enslave me, thereby puts himself into a State of War with me" (2.17). The subordinate has a right to destroy the threat to his preservation: "it being reasonable and just that I should have a Right to destroy that which threatens me with Destruction" (2.16).

Whoever practices this denial of equality, and the natural freedom, entailed, is to declare war on others. And by such a declaration one has "exposed his Life to the others Power to be taken away by him" (2.16). To put oneself in such an insecure state is most unreasonable and dangerous. One is open to being treated like a noxious beast:

One may destroy a Man who makes War upon him, or has discovered an En-mity to his being, for the same Reason, that he may kill a Wolf or a Lyon; be-cause such men are not under the ties of the Common Law of Reason, have no other Rule, but that of Force and Violence, and so may be treated as Beasts of Prey, those dangerous and noxious Creatures, that will be sure to destroy him, whenever he falls into their Power. (2.16)

It is more safe, more reasonable to acknowledge the equality of jurisdic-tion. Thus Locke refers to the law of nature as simply the law of reason and common equity (2.8) or the common law reason (2.16). The law of nature is the reasonable restraint of common equity that will establish mutual security (2.8) and preserve mankind (2.11). It is discovered through the person's own desire for safety and security.

The basis for restraint is fear of harm. The law is easily discovered through the threat of retaliation and revenge. Therefore, if one does not want to be harmed, one must not harm others. Locke quotes Hooker on the notion of equality to his own advantage. Hooker explains his concept of equality and moral law through a hypothetical mode: "If you want to receive good, then you must do good to others." Similarly, "if I do harm, I must look to suffer." Locke subtly changes the content of the law from mutual charity and affection to mere mutual restraint (2.6). The natural law is formulated as follows—no one ought to harm another in his life, health, liberty, or possessions. Why should one observe this law? In light of the previous quote from Hooker, the answer is obvious. If one does not do so, one must expect to suffer harm in return. Like Cain, the violator of equal right to freedom will understand his vulnerability: "he has declared War against all Mankind, and therefore may be destroyed as a Lyon or a Tyger, one of those wild Savage Beasts, with whom Men can have no Society nor Security: and upon this is grounded the great Law of Nature, Who so sheddeth Mans blood, by Man shall his blood be shed. And Cain was so fully convinced, that every one had a Right to destroy such a Criminal, that after the Murther of his Brother, he cries out, Every one that findeth me, shall slay me; so plain was it writ in the Hearts of all Mankind" (2.11). Locke here refers to revenge, lex talionis, as the "Great law of nature." Moreover, such a law is "written in the hearts of all mankind." This passage is crucial for under-standing the new approach to "natural law." The manner of the law's promul-gation, its content, and its effectiveness are all implicit here.

Locke's one specific formulation of the law is a principle of nonharm (2.6). More generally it is a principle of common equity, and mutual re-straint. At times, Locke identifies reason itself with the law.[16] A good di-alectical principle for definition is the use of contrast and opposition. Locke opposes the rule of reason to the rule of violence and criminality. The criminal has renounced the rule of reason, which demands restraint. Thus, the criminal is like a beast or noxious creature (2.16). But if mutual restraint is one part of the rule of reason, so is self-defense. It is also reasonable to kill a wild beast and rid oneself and mankind of the threat to preservation. So the natural law has two sides to it—mutual restraint on the one hand, and self-defense on the other. But in the order of discovery, the reasonableness of self-defense, or self-preservation, seems to come first. And in the order of right and jurisdiction self-preservation is also first. Although in the latter case, of right and jurisdiction, the primacy of self-preservation is shielded by the ambivalence of the law's formulation to preserve all mankind. First we shall discuss the way in which the law is discovered and by implication how the law is promulgated. Then we shall turn to the question of right and jurisdiction in the following section as part of Locke's new doctrine of individual execution of the natural law.

In what manner is the law of nature "plain" and "written on the hearts" of mankind (2.11)? Is Locke committed here to a doctrine of innate ideas and principles? What is plain, according to this passage, is a law of revenge to destroy a noxious beast. Following the lead of the inclination toward self-preservation, such a "law" is manifest. It does not take great intellectual awareness to comprehend the law, or to act according to it. At the very least, fear of others brings it to the fore as a possibility, as is the case with Cain's fear of retribution. The natural law is based upon the desire for self-preservation. The desire for self-preservation is an innate principle of action, as we learned from the "First Treatise." The precept of nonharm is not as such innate or written in the heart, as much as the desire for preservation and the fear of being harmed by others. The fear of harm leads one to act in self-defense. But self-defense requires no special study or enlightenment, other than strength and wiles. The principle of nonharm follows an enlightened pursuit of self-interest. It can be derived fully from the desire for self-preservation and the obvious danger that follows from a denial of mutuality or equality of rule.

The specifics of the law are not said to be innate or written in the heart. Reason must be "consulted" (2.6), and one must be a "studier of the law" (2.12). The law is intelligible and plain to a rational creature, but the degree of rationality is yet to be determined. The natural law is plainer than the "Phansies and intricate Contrivances of Men" (2.12). Men are just not always studiers of the law because they prefer to follow "contrary and hidden interests" (2.12). Custom is one factor that perverts clear reason, as we learned in abundant fashion from the *Essay*. Passion is another. Men follow their "interests"; they blindly follow their own bias and interests. Self-love makes men partial to themselves, and ill-nature and passion lead to extremism and violence (2.13). Men are not good students of the natural law; the law of nature does not appear plain to all; so it is obviously not innate. It is the function of government to make it plain and to specify its content through the civil law.

The law of nature is actually derived from a more fundamental right of nature. Freedom itself is understood as a protection for preservation. Men must be free in a state of nature, because to assume otherwise is to deny the right of self-preservation. To what degree and in what manner is self-preservation a right? Does not self-preservation also derive from the workmanship model? For Locke says that men are bound to preserve themselves by the natural law. But Locke takes up the issue of the enforcement of the natural law. The law is enforced by each individual in the state of nature. This admittedly "strange doctrine" (2.9) of the individual execution of the natural law exhibits the underlying meaning and implications of Locke's new doctrine of "natural law."

The doctrine of individual execution is asserted soon after the first few uses of the term natural law. Locke says that:

> And that all Men may be restrained from invading others Rights, and from doing hurt to one another, and the Law of Nature be observed, which willeth the Peace and preservation of all Mankind, the Execution of the Law of Nature is in that State, put into every Mans hands, whereby every one has a right to punish the transgressors of that Law to such a degree, as may hinder its Violation. For the Law of Nature would, as all other Laws that concern Men in this World, be in vain, if there were no body that in the State of Nature, had a power to Execute that Law, and thereby preserve the innocent and restrain offenders, and if any one in the State of Nature may punish another, for any evil he has done, every one may do so. For in that State of perfect Equality, where naturally there is no superiority or jurisdiction of one, over another, what any may do in Prosecution of that Law, every one must needs have a Right to do. (2.7)

The right of individual execution depends on a number of presuppositions, each of which helps to reveal the true character of Locke's natural law teaching. The obvious premise stated by Locke is the equality of jurisdiction. The doctrine of individual execution follows from the fact that no one is by nature designated to perform the action. It follows then that each individual must do so, as he sees fit. Individual execution involves a good deal of judgment, in addition to action. The individual must judge what the natural law is and how it pertains to the case at hand. The general precept is preservation—of "all mankind," as it is specified in this section. The individual has the right to punish transgressors. But a crucial ambiguity is contained here. Who is to judge who is a transgressor and who is acting in self-defense? Each individual must judge. The same ambiguity is contained in the first formulation of the natural law, stated in section six. No one ought to harm another, "unless it be to do justice to an offender." But the judgment of offense lies with each individual. The "offender" may well consider himself the "defender." Or again, in the section quoted above, the power of execution is for the "preservation of the innocent," and the restraint of the "offenders." The judgment of innocence and offense must be made by the individual. The natural law depends upon this "juridical crux," which is hopelessly subjective and biased. The necessity and character of a social contract derives from this crux. This shall be the topic for our next section.

The second crucial premise from which Locke derives the doctrine of individual execution is that the natural law must be effective in this world. The natural law would be "vain," Locke says, if there were no one to execute it "in this world." In light of the Essay, this premise is most telling. The natural law, as Locke defines it in the Essay, is the divine law. Its sanctions are, therefore, otherworldly. The meaning of natural law in the "Second Treatise," is therefore, not the same as the divine law. Divine law as such is superfluous. By simply following the strongest passion of self-preservation, as Locke calls it in the "First Treatise," the agent is following the will of God. This is mere confirmation of what is known through other means. Just as the precept of natural law, mutual restraint, is discovered through reflection on mutuality and war, so too is it enforced without the agency of God. The "workmanship model" is therefore superfluous. It is also interesting to note the choice of terms in the "Second Treatise" to describe compliance and violation of the natural law; Locke does not say "sinner" which according to the Essay would be the proper description of one who violates the natural law or divine law. Criminality and innocence refer instead to action as related to the civil law and the domain of life, liberty, and property.[17]

The so-called natural law must be restricted in scope to become effective through individual execution. The full-bodied natural law as divine law would be quite "vain" and ineffective in reliance upon individual execution. The goal or purpose of the natural law must be lowered to become effective. For example the virtues are not enforceable by "individual execution." But self-preservation is enforceable; so protection of life, liberty, and property become the sole domain of natural law. Compare this situation with Thomas

Aquinas' account of natural law. Thomas argues that the virtues are commanded by the natural law.[18] Moreover, Thomas posits three general levels of goods to be promoted and protected through natural law: preservation, procreation and education of children, and truth and fellowship.[19] Locke virtually eliminates the higher two levels of goods and restricts the natural law to the first, preservation. Thus, the demand for worldly effectiveness alters the meaning and scope of natural law.

The single goal for natural law, preservation, is ambiguously stated. The goal has a single content, but it may be variously described as to the object of preservation. As mentioned above, Locke variously describes the goal of preservation in terms of the self, all mankind, as many as possible, mutual security, and the innocent. In the first formulation of the precept Locke distinguishes the preservation of mankind and self-preservation and establishes an order amongst them: "Every one as he bound to preserve himself, and not to quit his station wilfully; so by like reason when his own Preservation comes not into competition, ought he, as he can, to preserve the rest of Mankind, and may not unless it be to do Justice on an Offender, take away, or impair the life, or what tends to the Preservation of the Life, the Liberty, Health, Limb, or Goods of another" (2.6). In this opening formulation, self-preservation takes clear priority to preservation of mankind. Yet Locke prefers to make preservation of mankind the basis for individual execution.[20] In this way, Locke deemphasizes the priority of self-preservation. And the approach works in the majority of cases. That is, the two goals, self-preservation and the preservation of mankind are often indistinguishable in the situations Locke presents.[21] Take the case of a violent man who "quitted reason" and becomes like a beast. The beast is a danger to everybody. Each individual has a right to kill him, and thereby preserve mankind. Thus in the fundamental conflict between men, mortal conflict, one appeals not directly to self-preservation, but to preservation of mankind. But in the heat of direct competition, the individual surely thinks of his own life, which is directly threatened and saved; mankind is but a distant afterthought. Nevertheless, everyone benefits, however self-centered the action.

An individual fulfills the "natural law" through the mere pursuit of self-preservation. But this cannot be considered a strict moral obligation at all. The natural law amounts to a set of precepts that are useful for self-preservation, and that arise from a passionate principle of action. A moral law as such must add something more—sanctions imposed from without. The right to self-preservation is literally "self-enforcing," as the doctrine of individual execution indicates. Men are enjoined to "preserve themselves" because they cannot really do otherwise. Self-preservation is the strongest passion and an innate principle of action. The execution of law pursuant to this end gives the so-called natural law its specificity. It is right reason, prudence, in the face of particular necessities and circumstances; it is "doing all reasonable things he can in order to that end" (2.11). What any may do in the prosecution of preservation, Locke says, "every one must needs have a right to do" (2.7). Locke often calls reason itself the law of nature. Reason determines what ought to be done to preserve oneself. The law of nature comes to light through the possibility of the threat to oneself. One has a right to harm or restrain another in self-defense. One affirms a right to destroy what is noxious (2.8). That is the extent of natural law; in so doing one may also preserve "mankind." But the foundation is autonomous judgment for autonomous interests.

Two Solutions

So which is the sure foundation of natural right, workmanship or autonomy? Hobbes most articulately challenged the fundamental presuppositions of the Thomistic synthesis of biblical theology and Aristotelian philosophy such as the sociability of man and the possibility of a common good, the existence of a highest good in virtue and contemplation, and the natural law derived from such human teleology. Hobbes, rather, began with a state of nature as a state of war, the futility of seeking a good higher than the pleasant preservation of the individual—comfortable self-preservation—and a natural law clearly derivative from more fundamental rights of nature such as the right to self-preservation. Following the early lead of Gerson, Hobbes defines "right of nature" (jus naturale) as "the liberty each man hath, to use his own power, as he will himself, for the preservation of his own nature."[22] Hobbes clearly distinguishes right (ius) from law (lex)—"right, consisteth in liberty to do, or forbeare; whereas Law, determineth, and bindeth to one them; so that Law, and Right, differ as much, as Obligation, and Liberty." For Hobbes, right (liberty) clearly takes precedent over law (obligation). The fundamental right or liberty of the self is unbounded or unlimited by anything; by the fundamental right of preservation, each man has a right to everything and anything done in the pursuit of preservation is without blame. The intolerable conflicts between individuals however amounts to a state of war. It is reasonable, therefore, to limit ones claim to things for the sake of self-protection. Morality exists by way of contract. Morality is a rational deduction of moral rules from the right of self-preservation.[23] Hobbes defense of individual rights required the existence of an absolute power in society to keep all potential wrongdoers in a state of awe such that they would obey the law. Hobbes' account was shocking in so many ways, not the least of which was its implicit antitheistic philosophy, that it was frequently decried and banned. The contrast between Hobbes and the biblical and philosophical accounts of moral and political order is clear. Is Locke more biblical or Hobbesian, or some strange combination of each?

Although there is a wide spectrum of interpretations of Locke's moral and political philosophy, they tend to gravitate to the poles marked out by the theological question. On one side of the spectrum lies the theological interpretation of Locke as a Christian apologist; on the other side lies a secular interpretation of Locke as a crypto-Hobbesian. Does Locke develop a rational moral law or does he rely on faith? Is the content of this law much like the traditional natural law or does it represent a departure?

Many scholars simply regard Locke as essentially a "religious thinker" who never could escape from the presuppositions of Christianity. Those of this school inclined toward a more "Gestalt" view of things, use terms like "theological framework," "theological matrix," "workmanship model," and "Christian worldview."[24] Those more inclined to a linear way of thinking simply say that Locke accepted natural law and God as a mere premise or presupposition.[25] The fall back to faith is therefore inevitable, for this is Locke's original position; he is forced to proceed in a circle.[26] According to each scholar's degree of personal insight into Locke's psychology they declare that he was more or less aware of the failure of reason in discovery of the divine law, but that he was not disturbed by it. For the whole is "coherent" and "hangs together" in faith. The dismal arguments for God's existence he found "satisfying" and he "feels" that he has demonstrated the existence of the Christian God because religion seeps into the demonstration.[27] It comes as no surprise therefore to this school of interpretation that Locke would downplay the notion of natural law, knowable by reason, in favor of a divine law known by faith alone. At the most extreme position we find the assertion that Locke attempted to show the very limits of human knowledge in order to bring out the necessity and importance of traditional Christian faith.[28] In other words, it is Locke's very design and intention to fall back on faith in the explication of natural law. A similar position is taken by Richard Ashcraft, who asserts that the purpose of the Essay is the "conservative" one of the "renovation and reinforcement of the faith."[29] Ashcraft introduces a subtle nuance of interpretation that is found to be the mainstay of most interpretations of Locke. He says that Locke may have believed that he presented a rational theological foundation for morality and natural law, but that he never questioned his fundamental religious assumptions; thus he argues in a circle, and never steps outside of the context or "circle of faith."[30]

'ine of interpretation of Locke involves the idea that Locke ..ed religious presuppositions. Although believing that he ,ished a work of rational explication, he unconsciously relied on ..aith of the day. The resulting doctrine is a collection of elements that are never fully consistent, at least from the outside; they may be "coherent" as a historical mind set. The interpretation of Locke, therefore, must proceed from a historical account of the religious beliefs of the day and a biographical account of Locke's own commitment to them, however tenuous or problematic this may have been for him.[31] Various shades of interpretation are found in this camp according to whether one posits some degree of awareness in Locke of the failure of his scheme for a rational morality. Thus some claim to trace a development in the thought of Locke from the *Essay* to the *Reasonableness of Christianity*. In the former work Locke entertains the idea of a rational morality; but by the time of the latter work he had abandoned the attempt, and explicitly appealed to scripture for the full and complete account of morality. Other readers note Locke's hesitancy in providing a rational morality and reliance on Christian belief, but still hoping for a rational basis.[32] In most of these cases, Locke's account is seen to be very similar to the "natural law tradition" of Thomas, Hooker, and other reformers. John Yolton says that Locke had a set of beliefs about man and God and deduced morality from these beliefs. Demonstration involves a kind of conceptual relationship between the various ideas and precepts acquired and held in faith. In addition to the failure to examine these fundamental beliefs, Locke also failed because he could not relate them all systematically. He relied on a haphazard listing of moral laws when it suited his purpose, a list that Yolton readily compiles from Locke's various works. The rules "disclose the moral framework in terms of which Locke examined society and civil government." Locke thinks that they are reasonable, but they are only reasonable to "an individual trained in Locke's educational system and growing up in his civil society." Each time the Christian faith set the framework or context for analysis.[33]

What is common to these various interpretations of Locke is the notion that his is a theological ethic developed from faith. It is more or less reasonable, more or less consistent within the context of his faith in God and a divine order. But the problem here is that these interpretations impose a coherence theory upon a foundationalist thinker. These readers surely cannot maintain that they get us closer to Locke's intention as a philosophical writer and historical actor.

Two other major interpretations of Locke stand at the extreme of the spectrum. These are the attempts of C. B. MacPherson and Leo Strauss to interpret Locke as a philosophical descendant of Thomas Hobbes.[34] Working independently of each other, with very different philosophical perspectives and historical methods, the two men have constructed interpretations of Locke very much at odds with the majority view. They make a case for Locke as a thoroughly modern liberal who shifts from natural law to a modern doctrine of natural right. Hobbes made the decisive break from the natural law tradition in positing a ground in human desire for self-preservation rather than the divine order of natural law and by taking his bearings from the radical and contentious individuality of men rather than from their sociability. Locke also adopts self-preservation and a contentious individuality as the basis for natural rights. Natural law is really nothing other than a means for social order protecting individual life, liberty, and property. Both Strauss and Macpherson agree that Locke opens up a justification of an unlimited appropriation of property and thereby undermines the traditional understanding of natural law.

Which of the two interpretations, Dunn or MacPherson/Strauss is correct? I believe that the *Essay* sheds an interesting light on the matter.

Perspective of the *Essay* Concerning Human Understanding

It is my understanding that the *Essay* is an important document in coming to terms with the failures and contradictions of Lockean natural law theory. It is by no means the definitive treatment of natural law (*Questions Concerning the Law of Nature* may be that work); but the *Essay* does show us Locke's intellectual workshop; in the *Essay* the various pieces and projects for ethics and natural law are quite in evidence. The doctrine of natural law cannot be divorced from the problem of its promulgation and its manner of intelligibility. So the understanding of his doctrine of natural law involves a question about the relation of faith and reason. Epistemological problems stand at the heart of the difficulty in interpreting Locke's ethical and political philosophy. Although the writing of the *Essay* was occasioned by Locke's discussion with his friends of just these topics—such as "the principles of ethics and revealed religion,"[35] the connection between the epistemological—and the ethical and political dimensions to Locke's philosophy are not immediately apparent. The attempt to provide a comprehensive interpretation of Locke's philosophy founders on the apparent divergence between the epistemology, on the one hand, and the doctrine of natural law on the other. Rosalie Colie considers the *Essay* as a failed attempt to reconcile various traditions.[36] Since the traditional natural law teaching was uncertain, Locke was led into major epistemological problems. She says that it was the major effort of his life to define and solve problems in two principal areas "traditionally subsumed under natural law—epistemology and ethics, or in Locke's language, 'human understanding' and 'civil government'." As he moved out of the natural law tradition, "the connection between two areas became less manifest and the conscious effort to connect the two subjects declined." The present day scholarship on Locke appears to accept this assessment.[37] The *Essay* does appear to provide a systematic study of the concept of natural law, although it is scattered throughout the extensive treatment of topics pertaining to epistemology.

The *Essay* poses the central problematic of Lockean natural law philosophy. It is that the attempt to construct a natural law in terms of divine law is a clear failure—clear that is, to Locke and to many readers. The problem of interpretation must the address the following givens in Locke's *Essay*.

1A. Divine law requires knowledge of a divine lawgiver and knowledge of the immortality of the soul.

1B. That the immortality of the soul cannot be known by reason is explicitly stated by Locke.

1C. The proof for God's existence is problematic and the attributes to which the *proof* leads are not sufficient for the providential law giver and the "workmanship model."

1D. The voluntarist notion of moral law makes it impossible to know with rational certitude what God commands.

2. The account of human action clearly abandons the Christian and premodern notion of the good and virtue. There is no natural basis for natural law as previously understood.

3A. Locke insists on the distinction between faith and reason and

3B. he claims that morality can be demonstrated rationally.

4. Locke puts forward all of the essential principles of Hobbesian human nature: hedonism, depravity, orientation to self-interest, rationality of mutual agreements to protect the self and maintain society.

5. Locke makes numerous pious assertions about his faith in divine law, divine order, and the divine being.

I have found no scholar to deny point 1A and point 1B. This is enough to create the crisis of interpretation. The points deserve some elaboration. It is a central notion of the *Essay* that moral ideas are "relations" by which an action is related and classified according to a law (2.38.4).[38] Locke further subdivides moral law into three types:

> The Laws that Men generally refer their Actions to, to judge of their Rectitude, or Obliquity, seem to me to be these three. 1. The Divine Law. 2. The Civil Law. 3. The Law of Opinion of Reputation, if I may so call it. By the re-

lation they bear to the first of these, Men judge whether their Actions are Sins, or Duties; by the second, whether they be Criminal or Innocent; and by the third, whether they be Vertues or Vices.

We must note that Locke assimilates "natural law" into the category of divine law. Divine law, Locke further states, requires that there be known sanctions, "rewards and punishments, of infinite weight and duration, in another life" (2.38.8). Thus, knowledge of divine law, viz., natural law, entails knowledge of immortality and eternal sanctions. In fact, Locke makes this very argument against the innateness of natural law; he argues that natural law cannot be innate because immortality and eternal sanctions are not innate ideas (1.3.12; see also 1.4.8). In the same fashion therefore, if natural law is to be known through reason and demonstration, these items must be known such. But Locke later in the *Essay* admits that the immortality of the soul cannot be known by philosophical proof (4.3.6). Of course, he hastens to add that the reader should not worry lest morality seem to be undermined, because it is "evident" that God "can and will restore us to the like state of sensibility in another world." The status of the "evident" statement is quite nebulous; for Locke states a few pages later that resurrection depends wholly on the determination of a free agent (God) and therefore cannot in principle be known with the rational certitude as the necessary truths of mathematics (4.3.29). We have a clear admission by Locke of the failure for divine law to be known by reason.

How does the reader of Locke deal with this failure to establish a divine law? The new scholarship employs a standard device: they say that Locke falls back on faith. But this stock response runs afoul of points 3A and 3B. Typically then the scholars will declare that Locke *thought* that he had given a good demonstration of God and the other conditions for natural law. Point 5 is frequently invoked for this position. At this point the scholar has ceased attempting to understand Locke as he understood himself and imposes a psychological hypothesis upon him, and employs a coherence/historicist supposition. This makes me very suspicious. On this account points 3A and 3B must be neglected or explains them away through a coherence theory of meaning. In fact, Locke himself taught a foundationalist theory, insisting quite strongly that the human mind can know the foundational truths of morality and arrive at the ground, or as Locke calls it, the "bottom" of things.

There is an alternative interpretation of this failure of Locke to establish divine law which does not rely upon the ad hoc psychological and historicist presuppositions. Locke very clearly and emphatically states that morality can be demonstrated with the certitude of mathematics.[39] This claim is actually the consequence and seal of his whole theory of ideas and mixed modes. Locke knew that divine law would falter, but he discovers an alternative, a grounding in self-interest properly understood.[40]

Locke provides two sketches of his demonstration of morality in the *Essay* (4.3.3 and 4.3.18). The one sketch proceeds from the supposition of divine workmanship and the obligations of the creature to obey the creator. The other sketch proceeds upon the basis of conceptual analysis of the terms government and liberty, and property and justice. Locke clearly knows that the first sketch of demonstration is a dead-end; or rather it is a quasi-proof requiring suppositions, as he calls them, of the divine being and our creaturely status. The other sketch entails an analysis of terms like government, liberty, property, justice. It follows the analysis of mixed modes. Locke does not complete the demonstration in the *Essay*. But it is clear that this line of demonstration is completable if one follows his method, knowing which terms to juxtapose as intermediaries. Eventually one arrives at the foundation or bottom of the concepts, which is self-consciousness and its own self-concern. In the *Essay* the knowledge of self is the absolute and certain ground of thinking. It is the basis for Locke's hedonistic psychology, also propounded in the *Essay*. The workmanship model is quite irrelevant for this sketch; although Locke does baptize the self-interest pursuit as the divine plan.

The traditional doctrine of natural law appeals to nature as a norm. Within the context of a teleological understanding of nature, the good is defined in terms of human perfection. The good attracts the human agent by its fullness and beauty. The good man performs his functions well and perfects his human faculties of reason and will. Locke constructs a science of ethics that does not depend on a notion of nature with purpose and fulfillment, nor does is depend on any notion of spiritual faculties to be perfected. A notion of "person," as a conscious self, replaces the traditional notion of soul. Consciousness of self has the highest degree of certainty according to Locke. This consciousness is not an abstract or pure mind, however. It is a consciousness of pleasure and pain; it is an agent's awareness of its own ease or uneasiness in the world and is defined in terms of the self's awareness of its own happiness and misery:

> Self is that conscious thinking thing, (whatever Substance, made up of whether Spiritual, or Material, Simple or Compounded, it matters not) which is sensible, or conscious of Pleasure and Pain, capable of Happiness and Misery, and so is concern'd for itself, as far as that consciousness extends. (2.27.17)

The certainty of existence of the entire external world rests upon practical truths connecting the operation of things with the pleasure and pain they produce in the agent. The certainty of things "existing in *rerum Natura*" is as great "as our condition needs" (4.11.8). Human faculties are not suited to a "perfect, clear and comprehensive Knowledge of things" but are suited rather to "the preservation of us, in whom they are; and accommodated to the use of Life: they serve to our purpose well enough, if they will but give us certain notice of those things, which are convenient or inconvenient to us." He goes on to say that the evidence for the external world is as great as we can desire— "as certain to us, as our Pleasure or Pain; i.e., Happiness or Misery; beyond which we have no concernment, either of Knowing or Being" (4.11.8). Locke avoids the "ocean of being" and speculative philosophy because it is not necessary for preservation. Personal convenience dictates Lockean sensibility.

From the perspective of personal consciousness and its own convenience, a rational ordering of choice is possible. The future consequences of an action must be taken into account. And so too must the conditions for continuance of any present good be assured into the future. The fear of loss extends self-consciousness into the future. Ethics is oriented not by a notion of duty or perfection, but by self-advantage and self-interest. Utilitarian calculation harmonizes the interest of the self with the interest of others. But this harmony can be established only by radically restricting the scope of ethics. The content of moral precepts must be pared down to a minimum. It must be made to focus on the civil goods of life, liberty, and property. Without these rules one can be neither safe nor secure. So despite the variability of and the subjectivity of happiness,[41] the precepts of this restricted morality are universal. Everybody requires the protection of their life, liberty, and property whatever their notion of happiness. By lowering the aim of ethics, restricting its scope, Locke can assure its effectiveness. By reorienting ethics to the demands of self-conscious temporal concern he can assure its certainty.

Even though the law of fashion is so diverse there is an important exception to be made for certain types of actions that have to do with "the general good of mankind" and self-interest. Despite the diversity of customs and manners, virtue and vice are "for the most part kept the same everywhere" (2.28.11). Locke's thesis is simple: men praise what is useful—that is, they praise what is to their own advantage. It is advantageous for others to be courageous and just; the courageous man may offer his assistance and the just man will not deprive one of his goods. Self-interest has a rationality that goes deeper than wayward fashion. On its basis a unity or universality of the law of fashion is found. Because men are "constantly true" to their interests, the "true boundaries of the Law of Nature" are preserved. The advantage of the true morality accrue to both individuals and the society at large. For Locke says that there is a visible connection between the "general good" and true morality. Again, rationality (the ability to perceive connections) is deeply embedded in the practical pursuits of life. Even the corrupt and depraved will give lip service to virtue because of the advantage that accrues to its observance by others.

After going through the litany of enormities practiced by men at different times and places, and playing up moral diversity, Locke makes a short aside: an exception must be made for those principles "that are absolutely necessary to hold society together" (1.3.10). In this case, the advantage to society is stressed. These principles are easily discovered because of a "visible connection" between public happiness and virtue. The same account of the praise accorded virtue is given here as well: the virtuous man is useful to others and for this reason he is praised. Similarly rules for the good order of society are useful and make one "safe and secure." No other basis is need for the knowledge of these rules than the reasonable pursuit of self-interest. Locke says that the divine basis for the laws need not be known explicitly as such.

This line of approach to ethics sounds a lot like Hobbes. Has Locke then baptized Hobbes and made him more palatable? Early in the Essay Locke outlines three possible grounds for moral precepts: the Christian, the heathen, and the Hobbist (1.3.5).[42] Each corresponds to one of three moral laws. The Christian appeals to the eternal sanctions of the divine law; the heathen appeals to virtue, which is the law of fashion; the Hobbist appeals to the requirements of public order and the power of the magistrate. As the Essay unfolds, Locke rejects the law of fashion as a stable or rational ground for morality. The divine law is too high and remote. Does Locke not embrace a form of Hobbesian natural law through the elimination of the other alternatives? Reason can only discover rules of social order that derive from self-interest. Indeed, in the following section Locke says that without them one cannot be "safe or secure" (1.3.6). This formula clearly echoes the "Leviathan" to which Locke had previously made reference.

The content of moral precepts must be pared down to a minimum. It must be made to focus on the civil goods of life, liberty, and property; a "thin theory" of good. The rules that protect civil goods can be universally appreciated and acknowledged as right even if not followed in action. Without these rules one can be neither safe nor secure. So despite the variability of fashion and the subjectivity of happiness, the precepts of this restricted morality are universal. Everybody requires the protection of their life, liberty, and property whatever their notion of happiness. By lowering the aim of ethics, restricting it scope, Locke can assure its effectiveness. By reorienting ethics to the demands of self-conscious concern and rational liberty he can assure its certainty.

Such is the ethic appropriated by faith: the rational pursuit of happiness, however happiness may be defined, is virtuous conduct. It is really an astounding remark, incorporating as it does, such moral relativism and concern for temporal convenience. The appropriation of the rational laws of utility by faith reorients that faith to the things of this world. The concern for the better world, an afterlife, is superfluous. For if by following the rules for happiness on earth one is de facto virtuous, no other special "religious" concern is called for. In some other passages Locke drops out the aim of finding the way to a better life after this one and speaks only of the aim of using knowledge to increase the stock of conveniences for the advantages of ease and health (4.12.10). And when the two aims are put into juxtaposition the greatest praise by far goes to the inventor as the "greatest benefactor." It does not go to the works of mercy and charity. Nor does it go to contemplation, philosophic or religious. He praises the discoverer of iron and deems him the "Father of Arts and Author of Plenty" (4.12.11). These are striking juxtapositions that could border on a form of blasphemy. At the very least, the judgment entails an elevation of human power and places God in the background. Technological "know-how" is to be esteemed above the quality of mercy. Technology saves men from the grave, Locke says. But we know that works of mercy may secure men's "eternal estate." Whatever Locke's interest in Christianity, it surely differs from the traditional Christianity in which works of mercy and charity are the stuff of sanctity, and not technological discovery and entrepreneurial ambition. Despite the acknowledgement of God and religious duty, the temporal focus of Locke's practical aim is manifest. Locke has constructed a purely secular ethic.

If faith is superfluous, then why is it even retained? Of course, this reading of Locke must deal with the fifth point above, concerning Locke's pious assertions, of which the *Essay* is full. Following Strauss one may say that they are part of Locke's rhetoric to appease and appeal to the Christian thinkers who would read his work. The new scholars reserve their special indignation for this hypothesis. Yet the plausibility of the claim, mentioned early on by Richard Cox and repeated by Horowitz, is nowhere refuted as a plausible hypothesis. Locke had a very valid concern for personal safety and social standing, but even more so for the honest reception of his philosophy. Whereas Hobbes and Spinoza were burned and decried, Locke's *Essay* met a less hostile reception. When one adds in internal evidence about rhetoric and civil discourse (3.9.15), it becomes a very solid hypothesis. We know that Locke wished to communicate his new ethic to various audiences, including Christian believers. The use of a familiar terminology is retained so that the new ideas are made "easie and intelligible to all sorts of readers," as Locke admits in his "Epistle to the Reader." John Yolton quotes approvingly a statement that "Locke secured for posterity advances by radical and progressive forces." Those who openly professed themselves "antithetical to revealed religion" found in Locke "tools to be exploited." Yolton notes that others of more moderate temperament, aligned to orthodoxy, effected more gradual and long lasting modifications:

> It was in the hands of these men, even more than in those of the Deists who appealed to Locke's epistemology, that the new tendencies within religion were most aided and abetted by the theoretical structure of the Essay. The application by the Deists was flashy and superficial; that of the traditionalists much more penetrating, perceptive, and positive.[43]

Locke found a way to enter into the most sacred and guarded of domains—such as theology, morality, and religious belief—and left his philosophic mark. Whereas Bacon, Descartes, and especially Hobbes and Spinoza, stirred up great resistance, Locke was able to introduce modern rationalism and the conquest of nature into the theological heart of the moral and political order. Indeed, Montgomery is right to assign to the "pious Locke," by way of the Puritans in the north and the enlightened statesmen in the south, the most devastating effect on American sensibility.

Conclusion

It is my contention that the *Two Treatises of Government* puts forward a new doctrine of natural law. Like Gerson and Hobbes, Locke begins with the identification of "*jus*" or right with "*libertas*," freedom. I agree with Strauss that he deliberately follows Hobbes here and essentially abandons the premodern, ancient and Christian, accounts of moral order. Locke has lowered the aim of natural law; he has reduced the precepts to a single one; he has placed the sanctions for the natural law entirely in this world in the right of individual self-preservation. In this latter step, Locke admits the novelty of his teaching. But the doctrine of individual execution is precisely the reason for the other novelties. Natural law is nothing other than a set of counsels for self-preservation: it includes the right to self-preservation and a right to war. It is reasonable to consent to the common authority of civil society when its laws will secure self-preservation. Thus the nature and extent for civil society is but a deduction from the fundamental individual rights of self-preservation and the execution of the right in the state of nature. Locke may turn around and declare that this is the will of God for us, and reflects his workmanship, but it seems to make it redundant.

Locke's conception of political society fits very well with agnosticism about God and human happiness. Comfortable self-preservation sets the goal for the civil society. The goal of protecting life, liberty, and property is not a substantive or a common good at all. Justice is simply the conditions necessary for the pursuit of happiness, whatever that may be from person to person. Political society does not set the standard or norm for human excellence nor see to the formation of character and virtue. It protects a private pursuit of happiness. Political action is the avoidance of the greatest evil, destruction of one's life, liberty, or property. It is significant that Locke talks about the inconveniences of the state of nature. Human beings are inclined toward civil society in order to avoid these inconveniences, not in order to attain a distinctively human and political good. Men take on themselves the obligation of civil society because it secures their property against the inconveniences of nature and war. The obligations of civil law are the full extent of Lockean *rational* morality. Such morality is not the high morality of religion, nor is it the noble ambition of an aristocrat or gentleman. But it is a morality appropriate to the "origin, certainty and extent of humane knowledge" as Locke expounds in the *Essay*.

The legacy of Locke is therefore ambivalent. The advocate of limited government, and an apparent friend of the theistic tradition, Locke nevertheless underwrote a model of radical human autonomy in which freedom dominates the moral order. Locke's philosophy of human rights is derived from a subjectivist account of the good; it lowers the goal of the state to a supposedly neutral position; it imposes a minimal obligation of nonharm; and must encourage self-interest. The minimal obligations embodied in civil law become the extent of morality; the wide sphere of private life must come to occupy the bulk of human energies. With Locke, such freedom was aimed at unlimited acquisition of property and the self found its affirmation in labor and the "work ethic," or what Leo Strauss called "the joyless quest for joy." But such terms as equal freedom and mutual respect came to be transformed under the inspiration of Rousseau and Kant to mean much more than civic liberty and protection of private property. They become terms designating a person who is self-creating and self-constituting through the imagination and will. In contemporary American jurisprudence they have come to promote the existence of what Professor Gerard Bradley has recently referred to as the "erotic self."[44]

And finally it provides a perspective on that central problematic for liberal democracy outlined at the beginning of the chapter by George Parkin Grant.

To put the ethical relation clearly: if avoidance of death is our highest end (albeit negative), why should anyone make sacrifices for the common good which entail that possibility? Why should anyone choose to be a soldier or a policeman, if Lockean contractualism is the truth about justice? Yet such professions are necessary if any approximation to justice are to be maintained. Within a contractualist belief, why should anyone care about the reign of justice more than their life? The believing Protestants provided the necessary moral cement which could not be present for those who consistently directed by contractualism or utilitarianism or a combination of both. . . . Clever people generally believed that the foundational principles of justice were chosen conveniences; nevertheless they could not turn away from a noble content to that justice, because they were enfolded more than they knew in long memories and hopes.[45]

So perhaps the real, the original, John Locke is both the old Locke and the new Locke by design; he enfolded a long memory around his contractual theory of justice; it was embraced by statesmen and scientists and preachers who gave it their own benign reading. Now after centuries of solid service the radical autonomy of true Lockeanism is coming into its own, shedding the larvae of Hooker and Aristotle and the Bible and emerging forth as the splendid liberal philosophy of our Rawls, Dworkin, and Richards. How benevolent it really is and how long it shall last is a topic for another day.[46]

Notes

This chapter extracted from a talk first delivered at the Southwest Political Science Association, San Antonio, Texas, in March 1994.

1. George Parkin Grant, *English-Speaking Justice* (Notre Dame, Ind.: University of Notre Dame Press, 1985), 58–68.

2. Marion Montgomery, *Why Hawthorne Was Melancholy* (La Salle, Ill: Sherwood, Sugden & Co., 1984).

3. Edward J. Harpham, ed., *John Locke's Two Treatises of Government: New Interpretations* (Lawrence, Kans.: University Press of Kansas, 1992), 1.

4. Richard Ashcraft, "The Politics of Locke's Two Treatises of Government," in *John Locke's Two Treatises of Government: New Interpretations*, Edward J. Harpham, ed. (Lawrence, Kans.: University Press of Kansas, 1992), 18.

5. C. B. Macpherson, "Locke on Capitalist Appropriation," *Western Political Quarterly* 4 (1951): 550–66; "Natural Rights in Hobbes and Locke," *Political Theory and the Rights of Man*, ed. D. D. Raphael (Macmillan: London, 1967), 1–15; *The Political Theory of Possessive Individualism: Hobbes to Locke* (Oxford: Oxford University Press, 1962); "The Social Bearing of Locke's Political Theory," *Western Political Quarterly* 7 (1954): 1–22. Leo Strauss, "Locke's Doctrine of Natural Law," in *What Is Political Philosophy* (New York: Free Press, 1959), 197–220; "Natural Law," *International Encyclopedia of the Social Sciences* 11 (1966): 80–85; *Natural Right in History* (Chicago: University of Chicago Press, 1952); *Persecution and the Art of Writing* (Glencoe, Ill.: The Free Press, 1952); *The Political Philosophy of Hobbes* (Chicago: University of Chicago Press, 1952).

6. Leo Strauss, "Locke's Doctrine on Natural Law," in *What Is Political Philosophy* (New York: The Free Press, 1959), 197–220; originally appeared in *The American Political Science Review* (June 1958).

7. For example, Thomas L. Pangle, *The Spirit of Modern Republicanism: The Moral Vision of the American Founders and the Philosophy of Locke* (Chicago: University of Chicago Press, 1988); John Locke, *Questions Concerning the Law of Nature*, ed. and trans. Robert Horowitz, Jenny Strauss Clay, and Diskin Clay (Ithaca, N.Y.: Cornell University Press, 1990); Richard Cox, "Introduction," in John Locke, *Second Treatise of Government*, (Arlington Heights Ill.: Harlan Davidson, Inc., 1982), vii–xliii; "Justice as the Basis of Political Order in Locke," *Nomos V: Justice*, ed. C. J. Friedrich and J.W. Chapman (Atherton Press: New York, 1963), 243–61; *Locke on War and Peace* (Oxford: Oxford University Press, 1960).

8. James Tully, A *Discourse on Property: John Locke and His Adversaries* (Cambridge: Cambridge University Press, 1980).

9. All citations are from Locke's *Two Treatises of Government*, a critical edition with introduction and notes by Peter Laslett, second edition, Cambridge University Press, 1970.

10. "Although men cannot be absolutely equal without being entirely free, and consequently equality, in its most extreme form, must merge with freedom, there is good reason to distinguish one from another. So men's taste for freedom and their taste for equality are in fact distinct, and I have no hesitation in adding, among democracies they are two unequal elements." Alexis de Tocqueville, *Democracy in America*, vol. 2, pt. 2, chap. 1. Trans. George Lawrence, ed. J. P. Lawrence (New York: Doubleday Anchor, 1969), 504.

11. "Suppositions without proofs put handsomely together in good Words and a plausible style, are apt to pass for strong Reason and good Sense, till they come to be look'd into with attention." (1.20).

12. See 2.6, 2.8, 2.10, 2.11, 2.12, 2.16.

13. See Robert A. Goldwin, "The State of Nature in Political Society," in *Essays in Honor of Jacob Klein* (Annapolis: St. John's College Press, 1968), 63–70.

14. Peter Laslett admits that the statement on property in one's own person, "almost contradicts" the workmanship model. "Introduction," 100. Yolton admits the problem here but states that Locke "apparently did not feel that fact to be incompatible." Yolton employs a distinction between man and person to resolve the issue, allowing God to have dominion over the man, and the person dominion over himself. This solution would seem to yield the case, since the person is now free of God." *Locke: An Introduction*, 69. See also Harvey Mansfield, "On the Political Character of Property in Locke," in *Powers, Possessions, and Freedom*, ed. A. Kontos (Toronto: University of Toronto Press, 1979), 23–28.

15. "God having made Man, and planted in him, as in all other Animals, a strong desire of Self-preservation, and furnished the world with things fit for Food and Rayment and other Necessaries of Life, Subservient to his design, that Man should live and abide for some time upon the Face of the Earth, and not that so curious and

wonderful a piece of Workmanship by its own Negligence, or want of Necessaries, should perish again, presently after a few moments of continuance: God, I say, having made Man and the World thus, spoke to him, (that is) directed him by his Sense and Reason, as he did to the inferior Animals by their Senses, and Instinct, which he had placed in them to that purpose, to the use of those things, which were serviceable for his Subsistence, and given him as a means of his Preservation. And therefore I doubt not, but before these words were pronounced, I Gen. 28,29 (if they must be understood Literally to have been spoken) and without any such Verbal Donation, Man had a right to a use of the Creatures, by the Will and Grant of God. For the desire, strong desire of preserving his Life and Being having been planted in him, as a Principle of Action by God himself, Reason, which was the voice of God in him, could not but teach him and assure him, that pursuing the natural inclination he had to preserve his own Being, he followed the Will of his Maker, and therefore had a right to make use of those Creatures, which by his Reason or Senses he could discover would be serviceable thereunto. And thus Man's Property in the Creatures, was founded upon the right he had, to make use of those things, that were necessary or useful to his Being" (1.86).

16. "And Reason, which is that Law, teaches all Mankind who will but consult it . . ." (2.6). See also 2.8, 2.10, 2.11, 2.12, 2.16.

17. "The Laws that Men generally refer their Actions to, to judge of their Rectitude, or Obliquity, seem to me to be these three. 1. The Divine Law. 2. The Civil Law. 3. The Law of Opinion of Reputation, if I may so call it. By the relation they bear to the first of these, Men judge whether their Actions are Sins, or Duties; by the second, whether they be Criminal or Innocent; and by the third, whether they be Vertues or Vices" (2.28.7). Cf. "That Men should keep their Compacts, is certainly a great and undeniable Rule in Morality: But yet if a Christian, who has the view of Happiness and Misery in another Life, be asked why a Man must keep his Word, he will give this as a Reason: Because God, who the Power of eternal Life and Death, requires it if us. But if an Hobbist be asked why; he will answer: Because the Publick requires it, and the Leviathan will punish you, if you do not. And if one of the old Heathen Philosophers had been asked, he would have answer'd: Because it was dishonest, below the Dignity of a Man, and opposite to Vertue, the highest Perfection of humane Nature, to do otherwise" (1.3.5).

18. *Summa Theologiae* I–II, q. 94, a. 5.

19. *Summa Theologiae* q. 94, a. 2.

20. See sections 6, 7, 8, 11, 16.

21. See Robert Goldwin, "The State of Nature in Political Society," in *Essays in Honor of Jacob Klein* (Annapolis: St. John's Press, 1976), 63–70: "The question, of the priority of self-preservation or the preservation of all, dissolves as Locke argues it. There need be no answer to the question in that form, because the two obligations merge and become one," 66.

22. Hobbes, *Leviathan*, chapter 14. In the Penguin edition edited by C. B. MacPherson (New York: Penguin Books, 1968), 189. See Richard Tuck, *Natural*

Rights Theories: Their Origin and Development (Cambridge: Cambridge University Press, 1979), 24–31; Richard Tuck, *Hobbes* (New York: Oxford, 1989).

23. See Hobbes, *Leviathan*; see also Richard Tuck, *Hobbes and Leo Strauss*; *Natural Right and History*.

24. See Geraint Parry, *John Locke* (London: George Allen & Unwin, 1978), 27, 36; James Tully, *A Discourse on Property*, x, 4; John Dunn, *The Political Thought of John Locke: An Historical Account of the Argument of the 'Two Treatises of Government'* (Cambridge: Cambridge University Press, 1969), 26.

25. See W. von Leyden, "John Locke and Natural Law," *Philosophy* 21 (1956), 27; Gough, *John Locke's Political Philosophy*, second edition (Oxford: Clarendon Press, 1973), 12: "The God of Christianity is the unquestioned ultimate presupposition." Similarly both Dunn (p. 88) and Colman (p. 2) claim that Locke accepted "unquestioningly" the belief in a "great chain of being." Just how far Locke did question and change this doctrine, all the while keeping up the appearance, see M. R. Ayers, "Mechanism, Superaddition, and the Proof of God's Existence in Locke's Essay," *The Philosophical Review* 40 (April, 1981), 234–40: "This deviation from Cudworth's notion of perfection covertly changes the whole character of the argument for God's existence. The similarities with Cudworth are, by contrast, obvious." Locke makes a similar covert change of Hooker; see Abrams, "Introduction," 69–70; thus Colman should know better than to make such a statement about Locke, see Colman, 238–43.

26. Parry, 34; Ashcraft, "Faith and Knowledge in Locke's Philosophy," in *John Locke: Problems and Perspectives*, ed. J. W. Yolton (Cambridge University Press: Cambridge, 1969), 205, 214; Dunn, 98; Gough, 19.

27. Again, see Dunn, 194–95, and Parry, 13. But on the feeling of satisfaction about the proof for God, see Locke's "Letter to Stillingfleet," quoted in Strauss, *Natural Right*, 207.

28. John Biddle, "Locke's Critique of Innate Principles and Toland's Deism," 417.

29. Richard Ashcraft, "Faith and Knowledge," 202.

30. Ashcraft says that Locke accepted Christianity "unquestioningly." Ashcraft, "Faith and Knowledge," 205.

31. As Michael Zuckert has observed, this approach is more explanation than interpretation, actually explaining Locke through the context of history and a "psycho-socio-biography." "The Recent Literature on Locke's Political Philosophy," *The Political Science Reviewer* 5 (Fall 1975): 300–3.

32. See for example James Gibson, "Locke's Theory of Mathematical Knowledge and of a Possible Science of Ethics." *Mind* V (1896): 50–52; Ruth Mattern, "Moral Science and the Concept of Persons in Locke." *Philosophical Review* 89 (1980): 35–36. Gibson and Mattern are to be commended for not neglecting Locke's continual insistence that morality can be a matter for demonstration.

33. John Yolton, *Locke and the Compass of Understanding* (Cambridge: Cambridge University Press, 1970), 172–78, and "Locke on the Law of Nature," *The Philosophical Review* 67 (October 1958): 487–88. See also his more recent, *Locke: An Introduction* (Oxford: Basil Blackwell, 1985), 47.

34. Macpherson, *The Political Theory of Possessive Individualism: Hobbes to Locke*; Strauss, *Natural Right and History* (Chicago: University of Chicago Press, 1953).

35. So reports Locke's friend James Tyrrell. See A. C. Fraser, ed., *An Essay Concerning Human Understanding* (New York: Dover, 1959), vol. 1, p. 9, note 2.

36. "The Social Language of John Locke: A Study in the History of Ideas," *The Journal of British Studies* 4 (1965): 31–33.

37. A notable exception is John Colman, *John Locke's Moral Philosophy* (Edinburgh: University of Edinburgh Press, 1983).

38. John Locke, *An Essay Concerning Human Understanding*, ed. Peter H. Nidditch, *The Clarendon Edition of the Works of John Locke* (Oxford: Oxford University Press, 1975). The citation refer to book, chapter, and sections numbers, respectively.

39. See 1.3.1; 3.11.16; 4.3.18; 4.4.7; 4.12.18.

40. 1.3.6, 10.

41. "The Mind has a different relish, as well as the palate; and you will as fruitlessly endeavour to delight all Men with Riches or Glory, (which yet some Men place their Happiness in,) as you would satisfy all Men's Hunger with Cheese or Lobsters; which though very agreeable and delicious fare to some, are to others extremely nauseous and offensive: And many People would Reason preferr the griping of a hungry Belly, to those Dishes, which are a feast to others. Hence, it was, I think, that the Philosophers of old did in vain enquire, whether Summum bonum consisted in riches, or bodily Delights, or Virtue, or Contemplation: and they might have as reasonably disputed, whether the best Relish were to be found in Apples, Plumbs, or Nuts; and have divided themselves into Sects upon it. For as pleasant Tastes depend not upon the things themselves, but their agreeableness to this or that particular Palate, wherein there is great variety" (2.21.55).

42. See above note 17.

43. John Yolton, *John Locke and the Way of Ideas* (Oxford University Press, 1956), 203–6.

44. Gerard V. Bradley, "The Constitution & the Erotic Self," *First Things* no. 16 (October 1991): 28–32.

45. George Parkin Grant, *English-Speaking Justice* (Notre Dame, Ind.: Notre Dame Press, 1985), 58–68.

46. See John P. Hittinger and Christopher Wolfe, *Liberalism at the Crossroads: An Introduction to Liberal Political Theory and Its Critics* (Lanaham, Md.: Rowman & Littlefield, 1994).

CHAPTER EIGHT

~

David A. J. Richards: Liberalism of the Autonomous Person

Toward a New Liberalism

David A. J. Richards is Professor of Law at New York University and Director of New York University's Program for the Study of Law, Philosophy and Social Theory. His publications cover a broad scope of interests especially including constitutional and criminal law, political philosophy, and ethics. This chapter focuses on his work entitled *Toleration and the Constitution*, and we shall make occasional reference to two books *Foundations of American Constitutionalism* and *Sex, Drugs, Death and the Law*; also two articles of interest for our purposes are "Human Rights and Moral Ideals: An Essay on the Moral Theory of Liberalism" and "Rights and Autonomy."[1]

The work of Richards may be appreciated as a continuation of the contract theory of Rawls and Dworkin; he applies the theory to an interesting set of legal and constitutional issues, focusing on privacy. In addition he provides a comprehensive philosophical base in a Kantian account of the person. This makes his work very engaging and challenging on multiple levels. There is a mission in Richards' work to purge American thought and culture of its religious influence; this includes what Richards calls its Calvinistic public morality and also natural law principles derived from Catholic morality and tradition.[2] One might say that Richards engages in a brand of revisionism, reinterpretation, and critique of the American tradition to arrive at its pure Enlightenment basis. Richards' work is animated by a grand democratic vision of a "national community of principle," based upon human autonomy and human rights; such a vision demands the radical critique and elimination of premodern communities and traditions that have practiced majoritarian tyranny and degradation of persons.[3] Indeed, Richards' liberalism is offered as a fundamental alternative to the ancient account of social and political life.

Richards stresses the radical departure in ethics and politics characteristic of the modern theory of rights elaborated by Locke, Rousseau, and Kant.[4] The new account stresses the autonomy of the person—a self-critical freedom to order one's own life. The person may claim a freedom from convention and a freedom from domination in the name of equal respect for persons. By way of contrast, the premodern view stresses "hierarchy of being" or "chain of being." Man has neither the radical freedom nor the absolute equality claimed by the modern account. Richards credits late medieval nominalism and voluntarism for shattering the notion of hierarchy of being and he credits the Reformation disputes over the interpretation of the Bible and tradition with bringing to the fore the "integrity of interpretative conscience" and the equal respect for persons as originators of claims.[5] The moral idea of personhood grounding human rights appears to be such a radical departure that premodern man may not actually have been a person as so defined. Consider the following remark:

> Persons originate claims when they make claims and demands as an expression of their own internal capacities of personal judgment, reflection, and will. Such capacities are not in play when persons are thought of as having preassigned places or roles, irrespective of such capacities or their exercise. For example persons are not thought of as having these capacities when they are defined solely by their functional utility in some larger design which alone specifies the status, place and worth of the person (for example their role in some political or social hierarchy or religious theocracy). (*Toleration*, p. 72.)

In this passage Richards gets close to denying the term person to people in premodern hierarchical societies. Perhaps there are some false dilemmas or disjunctions here, such as *sole* definition, *irrespective* of capacities, and the like. Elsewhere he says that the premoderns imposed a chain of being prior to empirical investigation. This is simply not true; for Aristotle, for example, it was a deduction from observations of nature. In fact Richards allows Locke to adopt the supposition of a great chain of being after empirical investigation. But Richards needs the stark alternative—for example, social convention may not allow one to exercise the capacity of freedom because of aristocratic or theocratic hierarchy. Claims are defined by an externally imposed system of appropriate roles; such a system is "contemptuous of the just liberties of a free person because it denies in principle the place or weight of such capacities of persons for rational freedom."[6] Such is the moral degradation of women today, Richards claims. Such degradation lies at the heart of alternatives to liberalism, whether it be ancient Greek, medieval Christian, or contemporary conservatives. Liberalism achieves the true and most pure form of morality and religion.

In his article "Rights and Autonomy," Richards elaborates on the deficiency of Greek political theory and practice in regard to its hierarchical systems and denials of equal respect for persons. The many were incapable of a truly ordered life and needed rule by the best. So too, Aristotle justified slavery and subordination of women as children little better than slaves.[7] This ancient and long-standing tradition was absorbed by medieval culture and continues to this day; it denies women their full personhood. The degradation of women continues to this day with the imposition of arbitrary structures of natural gender hierarchy and domination; the protection of women from such oppression is at the heart of American Constitutionalism. In fact, Richards expresses astonishment at the attraction of Aristotelian political philosophy, citing MacIntyre by name.[8] The alternatives must be studied and understood; Richards thinks the quarrel has been patently settled.

The ostensible subject and burden of Richards' work is the standard problem of judicial review and cases involving privacy rights; as a good liberal he wishes to demonstrate the constitutional legitimacy of the right to privacy, its rightful application in such cases involving contraceptive use in marriage (*Griswold v. Connecticut*), nonmarital contraceptive use (*Eisenstadt v. Baird*), pornography in the home (*Stanley v. Georgia*), and abortion services (*Roe v. Wade*); in addition he criticizes the court for its failure to apply privacy rights to consensual homosexual acts (*Doe v. Commonwealth's Attorney*): "*Doe* is deeply, morally wrong."[9] Homosexuals ought to be afforded the same rights to privacy, family, adoption, and so on as heterosexuals.[10] Such would forward the "great work of collective democratic decency that is the Constitution of the United States."[11] The logic of right to privacy leads to decriminalization of all consensual sex acts including prostitution, as well as drug use, and euthanasia.

Richards arrives at his justifications for judicial review, privacy, and his policy proposals by way of an intricate argument concerning interpretation of law and the foundations of political order: "The first traditional question of constitutional theory [judicial review] will, in my account, be answered last."[12] The prior questions to be explored deal with interpretation of law, the U. S. Constitution in particular, and the foundations of political order, and American federalism in particular. At the core of law, constitution, and political order Richards elaborates a doctrine of personhood derived from Kant. With the contractarian philosophy of Kant and Rawls, Richards aims to "bring to critical self-consciousness the humane legal developments" of recent note.[13] This philosophical approach is superior to the other modern accounts of political order. The modern alternatives to Kantian liberalism are utilitarianism and majoritarianism; they are variations of the same theme. Utilitarianism does represent an advance over the premodern tradition; indeed, Richards acknowledges that the great founder of liberalism, John Locke, advanced a view that actually mixed in both rights doctrines and a form of rule utilitarianism. The advance lies in its abandonment of hierarchical conceptions of the world and human life and its first grasp of a doctrine of equality. In addition, the nonharm principle, even advanced on utilitarian grounds, signified an appreciation of a theory of general goods and an attempt to limit the power of the state over individual liberty. The doctrine of utilitarianism is flawed because it misconstrues the nature of equality and the harm principle; and it is ultimately corrupted by the pursuit of aggregate interests which leads to grounds for violation of rights. The advances of utilitarianism have to be secured by placing them on the more true and firm footing of personal autonomy. Personal autonomy yields a true idea of equality and an intelligible and consistent reading of the nonharm principle. In addition it provides the essential constraints on aggregate interest violating personal rights and producing unjust outcomes in distribution of harms and benefits.[14]

Majoritarianism is more of a problem because it contains the seeds of the older premodern morality, the morality of the tribe. The norm of majority consensus provides an alternative to liberalism. But it is the demonic force of faction against which Madisonian political science must provide the corrective. As mentioned above, judicial review, a device for liberal constitutionalism, is antimajoritarian. Richards sees majorities as implicitly evil and incapable of judgement about the good of the whole.

The theory and practice of liberal constitutionalism are clearly superior to the alternatives, ancient and modern, in the eyes of Richards. What is the foundation for his view and what are its implications?

The Foundation of Liberalism

The Core Idea
Richards labels his position "liberal constitutionalism": the "cumulative weight of the argument of this book is that the rights characteristic of liberal constitutionalism converge in a certain way on a distinctive moral conception of thought, speech, and action."[15] Thus his position is best understood

as containing two major elements: an elaboration and application of characteristic human rights, *viz.*, freedom of conscience, freedom of speech, freedom of sexual expression, which he approaches through American constitutional law; second, a distinctive moral conception, *viz.*, equal respect for persons, which he derives ultimately from Kantian ethics. That is, he construes "equal respect for persons" in terms of autonomy; the general right of personal autonomy is said to be "the fundamental value of liberalism."[16]

Richards adopts a Lockean view, as he claims do the founders, on the legitimate scope of governmental interference with these human rights based upon the autonomy of persons. The only grounds for interference are the protection of "general goods" such as life, liberty, health, and property. Then following the Rawlsian conception of social contract he describes the general goods as those goods "that rational and reasonable people would want protected as conditions of whatever else they want."[17] Autonomy and general goods yield the notion of a neutral government; it cannot impose a substantive way of life upon the citizens nor act in behalf of such a vision; the government must be properly "neutral among diverse ways people may interpretively weight the pursuit of those goods in their vision of a good and decent life."[18] Autonomy is precisely the ability to form a plan of life; for the government to act on behalf of a distinctive conception of the good life would be to violate the equal respect for persons, many of whom choose diverse ways of life. In one article Richards draws upon Dworkin to summarize the core idea of liberalism:

> Fundamental political morality rests upon a neutral theory of the good for persons, which is compatible with broadly pluralistic life styles and forms, and the most fundamental right of persons is their right to equal concern and respect, compatible with a like respect for all, in defining their own visions of the good life.[19]

We need now to probe more deeply into this core statement of principle.

The Concept of Person

According to Richards, a theory of the person is both "empirical and normative," describing capacities and characterizing ideals and principles; the capacity is freedom, the principles are "rationality and reasonableness."[20] Richards follows Kant and Rawls in describing the person in terms of a capacity for critical reflection which allows freedom; that is, he distinguishes first order and second order desires; the first order desires are hunger, thirst, sexuality, desire for friendship, and the like; the higher order desires enable a person to self-critically evaluate the first order desires and thereby shape, plan, and adjust a way of life.[21] That is, each person has a capacity "to self-critically evaluate and give order and personal integrity to one's system of ends in the form of one's life."[22] The formulation in *Toleration* states the definition of freedom as follows: "the capacity of persons to formulate and act on higher order plans of action, which take as their self-critical object one's life and the way it is lived, changing or not changing one's life, as the case may be."[23] It is interesting to note that substantive goods are all equalized as first order goods—friendship is placed with hunger, for example. Indeed, Richards claims that the neutrality of the liberal ideal stems from the Kantian triumph of autonomy over desire.[24]

Autonomy defines the person, and respect for such autonomous persons is the foundation of liberalism. The implications of autonomy are that persons are independent from domination by others, independent of first order desires, and most of all, free to choose a plan of life such that the highest creative task is that of shaping one's own life as an individual free from custom and convention.[25] The person must be seen as an "originator of claims."[26] That is, persons must be seen as having the capacity to make judgments and thus to act.

This leads to the principles that characterize the exercise of the capacity of higher order reflection: rationality and reasonableness. Rationality includes both the practical and theoretical reason; the former he defines as prudence, aiming at realizing the good, the latter as epistemic rationality, aiming at true belief. Reasonableness is a moral capacity to consider the claims of others in terms of equal respect for persons. The principle of reasonableness often constrains that of prudential rationality. Autonomy as a moral ideal includes absence of constraint, rationality, and reasonableness.

The Derivation of Rights

Right of Conscience
The doctrine of human rights is derived from this definition of autonomous persons: "we may interpret equal respect for persons in terms of the principles that could be justified to every person understood as capable of rational and reasonable freedom."[27] Rights thereby secure "the essential distributive conditions of the self-respecting integrity of each and every person." Rights are the legal protection of the autonomy of persons, especially in the capacity for self-critical reflection and choice.[28] Freedom of conscience becomes

the first and paradigm right because it protects the capacity for rational free-dom itself; all other rights are "generalizations or elaborations" of this focal argument.

Richards goes through an extended historical account of religious freedom and the right to conscience. Augustine and Thomas Aquinas are criticized for their views on religious freedom. Although Augustine is said to have had a praiseworthy conception of the autonomous person, he failed to draw the inferences from this conception of the person. His view of religious freedom was based on a contempt for the freedom and rationality of persons; Richards claims that Augustine's suppression of the Donatists was motivated by an im-putation of demonic and moral failure to those with views different from his. This is the classic mistake of bigots; the doctrine of persons and equal respect for persons overcomes this error. It took the controversy of the Reformation to break open this truth. The disputes over biblical interpretation and the ad-vance of literacy gave every one an equal place in interpretation. Persons are now seen as originators of claims; respect for "integrity of interpretive con-science" and minimal conditions for epistemic rationality becomes the order of the day.[29]

According to Richards, Locke and Bayle came to formulate the essential principle, basing toleration upon a moral interpretation of respect for per-sonal integrity; their only mistake was a failure to extend the toleration to a universal scope. They mistakenly believed that the state required religion as a proxy for moral education and moral integrity; ethical independence, the Kantian ideal, is now clearly understood as an achievement independent of religion.

Jefferson and Madison came to see this full true view of religious tolera-tion based upon the autonomy of the person. Equal respect for persons is the organizing principle of the First Amendment. Freedom and rationality, Richards claims, are the "background rights" in light of which we must con-strue the First Amendment.

Richards thus construes the First Amendment as an attempt to "guarantee and secure to a person the greatest equal respect for the rational and reason-able capacities of the persons themselves to originate, exercise and express and change theories of life and how to live it well."[30] The state must make sure that it does not infringe upon the formation of belief, the expression of belief, and the revision of belief. Richards construes the free exercise clause to be aimed at the right to express a current belief and the antiestablishment clause to protect the right of freedom in the formation and revision of conscientious beliefs. The deepest value protect therefore is not religion per se, but the higher powers of the person, the capacity for critical reflection as in a rational and reasonable person. The state should not attempt to construe this in terms of the content or definition of religion. Rather it should be construed as protecting any conscientious belief and the action that derives from it, if the action does not harm the equal rights of others or some compelling state interest that involves the general or basic goods. Thus the right of conscience exercises a "gravitational pull" on the First Amendment such that the original meaning may be transformed. Richards believes that his account of the First Amendment clarifies the essential correctness of decisions concerning released time to teach religion, school prayer, teaching Darwin vs. creationism, aid to public school, and the like; and he chastises the court for restricting the scope of actions protected by the free exercise clause when it attempts to define religion in institutional terms and for permitting tax exemptions for churches since this amounts to "multiple establishment."[31]

The right of conscience is the primary right and the paradigm for all others; expanded to include any conscientious belief or actions derived therefrom, so too other rights are similarly expanded and developed in light of the principle of autonomy and respect for persons. The scheme is applied to free speech, with some interesting results such as the defense of a right to pornography; indeed pornography is extolled as the higher option against the repressed Catholic and Puritan public morality.[32]

The Constitutional Right of Privacy

The very legitimacy of the right to privacy or the range of the right has been challenged by a number of thinkers and Richards seeks to refute them. Richards sees a clear line from Griswold on contraception through other cases involving nonmarital sex and abortion rights extending to the eventual liberation of homosexuals and prostitutes. He rejects the attempts to explain decriminalization on the grounds of a changing moral consensus or the utilitarian principle of nonharm. The former attempt to explain Griswold or other forms of decriminalization begs the question because there must be an appeal to a critical standard outside of convention itself; moreover, an appeal to the moral consensus misconstrues the role of the judiciary as a counter-majoritarian institution which is debased if it simply tracks a moral majority. The harm principle represents an advance since it clearly lays out restrictive conditions for state interference.[33] But an efficiency-based argument is not sufficient; it may concede the immorality of the action or it may have to consistently act on utilitarian grounds if there is sufficient offense to a sizable majority. Thus the nonharm principle must be based upon the right of personal freedom or personal autonomy. Privacy interests are connected to the higher order interest of personal autonomy. Richards claims that the resources for higher order choice include "capacities for thought, emotion and action as integral to the self-image of a person exercising moral independence in the formation of intimate relationships."[34] The state may not intrude into this domain of intimate personal relationships since it is connected to "moral independence."

The state may only intrude to protect general goods and it cannot impose the standards of one group or sect. The general goods, as explained above, allow diverse visions of a decent and good life. The right to privacy therefore runs parallel to the right to conscience; it must include belief and action; and the state must be neutral as to the various conceptions of the good life and avoid the imposition of sectarian points of view. To deny the legitimacy of the right to privacy concerning intimate relations debases the "essential moral powers of a just personal life."

According to Richards the jurisprudence of privacy confirms this construal on the basis of personal autonomy. If the Griswold case acknowledges the unenumerated right of marriage, it is because the abstract background right concerns intimate personal relationships, "through which we express and realize a wholeness of emotion, intellect and self image guided by the just play of the self-determining powers of a free person."[35] Thus for good reason is the right to privacy extended to nonmarital relationships, the use of pornography, and abortion services. Richards believes that the Griswold case exposes the groundlessness of the religious (especially Catholic) objections to contraception,[36] highlights the great good of sex as an end in itself, and enhances the rational dignity of women who are freed from prejudice and traditional duties of the procreative function. So too abortion, pornography, and homosexual acts are liberated from false moral condemnation and individuals freed from the oppressive weight of tradition and convention. The moral powers of the person are thereby protected and nourished.

Richards concedes that abortion may be the harder case because there is an apparent harm involved; but on examination he legitimates the abortion cases; restrictive abortion laws infringe upon "essential moral powers in the service of nonneutral values." He argues that a case cannot be made for the full "moral" personhood of the fetus—it lacks self-conscious agency. It is a potential person; only religious premises bestow actual personhood on it. He rejects the slippery slope argument back to conception and declares that such a capacity clearly arises late in pregnancy. No evidence nor argument is provided for these claims.

The real issue for Richards, if we may judge by the degree of passion and evidence invoked, is the larger cultural war over gender roles: abortion is a proxy for other issues and a "controversial powerful sectarian ideology about proper sexuality and gender roles" is being foisted upon society at large. It is a vision that degrades women. Thus the abortion decision is "clearly a just application of the constitutional right to privacy, because the right to abortion choice protects women from the traditional degradation of their moral powers, reflected in the assumptions underlying the antiabortion laws."[37] Richards seems to imply that the greater moral vision has prevailed in *Roe v. Wade*. But no, he insists that the theory of general goods keeps the state at a neutral point. The state should remain neutral and thus allow freedom of choice; antiabortionists may try to persuade others that their vision is more beautiful, good, or true, but they may not use the power of the state to enforce it.

A similar approach is used to explain the right of privacy and homosexual activity. Richards refutes the moral arguments, in this case citing novel interpretations of the Bible, but also attacking the procreative model of sex. He connects intimate association with the just moral powers of forming a higher order plan of life. The laws against homosexuality are brutal and callous, he declares; they constitute a functional equivalence of heresy prosecution. This is a serious remark. Right to intimate association is an elaboration of the right to free exercise of religion construed as a protection of conscientious belief and action that follows from it. So too, the state endorsement of heterosexual relations through law and tax breaks is a functional equivalent of state establishment of religion. The courts must go much further in the legal protection and recognition of homosexual ways of life.

The paradigm right of conscience may finally be traced through the jurisprudence of equal protection and suspect classifications. It is a substantive right protecting equality of moral powers. In *Toleration*, Richards makes a few suggestive remarks about fighting stereotypes and extending equal protection to poor people, women, et al.; in *Foundations*, he follows this through. Indeed, for Richards the claims of feminists, gays, and other minorities are the vanguard for restoring the United States to its "community of principle"— they reveal the true moral gravity of American constitutionalism, that is, respect for personal autonomy and the freedom to choose one's way of life. The marginalized groups in American society will lead the country to its promised land of equal respect for persons:

The deepest level of American consensus is about the Constitution. All Americans have a place in that enterprise, because it supplies the grounds of the principle that dignify the lives of outcasts (e.g., blacks or women or homosexuals) from majority factions in terms of respect for the rights and common interests of all persons.

America's moral community is a "community of principle." Accordingly he says "our bonds of community are neither ethnic nor racial nor sexual nor familial nor religious nor any other of the 'natural' groups around which most polities organize their identities, but a new vision of republican political community the morality of which is democratic reason."[38] The work of democratic reason is a function of the judiciary and is embodied in the institutions of liberal constitutionalism.

The Institutional Features of Such Rights

The institutional arrangements of the American Constitution are likewise construed in light of the Kantian principle of equal respect for persons: the "institutions of democratic self-rule" are an attempt to realize a stable justice; and justice aims "to protect an idealized moral conception of persons as free, rational, and equal," as Rawls has rightly outlined.[39]

Judicial review, for example, is a necessity because such a public philosophy requires discipline and independence; only a judiciary branch free from majoritarian pressures could maintain the critical independence.[40] The court thus must "vindicate best arguments" of principle essential to our constitutional tradition. This is the work of democratic reason.

So too, the separation of powers and the federal structure is an attempt to protect equal respect for persons by combating faction and its "corruptive and demonic effect" whereby other persons are considered evil and less than persons. Madison's concern for faction was nothing less than a concern over the "Augustinian contempt for moral powers of those with whom one disagrees."[41] In addition, Madison construed "the people" not simply in terms of a majority, but in more fundamental terms of "the basic rights of the person which the contractarian state exists to defend." Popular sovereignty means the sovereignty of the individual right of conscience.

Conclusion

Richards' attempt to formulate a new liberalism is a formidable account that unfolds the logic of the core liberal idea of the autonomous person. Although many subscribe to the core idea, few would wish to trace it out as far as Richards has done. But his account and recommendations deserve the serious consideration of liberals and critics of liberalism alike. Richards in fact responds to a number of criticisms of liberalism proffered by the "communitarians." Is the doctrine of neutrality such that liberalism is unable to recommend or educate in positive moral ideals?[42] Does liberalism alienate one from community and authentic life?[43] Is liberalism antireligious? Does the Kantian ideal of the person downgrade love and personal relationships.[44] Richards believes that liberalism can be defended against these charges.

There are other questions of fundamental import that a critic of Richards' account of liberalism should consider as well. The foundational notion of person is invoked as a postulate. He admits that the notion is both empirical and normative. On both counts the theory of the person is open to challenge. For example, can the person be defined in terms of freedom alone and with a neutral account of the good life? Finnis, Raz, Taylor, et al. have made serious arguments to the contrary. The doctrine of state neutrality combined with the aggressive pursuit of equal respect for persons also seems to indicate the problems with a form of liberalism based upon neutrality with respect to the good. From a political perspective, there exists a tension between the temper of his democratic optimism and the elitist account of judicial review; this leads to a somewhat peculiar account of republican institutions, especially in relation to questions of federalism and faction. It is not so clear that founders of the American constitution wished to push individual autonomy to the point of the destruction of traditional communities and majorities, nor is this clearly a politically good or humane outcome. His account of liberalism may perhaps ultimately be too rash in theory and in practice.

Notes

This chapter was originally presented as a paper at the American Public Philosophy Institute, Newark, N.J., October 24, 1990. It is extracted from "David A. Richards and the Liberalism of the Autonomous Person," in *Liberalism at the Crossroads: An Introduction to Contemporary Liberal Theory and its Critics*, ed. John P. Hittinger and Christopher Wolfe (Lanham, Md.: Rowman & Littlefield, 1994).

1. David A. J. Richards, *Toleration and the Constitution* (New York: Oxford University Press, 1986); *Sex, Drugs, Death and the Law* (Totowa, N.J.: Rowman & Littlefield, 1982); *Foundations of American Constitutionalism* (New York: Oxford University Press, 1989); "Human Rights and Moral Ideals: An Essay on the Moral Theory of Liberalism," 5 *Social Theory and Practice* 461 (1980); "Rights and Autonomy," 92 *Ethics* 3 (1981). See also *A Theory of Reasons for Action* (Oxford: Clarendon Press, 1971) and *The Moral Criticism of the Law* (Encino, Calif.: Dickenson-Wadsworth, 1977); "Aims of Constitutional Theory," 8 *University of Dayton Law Review* 723 (1983).

2. On Calvinism see *Sex, Drugs, Death and the Law*, 2, 14, 90, 126, 194; *Foundations of American Constitutionalism*, 25, 54; *Toleration and the Constitution*, 235, 240. On Catholicism see *Sex, Drugs, Death and the Law*, 52; *Foundations of American Constitutionalism*, 217; *Toleration and the Constitution*, 207, 259–60, 277–78.

3. On the community of principle, see Richards, *Foundations of American Constitutionalism*, 295–99. On the degradation of traditional communities, see *Foundations of American Constitutionalism*, 277; "Human Rights and Moral Ideals," 485–86: "The detailed casuistry of one's personal life, typical of older moral traditions, imposes unreal and factitious constraints which deny and disfigure the moral freedom that we, as persons, possess. To deny such freedom is to impose a false passivity and resignation, a slavery of the spirit which is neither natural nor humane."

4. Richards, *Sex, Drugs, Death and the Law*, 1; "Rights and Autonomy," 3.

5. Richards, *Toleration and the Constitution*, 62. See Charles Taylor, *Sources of the Self*.

6. Richards, *Toleration and the Constitution*, 81–82.

7. See also Richards, *Foundations of American Constitutionalism*, 276–77.

8. "Plato and Aristotle were not liberals or democrats in our sense, and an exploration of how the founders critically appreciated this fact might debunk the kind of fashionable appeal these thinkers enjoy in general and in constitutional theory." Richards, *Foundations of American Constitutionalism*, 296.

9. Richards, *Sex, Drugs, Death and the Law*, 63. "Certain of the traditional moral condemnations of homosexuals, appear, on analysis, to be vicious forms of social and legal persecution." "Human Rights and Moral Ideals," 479.

10. See Richards, *Foundations of American Constitutionalism*, 246–47.

11. Richards, *Foundations of American Constitutionalism*, 246–47.

12. Richards, *Toleration and the Constitution*, 64.

13. Richards, *Sex, Drugs, Death and the Law*, 5.

14. Richards, *Toleration and the Constitution*, 69–71, 237–42; "Rights and Autonomy," 5, 17–19; *Sex, Drugs*, 9–10.

15. Richards, *Toleration and the Constitution*, 68.

16. Richards, *Sex, Drugs, Death and the Law*, 8, 19.

17. Richards, *Toleration and the Constitution*, 245. See Richards, *Sex, Drugs, Death and the Law*, 12–13.

18. Richards, *Toleration and the Constitution*, 246.

19. Richards, "Human Rights and Moral Ideals," 461.

20. Richards, *Toleration and the Constitution*, 71–85; see *A Theory of Reasons for Action*, passim.

21. Richards, "Human Rights and Moral Ideals," 466.

22. Richards, *Sex, Drugs, Death and the Law*, 10.

23. Richards, *Toleration and the Constitution*, 71–72.

24. Richards, *Sex, Drugs, Death and the Law*, 9; "Human Rights and Moral Ideals," 467.

25. Richards, "Human Rights and Moral Ideals," 465–66.

26. Richards, *Toleration and the Constitution*, 72.

27. Richards, *Toleration and the Constitution*, 84; see "Human Rights and Moral Ideals," 467–68: "The idea of human rights is a corollary of the Kantian interpretation of treating persons as equals in virtue of their autonomy."

28. Thus Richards summarizes the doctrine as follows: "In view of the fundamental importance to liberalism of the autonomy based interpretation of treating
persons as equals, the content of these constitutional rights clusters around the
idea of respect for the independent and self-critical mind (freedom of expression;
religious tolerance) which takes responsibility for directing its common life with
others (political rights) and its personal life on its own (autonomy rights) and is
guaranteed the greatest extensive liberty, compatible with a like liberty for all, in
understanding both the law and its reasons so as to plan one's life accordingly (due
process; and so forth)." Richards, "Human Rights and Moral Ideals," 470.

29. Richards, *Toleration and the Constitution*, 26–27, 88–89.

30. Richards, *Toleration and the Constitution*, 136.

31. Richards, *Toleration and the Constitution*, 160, 170.

32. Richards, *Toleration and the Constitution*, 206–10.

33. The conditions are: 1. there must exist concrete harms to assignable persons;
2. the state cannot interfere on paternalistic grounds to protect the agent for his own
good; 3. the state cannot interfere simply because the mere thought of the act offends
someone. Richards, *Toleration and the Constitution*, 237–42. See Richards, *Sex, Drugs,
Death and the Law*, 3, 7.

34. Richards, *Toleration and the Constitution*, 243.

35. Richards, *Toleration and the Constitution*, 255–58.

36. Richards rehearses a very limited type of argumentation made against contraception; the sustained arguments of Anscombe, Finnis, Grisez, or Wojtyla are not
considered.

37. Richards, *Toleration and the Constitution*, 268. These assumptions pertain to
gender hierarchy and biologically imposed roles on women.

38. Richards, *Foundations of American Constitutionalism*, 299.

39. Richards, *Toleration and the Constitution*, 41.

40. Richards, *Toleration and the Constitution*, 290–92; Richards, *Foundations of
American Constitutionalism*, 292: the judiciary protects against the "self-blinding
views of majority faction."

41. Richards, *Toleration and the Constitution*, 300.

42. Richards, "Human Rights and Moral Ideals."

43. Richards, *Toleration and the Constitution*, 82–83.

44. Richards, "Rights and Autonomy," 15–16.

CHAPTER NINE

Approaches to Democratic Equality

Yves Simon states in *Philosophy of Democratic Government*:

> During the phase of democratic struggle against the old aristocratic and
> monarchical order, liberty and equality are considered inseparable. . . . The
> will to be free and the claim for equality seemed to be but two aspects of the
> same enthusiasm. . . . But soon a split takes place within what was the Third
> Estate. The Fourth Estate has arisen, with a new claim for equality—a claim
> which sounds unintelligible to its former allies of the bourgeoisie. . . . The
> formula which attributed basic unity of meaning to freedom and equality
> seems to have been lost as soon as the defeat of the old hierarchies was cer-
> tain.[1]

Tocqueville argues that equality, and not freedom, was the aim of modern
democracy all along. As much as freedom and equality share a common
ground, they diverge at many points. He understands the challenge to liberal
democracy to be the protection of freedom and excellence in the face of its
egalitarian trends.[2] American political history could also be viewed as an unfolding of the tensions inherent to its founding concepts and symbols.[3] The
patriot's perorations and flags were emblazoned with liberty. But the philosophical origins seem to be partly rooted in claims to "equal station" and
"equal creation."[4] Both sides of the American Civil War made legitimate
claim to the flag of freedom, as James MacPherson has recently shown. But

the degree to which liberty's twin, equality, could be separated was really the issue, as Lincoln so eloquently expressed it in his Gettysburg Address. And this struggle in turn continues to haunt our life together. Added to this are new claims to freedom, now called "liberation," but whose inner appeal is really a claim for equality of conditions, if not in some respect an equality of results. Surely this is enough to suggest the importance of the problem of equality and its inclusion in a discussion of freedom in the modern world. Thus, Simon warns us that the issue of equality, and its relation to freedom, is too vital to be dodged.

In fact, contemporary literature is filled with debates about equality and liberty. Variations of the Rawls and Nozick debate fill the journals and anthologies. But this debate seems to be interminable and for good reason, as MacIntyre shows in his book *After Virtue*. Claims based on legitimate entitlement, he says, are incommensurable with claims based upon need. But more fundamentally, the contemporary debate is flawed by an inability to account for desert; because desert presupposes a "shared understanding both of the good for man and of the good for that community and where individuals identify their primary interests with reference to those goods."[5] Maritain, Simon, and Kolnai draw upon a premodern, Aristotelean tradition in which a normative good is shared by a community. Their disagreements therefore are fruitful in light of the shared assumption about a common good. Simon and Maritain are known for their attempts to embrace the modern liberal tradition and its egalitarian dynamic; they attempted to purify and elevate it in terms of the Aristotelean/Thomistic political science. Thus they represent a new orientation of Catholic political philosophy, which hitherto had been somewhat skeptical of the liberal tradition in politics. Indeed, Paul Sigmund has recently commented about the importance of Maritain in this development.[6] Kolnai, on the other hand, highlights and defends the aristocratic element in the tradition and points to some inconsistencies and weaknesses in the liberal position, however purified or elevated.[7]

The thinkers in question share not only a common orientation, but also a profound feel for the historical reality of twentieth-century political life. In Maritain we find a glowing hot praise of progressive liberal democracy and the seeds of the "New Christendom"; Simon sets the fervor of progress and social justice in the sober forms of Aristotelean regime categories; Kolnai questions the theoretical consistency of the Aristotelean forms with modern terminology and the practical wisdom of so doing. A comparison and contrast may yield some very fruitful results, both for political theory and for political practice.

Thus we plan to proceed in our inquiry as follows. We shall examine Maritain, Simon, and Kolnai in order and in each one give a summary of their account of equality and any moderating or counter-tendency. That is, we shall look for their idea of equality, and consider also whether and to what degree equality is desirable and possible. At stake, we believe, is the nature and meaning of contemporary democracy and its prospects for success.

Maritain: The "Realist" Approach to Equality

Maritain's key writing on the question of equality is an essay entitled "Human Equality."[8] Maritain develops his notion of equality through his typical method of analysis; it involves an examination of two extremes and the virtuous middle position. We find this approach in his *Person and the Common Good* and it is thematic in his *Introduction to Philosophy*.[9] And in this case, the approach draws upon his epistemological categories. The essay is abstract and raises many questions about application, which must be garnered from his other works.

The three approaches to human equality outlined by Maritain are first, the nominalist/empiricist approach, which denies the reality of a universal human nature. It permits the enslavement of one part of humanity by another. The second approach is the idealist one; it denies particularity with its concomitant inequalities. It may be labeled egalitarianism. The third approach is called "realist": it allows for unity and diversity in the human species, for equality and inequality.

The nominalist or empiricist approach is so taken with concrete inequalities that it denies any validity to the idea of a common humanity. Instead it erects biological or social divisions into essential differences, dividing the truly human from the subhuman. "False hierarchies of pseudo-specific gradation which establish between men inequalities in the same order as those which apply to a lion and an ass, an eagle and an ant."[10] The divisions may correspond to social privilege such as those of aristocratic birth or bourgeois wealth or to supposed differences in race or ethnicity. The error lies in the rigid ideological posturing by which common humanity is denied of an entire segment of the species, and a group thereby "concentrates into itself" all the dignity and privileges of human nature. The lower group exists only for the higher group. But as Maritain readily argues, the claimed superiority for a group or bloc is always undermined because of the aggregate nature of the excellence or inequality. That is, the values are on average or on whole. Moreover, there may be overlapping

from one group to the next. Aristotle uses a similar argument against conventional slavery and hereditary privilege.[11] The boundary separating the
groups is usually so variable and fluid that it can be "broadened or con-
tracted as the mind wishes." Lincoln uses a similar argument against black
slavery: if skin color grants one a warrant to despotic rule, then a yet more
white man may justly enslave him. Finally, Maritain points out that an inferior group can improve; and in fact, both groups share "a common natural pattern which they more or less fully realize."

Maritain's critique of the nominalist approach makes the standard case
against slavery or tyranny. Basically, no men should be treated as beasts. It
would stand against extreme forms of oligarchy, which Aristotle argues bor-
ders on tyranny. But Maritain's argument only grazes the superior claims of
the aristocrat or monarch. It does not touch them if their claims do not entail superiority in essence or a reduction of the other to the status of slave. If
the claim of superiority is detached from the ethnic and/or hereditary basis,
and is rather claimed by an individual, such as Lincoln's "family of the lion
or the tribe of the eagle," its high reach is left open.

The relevance of this false "nominalist" approach was quite pressing in the
face of National Socialism and its racist creed, and it remains so to challenge
any form of racial exploitation. Also, if economic conditions of some segments of a regime are oppressive to the point of slave-like exploitation, the
critique is operative. Maritain does not make the relevant applications in this
essay. In some places he terms the capitalist in this way. Simon discusses the
possibility of "oligarchic exploitation," and he makes a careful analysis of
equality in exchange.[12]

The idealist approach to equality excludes empirical inequalities and
treats the unity of mankind in the abstract. Maritain charges this approach
with a "speculative denial" of natural inequality because it considers inequalities as solely the result of the artificial stratification of social life.
Hence, inequality is a "pure accident" suggesting no intelligible patterns for
the mind. This leads further to a practical denial of inequality because it is
"an outrage against human dignity." The egalitarian idea of equality demands
simple equality and uniformity. Its instinctive tendency, Maritain says, is hatred of superiority and a leveling spirit. "In mental patterns which correspond
to this, there develops an uneasy touchiness regarding any possibility of a hierarchy of value among men."[13]

Maritain's analysis of egalitarianism is very pointed; its major thrust runs
counter to the claim of pure democracy. And it certainly allows no room
for a democracy based upon value relativism. Maritain's critique of its abstract reduction of particularity resonates to some contemporary develop-

ments in the critique of democratic theory concerning the unencumbered self.[14] Maritain's critique of the two extreme approaches to equality comes down hardest on the egalitarian approach. It seems to be more spirited and better aimed at real types. He says that the nominalist approach is more hateful, but the idealist approach is more treacherous and leads to worse forms of slavery because it embodies a "bitter passion counterfeiting Christian charity."[15]

The realist approach to equality leads Maritain to eschew the idealist in favor of an "existentialist one." Equality is found not in an abstract ideal, but in "the root energies and sources of being" that lead human beings to seek communication with each other. Rather than use the notion of equal nature, Maritain favors the notion of community in nature. He would found equality on the natural sociability of men, and specifically in a tendency to love one's own. It is similar, I would say, to Aristotle's notion of natural friendship, or philanthropy.[16]

Maritain adroitly develops a defense of inequality out of the same unity in nature that grounds equality. Sociality demands differentiation and differentiation demands inequality. Maritain gathers up and develops the various reasons for inequality in a human community. I refer to them as the metaphysical principle of variety, the principle of individual merit, and the social principle of differentiation. Maritain cites Thomas' argument that inequality, order, and hierarchy are part of divine creation.[17] As for individual merit, Maritain points to moral, psychological, and even biological origins. In *Art and Scholasticism* Maritain refers to the "*habitus*" of virtue as a "metaphysical title to nobility" which makes for inequality among men.[18] Finally, diversity of internal structures in society and diversity of conditions result from social life itself; in fact he says that inequalities testify to the "inconquerable originality and vitality of social life."

Maritain makes a strong affirmation of the necessity and value of inequality. He says further that Christianity does not iron out social inequalities, but brings them into "true proportion."[19] The true proportion of inequality is its twofold subordination to equality. It must not obscure the foundational value of equality nor must it impede the progressive development of equality in society. Social inequality, he says, must not be a principle of exclusion but one of communication; the inequalities must not be erected into a state of social servitude; nor should the man in the lower condition be considered an inferior man without dignity.[20] Maritain reminds the reader of his criticism of the nominalist approach to equality which would "harden" the inequalities and become oppressive. The primordial unity of human nature is the basis for the inequalities—the latter are justified in terms of the community. But as well noted above this amounts to nothing more than strictures on tyranny or exploitation. But the "true proportion of equality to inequality" also includes something more. Maritain now introduces his notion of progressive social equality as an aim and purpose of society.

Social equality, he writes, "rises up progressively in the midst of society, like a social flowering forth or fructifying of the equality of nature." For example, although fundamental rights of the person are anterior to society, the legal order must increasingly embody protection for them. Further, the rights of the person in the political and economic spheres require continual progress in awareness of the rights, conditions for fulfillment, and embodiment in law and fact. The inequalities in society must be compensated for by a "redistribution" of benefits such that the higher benefits are open to all and such that the dignity of the lower level is acknowledged through a proportional equal opportunity for fulfillment. Further, Maritain states that all should "in so far as possible participate 'free of charge' in the elementary goods needed for human life." The telos of political community is equality, not the perpetuation of inequalities. Thus, through this second subordination of inequality to equality, Maritain surmounts the aristocratic orientation of the Aristotelean-Thomistic tradition from which he derives his basic concepts. Of course it is crucial to Maritain's own account that the principal qualities dominant in monarchical and aristocratic regimes are "preserved" in the democratic regime, even while being "transcended."[21] How are these qualities preserved? Does it not require the presence of countervailing principles within the democratic regime? Has Maritain paid sufficient attention to the problem and the tensions inherent in the mixing of political principles?

Maritain acknowledges the many obstacles that frustrate the ready achievement of the democratic principle of equality. Progress toward social equality is a long arduous road. The democratic principle of equality is marked by a "dynamism." It requires the "conquest of man over nature and over himself." It is "an end to struggle for, and with difficulty, and at the price of a constant tension of the energies of the spirit." The tensions are indeed real. For Maritain, by linking equality with his high idea of liberty, keeps an elevating tone to its progress. That is, excellence and standards are held firmly in place by his account of liberty. His is not a "leveling equality." Further, the qualification of social equality with the "proportion" to condition and function is bound to disappoint the contemporary egalitarian movement. Maritain states that identical opportunity, strict equal opportunity I take it, is an illusion. What are the conditions, the merits, and functions that would limit proportionately equal opportunity? His remarks on equality for women are very instructive on this point.[22]

Other tensions emerge from Maritain's account. The progress to the free participation in the goods needed for human life raises many questions. Is it a call for state socialism, socialized health care for example? It is not clear. Simon has more to say explicitly about "free distribution." The problem is, of course, that this tendency, if centralized, can run counter to the principle of differentiation and pluralism. How is equality to be achieved? Maritain's metaphor of "flowering" is too vague: the hard question of means, such as affirmative action, quotas, and the like, are not treated in his account. It is hard to gauge his position given the dynamism toward equality on the one hand and the desire for pluralism and a high liberty on the other. Tocqueville saw this as the overriding tension and issue. Maritain seems to view the two in tandem and therefore fails to acknowledge the deeper tension in democratic theory and practice.

Perhaps the greatest tension surrounds his notion of progress. Even though Maritain speaks about the law of twofold contrasting progress of good and evil in history, he often fails to acknowledge the presence of intrinsic limitations on progress, particularly in political life.[23] Will progress overcome the tensions in political life or are we faced with inherent tensions whose resolution must be managed? Plato speaks about the paradox of philosopher-king, Aristotle of the incommensurable claims to rule, Madison of self-interest, faction, and common good, Tocqueville of glory and welfare; and thus they accommodate themselves accordingly by means of the noble lie, the mixed regime, checks and balances, self-interest properly understood. These political thinkers would certainly not claim that democracy replicates the qualities of monarchy or aristocracy in any pure form, let alone would they claim that democracy transcends them to a superior level of achievement in their own line or according to their distinctive principle. The qualities are replicated in some analogous but less pure form, and only as the result of mixing in a principle which counteracts the pure democratic principle.

The polarity of individual and person plays a central role in Maritain's philosophy, but this polarity lends weight to the progressive resolution of the tensions themselves. The trajectory of realization is potentially unlimited, according to the "conquest" of man over nature and over himself, the conditions Maritain names as the engines or dynamism for the progress toward greater equality. Does his account give too much sail to the prospects for democratic achievement?

Simon: The Egalitarian Dynamism
and the Principle of Autonomy

Simon's political philosophy reflects a greater awareness of the inherent tensions of political life as such and he explicitly deals with the tension of equality and liberty. More specifically, he affirms Maritain's ideal of social equality, but he has a much better-defined counter-tendency in the principle of autonomy. The latter principle is also important to Maritain; he even cites it in his book *Man and the State*.[24] But Simon carefully works through the tensions and arrives at well-defined principles of compromise. He does not speak of a brotherly city of the future; if anything, his concluding chapter on technology carries an undertone of very limited expectations.

Simon begins his account of democratic equality with Maritain's idea of the notion of equality as a common human nature, rejecting the nominalist bias of doctrines of inequality. He excludes the doctrine that human kind can be divided essentially by race into higher and lower. Equality is grounded in potential for community life. He then turns the account more directly to the problem of equality and its tensions. The ideal of equality deriving from common humanity can be applied in a strict fashion and in the fashion of a tendency. For example, all men are covered by the norm prohibiting the killing of innocent life. Race, social standing, wealth, and so forth are irrelevant considerations here. Any excepting conditions are made on principle, like self-defense, not on an arbitrary basis. Simon, writing in 1950, prophetically mentions abortion and euthanasia as great violations of the ideal of equality and common humanity. Similarly, fair exchange demands a strict equality, for again race, wealth, and the like are not relevant factors. But in other demands for equal consideration, limitations must be acknowledged. Hence in some cases equality must be adopted as a "progressive tendency" to greater realization. The two examples considered are health care and education. All human beings ought to be protected from disease and death. The desire for life is equal in all segments of society, Simon says. On this point Simon claims that our conscience has improved.[25] But it does not follow, he says, that it is in our power to provide equal protection to all, nor is it "necessarily iniquitous that it [society] fails to do so." But society must be on a "track" leading to equal protection for all. This is "the equalitarian dynamism contained in the unity of human nature." But this dynamism he says is often lawfully restricted and delayed. Why? Its implementation may require "an enormously increased weight of bureaucratic organization [and a loss] of a considerable amount of liberty." He gives a similar account of education; society must be on track to greater opportunity, but the recognition of different abilities and conditions, and the problem of freedom and taxes may restrict its implementation.

Despite these "lawful restrictions and delays" in the realization of equality, Simon insists that democratic theory and practice be gauged above all in terms of progress in equality. Conservativism, he warns, simply seeks to maintain the advantages of small minorities. At best, Simon would allow for a form of "fiscal conservativism" from what he has said about lawful restrictions. Does it follow then that democratic theory and practice must posit as a regulative ideal the eventual suppression of all advantage and privilege with the inequality that accompany them? That is, has Simon reduced the "conservative" objection to that of means and efficiency? Could greater power and technical prowess enhance progress in equality and pare down the conservative objections? Should democratic regimes be ever in search of greater power and take of advantage of any possible advance in equality?

Simon argues very strenuously against this conclusion on the basis of the principle of autonomy or subsidiarity. Simon entertains the following proposition: "inequality should never be determined by any consideration foreign to individual merit." Simon says that this well-sounding vague notion has the "character of radicalism made inconspicuous."[26] Yet it would seem one is driven to this point by a certain logic in the equalitarian dynamism. For legal equality and open opportunity can neutralize aristocratic privilege. But then education, position, and other factors such as wealth can still leave great gaps in equal opportunity. Strict equal opportunity must eradicate "all privilege or handicap attaching to hazard of birth." If so, the right of inheritance and any family influence would stand in the way of equality. But the elimination of the family is a utopian scheme that would subject men to a far greater arbitrariness; hence Simon's fear of "radicalism made inconspicuous" in the claim of equality.

Simon backs off to a larger context in order to resolve the antinomy. The problem is biased by "an individualistic preconception." The family and social being is part of the good life desired for each citizen. Thus, "some of the things for which opportunity is sought are of such a nature as to balance and restrict the principle of equal opportunity." Equal opportunity is carried too far when "it threatens to dissolve the small communities from which men derive their best energies in the hard accomplishments of daily life." From the perspective of human flourishing, the principle of equality is limited by more than technical efficiency, but also by a positive notion of the good life.

Simon concludes with three principles pertaining to equal opportunity, thus gathering the various elements in tension: a democratic regime must strive for legal equality; it must take positive measures to avoid factual exclusion from any function (e.g., financial help for education); it must allow the greatest possible autonomy to prevail. The first principle reflects the strict equality of common humanity; the second principle reflects the equalitarian dynamism of a democratic regime; the third principle, Simon says, makes the principle of equal opportunity less absolute; without it, equal opportunity would be "a first class factor of atomization and a formidable wrecker of democratic communities."

What is the principle of autonomy or subsidiarity. It is stated most succinctly in the chapter of democratic freedom:

> The metaphysical law which demands such diversity demands also that no task which can be satisfactorily fulfilled by the smaller unit should ever be assumed by the larger unit. . . . It is perfectly obvious that there is more life and, unqualifiedly, greater perfection in a community all parts of which are full of initiative than in a community whose parts act merely as instruments transmitting the initiative of the whole.[27]

Simon does not denounce state intervention in principle—it could well serve freedom from exploitation and even strengthen autonomic institutions. Further, he does not want to suggest that the state is evil in essence or adopt the individualist preconception on the libertarian side which he sought to avoid on the egalitarian side. But given the tendency of the modern state to expand, Simon cannot overemphasize the principle of autonomy. Concerning the problem of "free distribution" mentioned above, Simon also invokes the principle of autonomy, so as to rule out a socialist interpretation. The great problem he says is to make it "independent of the arbitrariness of individual whims without delivering it up to the arbitrariness of public powers and their bureaucracy." In all facets, the "absolutism of the state must be held in check by forces external to the state apparatus."[28] Church, press, private school, labor unions, cooperatives of different sorts, and private property and free enterprise are all conditions of the principle of autonomy. Simon uses Tocqueville's intermediate associations as a device for liberty.

Simon's principle of autonomy leads him beyond democratic regime to an idea of the mixed regime as the best. Any regime, he says, may need the operation of a principle distinct from and opposed to its own idea. The association of democracy with nondemocratic, which must mean nonegalitarian, principles may be necessary to serve the common good and to check its own weaknesses. In fact, Simon's ultimate defense of democracy, universal suffrage, rests upon, not the claim of the common man as such, but a "pessimistic" reason—resistance to the power of the state and elites.[29] That is, after surveying the various reasons for universal suffrage from the standpoint of democratic optimism, he concludes that the best reason is distribution of power—that is, the principle of autonomy. For each of the reasons for democratic rule through universal suffrage, named by Simon the "statistical" and the "sociological," can be countered by the aristocrat or monarch. For example, if the many can claim that they are less apt to be corrupt, the aristocrat can still claim they he is more apt to produce high excellence. Or if the many can claim to muster a combination of gifts and talents into a wise virtuous decision, the few or the one great man can stake an even greater claim. Simon develops very adroitly the arguments found in Aristotle's *Politics* for the various claims to rule.[30] He also rejects romantic arguments postulating a superior virtue in the proletariat or a supposed elite. Simon fully realizes that the claim of universal suffrage is not based upon a new virtue of the common man, but the sheer power of numbers. And this is a legitimate factor to be reckoned with in the political association. It is one of the incommensurables present in all regimes. The principle of equality alone cannot bear the burden of justifying the claims of democracy.

In Simon we find a more direct acknowledgement of the inherent tensions in the egalitarian claims of democracy. In his account we find a statement of the equalitarian dynamism, but it is held in check by a counter principle of autonomy. Simon, even more than Maritain, emphasizes the conservative element in political theory. But does his reading of the egalitarian dynamic set up a dialectic in which the citizens are always discontent and disappointed? Tocqueville observed that the idea of equality promotes envy precisely because the means for achieving equality are "constantly proving inadequate in the hands of those using them." Further, he says:

> Democratic institutions awaken and flatter the passion for equality without ever being able to satisfy it entirely. . . . [The people] are excited by the chance and irritated by the uncertainty of success; the excitement is followed by weariness and then by bitterness. In that state anything which in any way transcends the people seems an obstacle to their desires, and they are tired by the sight of any superiority, however legitimate.[31]

Concerning the problems of envy and mediocrity Simon says simply that "these risks are well known and do not call for any elaboration." But without further elaborating does Simon not run the risk of jeopardizing the principle of autonomy? By stressing the equalitarian tendency in contemporary democracy he must then place the principle of subsidiarity/autonomy in the position of a check or a drag against the expansion of equality. Are they doomed to fight a rear-guard action and forever face the wrath of the discontent and disappointed egalitarians?

Kolnai: Pluralism as a Conservative Principle

Aurel Kolnai was born in Budapest Hungary in 1900; he studied philosophy at the University of Vienna where he converted to Catholicism, in part due to the influence of the writings of G. K. Chesterton and the German Phenomenological School. For about twenty years he worked as a writer and journalist. Of Jewish extraction, Kolnai viewed the rise of National Socialism with particular alarm; he spent six years writing a critique of their doctrines, a book later published as *The War against the West.*[32] He left Austria in 1938, and his citizenship, and he worked as a journalist in England and North America during the war. From 1945 to 1955 he taught at Laval University. In 1955 he moved to London, became a British national, and he taught ethics at Beford College, University of London. He died in 1973. His output was not as vast as Maritain or Simon, but he produced some very good essays in the fields of ethics and political philosophy. Some of his articles are collected in a volume edited by Bernard Williams and David Wiggins, published by Hackett Press, and a book, *The Utopian Mind,* is scheduled for publication next year. The influence of phenomenological and analytic method is apparent. His experience of the world wars and his years of journalism gave him a keen feel for political reality. For our account of equality, we are interested in some pieces written while at Laval; they are his review of Maritain's *Man and the State,* and two articles "The Meaning of the Common Man," and "Privilege and Liberty."

Kolnai's criticism of Maritain is admittedly captious in tone and not entirely fair in representing the balanced sweep of Maritain's political philosophy as a whole. On the other hand, *Man and the State,* with its democratic creed and its praise of shock troops like John Brown, is open to criticism. Kolnai identifies some critical weak points in Maritain's philosophy. He accuses Maritain of wishing to have his cake and to eat it too. That is, he attempts to harmonize a progressive democratic theory with Christianity and Thomas Aquinas. Of course others have spotted this tension in Maritain's philosophy. Maritain does not recognize the tension between the "orderly life of democratic institutions" and the "spirit of mass subjectivism . . . which is the driving force of the democratic creed." Or further, he clings to a dogma of "boundless terrestrial optimism." Maritain has a ready response to these charges. But there is something in his orientation that causes such an impression. Perhaps Kolnai scores the most direct hit in his praise of Maritain's concern for "pluralism."[33] A pluralistic society Kolnai says "relies precisely upon given realities in their manifoldness, contingency and limitation," and is therefore "refractory" and opposed to a streamlined creation of social reality. "In other words," Kolnai says, "pluralism, if taken seriously, involves a conservative outlook."

Kolnai's claim is not simply a matter of labels. Russell Kirk outlines six principles of conservative thought as follows—a belief in a transcendent moral order, social continuity, prescription, prudence, variety, and imperfectibility.[34] Maritain and Simon affirm all of these principles in one way or another; and indeed, they rely on them to structure the life of the city and to check and even brake the progressive spirit of social equality as shown above. But does this not put the conservative value always in the rear-guard, always catching up, and on the defensive? The position of Simon and Maritain would seem to encourage ardent hopes for equality which must then be dashed by the hidden conservative principle. Kolnai notices that when conservative forces and conceptions serve as mere "brakes" on progress an ambivalence and impatience is evoked toward them. Democratic society is faced then with an alternative: "maintenance of institutional freedoms and the full acceptation of the religion of the Common Man."[35]

Kolnai reveals an internal weakness in the philosophy of democratic government which emphasizes the principle of equality and aims at the surpassing or neutralizing of privilege. Liberal democracy he says will always appear in this light as insufficiently democratic, as insufficiently advanced "in its own direction." And this sets up a temptation to abandon "mere formal or political democracy" for real, substantial, or social democracy. Thus a certain emphasis within democratic theory can serve as a bridge from progressive democracy to communism. Communism is seen as a rival brother, "laboring under imperfections but yet representing the self-same triumphant march of Man."[36] The contradiction between formal equality and socioeconomic privilege leads to an attack upon privilege and the advocacy of a democracy of the common man. But Kolnai claims that this strikes at the very root of order and hastens its collapse.[37]

Kolnai's proposal is to approach the defense of democracy and equality from another perspective, stressing the principle of pluralism and autonomy as the leading idea. He says:

> What we have in mind is not, of course, a proposal to substitute for Western Democracy along with its ideological biases, a fancy system of Conservative Constitutionalism, nor a return to this or that specified stage of the past, but a suggestion to displace the spiritual stress from the "common man" aspect of

democracy to its aspect of constitutionalism and of moral continuity with the high tradition of Antiquity, Christendom and the half-surviving Liberal cultures of yesterday.[38]

Kolnai wishes to emphasize rule of law, balance and limitation, responsible government, federalism, and the consent of the governed. He defends universal suffrage, as Simon does, as a check to the power of rule.[39] But checks and balances are not sufficient to maintain a regime of liberty, Kolnai argues. He calls it a "fallacy of federalism" to believe that "plurality of forms" and decentralization alone is sufficient to defend liberty. Administrative decentralization, he points out, could simply deal with a subsection of a still uniform whole. Moreover, equality as such tends to "centralization and uniformity." Tocqueville demonstrated this trend in democracy. In addition to federal or plural forms, an appreciation of difference and inequality is required. For the substance and savor of an intermediate group is constituted by "its particular structure of authority, of loyalty and allegiance, or tradition and formative power, of 'rulership' and obedience."[40] In short, vertical relationships with patterns of privilege within various groups and within society as a whole are essential to true autonomy and federalism.

Natural inequality, he argues, is "essentially inseparable" from artificial inequality. Further, natural distinction is a fruit of privilege and generative of new privilege.[41] The moderate equalitarian position, he says, fails to see this, and thus must remain hostile to privilege. The ideal of equality demands the elimination of privilege. Kolnai objects that not only does this approach to equality rest upon an individualist premise, it is also an approach that tends to a reductionistic and uniform view of the good. And finally, the approach requires a centralized consciousness to administer and ensure equality. On these points, the equalitarian ideal is opposed to any principle of autonomy.

The role of hierarchy and privilege must be understood in their full social valence and not simply as a "necessary evil." Kolnai defines privilege as: "a positional value in society relatively independent of the will of society."[42] Social hierarchy does not and is not meant to correspond univocally with the hierarchy of moral or intellectual values. Rather hierarchy expresses the bondage of all men to what is intrinsically better than they. That is, social values are not good simply as an immanent unfolding of my volition and needs, but objectively good.[43] The equalitarian tendency in its objection to privilege often masks a rejection of an objective order of values and limited power of man. Kolnai sees here a metaphysical rebellion at the heart of the enterprise. And this is why a more radical assertion of human power in communism is a possible outcome of the trajectory of progressive democracy.

Kolnai thinks that liberty cannot be defended nor maintained without a vertical limitation on its use. He shares the concern of Solzhenitsyn about the abuse of liberty permitted within the context of its horizontal limitation by equal right alone. We need not only a theocentric humanism to provide the notion of liberty under God, but also the entire range of intermediary groups with their embodiment of high moral value and authority. The liberal conception of society, he argues, cannot support and protect liberty "except in a precarious and self-contradictory fashion." It must rely on conservative values such as autonomy, pluralism, et al. But such values, while "unofficially tolerated," they are "continually harassed and eaten away, by the immanent dialectic of liberal society as such." The university and the church are perhaps the key intermediate groups to resist this harassment. It is the mission of these institutions, Kolnai urges, to "inoculate the national mind with the seeds of objective value reference, of a vision of things 'sub specie aeterni,' of intellectual independence and moral backbone."[44]

Kolnai thus would have us use the principle of pluralism and differentiation not in the rear-guard as a mere check to equality, but as a vanguard in the promotion of excellence and the things that make a human life worth leading.

Conclusion

Maritain, Simon, and Kolnai have political philosophies and approaches to democracy which share the same essential elements. However, the stress within each approach is different. The former two stress the equalitarian tendency of modern democracy, which they check with the principle of autonomy or subsidiarity, among other things. Kolnai raises a very legitimate point. This approach to autonomy and liberty, in a political perspective, appears as a mere brake or counterprogressive element. As a result it seems like a reactionary position opposing the march of progress. Further, the use of autonomy as a principle of greater efficiency may prompt dreams of greater human power which allows for greater achievement of equality without seeing its countervalue. I believe that the intention of Maritain and Simon is to defend true hierarchy of value and to defend the social principles necessary to defend it; Kolnai does overstate his case against Maritain. The idea of freedom as self-mastery and virtue, the belief in an objective order of values and natural law, and the principle of freedom all radically transform his idea of equality.

Kolnai's proposal to lead with the idea of virtue and pluralism allows political philosophy to be countercultural with respect to the democratic tendencies even in order to serve it well. That is, the principle of hierarchy can be adapted to a democratic regime defined in terms of rule of law and the society of free men and women. The ideal of equality can then be absorbed through the system of balanced society in which each segment of society should be nourished but checked for a common good; that is, the idea of mixed regime in which all claims to rule are duly regarded provides grounds for opposing oligarchical exploitation and a defense of equal rights. How far can we take this in establishing justice for all sectors and levels of society without invoking the progressive tendencies that lead to envy and disappointment?

The three thinkers together represent a remarkable philosophy of government with many fruitful tensions. Thus, Heinrich Rommen has correctly observed that:

> Political philosophy in Catholic thought with its constitutive polar system will, through all of its eras, show a conservative and a liberal strain; it will depend upon the particular circumstances of an era which of them will be more outspoken. Furthermore, each of them keeps the other from falling into extremes. The continuous defense and attack that each needs and makes against the other prevents either from monopolizing political philosophy.[45]

Indeed, so much depends upon the circumstances of our era. I should conclude with Tocqueville who said—"I think that at all times I would have loved freedom; but in the times we live, I am disposed to worship it."[46] I do not think that we have to go that far in our defense of inequality; but it is at least worthy of our admiration.

Notes

Excerpted from "Approaches to Democratic Equality," *Freedom in the Modern World*, ed. Michael Torre (Notre Dame, Ind.: University of Notre Dame Press, 1989).

1. Y. Simon, *Philosophy of Democratic Government* (Chicago: University of Chicago Press, 1951), 195–97.

2. Alexis de Tocqueville, *Democracy in America*, trans. G. Lawrence (New York, 1969), 503–6, 690–705. See M. Zetterbaum, *Tocqueville and the Problem of Democracy* (Palo Alto, Calif.: Stanford University Press, 1967).

3. See the dispute between H. Jaffa and M. Bradford. W. Kendall and G. Carey, *The Basic Symbols of the American Political Tradition* (Baton Rouge, La.: LSU Press, 1970); M. E. Bradford, *A Better Guide than Reason* (LaSalle, Il.: 1979); H. Jaffa, *How*

to *Think about the American Revolution* (Durham, N.C.: Duke University Press, 1978); see also R. Hoffstadter, *The American Political Tradition* (New York: Vintage, 1948).

4. And this in turn rests upon a fundamental ambivalence about equal dignity of humans under God, or equality of all desires and goods. John Locke is the true origin of the tensions and conflicts of interpretation and practice. See L. Strauss, *Natural Right and History* (Chicago: University of Chicago Press, 1951), 202–50; J. Tully, *A Discourse on Property* (Cambridge: Cambridge University Press, 1980).

5. A. MacIntyre, *After Virtue* (Notre Dame, Ind.: Notre Dame University Press, 1981), 228–33.

6. P. Sigmund, "Maritain on Politics," *Understanding Maritain* (Macon, Ga.: Mercer University Press, 1987), 153–55; for a discussion of the Catholic political tradition see H. Rommen, *The State in Catholic Thought* (St. Louis: Herder, 1947), 483–503.

7. A. Kolnai, "The Synthesis of Christ and the Anti-Christ," *Integrity* V (1951) 40–45. See also, L. Strauss, *What Is Political Philosophy?* (New York: Free Press, 1959), 306–11, and E. Goerner, "Aristocracy and Natural Right," *The American Journal of Jurisprudence* XVII (1972): 1–13.

8. Found in *Ransoming the Time*, trans. H. Binsse (New York: Charles Scribner's Sons, 1941), 1–32. It is a much-neglected essay. A nice treatment is found in Donald Gallagher's introduction to the reissue of *Christianity and Democracy and Rights of Man and Natural Law* (San Francisco: Ignatius Press, 1986), xxviii–xxxii.

9. *Person and the Common Good*, trans. J. J. Fitzgerald (Notre Dame, Ind.: University of Notre Dame Press, 1966). *An Introduction to Philosophy*, trans. E. I. Watkin (New York: Sheed and Ward, 1962); see especially section on nominalism and realism, 111–13.

10. "Human Equality," 4–5.

11. Aristotle, *Politics*, 1255b1.

12. Simon, *Philosophy of Democratic Government*, 196, 230–59.

13. "Human Equality," 14.

14. See MacIntyre, *op. cit.*; M. Sandel, *Liberalism and Its Critics*, (New York: Cambridge University Press, 1984).

15. "Human Equality," 16. See *Three Reformers*, (New York: Scribner's, 1929), 130, 140, 145.

16. *Nic. Ethics*, VIII, 1, 1155a20.

17. Thomas Aquinas, *Summa Theologica*, I, 85, 7; I, 47, 2.

18. "*Habitus* are, as it were, metaphysical titles of nobility, and as much an innate gifts they make for inequality among men." Found in *Art and Scholasticism and the Frontiers of Poetry*, trans. by J. Evans (Notre Dame, Ind.: University of Notre Dame Press, 1962), 11.

19. See *Three Reformers*, 145–46. The order of grace is said to reverse the positions of the humble and the exalted, "without doing any hurt to the order and hierarchies of nature."

20. See D. Gallagher, "Introduction," to *Christianity and Democracy and the Rights of Man and Natural Law*, xxviii.

21. *Rights of Man and Natural Law*, 51–52.

22. *Integral Humanism*, trans. J. Evans (Notre Dame, Ind.: University of Notre Dame Press, 1973), 196–99.

23. J. Maritain, *On the Philosophy of History*, trans. J. Evans (New York: Charles Scribner's Sons, 1957), 43–57. See Thomas Flynn, "Time Redeemed: Maritain's Christian Philosophy of History," in *Understanding Maritain*, 307–24.

24. *Philosophy of Democratic Government*, 130. See J. Maritain, *Man and the State* (Chicago: University of Chicago Press, 1951), 68.

25. Maritain, *Man and the State*, 205. See also L. Strauss, *What Is Political Philosophy*, 309, and Aristotle, *Nic. Ethics*, 1117b10.

26. Maritain, *Man and the State*, 223.

27. Maritain, *Man and the State*.

28. Maritain, *Man and the State*, 252, 137.

29. Maritain, *Man and the State*, 98.

30. Aristotle, *Politics*, III, 6–17.

31. Tocqueville, *Democracy in America*, 198.

32. For a biography and bibliography see A. Kolnai, *Ethics, Value and Reality*, introduction by Bernard Williams and David Wiggins (Indianapolis: Hackett Publishing Co., 1978). For the review of Maritain, see "The Synthesis of Christ and the Anti-Christ," *Integrity* V (1951): 40–45; "The Meaning of the Common Man," *Thomist* (1949): 272–335; "Privilege and Liberty," *Universite Laval Theologique et Philosophique* V (1949): 66–110. See also, his *War against the West* (New York: Viking Press, 1939).

33. Kolnai, "The Synthesis of Christ and the Anti-Christ," *Integrity* V (1951) 41.

34. R. Kirk, "Introduction," *The Portable Conservative Reader* (New York: Viking Press, 1982), xv–xviii.

35. Kolnai, "Privilege and Liberty," 88–89.

36. Kolnai, "The Meaning of the Common Man," 273. In a similar vein see L. Strauss, *The City and Man* (Chicago: University of Chicago Press, 1964), 4–5. Also, A. Solzhenitsyn, *A World Split Apart* (New York: Harper and Row, 1978).

37. Kolnai, "Privilege and Liberty," 93.

38. Kolnai, "The Meaning of the Common Man," 274.

39. "It is indubitably true that a system of government in which the 'plain man' as such 'has a say' is intrinsically better than government by an esoteric caste of public officials no matter how well bred, 'cultured' or 'public spirited.' This is what perennially validates Democracy in the sane sense of the term, as contrasted to its erection into a false religion of secular messianism. Democracy, in that same sense, means participation at various levels of the broad strata of the people in the shaping of public policy." Kolnai, "The Meaning of the Common Man," 309.

40. Kolnai, "Privilege and Liberty," 97–98.

41. Kolnai, "Privilege and Liberty," 86–87.

42. "A society in which liberty is to thrive can only be a society rich in privileges, affording manifold means of redress and opportunities (not devised in the spirit bent

upon effacing the framework of privileges) to the 'underprivileged': a society capitalistic in the sense of containing and recognizing finite power factors and formative influences in their own right, besides state power and the prevailing mood of the collective; a society ennobled and oriented by a plural system of 'hierarchies' pervading it with supra-social value references as contrasted with its totalitarian self- worship—hierarchies limited in their scope, but also sustained, by their mutual action and interpenetration, and again balanced by, but on their part helping to support and vitalize (as social realities), the constitutional design of public power, the validity of universal moral law, the protection of general human and civil rights, and the plane of Christian equality among men." Kolnai, "Privilege and Liberty," 96.

43. Kolnai, "The Meaning of the Common Man"; see also "Privilege and Liberty," 72–73.

44. Kolnai, "The Meaning of the Common Man," 288–89.

45. Rommen, The State in Catholic Thought, 500.

46. Tocqueville, Democracy in America, 695.

CHAPTER TEN

~

Aurel Kolnai and the Metaphysics of Political Conservatism

The political thought of Aurel Kolnai is difficult to classify. He identifies himself as a "conservative" and that designation is apt; but it is of course terribly vague and subject to emotive connotations and partisan distortions. The American landscape alone is filled with a wide spectrum of "conservative thought;"[1] and when one adds the British and continental varieties the term conservative no longer holds a coherent center of meaning. The purpose of this chapter is in part to outline and display the unique brand of conservatism that marks Aurel Kolnai. It bears some affinities to Alexis de Tocqueville and Edmund Burke, and shows the imprint of G. K. Chesterton, but it bears its own distinctive mark. This is due in part to Kolnai's philosophical method that is neither textual, nor sociological, nor historical. It uses linguistic analysis but soon passes into a phenomenological approach, ultimately yielding a metaphysical perspective. I shall say a word about his method in due course, but first, further elaboration on Kolnai's conservatism, which I have labeled a "metaphysical" conservatism. I mean by this that his analysis arrives at a very fruitful notion of "participation" by which he penetrates the ideological core of modern liberalism and at the same time retrieves the basic principles of premodern political philosophy, which become a most flexible and adroit tool for analysis and open to various applications.

The metaphysical perspective is not that of an a priori system, nor is it a detached abstract system which he brings to bear on politics; rather we find in Kolnai a man of unique political experience who through keen observation and reflection arrives at some essential core principles of political life. In a statement of method Kolnai said that his was a "phenomenological temper averse to speculative dogmatism but in revolt against the tyranny of the positivisitic, monistic, and naturalistic outlook."[2] "Let the phenomena speak" Kolnai elsewhere counsels.[3] And indeed it is to phenomena that Kolnai's keen mind tends—the irreducible and diverse strands of a rich and broad human experience that characterize his own life's journey. His own statement of nationality reflects this broad experience: "Until 1929, Hungarian; 1929–1938, Austrian; thereafter stateless; 1951–1962, Canadian; thereafter British."[4] He wrote numerous articles in various languages attending to particular political issues of the day. His massive work *War against the West* is an intricate exploration of particular Nazi writings, persons, and proposals.[5] Kolnai knew politics first hand and from the front seat. He was well acquainted with its various forms, its different appearances, and the distinctness of its ontological texture, as distinct from ethics per se, art, religion, etc. So Kolnai's metaphysics of conservatism is well grounded in human experience and aided by careful analysis of precise meanings. Yet his political philosophy is a bold and daring attempt to view political life in its metaphysical depth.

In addition to metaphysical depth, Kolnai's political thought achieves a high degree of purity and freedom from cant and political slogan. This is not to say that Kolnai is not a man of deep political passion; at times he engages in harsh critical judgment.[6] Perhaps his condition of being stateless for twelve years offered an opportunity for political detachment; whatever the reason, Kolnai is also a writer remarkably free of partisan spirit or an ideological program. He wrote a fine article entitled "The Moral Theme in Political Division," in which he explores the various shades of meaning and connotations of the terms "right" and "left" as they pertain to morality.[7] From reading this article, one could not tell where Kolnai himself stands; he views them as complementary positions with different takes on the conditions and implications of morality, both of which have strengths and weaknesses. Let the "phenomena speak" Kolnai counsels. From other writings, as we shall soon explore,[8] it is perfectly obvious that Kolnai considers himself to be a man of the right or a conservative; but he is well aware of the special illusions, shortcomings, and exaggerations to which that political side might fall prey.[9] To conclude this opening attempt at orientation to the political thought of Aural Kolnai we should consider his own qualification of his designation as "conservative": "What we have in mind is not, of course, a proposal to substitute for Western Democracy along with its ideological biases, a fancy system of Conservative Constitutionalism, nor a return to this or that specified stage of the past, but a suggestion to displace the spiritual stress from the 'common man' aspect of democracy to its aspect of constitutionalism and of moral continuity with the high tradition of Antiquity, Christendom and the half-surviving Liberal cultures of yesterday."[10] Exactly what is the "common man aspect" of democracy is the great theme of Kolnai's critical political thought, and the prospect of "moral continuity" the great theme of his constructive sociopolitical vision.

The core of Kolnai's philosophy, which we shall explore in detail below, may be stated in two broad statements. The first is that political liberty, and democratic regimes, requires a respect for various forms of "privilege." Indeed as he forcefully argues "Privilege is the rampart of liberty, —not the liberty of the 'privileged' only, but of all classes of the people, of the whole multitude,—because it safeguards the existence of relatively independent persons." And further, privilege inextricably entwines both natural and artificial excellence: "there is no 'natural' distinction which is not the fruit of various 'privileges,' and none which not generative of new privileges." Contra Thomas Jefferson, Kolnai seeks to demonstrate, not the need for aristocratic government, but the appreciation of diverse pockets of excellence, many of which have been sheltered in the folds of social privilege.[11] Kolnai's second basic thesis is that the hatred of privilege and hierarchy is the bridge to a totalitarian form of democracy.[12] In more poetic form, the thesis states that a "dialectical chrysalis is hidden from the outset" in modern political liberalism, which "ready to develop while feeding, by virtue of the original kinship of stuff, on the flesh of the host, may assume full life and cast away the carcass of its devoured relative." In more conceptual terminology he shows that liberal individualism united at birth with collectivism and Machiavelli, Hobbes, Rousseau, and Marx merely works out the logic of the democracy of the common man.[13] Or to reverse the metaphor, Kolnai said that "the graceful butterfly of personal dissimilarity can[not] alight directly on the drab fabric of social homogeneity" but it requires a "congenial framework of social hierarchy and the 'fields of tension' implicit therein" (CM 293). To finish the broad stroke of Kolnai's philosophy—as a post-war writer, Kolnai has the experience of Nazism directly behind and Stalinism ahead; but he foresees an eventual demise of the Soviet scourge and the same threat of political danger to liberal democracy from within. At stake is a "metaphysical substructure" of sound political order and the contrast of a "metaphysical subversion" (PL 75) of the highest order which comports not simply with a Hitler, a Lenin, or a

Mao, but an "inherent tendency toward anticonstitutional, monistic, to-talitarian types of power," which tendency may be discerned in America, Britain, or Germany (CM 317).

Hierarchy, Privilege, and Liberty

Kolnai's understanding of political life centers on the presence of social hier-archy and various forms of "privilege." He shows the vital connection of hi-erarchy and privilege to political liberty. This connection is historical, ana-lytic, and phenomenological. His vision of the best regime is not aristocracy per se, but some form of mixed regime which has the broadest possible par-ticipation of people but which maintains intermediate groups and sources of influence on social and political life which are independent of a central power—these groups and centers of influence he thinks operate through "privilege" and often exhibit hierarchical patterns of organization and oper-ation. Thus, like Tocqueville, he thinks that the existence of political liberty requires such things as intermediate groups, religious activity, and thoughts, sentiments, and mores that may counter the relentless trends of egalitarian-ism. To explore this area of Kolnai's thought we shall elaborate on his notions of hierarchy, privilege, and liberty.

Hierarchy

Kolnai subjects the notion of hierarchy to a thorough linguistic and phe-nomenological analysis. He explains the vital social role played by hierarchy. And finally we must understand a metaphysics of "participation" by which hierarchy plays such a vital role.

The notion of hierarchy is a complex one which includes quantitative (higher number), qualitative (higher study), social subordination of com-mand and obedience, social prestige based on excellence, higher forms of life and activities, and finally the notion revealed by the etymology (the Greek ιεροσ)—the sense of the sacred, that which transcends the human as outside and "above" man (CH 170–175). He also explores the metaphor of vertical-ity and its contrasting meanings of height and depth; finally he considers the phenomenological approaches to hierarchy of values and marks "noble" not as a sheer vital value a la Scheler, but as a "compenetration between a con-crete being and some salient of vital, aesthetical, intellectual or moral val-ues" (CH 181). He finishes the phenomenology of hierarchy with a brief consideration of nobility in society; his thesis that "division, equilibrium, control and manifoldness of social hierarchies, positions of authority, power, rank, prestige, wealth, etc. deserved being respected and honored not be-

cause they warrant personal excellence but because they stand for a vital necessity of social order and are conducive to the recognition by and in society
of the hierarchical distinction of values" (CH 185). Kolnai admits both that
the presence of hierarchy is irksome in the "egalitarian atmosphere" of the
present world and that a democratic corrective is necessary for the aristocratic features of hierarchy as such. These political ties are explored in great
depth and with great vigor in his political philosophy. But by establishing the
phenomenon of hierarchy, Kolnai provides a certain grounding for the political analysis.

To begin with the social phenomenon already touched on above, the
so-called social hierarchy results from a natural leadership in various sectors of human endeavor. Kolnai notes that a noble is a notable—one who
is known and is not anonymous (CM 297) and therefore exists and acts
with a degree of independence. Kolnai points out that a notable is not restricted to "medieval feudality" or "modern age rural squirearchy" (CM
299). Notables are members of the higher middle class, urban patriciates,
and church organizations—as well as found in "military, academic, and
even trade union milieux." Such notables have a claim to social preroga-
tive or leadership in virtue of a "value intrinsic, distinctively qualitative,
pervading the essence of its bearer." Yet the sense of hierarchy does not as
such mean the noble persons are higher morally or even metaphysically
better than another; but they do serve as "a stimulus and a gross provi-
sional measure of value." The noble represents a higher value; there is an
exemplariness—such as the general of conspicuous courage, the scholar's
devotion to truth, the monk's dedication to prayer, the union leader's
commitment to justice, and so on. The idea of exemplar now strikes to the
depth of the metaphysical substructure of a well-ordered society. Kolnai
says that nobility simply means "the reception by society of a structural
principle of order that is not of its own making or positing but originates
in a supra-social quasi-entitative human value. . . . it is a recognition of
what is higher and better than its own 'thesis,' 'volition,' or appointment
may be" (CM 299).

This notion of participation is quite profound. It means that we receive
the good; we hold it precariously and tentatively; we are stewards if you will
of the good. The notion of participation implies analogy—that is, diverse
modes of fulfillment of the value, with various sets of primacy and secondary modes of fulfillment and responsibility. Hierarchy and participation may
mean that "certain personnel, by virtue of its very constitution and in a
sense penetrating its distinctive being as it were is primarily ordained to ac-
tualize and to cultivate a certain set of higher values; to attend to and to

serve certain aspects of the common good" (PL 72). This notion is embodied by the professions. The importance is that there are higher values—indeed the noble stands for the idea of "man's participation in values higher than those universally and actually obtainable for man, and with it, Man's bondage to an objective order of natural being which essentially and metaphysically surpasses his power and outranges his sovereignty" (CM 302; PL 73). At the end of the day "we are merely creatures and guests of God even on earth, not in any sense claimants on Him . . . and we are also ineliminably and most fortunately for us all, beneficiaries and benefactors, servants and masters, pupils and teachers, imitators and exemplars of one another . . . always in a more proper sense receivers and followers than as 'privileged' spenders or leaders" (PL 70). Response not fiat is the primary gesture of man. The notion of hierarchy then leads to that of privilege.

Privilege

The notion of privilege parallels that of hierarchy. Kolnai says that "privilege means the social projection, institutional recognition, traditional embodiment of the essentially insurmountable dividedness, imperfection and subjectivity (in the face of a transcendent Object and Good) of Man" and a correction of our smallness and fallenness—in fact, he says, very few or rather "very many men in different ways transcend the common level" and those who have achieved in some limited respect may be their instrumentality have others reach out "beyond their own immediate possession or proper nature and enrich themselves" (PL 69). What Kolnai has in mind here by privilege would be something like privilege of rank, privilege of attaining a social position such as a tenured faculty member, member of the bar, physician; or alternatively students at a college, traders in a market, and so on. They are able to carry on their business or profession without external interference and to gain access to the information, tools, etc. which they need to perform such activities. It is the very independence of the actual will or appetites of society that allows the privilege to serve such an enriching function in society. Privilege Kolnai says is an established positional value in society that relatively independent of the will of society, yet fundamentally in tune with it. Privilege allows "a pattern of concrete and specialized 'points of interblending' between private and common good." It implies intermediate groups, classes, bodies with their own "perspectives, insights and devotions, virtues and loyalties, responsibilities and vocations, standards of honor and accumulations of value" (PL 93). The vital functioning of a society will have many diverse such groups with their hierarchy, leaders, and privileges. But no elite group is the only one, nor does any such group excel the rest of society in all humanly relevant values and achievements. Not every group will be equal in all respects, nor will every individual be equal in all respects as they are members in various groups and participate at various levels within each group. And as we said above, there is no natural distinction that is not a fruit of privilege and none that is not generative of privilege (CM 289). So sons and daughters of a physician may have a privilege (social, not legal of course) to gain the habits and knowledge to enter medical school and become a physician. So too sons and daughters of an Ivy League school may have a certain privilege that leads to their entry into the same Ivy League school.

Kolnai points out that privilege derives from the notion of exemption from the law granted to a particular category of persons; they are set apart, not set above the law. "Privilege means in the first place, 'distinction' and hence limitation" (PL 99). Thus it is not simply a favor but a confirmation of the distinguished. Kolnai thus exhibits the connections between hierarchy (distinction), privilege (exemption), and liberty (relatively autonomy to act). The metaphysics of participation is how the various notions are united, and it is worth quoting Kolnai at length on this matter:

> In all true participation there must be present some element embodying a specific stress on the dissimilarity and distinction between what participates and what is participated in; this indeed is what Privilege chiefly signifies on the level of social reality, in a three fold sense: (a) as regards the participation of the privileged qua private parties, in public authority and rulership; (b) as regards the participation of the "common" or relatively underprivileged citizens in the possibilities and benefits of a more excellent mode of life as realized, adumbrated, or tried out by the holders—that is, the prime beneficiaries and trustees as it were of privilege; (c) as regards participation of human reason, by its proper use including its acceptance of the irrational and contingent as well as the fact of its own social dividedness in a Reason infinitely surpassing man's own. (PL 100)

Privilege therefore is not a position generated for its own sake or for the pleasure and private good of the individual holding the privilege; but it is a function of the common good.

Liberty

Kolnai understands liberty politically as a certain independence from the central power; it first appears as an exemption. Privilege serves as the rampart to liberty; again because of its social role and because of the metaphysics of participation and the dispositions it cultivates in a social body.

The historic root of political liberty lies in "privilege" and its extension (PL 89). There were privileges of the barons against the crown; or privileges of universities from political and ecclesiastical control; so citizens rights are in some way "geared to and dependent upon the subsistence of certain 'exemplary' privileges necessarily limited to a minority." In this way then privilege is the "rampart of liberty"—for all classes of people "because it expresses and safeguards the existence of relatively independent persons as quasi finite parts of society, as principles of the community" (PL 94).

A free society will be a society "rich in privileges, affording manifold means of redress and opportunities (not devised in the spirit of effacing the framework of privileges) to the 'underprivileged'" (PL 96). It should be a balanced society involving a plurality and limitation of all social powers and political prerogatives, and an ordering "in deference and reference to a Power radically beyond and above Man in his social reality, in his political dignity, and in all manifestations of his 'will'" (CM 274). Freedom is a "high good" because it is the signature of the "civic status of man." It implies a constitutional state because this limits the power of the state to allow manifold privileges to the citizens. Kolnai explains the notion of "liberty under God." It is an "intrinsically limited freedom" susceptible to be developed in concrete social institutions, and attached to a moral order in which man is a responsible agent (PL 86). Limitation and balance are essential to the very idea of freedom.

Kolnai's notion of hierarchy, privilege, and liberty does not at all entail an aristocratic society. He emphatically insists that the conservative concept of liberty entails a mixed regime, balanced in the fashion outlined above. It requires equilibrium among "finite, limited and unequal weights" (PL 90). In fact Kolnai sees Aristotle's mixed regime, preponderantly democratic, in a "spirit of time-conditioned, 'realistic' compromise" as the ideal. Indeed he says that the "participation at various levels of the broad strata of the people in shaping public policy is essential to remind the elites of their 'limits' and to restrain them from "one sided vagaries and predilections" etc." (CM 309).The high and low are complementary and not even a designation of better Kolnai points out in his analysis of hierarchy—the low view is as essential as the high (CH 174).

Thus Kolnai's initial analysis and proposals are in tune with liberal democracy; but as we shall see, they are counter to the stress of the common ideology, which seeks to eliminate all privilege, equalize all sectors of society, and use a central consciousness and will to bring about a more just society. Against this totalitarian tendency, Kolnai thinks the direct argument for hierarchy, privilege, and liberty is the only counter.

Equality as Identity

Beyond Envy

Why is the presence of "privilege" and "hierarchy" so irksome to contemporary liberal democracy? Why is it so relentlessly under attack? It is a truism concerning democracy that envy is a special problem insofar as it champions the many against the few. Indeed, Alexis de Tocqueville noted the various manifestations of envy in American democracy.[14] Kolnai explains that the dynamic of democracy springs from a source deeper than envy as such. That is, modern democracy contains a sentiment, an ideology, a spiritual orientation that go beyond the classic understanding of the relative claims of the many, or the poor, or a lower class against the few, the rich, the upper class. This new democratic spirit showed itself most distinctively, of course, in the ideological claims during the French Revolution. Kolnai is fond of citing Sieyes's formula "What is the Third Estate? Nothing; —What ought it to be? Everything;" thus Kolnai says "the quasi-religious impetus of Total Equalitarianism draws on deeper forces than envy and jealousy, competitive self-assertion, the need to overcome for one's inferiorities, and craving for material comforts" (CM 281; PL 90). The deeper source lies in the new metaphysical conception of the common man. Tocqueville also connects the vehement hatred of privilege with a new conception of man and its concurrent trend toward centralization;[15] but Kolnai's analysis is more trenchant, on the one hand being less sociological than is Tocqueville's, but on the other it gains in conceptual and phenomenological clarity.

At the outset of his best account of the issue, "Privilege and Liberty," Kolnai lists three false presuppositions of the new egalitarianism: (1) goods of society are solely goods for consumption, such that the possession by one entails the want of another; (2) strict proportional equality must obtain in the distribution of goods based upon some evident test of contribution to society; (3) sameness of reference, use, enjoyment, and immediacy (CM 68–69). The first false presupposition is the standard condition for envy; classical writers from Aristotle through Augustine and Dante noted the problem of reducing the good to the material and exclusive; and it drives in part the Hobbesian conception of the state of war.[16] This notion can be overcome by a number of political and moral devices including a more expansive notion of the common good, the expansion of the material goods themselves; the second notion is more challenging and starts to formulate the ideology of the common man. It does pervert the notion of justice, Kolnai explains, by taking a pattern of commutative justice and strict rectification and applies it to distributive justice (CM 282–83). Kolnai notes that greater access and opportunities for ascent, for greater participation in social benefits and privileges is an important part of democracy properly understood (PL 96)[17]; further, political democracy need not have a direct bearing upon socioeconomic, cultural, and traditional gradations within its prepolitical structures (CM 279). The notion of strict proportional equality will wreak havoc when combined with the demand for a central consciousness to determine and equalize the just shares; and this can be set in motion by a sloppy notion of equal opportunity and equal chances to advance and acquire privilege and social benefits. But the sloppy notion of equal opportunity often resolves itself back to elimination of legal bars to participation and means of encouragement for development among some classes of society. That is, even this presupposition need not drive the new vision of totalitarian equality. It is the third presupposition that is "more recondite" and "carries us straight to the core of the matter" (PL 67).

The basic false presupposition is that the common good must be interpreted in terms of "sameness of reference, use, enjoyment, and immediacy." This very thesis is hard to grasp at first, yet it has the farther-reaching implications (PL 68). It can only be grasp by way of opposition to the metaphysics of participation; it substitutes a metaphysics of identity. It involves the dialectic of modern political philosophy of individualism versus collectivism, both inextricably combined when drawn into the orbit of the identarian schema: "individualism prefigures collectivism from the outset and collectivism is only individualism raised to the high power of an absolute monism centered in 'all and every one'" (PL 68). The core notion is the thesis that "no man must hold more or be more than his fellow man" and if he does happen to "hold more or represent more" this be "on behalf, and in the name and jurisdiction of Society as an actual Unit of Consciousness, an actual Subject of Will entirely contained in the collective thoughts, moods, decisions of the moment." It is the notion of common man that allows this fundamental sameness of reference, rationale for centralization of power. The common man is more than a plaintiff, nor simply a victim of spoliation; the common man is the construction of preferable type of man, indeed "a hero, if not a new god" (CM 279). The notion of common man embodies the modern aspiration to overcome limitations and contingency; to become the master and owner and nature; to be free in the most radical sense of free from limitation of nature and God. Thus Kolnai claims that the "war against nobility" (hierarchy and privilege) is "in truth an essential and metaphysical rebellion leveled at something that towers infinitely above kings, dukes, barons, squires, factory owners, generals and admirals, fops or usurpers" (CM 302). We must therefore carefully trace the contours, origins, and effects of this notion of the common man.

First, Kolnai's attempt to account for political life in terms of a type of man hearkens back to classical political philosophy; Plato and Aristotle traced the essential formality of political life to the *politiae* or regime, which reflects a purpose and form of good life, as well as a distinct notion of justice. Leo Strauss explains this idea as follows:

> The character or tone of society depends upon what the society regards as most respectable or most worthy of admiration. But by regarding certain habits or attitudes as most respectable, a society admits the superiority, the superior dignity of the those human beings who most perfectly embody the habits or attitudes in question. That is to say, every society regards a specific human type as authoritative. When the authoritative type is the common man, everything has to justify itself before the tribunal of the common man; everything that cannot be justified before that tribunal becomes, at best, merely tolerated, if not despised or suspect.[18]

What is the "tribunal of the common man"? Kolnai provides a very sharp description. First, the common man is very different from the plain man, but may be rightly described as "any man"; second, the common man requires the sameness of reference mentioned above, entailing an equality of similarity or identity (entitative equality); third, the common man must be the generator of value, not submissive to any higher value. The tribunal of the common man, so constituted, must lead to the utopian goal of abolishing alienation and rely on the means of centralizing a mass consciousness and will.

The first point, that the common man is a "construct of subversive sophists and power seekers" and quite different from the "plain man" shows Kolnai at his best in attending to the nuances of language and phenomena of every day political life. The "plain man" Kolnai says has a center of gravity in "his practical concerns" but is attached "by firm if somewhat elastic ties to 'things higher than himself'" (CM 310); the plain man is embedded in particular background; the plain man may be distrustful of the elites; he may be indifferent to the concerns of higher culture. As such, Kolnai says the plain man is necessary as a corrective and supplement to the "higher" or notables of society (CM 309). In his phenomenology of hierarchy, Kolnai even points out the positive good embodied by the "low" view as well as the limitation of a strictly "high" perspective; thus the plain man "presupposes distinction [and] embodies a complementary relation to it" (CM 311). The common man, on the other hand, is what philosophers now call the "unencumbered self"—Kolnai says this "anyone" implies a standard "without the implication of either mature personal judgment or a particular creed or tradition which most members of a community happen to share. It is precisely this foundation of an empty humanistic 'universality' in the sense of 'any-oneness' upon which this 'creed' the cult of the Common Man and the mentality bred by that cult, is erected" (CM 323). He is indeed not a notable (without distinctions of wealth or social position) but can be "anyman." Any particular commitment or perspective is a limit to his commonness. He is not only distrustful of power, but is intolerant and covetous of the higher ranks. He cannot appreciate the meaning of any ideal point of view "not assimilable to his welfare" (CM 310).

Second, the tribunal of common man requires that sameness of reference for all benefits and achievements. This encourages and breeds a reductionist and materialist ethos; only with a uniform scale of value, identical standards of value and "habits of valuation" can there be quantification, "calculation and functional regulation" (CM 290). The subtle, the immaterial, the qualitative are soon lost. In addition, the notion of equal opportunity or equal chance leads to a positing of similarity: "once we fall prey to the illusive ideal of an absolute 'formal' equality, that is, of a neutral and homogeneous medium of equal 'rights' and 'chances'—we cannot help sliding down the path that leads to the abyss of material equality, with its concomitants of an impoverishing, oppressing, suffocating and deadening uniformity." Indeed, it is the contradiction between the claim of formal equality and the absence of social or material equality that long gave fertile ground for Marxist critiques of bourgeois society. This antinomy is rooted in the role of contingency, limitation, and dividedness of the human condition; it is only the structural role of privilege and hierarchy that leads us to give a realistic appreciation of this condition.

Thus finally the tribunal of the common man can brook no superiority: the common man is "Man Divine as mere man . . . Man above whom is set no Order, no Power, no Being essentially different from him, impervious to his reason, independent of his will; no social authority, therefore, either, which symbolizes, expresses, and fructifies, illuminating its various aspects and corollaries, this fact and this sense of metaphysical subordination" (CM 318). Indeed, Kolnai sees the political power of the common man become but "the ensemble of human consciousness moving and decreeing in complete unison throughout all individual minds" (CM 319), or again, the common man must represent "humanity pure and simple, sheer humanity" such that "all particular determination must be broken up [as] it implies Man's creaturely limitation" (CM 281). The metaphysics of participation must be replaced by a metaphysics of identity: the tribunal of the common man is just the standard of the good, the maker of right. If hierarchy and privilege stand for "submission of man to what is highest in man" (participation), then equality of the common man proclaims the "equal and joint sovereignty of men" and speaks the idiom of identity which taunts "man with the mirage of 'positing' and 'generating' reality, including his own, of absorbing the infinite into one human consciousness, of supplanting or indeed 'creating' God" (PL 73). The true goal of the regime of the common man must be that utopian goal of overcoming alienation.

Alienation and Utopianism

In a brief marvelous, but unpublished, essay entitled "Utopia and Alienation" Kolnai attacks this issue directly. Utopia is defined as "Life without alienation." Alienation is man's "being confronted with what is not himself: the landscape of Alteriety which constitutes his world." In fine phenomenological style Kolnai lists out various features of alienation: objective categories; works of man; distinctness of human wills and their precarious harmony; the caducity of individual life; the "very fact of conscience; problematicity of practice; contingency of social process." Each is elaborated upon. But in the core, alienation means "man's dependence on human reality that is not the expression of his mind and will" nor the expression of "any self-identical and unitary human essence and will with which he may identify himself." He goes on to expound on the utopian temper which is hypersensitive to alienation. This is the tribunal of the common man.

The secret motive beyond envy lashes out at hierarchy and privilege because of the sheer otherness, alterity, of them, that is the contingency and divideness of the social reality. It is not masterable or controllable by the immediate reason and will of the common man. Therefore the ideology leads to an "active suppression" of what is alien to self; this suppression may involve branding the other as an outcast or pariah, or an "immature" section of mankind in need of reeducation. Kolnai observes that every human face in which the common man cannot recognize his own reflection is "crazy" or "uncanny" (PL 75–76). Hierarchy and privilege are most irksome in their claim to represent some higher demand and its fragility and tentativeness to human possession. The superior or higher must be brought down and neutralized; that is, whereas the "plain man" may register some indifference or avoid contact with the higher claim, the common man must either eliminate them, or better yet, "annex" and "remodel them" thereby bending them to "the measure of his requirements, with the pretension of thus enhancing and intrinsically improving them" (PL 70, see also CM 311). For example, the institutions of religion and education are particular vulnerable to the process of annexation and remodeling. The idea of the common man as just "anyone" means that "any subjectivity as such is—equivalently to others—a judge of truth, and similarly any human need an immediate sovereign determinant of the good" (PL 76). The rampant spread of subjectivism and relativism in ethical thought reflects this trend—"who is to say what is right or wrong?" since anyone's judgment is as good as anothers; and so too the notion of a therapeutic society places any felt need as a prima facie right to be reckoned with. Kolnai perceptively notes that unity becomes a "self contained theme of society" no longer is it "a function of the convergence of minds towards a transcendent cause, measure and end" (PL 77). Thus religious differences do not require true civility and dialogue, but rather such differences are suppressed as divisive or are remodeled along the lines of a new age substitute for religion, a generic unifying spirituality that substitutes for divided, particular faith traditions.[19] The utopian goal is that of a "tensionless common subjectivity" (CM 320) and this means the destruction of any "objectivization" be it religious, philosophical, juridical, or social. This goal reflects the metaphysics of identity.

Participation presupposes division and contingency, form and limitation; man receives the good and the standard and in turns renders an appreciative response; there is an acknowledgment of the tentative hold on the higher value; and an acknowledgment of realities beyond self, higher than self, such as common good, human good, etc. The metaphysics of identity, on the other hand, projects human mastery and unity, and progress and emancipation. It is by the fusion of all into one, the mediate into the immediate, that such mastery and emancipation appear possible. But in fact, Kolnai considers this utopian projection to be an "impossibility on the border of the 'analytic' and empirical"—it violates the "basic constitution of man" and leads to an "incurable self-contradiction."[20] The violation of human nature involves the very requirement of an object for human activities of "love, fight, curiosity, understanding, virtue, possessions, rank, equalization, conquest, adaptation;" and further "alienation constitutes a fount of pleasure, thrill, happiness, vitality, [and] sense of being alive." As Kolnai explains it in his published work:

> By claiming Identity, we stop ourselves, as it were from participation; by asserting man's absolute and all-comprehensive Actuality we foil the manifold real potentialities in man which can only thrive in spheres remote from a totalitarian concentration on the evident needs of the moment, and prevent them from actualization; by "emancipating" man from "divisions," "tensions," "contradictions," *Verdinglichen* and "alienations" that are inherent in his natural condition we isolate, "divide" and "alienate" him integrally from his proper humanity, set him against whatever represents the reality of freedom

and dignity—of nobility and sovereignty, of virtue and wisdom, of perfection and progress—within him (and can never be simply he, anymore than his) and reduce him to an abject Thing while inflating him into a self styled Deity. (PL74)

The violation of human constitution leads to the great contradiction: it leads to a super-alienation, it requires an all-powerful central consciousness which can overcome the alienation and rectify the injustices of privilege and liberty.

The Central Consciousness
We return full circle now to Kolnai's claim that "privilege is a rampart of liberty." Its destruction requires and encourages a central consciousness and power to achieve the utopian goal of equality as identity. The step toward the utopian goal is already taken by liberal democracy when it proclaims formal "equal opportunity" and must thereby arrange for equal chances and opportunities—the contradiction arises because "an omnipotent leveling power itself needs a distinct supremacy over the power of the common man" (CM 289). How else shall we secure true equal conditions; who shall cleanse "the tissue of society" from power relationships ("relations of dependence and from 'vertical' principles of articulation." We must be led to concentrate power in the hands of "'One Subject' of consciousness and will: the subjectified, totalitarian collective; to make all social order dependent on the decree of one human agent supposed to incarnate the 'rational will' of 'us all'" (PL 95). Kolnai is most amazed at the ultimate willingness to be directed by the central consciousness; it amounts to a self-enslavement of man. This is the temper of the utopian mind.

The power must be centralized in order to suppress any "private factors" of public relevancy and influence because these would introduce privilege, division, superior standard, and so on. Kolnai views the tendency toward centralization as something more than a sociological trend or fact; it is part of the logic of the common man. The real object of hatred is the idea of "a concrete natural order of society's life; of an artificial texture of social relationships and appreciation's reposing on a receptive incorporation of 'natural' data of value rather than on the opinion and will of an omnipotent collective subject" (CM 301). Although liberals are adverse to totalitarianism and certainly to methods of terror, Kolnai thinks that the liberal has virtually become totalitarian in the war against privilege in the name of the common man. How the dialectic of the common man unfolds itself in the life of Western liberal democracy is our next topic for consideration.

Western Liberal Democracy

The Forms of Democracy and Models for Interpretation

As we emphasized at the outset of this chapter, Kolnai is not about a reactionary return or conservative utopianism; his sights were trained on Western liberal democracies as high historic achievements requiring support. His main concern is the preservation of liberty against the ideology of the common man. We can review some of the points made already. The historic roots of political liberty are to be found in privilege and the extension of privilege. As such privilege still holds out a standard for political liberty and shelters in it more good than bad. Kolnai does not have in mind an aristocracy let alone an oligarchic defense of privilege. The best arrangement for liberty lies in a mixed regime, first recommended by Aristotle. The form of mixed regime Kolnai has in mind is of course a popular democracy in which a broad strata of society are enfranchised and participate in the political process. It is a society that most of all reflects balance; political checks and balances as well as division of social power. And we should add, Kolnai saw capitalist and market economy as a support for liberty:

> Their power [capitalists]—obnoxious as are many of its effects, and howsoever desirable its curtailment may be in itself—is radically inseparable from a certain groundwork of division, independence and competition of the liberal bourgeois type, as inherent in the structure of market economy.

So Kolnai concludes that the case of capitalism versus socialism represents the case of "human dignity and political liberty, of Constitutional Society, as against the self-enslavement of man" (PL 95; see long note, p. 107).[21] At least Mammon is "an outgrowth of polytheist hethendom" whereas socialism amounts to a monotheist worship of himself.

Since Kolnai understands prudence and does not seek a utopian refashioning of Western liberal democracy, we must understand his work to be involved with the interpretation of those basic institutions and historic roots. At stake are two fundamental models of democracy rooted in political philosophy. We have given a brief sketch of that political philosophy which uses a model of participation, recognizing a true common good, indeed a good higher than immediate human needs and moods. Kolnai does not often refer to textual sources for this view. In part this is his phenomenological method. From time to time he does mention Aristotle and Aquinas. I have suggested an affinity with Tocqueville. His own formulation runs as follows: what has made "the concrete reality and duration of liberal democracy, with its manifold compromises and elements of sanity, possible and practicable has been

'Conservative'—the Christian, hierarchic, pluralistic, and realistic—as it were 'finitistic' substance of our civilization" (PL 87).

The alternative view he traces to a certain dialectic of individualism and collectivism that originates with Hobbes; he also mentions Descartes, Machiavelli, Rousseau, and Kant as sources for understanding the humanistic and rationalistic orientation that gives rise to the philosophy of the common man. Although Kolnai does not write as a theologian or as a Catholic apologist, he does see the role of religion as an important component in the new philosophy. In the more polemical "Cult of the Common Man" he attributes many features of the new philosophy to the imitation or substitution for religious concepts—universalism, monotheism, will of God, providence, and Christendom all have their equivalent in the new philosophy as totality, monism, will as God, planned economy, and collective security. Elsewhere Kolnai does allude to a "humanistic misreading of the gospel" that holds out a promise of a terrestrial paradise and a divinisation of reason and will (PL 90). And indeed interpretations of Bacon and Descartes have come to recognize this new interpretation of charity as benefaction for human progress.[22] There is no doubt that Cartesian rationalism has had a devastating impact upon political philosophy and this constitutes a great topic for conservative political writers like Oakshotte and Russell Kirk. But the key issue concerning religion is that of the question of objective value and moral obligation over and above human desires (PL 96). Hierarchy and privilege, the metaphysics of participation, reflect this philosophical orientation. Religion has an important role in being the most direct reminder of this metaphysic. Kolnai has written a very perceptive and careful analysis of the religious and humanitarian attitude, the details of which we need not belabor at present.[23]

He sees liberty as a fruit rather than the foundation of civilization; it requires a finitistic notion of the human condition and a scheme of participation. Or again, he says no organization of freedom can guarantee freedom. The most direct account he gives lies in the dialectic of individualism and collectivism: the mere horizontal limitation of freedom—that is, freedom limited by the equal freedom of others cannot support liberty. Individualism and collectivism are not "point and counterpoint" but "essentially the self same thing" in Hobbes, Rousseau, Kant, and Marx. "The combination of 'popular sovereignty' with the 'rights of the individual' is not a purely arbitrary mixture of two contradictory schemes, [since] they are both meant to express one basic dimension, respectively of the sovereign self-determination of man as shared equally by every man as such" (PL 85). Kolnai was struck by the claim of Communist citizens to have greater freedom; they meant that the state is not so limited by dividedness, contingency, etc. The habits and customs in liberal democracy are to reject the notion of central power; yet it is called forth by the notion of the common man as was showed above.

Kolnai anticipates the communitarian critique of liberalism now making its way through contemporary political philosophy.[24] The common man is naught but man, rescinding from "local, racial, cultural, professional or other particularizing and limiting data" (CM 307). He has a remarkably incisive description of what Rawls would later construct as the "veil of ignorance"— the neutrality and shedding of "pre-established biases" to use morality as leverage for moralization of life (MT 246). Beginning with isolated individuals, a collective approach is demanded. How will their actions and interests be coordinated without the central authority; the classical liberal notion of the market or invisible hand will disappoint because of the inequalities and privileges it will generate. The contradiction between formal equality and the material chances, with "no socially meaningful inequality of status, no qualitative 'pretension of value' to support it" pushes the dialectic of the common further toward identity and centralizing power: the "'liberal axiom conceives of human life as a welter of discrete 'points' which 'meet' accidentally as it were in an empty space . . . the assertion of an 'equally absolute freedom'—the divinization of the subjective will as such, in the sense of a rigorous formalism, independently of its intrinsic quality and its specific object must needs take a turn toward identity in the place of mere mutuality; toward an actual fusion in the place of harmony or arrangement" (PL 87; on formalizing morality see HR 446–47).

Present Dynamic

Kolnai characterizes the contemporary (1945–1970) dynamic of liberal democracy as a three fold situation: i. the reduction of good to desire and want fulfillment and the interpretation of freedom as a means for comfortable preservation; ii. the restless spirit caused by the gap between the formal rights and the material conditions and outcome; iii. the growing attack on the very conservative values (i.e., privilege and hierarchy as reflecting an objective, transcendent order of value).

Kolnai marks the beginning of the end of the dialectic of the common man the emergence of welfare state. We have become, he says, a democracy of wants. He was appalled by the American rhetoric of freedom from want and fear. The idea of freedom from want transformed freedom as a high good, a constitutional value for limited government, to the idea of freedom through government (PL 82). Government must do something to make me happy, equal, free, etc. The loss of an objective axiology, the reduction of good to appetite is also part of the issue (CM 315; 327). Of course the seeds of this corruption are directly traceable to Hobbes and to the revered John Locke.[25] The desire for comfortable self-preservation sets the dynamic for at least what Tocqueville calls a "soft despotism."[26] Kolnai says the common man "craves security, comfort, and the bliss of never being denied a need" (PL 82).

But it is the contradiction between the formal equality and the material conditions and outcome that creates an unrest and conditions the people to embrace more and more state intervention, uniform conditioning, in short, the soft despotism.

Kolnai's plea is for the recognition of the importance of conservative values, in the form of the metaphysics of participation, to offer any limitation on the power of government and the centralizing consciousness and will. The liberal democratic order reposes on preliberal axioms, conventions, and traditions that limit the excess of individual liberty and popular sovereignty, and it is not the automatic mechanisms of constitutional order.[27] The liberal state must destroy the very thing that gives it balance and sanity; the "liberal conception of society" cannot support and sustain liberty "except in a precarious and self-contradictory fashion" because it must rely on conservative values "unofficially tolerated yet continually harassed, and eaten away, by the immanent dialectic, the law of evolution, of liberal democratic society as such" (PL 86).

Kolnai and the Present Crisis

Kolnai's metaphysical approach to political liberalism and conservatism still provides a very insightful and useful heuristic for understanding the state of politics today. His core project appears all the more relevant today as it was in 1945. We must "displace the spiritual stress from the 'common man' aspect of democracy to its aspect of constitutionalism and moral continuity with the high tradition of Antiquity, Christendom and the half surviving Liberal culture of yesterday" (CM 274). We do this by emphasizing "Balanced Society" or "finiteness of all human power, the plurality and limitation of all social powers and political prerogatives; and the ordering of society in deference to a power radically beyond and above Man in his social reality." The defense of privilege and hierarchy is as timely as ever; it must be done with the same dialectic finesse as Kolnai's so that the case can avoid the inevitable charges of craven protection of interests alone. But the protection and support of true diversity and the vitality of intermediate groups was again a great concern of Tocqueville a hundred years earlier.[28]

But Kolnai's defense is more penetrating. First he criticizes the "Federalist Fallacy." The mere demand for more decentralization is not sufficient; if the overall cultural and mental climate reflects the homogeneity of the common man ideology; if the administrative tasks are given over to subsidiary groups while the central consciousness and will retains directives, standards, etc., then the federal scheme is of no avail. Further, the intermediate group and the communitarian goals of contemporary political philosophers still emphasize the voluntary, the free power, and the lack of verticality and nonvoluntary relationships. I think Kolnai envisions the wider range of preliberal culture that was necessary to sustain liberty. Although he did not have much to say about the details, Kolnai did anticipate the possibility of family relationships being undermined by the gender and gay liberation movements. He noted in passing that it is inevitable that equalitarianism would move into this area and thereby "strike even more fundamentally at the root of the concept of social order" and impose "artificial similarity upon natural similarity in the place of 'artificial' mores shaped in reverent awareness of natural order and elemental differences" (CM 301). The reference to the homosexual movement is more brief—but he says that sexual promiscuity of all forms, as well as perverse forms of it, symbolize both the absolute sovereignty of man over the universe—the negation of his creatureliness of the limits and laws imposed on him by a concrete order of nature he has not made—and the joyous descent of man to the level of "blind urges" and physical forces or pressures (CM 326).

Kolnai's analysis of liberal democracy in terms of the metaphysics of identity versus participation is remarkably rich for understanding the "culture wars" in America and the fundamental fault line which is uncovered therein.[29] Indeed, the role of a central consciousness has been assigned of late to the U.S. Supreme Court by a group of thinkers who argue the "judicial usurpation of democracy."[30] Justice Kennedy's recent opinion concerning the right to define one's own view of existence and meaning of the universe is a remarkable statement passing over to the metaphysics of identity and against hierarchy and participation in an objective order of value.

At the end of the day, Kolnai's account places education and religion as the core institutions for sustaining liberty in our Western regimes today; they have the "privilege" so to speak of "inoculating the national mind with the seeds of objective value-reference, of a vision of things 'sub specie aeterni,' of intellectual independence and moral backbone" (PL 97). At least for the United States, the educational institutions have abandoned the field to the common man ideology and the metaphysics of identity. Religion maintains a primal vigor, when it is not given over to the generic new age spiritualities or the therapeutic mentality. Kolnai's vision of a sound democratic regime depends upon a conception of "liberty under God" (PL 86). Perhaps for Kolnai's political philosophy to be persuasive a prior change in perspective is needed. It was Chesterton who had a decisive impact on Kolnai's religious thought and sensibility. Perhaps Chesterton is needed to keep alive that vision of the "ragged rock" of orthodoxy still balancing itself throughout the centuries. Aurel Kolnai saw it and by its light he relentlessly sought to show the imbalances of the present day and what might be their fateful consequences.

Notes

This chapter extracted from "Kolnai and the Metaphysics of Political Conservatism," *Appraisal* II no. 1 (1998): 26–36.

    1. See George H. Nash, *The Conservative Intellectual Movement in America: Since 1945* (New York: Basic Books, 1976).

    2. "The Concept of Hierarchy," in Aurel Kolnai, *Ethics, Value and Reality*, introduction by Bernard Williams and David Wiggins (Indianapolis, Ind.: Hackett Press, 1978), 167; he also says "Phenomena, especially such as play a great and manifold part in man's mental and practical life, after all do exist and cannot be explained away as 'mere appearances' or reduced to more massive and more universally indubitable data of experience," p. 166.

    3. "The Meaning of the Common Man," *Thomist* (1949): 275.

    4. Kolnai, *Ethics, Value and Reality*, xiii.

    5. *War against the West* (New York: Viking Press, 1939).

    6. Interestingly, the harsh judgment is often reserved for fellow Catholic intellectuals , such as Jacques Maritain, who would sometimes exhibit an excessive zeal for rapprochement with liberalism. See Kolnai's review of Maritain's *Man and the State*, "The Synthesis of Christ and the Anti-Christ," *Integrity*, V (1951): 40–45; and my article exploring these two thinkers entitled "Approaches to Democratic Equality," in *Freedom in the Modern World*, ed. Michael Torre (Notre Dame, Ind.: University of Notre Dame Press, 1989) and "Maritain and Simon's Use of Thomas Aquinas in the Justification of Democracy," *The Legacy of Aquinas*, ed. David Gallagher (Washington, D.C.: Catholic University of America Press, 1993); another of Kolnai's works aimed at Christian liberalism is "The Cult of the Common Man and the Glory of the Humble," *Integrity* 6, no. 2 (November 1951): 1–43.

    7. *Philosophy*, XXXV, 1960, 234–54.

    8. "The Meaning of the Common Man," *Thomist* (1949): 272–335; "Privilege and Liberty," *Universite Laval Theologique et Philosophique*, V (1949): 66–110.

    9. See "Privilege and Liberty," 66, on "reactionary aestheticism and fascist hysteria" and 99, on Platonist and romantic misconceptions of social hierarchy; as well as "Moral Theme," op. cit. on right-wing hypocrisy, inertia, and dangerous "holism."

10. "The Meaning of the Common Man," 274.

11. "I agree with you that there is a natural aristocracy among men. The grounds of this are virtue and talents. Formerly, bodily powers gave place among the aristocracy. But since the invention of gunpowder has armed the weak as well as the strong with missile death, bodily strength, like beauty, good humor, politeness and other accomplishments, has become but an auxiliary ground for distinction. There is also an artificial aristocracy, founded on wealth and birth without either virtue or talents; for with these it would belong to the first class. The natural aristocracy I consider as the most precious gift of nature, for the instruction, the trusts, and government of society." Thomas Jefferson, *Letter to John Adams*, October 28, 1813.

12. "Privilege and Liberty," 66, 86, 88; "The Meaning of the Common Man," 273.

13. "Privilege and Liberty," 66, 86, 88; "The Meaning of the Common Man," 273.

14. Alexis de Tocqueville, *Democracy in America*, ed. J. P. Mayer, new trans. George Lawrence (New York: vol. 2, part II, chapter 13, 537).

15. Tocqueville, *Democracy in America*, vol. 2, part IV, chapter 3, 672. Tocqueville discerns the same fundamental metaphysics as Kolnai—see for example his analysis and denunication of "pantheism" as the typical democratic religious framework, vol. 1, part I, chapter 7, 451.

16. St. Augustine, *Free Choice of Will*; Dante, *Purgatorio*, canto XVI; Hobbes, *Leviathan*.

17. See Tocqueville on two types of passion for equality, op. cit., vol. 1, part 1, chapter 3, 57.

18. Leo Strauss, *Natural Right and History* (Chicago: University of Chicago Press, 1953), 137.

19. On the issue of religious indifference and toleration, see Kolnai's "Cult of the Common Man and the Glory of the Humble," *Integrity*: 36–37.

20. From the unpublished manuscript, "Utopia and Alienation," 4; I wish to acknowledge my debt to Margaret Calderon Miller and her father Joseph Calderon who, in 1975, kindly introduced me to the writings of Mr. Kolnai and provided me with copies of some of his unpublished manuscripts.

21. On the inherent divisions see Michael Novak, *The Spirit of Democratic Capitalism*.

22. Descartes' discourse on method, part VI for example, as interpreted by Richard Kennington in "Descartes and Mastery of Nature," in *Organism, Metaphysics and Medicine*, ed. S. F. Spicker (Dordrecht: D. Reidel Publishing Co., 1978), 201–23.

23. "The Humanitarian versus the Religious Attitude," *Thomist* VII, no. 4 (October 1944): 429–57.

24. See *Liberalism at the Crossroads: An Introduction to Contemporary Liberal Theory and Its Critics*, ed. John P. Hittinger and Christopher Wolfe (Lanham, Md.: Rowman & Littlefield, 1993).

25. John P. Hittinger "Why Locke Rejected an Ethics of Virtue and Turned to an Ethic of Utility," *American Catholic Philosophical Quarterly* 64 (1990): 267–76.

26. Tocqueville, *Democracy in America*, vol. 2, part IV, chapter 6, "What Sort of Despotism Democratic Nations Have to Fear."

27. See George Grant, *English Speaking Justice* (Notre Dame, Ind.: University of Notre Dame Press) on the role of theological traditions that supplemented the threadbare philosophy of social contract of Hobbes and Locke.

28. Tocqueville, *Democracy in America*, vol. 2, part 2, chapter 5, "On the Use of Associations in Civil Life."

29. See Robert Bork, *Slouching Towards Gomorah*.

30. Richard John Neuahus, et al., *The End of Democracy? The Judicial Usurpation of Politics* (Dallas: Spence Publishers, 1995); first appeared in *First Things*.

PART III

~

Wisdom and Grace

Where is the wisdom we have lost in knowledge?
Where is the knowledge we have lost in information?

—T.S. Eliot, "The Rock"

The spiritual dynamism at work in human culture implies a twofold movement. First, there is the movement of descent, the movement by which divine plenitude, the prime source of existence, descends into human reality to permeate and vivify it. For God infuses in every creature goodness with lovability together with being, and has the *first* initiative in every good activity. Then there is the movement of ascent, which is the answer of man, by which human reality takes the *second* initiative, activates itself toward the unfolding of its energies and toward God. . . . A new age of civilization will realize again that the descent of divine plenitude into man matters more than the ascent of man toward self-perfection. In this new age the movement by which the human being answers God's movement of effusion would not take place, as in the Middle Ages, in a childlike, ignorant-of-itself humanity. Its new simplicity would be a mature and experienced, self- awakened simplicity, enlightened by what might be called a free and evangelical introspection.

—Jacques Maritain, "A New Approach to God"

~

CHAPTER ELEVEN

John Paul II and the Exorcism of Descartes' Ghost

In *Fides et Ratio* Pope John Paul II invites us to consider both the ways of faith and the ways of reason in overcoming the crisis of our time—the crisis of meaning and truth which has issued in human degradation—called "nihilism." This crisis of modernity has led people to face the untenable options of "a destructive will to power or to a solitude without hope" (§90). The roots of this crisis lie deep in historical decision and philosophical reflection in the encounter of human beings with their own conscience, with the question of being and God. The contemporary crisis recapitulates in the depths of the soul of modern man, the foundational and originating questions of modern philosophy. In brief, the crisis is spawned by a hyper-rationalist mentality which separated itself from the wisdom of faith, claiming for itself more than the legitimate autonomy of the ancients, but a self-sufficiency, closed in and hostile to faith (§75). The modern philosophy required the abandonment of a living faith, a faith that provides guideposts that beckon along the way and transform the interiority of the search. And by the great irony of history, the result has led to an abandonment of reason. Thus, by the same dynamic, working in reverse, a recovery of reason—a bold philosophical reason—is in some way connected to a revitalization of faith: "each without the other is impoverished and enfeebled" (§48). There are many ways to approach this rich text of John Paul II, the philosopher Pope.

I propose to read this encyclical as a venture into the philosophic quarrel of the ancients and moderns, a quarrel which has been engaged by such seminal thinkers as Jacques Maritain and Leo Strauss.[1] Specifically, I propose to trace certain themes in *Fides et Ratio* which we must come to identify as "Cartesian." We must then come to understand the nature of Descartes' quarrel with premodern philosophy and the problematic character of its resolution; this should help us to appreciate what positive gains were made by Descartes and what important things were lost. An authentic "postmodern" position must continue to hold these gains and losses in tension and perspective. That is, John Paul II's critique of modernity seeks to rescue the advances and aspirations of the modern age and yet to understand them in a larger perspective in which the wisdom of the ancients and medievals can be reappropriated and provide some ways out of the present crisis. In order to explore John Paul II's account of the philosophic crisis of the modern age, I propose to do the following: first, gather together the various signs of the times which indicate the crisis of modern philosophy and culture; second, match up such signs with their philosophic roots in the modern project as found in Descartes' *Discourse on Method*; third, review the important critique of Descartes made by Jacques Maritain, one of five Western thinkers put forward by John Paul II as an exemplar of the successful integration of fides et ratio.

Signs of the Times: The Crisis of Modernity

John Paul II approaches the crisis of modern philosophy in terms that Nietzsche revealed long ago—the crisis of nihilism. Modern man has lost a sense of the meaning of life and the cosmos. The very search for meaning is made "difficult and fruitless" because of the fragmentation of knowledge and the proliferation of theories (§81). Many can remain content within a purely utilitarian point of view "locked in the confines of immanence" with an indifference to the very question of transcendence and "ultimate and overarching meaning" (§81). John Paul II is concerned for the younger generation who find themselves at a loss in contemporary culture: "For it is undeniable that this time of rapid and complex change can leave especially the younger generation, to whom the future belongs and on whom it depends, with a sense that they have no valid points of reference. The need for a foundation for personal and communal life becomes all the more pressing at a time when we are faced with the patent inadequacy of perspectives in which the ephemeral is affirmed as a value and the possibility of discovering the real meaning of life is cast into doubt. This is why many people stumble through life to the very edge of the abyss without knowing where they are going. At times, this happens because those whose vocation it is to give cultural expression to their thinking no longer look to truth, preferring quick success to the toil of patient enquiry into what makes life worth living. With its enduring appeal to the search for truth, philosophy has the great responsibility of forming thought and culture; and now it must strive resolutely to recover its original vocation" (§6). For the sake of the young, if not for the older generations, John Paul II considers it a time to take stock of modern philosophy. If the path of modern philosophy has led to nihilism, is it not time to reconsider some of its fundamental principles, specifically its very self-conscious rejection of the ancient philosophy?

John Paul II discusses at least three points in which modern philosophy has resolved its quarrel with the ancients in ways that now have become problematic in their connection to nihilism. The three points are: (1) the emphasis upon subjectivity; (2) the method of separation and reduction; (3) the project of mastery of nature. Each of these items contributes some share to the nihilism of the present age. Perhaps then we could see better the need for: (a) a rediscovery of being, (b) a refashioning of an integrative and expansive approach to knowledge, and (c) a reaffirmation of a moral and contemplative good beyond mastery and utility. In other words, a serious look at the crisis of the modern age recommends to us a reconsideration of ancient philosophy as a constructive task.

It is part of John Paul II's great achievement to combine the old and the new, he has done so philosophically as well as theologically. The discovery of subjectivity he acknowledges to be an advance of modern philosophy[2] which "clearly has the great merit of focusing attention upon man. From this starting-point, human reason with its many questions has developed further its yearning to know more and to know it ever more deeply" (§5). But he adds that this advance has been "one sided," thereby obscuring other important truths: "Yet the positive results achieved must not obscure the fact that reason, in its one-sided concern to investigate human subjectivity, seems to have forgotten that men and women are always called to direct their steps towards a truth which transcends them. . . . It has happened therefore that reason, rather than voicing the human orientation towards truth, has wilted under the weight of so much knowledge and little by little has lost the capacity to lift its gaze to the heights, not daring to rise to the truth of being. Abandoning the investigation of being, modern philosophical research has concentrated instead upon human knowing. Rather than make use of the human capacity to know the truth, modern philosophy has preferred to accentuate the ways in which this capacity is limited and conditioned." Or again, John Paul II says that some moderns have simply abandoned the search for truth as they make their "sole aim the attainment of subjective certainty or a pragmatic sense of utility" (§47).

John Paul II uses the same language again saying that this modern turn leads to an "obscuring" of "the dignity of reason" equipped as it is to know truth and the absolute (§47). The crisis of modern philosophy is due in part therefore to loss of a sense of being, and a sense of the absolute in whose mystery we live and move and have our being. John Paul II does not of course deny that human mind suffers from limit and condition. But modern philosophy has so emphasized this aspect, that the very quest for being is atrophied—it does not "dare to rise to the truth of being" (§5). Using the poetry of Gerard Manley Hopkins we may say that the moderns have discovered how much our knowledge "wears man's smudge [&] shares man's smell; the soil/ Is bare now, nor can foot feel, being shod." And thus does the modern soul despair of the richness of transcendent meaning and objective truth. They do not see that "for all this, nature is never spent;/ There lives the dearest freshness deep down things," which nature and freshness reason could discover. Nor can they see anymore that morning of faith which comes because the "Holy Ghost over the bent/ World broods with warm breast [&] with ah! bright wings."[3] They look not to the wings of the spirit, neither reason energized by nature and its deep freshness nor the bright and warmth effects of faith. It is the loss of the élan of knowledge, the weariness with reason, which John Paul II seeks to counter and revive: "Faith and reason are like two wings on which the human spirit rises to the contemplation of truth; and God has placed in the human heart a desire to know the truth—in a word, to know himself—so that, by knowing and loving God, men and women may also come to the fullness of truth about themselves" (§1).

The second point concerning modernity, needing fundamental reconsideration, accompanies the first. It is the separation of thought from faith and a reduction of the richness of human experience. Philosophy rightly seeks its own "autonomy" or distinction from theology and so too are the various disciplines to be distinguished each from the other. Each seeks an authentic "autonomy" in the sense of following a proper method and tracing distinct lines of causality and intelligibility: "If by the autonomy of earthly affairs we mean that created things and societies themselves enjoy their own laws and values which must be gradually deciphered, put to use, and regulated by men, then it is entirely right to demand that autonomy . . . all things are endowed with their own stability, truth, goodness, proper laws and order. Man must respect these as he isolates them by the appropriate methods of the individual sciences or arts."[4] Thus, philosophy is rightly distinguished from faith and seeks to follow its own methods and demand its own evidence and proof. But in modern philosophy the quest for distinction has becomes separation. John Paul II calls this position a form of rationalism—the philosopher seeks to be "separate from and absolutely independent of the contents of faith" (§76). Complete independence or self-sufficiency are other terms used by John Paul II to describe this approach of modern philosophy. It is an exaggerated sense of autonomy.

It is a "false autonomy," say the Council Fathers, which seeks to cut off temporal and secular affairs from their deeper roots and ultimate goals, to suppose that created things do not depend on God and that man can use them without any reference to their Creator. Nihilism follows as a consequence of this separation, for without the Creator the creature disappears. One finds in modern method a dogmatic separation; a reductive approach which excludes the very possibility of faith. This is done because faith is considered to be a threat to the autonomy of the mind. The third factor in the crisis of modernity may well be the most decisive. It is the capstone; the other two themes, the focus on subjectivity and the reductive method, are often mentioned as dynamically connected to the quest for mastery over nature. The modern age is characterized by great technological progress. The technical advances grant what seems to be "a quasi-divine power over nature and even over human beings" (§46). The desire for mastery most engenders the crisis of meaning. Nihilism results from the denial of limitation, ethical principle, and a higher being. The technological mentality moves away from "contemplative truth," abandons the search for ultimate goal, and substitutes instead an "instrumental" conception of reason that promises to procure for man "enjoyment or power" (§47). In his first encyclical John Paul II mentioned this problem as indicating the crisis of our time, and he refers to that very text here in *Fides et Ratio*.[5]

The deep fear of technology bringing with it a widespread tyranny or degradation is one of the deepest signs of the times and an indication of the crisis of modernity. Philosophy must recover a "sapiential dimension" so that the "immense expansion of humanity's technical capability—[be] ordered to something greater lest inhuman and destroyer of human race" (§81). The great evil of this century, a century of technological progress, causes a sense of despair in reason (§91). We now have an opportunity for recovering the sapiential dimension precisely because we have come see the illusion of "technical progress making us a demiurge, single handedly and completely taking charge of destiny."[6] These three themes resound throughout *Fides et Ratio*: the turn to subjectivity, a reductive and separatist method, and mastery of nature. It does not take too much reflection to detect here the presence of Descartes. John Paul II does not mention him by name, but this constellation of philosophical themes puts us on the trail of Descartes; and it is John Paul II's mission to exorcise his ghost.

The spirit of Descartes—subjectivity, rationalist separation, and mastery—continues to haunt modern and contemporary philosophy; now one, now another element may be denounced or shaken off by this or that thinker claiming to be "postmodern." Descartes is a favorite object of critique by postmodern philosophers; and yet they continue to employ one or the other theme. But it is rare indeed to find a bold thinker who would throw them all off at once. John Paul II urges us to do just that and begin anew in our philosophical quest for first things. In an official document of the church, it would be not be fitting to name names, but rather to sketch trends and identify principles. But we may surmise that John Paul II has Descartes in sight from looking at names he does mention favorably. Jacques Maritain is held up as an exemplar of a thinker who well integrated faith and reason (§74). We know that Jacques Maritain sketched out his philosophical project of recovery of Aristotle and Aquinas in explicit contrast with Descartes and modern philosophy. This is evident from his great work *Degrees of Knowledge*, to his treatments of Descartes in *Three Reformers* and *The Dream of Descartes*.[7] In addition to thematic analysis and the indirect link through Jacques Maritain, we have direct indications of John Paul II's concern with the ghost of Descartes in his more informal work entitled *Crossing the Threshold of Hope*. We find a striking similarity in the use of the three themes of modernity in the sections entitled "If God exists, why is he hiding?" and "What has become of the History of Salvation?"[8] John Paul II claims that the very demand for the total evidence of God stems from a way of philosophy "that is purely rationalistic, one that is characteristic of modern philosophy—the history of which begins with Descartes, who split thought from existence and identified existence with thought itself."[9] John Paul II detects impatience with mystery. The term rationalism embraces the first two of the themes mentioned above: the turn to subjectivity and the reductive method. The turn to subjectivity evinces a rebellion against our creaturely status and an attempt to overcome the distance between God and man.

Picking up on this theme a few pages later John Paul II claims that the very idea of salvation history is forgotten, obscured if you will, because of Descartes; while he does not claim that Descartes lacked faith or even sought to destroy it, at least we can say that Descartes created a "climate in which, in the modern era, such estrangement became possible."[10] What is this era, and what characterizes the climate hostile to faith? The new era is characterized by a "great anthropocentric shift" in which subjectivity and reduction prevail—the *cogito* as the motto of modern rationalism signifies the plan for subjectivity and separation—the Cartesian method.[11] John Paul II says that the trajectory of modern philosophy, anglo and continental—is but an expansion of the fundamental Cartesian position. John Paul II finds its root in the *cogito*: "by making subjective consciousness absolute, Descartes moves instead toward pure consciousness of the Absolute, which is pure thought." That is, compared to Thomas' philosophy of existence and God as *Ipsum esse subsistens*, Descartes unfolds "autonomous thought." Human thought must measure existence and banish mystery. Objectivity is lost in favor of human consciousness. Hence, John Paul II says Descartes put us "on the threshold of modern immanentism and subjectivism."[12] The transcendence of truth and of God are lost. As we have seen, these themes echo throughout *Fides et Ratio*. Now John Paul II does not name Descartes and the theme of mastery, but it follows close behind his treatment of Descartes as "father of rationalism." That is, the rationalism of subjectivity and reduction, is the rationalism of mastery. Thus in the following section of *Crossing the Threshold*, "The Centrality of Salvation," John Paul II says that the Enlightenment mentality does not need God's love. No one needs his intervention, he says, in a world that is "self-sufficient, transparent to human knowledge, free of mystery thanks to scientific research, that is evermore an inexhaustible mine of raw materials for man—the demigod of modern technology."[13] It is clear that John Paul II's *Fides et Ratio* seeks to reopen the quarrel with modern rationalism, with the Enlightenment mentality, which has banned faith and which is rooted squarely in Descartes. It would be worthwhile therefore to make a brief survey of Descartes' own account of this new philosophy, which created the climate for loss of faith.

Revisiting the Quarrel of Ancients and Moderns: Descartes' Discourse on Method

Descartes' *Discourse* is one of the founding documents for modern philosophy. Descartes surveys his training in the ancients and self-consciously proclaims the need for a new method, indeed a new goal for philosophy and all learning. With good reason then does Albert Borgmann, *Crossing the Postmodern Divide*, name the *Discourse* as one of three key works, the others being Francis Bacon's *New Atlantis* and John Locke's *Second Treatise of Government*.[14] Borgmann rightly notes that any attempt to get through the "post" of postmodern must first understand what is distinctively modern. Just the briefest review of Descartes' *Discourse on Method* will show us that the problematic of *Fides et Ratio* involves the way of philosophizing initiated by Descartes. The question of Descartes' deepest intention as an author, and the question of his relationship to the faith of the Catholic Church, is beyond the scope of this brief chapter.[15] But we can show how Descartes did indeed create the intellectual climate for the eventual loss of faith.[16] René Descartes outlined the philosophy which gave a charter to the growth of modern technological society in his *Discourse on Method*. Rejecting the ancient philosophy for its lack of effective control, Descartes says that he wishes to found a new practical philosophy; by "knowing the force and actions of the fire, water, air and stars, the heavens, and all other bodies that surround us, just as we understand the various skills of our craftsmen, we could make ourselves the masters and possessors of nature."[17]

Surely, John Paul II looks out at Europe and the West and sees that we are now approaching the fulfilled dream of Descartes' modern project. Descartes promised, as the fruit of his new philosophy, "an infinity of devices that would enable us to enjoy without pain the fruits of the earth and all the goods one finds in it, but also principally the maintenance of health."[18] John Paul II sees rather a society "completely centered upon the cult of action and production and caught up in the heady enthusiasm of consumerism and pleasure seeking."[19] Technology has fulfilled its dream, only to find a life now emptied of higher purpose or deeper meaning. Faith suffers in such a climate "free of mystery thanks to scientific research, that is evermore an inexhaustible mine of raw materials for man—the demigod of modern technology."[20] The Pope seems to indicate his awareness too of the source deeper than Descartes, namely Machiavelli, who counseled the mastery of fortune and chance and providence itself. Furthermore, is faith also not cast into oblivion in light of the other great criterion for the modern philosophy—mathematical certitude? In order to reach this goal, Descartes recognized the need to reform the entirety of education and the social role of the intellectual in society such that expertise would be more readily developed and experts be revered as great benefactors who are free to pursue their study. He evaluated the curriculum of studies in terms of certitude and utility: he sought "a clear and assured knowledge useful for life."[21]

Poetry, theology, philosophy, ethics, and a few other disciplines were cast aside in light of these new criteria of certitude and utility. In fact, the disciplines that would lay the basis for the experts, scientific studies, would have to be built from the ground up. On the basis of mathematical science, Descartes proposed his famous new method for the conduct of inquiry. It would begin with a universal doubt of anything not clear and distinct; again, traditional opinion would be swept aside in all areas in order to make room for the useful and certain knowledge of science. The certitude of science would be assured by the use of simple nature and forms such as principles of mechanics. In its streamlined form, the method for arriving at knowledge would follow the analytical method, breaking apart a problem into its simplest terms and then building up to greater levels of complexity. Descartes' project and method have been tremendously successful. But its success is marred by an ambiguity about its goal or purpose. For when Descartes turned to human production he praised projects that followed a rational and effective plan, whatever their end. For he admits that in the political order he must admire Sparta even if its ends or purposes were not sound. At least they were organized effectively. The crack in the system appears here. For the end is not subject to the same clarity as the method. The end is left ambiguous since it is not within the competence of the new science to determine it; as Richard Kennington puts it, "the utility goal can never be brought within the charmed circle of certitude."[22] Descartes simply adopts the lowest common denominator by appealing to that which is most universally desired: health and life and convenience of living. To cite Kennington again, "the benefits are as universally available to humanity as they are devoid of exacting duties or self-sacrifice."[23] But this begs the question about the nature of the good life. The technical skills appear to be neutral to an end, but, in fact, they point to one end and encourage us to judge in terms of a utilitarian and hedonistic ethic. The criterion for the new knowledge is certitude that entails a skepticism toward traditional modes of opinion and grants to the expert a special status.

The method is not only inherently set against tradition and opinion, it requires a reductive approach to the material in the name of "objectivity." And it further requires specialization and a narrow or partial vision in the name of competence. Most of all, the Cartesian project is problematic because of the ambiguity about the end or purpose. On the one hand, the expert must appear neutral; for the question of end or purpose is beyond his competence. This is the contradiction at the heart of the project. Every technique is put to use for some end, but the end is not determined by a technique. The expert easily assumes an end for technique by appealing to what people want. Thus, on second look, the expert appears as a humanitarian who simply appeals to universal human desires and passions. The expert is therefore unproblematic. But when it is seen that the method requires a reductive approach and that it encourages the lowering of human goals, it becomes problematic in the extreme. The reductive approach to human affairs is potentially dehumanizing and degrading. It may well lead to the "abolition of man."[24] Man no longer dares to know the truth of being, says John Paul II. This ghost of Descartes needs to be exorcised by a return to and recovery of the premodern traditions of the ancient Greeks and medievals. A climate must be restored in which we dare to seek the truth of being. Thus we shall finish our presentation with a turn to the philosophy of Jacques Maritain. Maritain took upon himself the task of working through the modern philosophy and finding those places at which the perennial philosophy of Thomas Aquinas, and Aristotle, could assist us in restoring a sound philosophy of being.

Maritain on Descartes' Fides et Ratio

Maritain provides a thorough and detailed critique of Descartes in *The Dream of Descartes*. It is beyond the scope of this brief chapter to explore the long list of texts of Descartes in which Maritain finds the deep betrayal of Catholic intelligence made in the name of the modern project. Fortunately, there are variations of his critique to be found in his more popular work, *Three Reformers*, as well as in his *Saint Thomas Aquinas*.[25] Maritain's general accounts of the Cartesian origins of the crisis of modernity match the basic account of the crisis of our time provided by John Paul II in *Fides et Ratio*. That is, Maritain says that the Cartesian heritage has bequeathed to us a distorted philosophy because of (1) idealism, (2) rationalism, and (3) dualism.[26]

These three problems bequeathed to us by Descartes correspond to the themes of *Fides et Ratio* identified above: subjectivism, methodological reduction, and mastery of nature. Idealism is the separation of thought from being, the very root of modernity identified by John Paul II in *Crossing the Threshold of Hope*. Indeed, Richard Kennington has argued that Descartes' *Meditations* is metaphysically neutral, that is, the precise nature of being human or the scope of nature and being themselves are secondary to the utility of our understanding of nature. Maritain pursues the problem in terms of the basic orientation of the mind to things. It is the angelic mode of knowing which can proceed as if independent from things, in a fully intuitive mode, with eventual power over natural forces. Although Maritain and John Paul II seem to think that the mind's orientation to being is the root issue for understanding the relationship of faith and reason—it is the second item, rationalism, which must be of more immediate concern. Maritain's account of this notion of rationalism is quite thorough and shows the reason why our intellectual climate is so hostile to faith. In his chapter entitled "The Revelation of Science," Maritain points out the reductive method of Descartes imposes mathematical intelligibility on all knowledge.[27]

The premodern tradition recognized that human knowing is diverse and requires various methods or modalities. It would be foolish to demand the same level of certitude in all matters (See Aristotle's *Ethics*, *Metaphysics*).[28] The mind has an expansive range of objects of thought, but not every object can be made to conform to the same method without suffering a distortion or obscuring of its true being. Thomas also discusses the divisions and methods of the sciences and he speaks rather of "modes" not methods of science, to indicate the need for the human mind to approach the levels of science in diverse, analogous ways. The third consequence of Cartesian philosophy, dualism, stems from the split between consciousness and body. It allows the body to be exploited by technical means serving the enjoyment of a detached consciousness. John Paul II argues that dualism has obscured the importance of virtue as a habit of personal choice and self-mastery.[29] Maritain previously saw the impending nihilism. Man has been "split asunder" and "nothing in human life is any longer made to man's measure, to the rhythm of the human heart." Man is at the center of a world "inhuman in every respect."[30] Maritain and John Paul II both see the greatest sign of the time to be this fear of technology. It is the confusion brought about by the originating principle of modern philosophy in Machiavelli and Descartes—the mastery of fortune and nature. The first work of renewal requires a return to moral self-mastery as taught by the ancients and medieval. Perhaps C. S. Lewis was not far off when he said that what we need is something like repentance if we are to find our way out of the modern crisis.[31] For grace (*fides*) not only presupposes and perfects nature (*ratio*); but grace also restores and heals nature. Reason will be restored by faith. Perhaps the deepest lesson we learn from John Paul II, Maritain, and Lewis is that the nihilistic spirit of modernity, the ghost of Descartes, can only be cast out by prayer and fasting.

Notes

This chapter extracted from "Fides et ratio: Exorcizing the Ghost of Descartes," in *Faith and Reason*, ed. Timothy L. Smith (South Bend, Ind.: St Augustine Press, 2001), 217–29.

1. See Jacques Maritain, "Integral Humanism and the Crisis of Modern Times," *Scholasticism and Politics* (New York: Macmillan, 1940), 11–32; Maritain, *Integral Humanism: Temporal and Spiritual Problems of New Christendom*, trans. Joseph W. Evans (Notre Dame, Ind.: University of Notre Dame Press, 1973); Leo Strauss, *Natural Right and History* (Chicago: University of Chicago Press, 1953); idem, *What Is Political Philosophy?* (New York: The Free Press, 1959).

2. See Charles Taylor, *Sources of the Self: The Making of Modern Identity* (Cambridge, Mass.: Harvard University Press, 1989).

3. G. M. Hopkins, "God's Grandeur," in *Gerard Manley Hopkins: A Selection of His Poems and Prose*, ed. W. H. Gardner (New York: Penguin, 1953), 27.

4. *Gaudium et spes*, §36.

5. *Redemptor Hominis*, §15.

6. "[P]ropter reperta scientifica et technica, homo veluti demiurgus assequi ex se solo possit sibique obtinere plenum suam in fortunam dominatum" *Fides et Ratio*, §91 (Emphases added).

7. Jacques Maritain, *Three Reformers* (New York: Apollo, 1970); idem, *The Dream of Descartes*, trans. Labelle L. Andison (London: Editions Poetry, 1946).

8. John Paul II, *Crossing the Threshold of Hope*, ed. Vittorio Messori (New York: Alfred A. Knopf, 1994), 37–41, 50–53.

9. John Paul II, *Crossing the Threshold*, 38.

10. John Paul II, *Crossing the Threshold*, 52.

11. John Paul II, *Crossing the Threshold*, 51.

12. John Paul II, *Crossing the Threshold*, 51; Cf. *Fides et Ratio*, §81.

13. *Crossing the Threshold*, 55.

14. Albert Borgmann, *Crossing the Postmodern Divide* (Chicago: University of Chicago, 1995), 22–26.

15. I wish to thank Cyrille Michon for raising the issue of Descartes' knowledge and commitment to Catholic principles, as indicated in Descartes' "Notes directed against a certain programme" (Cf. *Discourse on Method, The Philosophical Works of Descartes*, ed. and trans. E. S. Haldrane and G. R. T. Ross [Cambridge: University Press, 1972] vol. 1, 438–39). In this text he provides a role for the faith to give a negative influence, that is, reason may be used to disprove contradictions to itself. It may be close to but does not really reflect the Thomistic view. Cf. *Fides et Ratio*, §76.

16. I shall be drawing on many points which I learned from Richard Kennington, my professor at the Catholic University of America, from class and from his published articles: Richard Kennington, "René Descartes," in *History of Political Philosophy*, ed. Leo Strauss and Joseph Cropsey, third ed. (Chicago: University of Chicago Press, 1987), 421–39; Richard Kennington, "Descartes and the Mastery of Nature," in *Organism, Medicine, and Metaphysics*, ed. S. F. Spicker (Dordrecht, Holland: D. Reidel, 1978), 201–23. I take responsibility for this interpretation as applied to John Paul II and the problem of Catholic philosophy in the contemporary context. Some material is drawn from my articles "The Moral Status of the Expert in Contemporary Society," *The World and I* 4:8 (August 1989): 560–85; and idem, "Why Locke Rejected an Ethics of Virtue and Turned to an Ethic of Utility," *American Catholic Philosophical Quarterly* 64 (1990): 267–76.

17. Descartes, *Discourse on Method, The Philosophical Works of Descartes*, ed. and trans. E. S. Haldrane and G. R. T. Ross (Cambridge: University Press, 1972), vol. 1, 119 (§6).

18. Descartes, *Discourse on Method* VI, 83.

19. John Paul II, *Reconciliation and Penance*, §18.

20. John Paul II, *Crossing the Threshold*, 55.

21. Descartes, *Discourse on Method*, 83.

22. Kennington, "René Descartes," 212.

23. Kennington, "René Descartes," 221.

24. See C. S. Lewis, *The Abolition of Man* (New York: Macmillan, 1947), 80–91; Michael D. Aeschliman, *The Restitution of Man: C. S. Lewis and the Case against Scientism* (Grand Rapids: Eerdmans, 1983); Peter Kreeft, *C. S. Lewis for the Third Millenium* (San Francisco: Ignatius Press, 1994).

25. Maritain, *Dream of Descartes*; idem, *Three Reformers*; idem, *Saint Thomas Aquinas*, trans. J. F. Scanlan (New York: Sheed & Ward, 1931); idem, *Peasant of the Garonne*, trans. M. Cuddihy and E. Hughes (New York: Holt, 1968); see also work by Peter Redpath, *Cartesian Nightmare: An Introduction to Transcendental Sophistry* (Amsterdam and Atlanta: Rodolpi, 1997).

26. This is from his most thorough critique in *Dream of Descartes*, 130–50. In *Saint Thomas Aquinas* (58–59), Maritain works the trilogy of Agnosticism ("by cultivating a more or less refined doubt which is an outrage both to the perception of the senses and the principles of reason, that is to say the very things on which all our knowledge depends"), naturalism ("The mind at the same time refuses to recognize the rights of primary Truth and repudiates the supernatural order, considering it impossible—and such a denial is a blow at all the interior life of grace"), and individualism/angelism ("the mind allows itself to be deceived by the mirage of a mythical conception of human nature, which attributes to that nature conditions peculiar to pure spirit, assumes that nature to be in each of us as perfect and complete as the angelic nature in the angel and therefore claims for us, as being in justice our due, along with complete domination over nature, the superior autonomy, the full self sufficiency, the *αὐτάοχελα* appropriate to pure forms"). In *Three Reformers* (55ff) he emphasizes that the root of "angelism" is something that embraces all three in many respects.

27. Maritain, *The Dream of Descartes*, 37–42.

28. Aristotle, *Ethics* I. 3 1094b20–27; idem, *Metaphysics* II. 3 995a5–20.

29. John Paul II, *Reflections on Humanae Vitae* (Boston: Daughters of St. Paul, 1984), 36–38.

30. Maritain, *Dream of Descartes*, 146.

31. C. S. Lewis, *Abolition of Man* (New York: Macmillan, 1947), 89.

~

CHAPTER TWELVE

Maritain on the Intuition of Being

In *Existence and the Existent* Maritain says that an "intuition of being makes the philosopher."[1] In *The Peasant of the Garonne* his words are more emphatic. He says, "the intuition of being is not only, like the reality of the world and of things, the absolutely primary foundation of philosophy. It is the absolutely primary principle of philosophy." The intuition of being is really the key to Maritain's work; to his mind it is the key to St. Thomas and philosophy as such.

We must try to recapture that germinal insight which bears so much weight in Maritain's philosophy. He was fond of recounting numerous ways or roads to the intuition of being. In *Existence and the Existent* he merely lists some of these. For example, he mentions the way of Thomas Aquinas who grasped the being of things through an "imperial intelligence serenely relying on its limpid strength." He mentions also a "natural grace" at the sight of a blade of grass; the sudden perception of self; the sense of the contingency of the world; the inner experience of duration, anguish, or fidelity. Many of these concrete ways are fleshed out in other works.[2] He was fond of recounting his wife's vivid experience of self-awareness. He often elaborated upon the sense of contingency in his proof for God's existence. The writings of Bergson, Marcel, and Heidegger he used for the way of inner experience. And we cannot fail to mention his praise of poets like Wordsworth and Hopkins for their appreciation of singular beauty.

The following is Maritain's own attempt to render in metaphoric terms the intuition of being:

What I then perceive is like a pure activity, a consistency, but superior to the whole order of the imaginable, a vivid tenacity, at once precarious (it is nothing for me to crush a gnat) and fierce (within me, around me, mounts like a clamor the universal vegetation) by which things surge up against me and triumph over possible disaster, stand there, and not merely there, but in themselves, and by which they shelter in their thickness, in the humble measure meted out to what is perishable, a kind of glory demanding to be recognized.[3]

The act of existing in things is a "glory to be recognized." In each case of the concrete approaches, including his own metaphorical description, the intellect must "release in one authentic intellectual intuition, the sense of being, the sense of the value of the implications that lie in the act of existing."[4] *Existence and the Existent* is one such attempt to release this intuition and to unfold its implications through various metaphysical issues like act/potency, causality, and evil.

What are we to make of this claim to an "intuition of being"? Any claim based on intuition is immediately suspect to philosophers. Perhaps it is nothing more than "mere poetry." It bespeaks vague feeling or easy and gratuitous assertion. It is a term more suited to poetry, not the stern stuff of metaphysics and logic. Moreover, for Thomist philosophers, the question arises as to Maritain's faithfulness to the master. Is this notion of an intuition of being derived from or compatible with St. Thomas?

In this chapter I shall assess Maritain's intuition of being by examining its Thomistic origins and by noting the similarities and differences between poetry and metaphysics in Maritain's philosophy. I shall argue that the charge of "mere poetry" is formally incorrect; that the "intuition of being" as a fundamental habit of mind is essential to any Thomistic philosophy, as well as to any realistic metaphysics; and lastly, that the charge ironically displays a dissociated sensibility that Maritain sought to overcome.

The Thomistic context and warrant for the "intuition of being" is well laid out in *Existence and the Existent*. As a preliminary to the intuition, Maritain goes over the familiar ground of the role of judgment in Thomistic epistemology.[5] Simple apprehension abstracts an intelligible note from things and forms a concept. But the act of knowing must return through judgment to the sensible being in order to judge the truth of things. The intellect does more than contemplate the picture of essences in ideas: it must restore them to existence through judgment. The concept, the universal, exists only in the mind; what actually exists is a "subject," a being. The reality known derives from a "trans-objective subject." Thus the function of judgment is "existential": judgment "transposes the mind from the plane of simple essence of the simple object of thought, to the plane of the thing, of the subject possessing existence."[6] Judgment is fundamentally an affirmation of existence.

But, since existence is of another order than essence, existence is not an intelligible or object-like essence. It cannot be grasped conceptually, but only in judgment. The concept of existence cannot be visualized apart from being. Being contains within itself the two-fold valence of essence and existence, a notion of "what something is" and the judgment "that it is." In the intuition of being, the mind surges beyond the grasp of essence to the existence of things. But the existence of the being draws the mind to consider something more than brute facticity or a dark surd. The intuition of being grasps the formality of existence, a "super-intelligible" datum for the mind.

A difficulty in assessing Maritain's intuition of being comes in the interpretation of the nature of metaphysical judgment. As he acknowledges in a long footnote in *Existence and the Existent*, metaphysical judgment is a judgment of "separation." That by virtue of which a thing is what it is, is different from that by which a thing is said to be as such. Thus, the intelligibility of being is seen to be free from the intrinsic determination of matter; that is, being need not be material. There is a dispute among Thomists as to the conditions necessary for this judgment. Does it require prior knowledge of immaterial substances such as angels or God? Or does it require merely an understanding of intellectual immateriality? Or can it be derived from the distinction of essence and existence as separate intelligibilities?[7] Maritain seems to think that the last is true, and this has drawn some criticism, which has been directed also at many existential Thomists, who are accused of seeking to pull being out of a chair, somehow short circuiting the long arduous path to metaphysics. Others may reject this approach because it operates in the sphere of naïve understanding without critical awareness. The notion of being must be derived, they would say, from a transcendental analysis of the structure of human knowing. Others may even argue that the notion of being is derived from the Christian distinction between God and creatures, and thus the intuition is sensible only within the ambiance of faith. Although Maritain did intend the intuition to constitute the entry into metaphysics, he also considered it the formal habit of mind that must constitute the basis for any Thomistic philosophy.

The intuition of being is the beginning of philosophy; it is a "beginning" in both senses of the word, genetically and formally. It is the *arche* of philosophizing, as in Socrates' remark that "wonder is the beginning of philosophy." Indeed, the intuition of being is the experience of wonder at the "inexhaustibility" of the real and the "super-intelligiblity" of being. The intuition of being is first and foremost a habit of mind, a disposition toward the world that envelops the entirety of the intellectual life, giving it a certain tone. Maritain does not mean to suggest that all of reality can be seen at a glance or deduced from this simple but profound intuition, thereby obviating the need for any science or logical analysis. Maritain is not guilty of such romantic or *a priori* excess. Rather, the intuition of being is a testimony to the integrity and wholeness of things, the depth of reality that will always elude our final grasp, which yet gives the thinker a hope to inquire further, striving for greater integration of knowledge of the real. It is the source and inspiration of "Thomistic realism."

As a habit of mind, the intuition of being is the proper "dwelling place" or "modus" for any type of Thomistic metaphysics, and, as Maritain would argue, for any realistic metaphysics. By whatever process one deems metaphysical judgment to be legitimately effected, the effect in the knower is a habit of mind by which the intelligibility of being in "its full amplitude" is acknowledged. In the *Preface to Metaphysics*, Maritain speaks about the intellectual virtue of the metaphysician. In addition to the objective light constituted by the degree of immateriality that specifies a science, there is a "subjective light perfecting the subjective activity of the intellect, by which the intellect is proportioned to a given object, fitted to apprehend it."[8] I believe that this is a key to the importance and relevance of Maritain's notion of the "intuition of being." By a habit one is disposed to think or to act in a determinate and stable way; in this case one becomes disposed to recognize and acknowledge the presence of being and the full amplitude of being as such. Thus by whatever means one comes to the judgment of metaphysics the effect is the same acknowledgement of the intelligibility of *esse* as "the act of all acts" and "the perfection of all perfections."

And the intuition of being should be appreciated in the order of the formality, as much as in the order of the genesis, of metaphysics. That is, even if one is uncomfortable with the attempt to base metaphysics in an intuition of being, without the steps of natural philosophy or other discipline, the result of any Thomistic metaphysical system must be the return to the intuition as the stable habitual center of the intellectual life. We must begin with the "sense of the value of the implications that lie in the act of existing.

We have a further clue to the habit of being in the distinction between "*ratio*" and "*intellectus*" or reason and intellect.[9] In Maritain's account the "*intellectus*" is rendered as "intuition." There is textual warrant for translating "*intellectus*" as intuition.[10] Perhaps this term is misleading and would be better served by vision or understanding. Maritain would have philosophy begin with a vision, acknowledgement, or awareness of the being of things.

At the heart of the distinction is Thomas' insistence upon a nondiscursive moment in intellection. In addition to the complex apparatus of dialectic and abstraction, demonstration and reasoning, the human knower must be said to "see" simply. In fact, Thomas says that reason begins and ends with intellection; "*ratio*" is related to "*intellectus*" as motion is related to rest, and as the imperfect is related to the perfect, and even as time is eternity. The process of reasoning terminates in vision of what a thing is or the truth of some conclusion. Reasoning without some terminal insight, at least in aspiration, is nonintelligible in Thomas' scheme. All human knowledge, all human science, aspires to fruition in metaphysical knowledge. The labor of reason aspires for the intuition of being. Hence we arrive again at the dynamic character of the intuition of being as a habit of mind. For Thomas describes the relation of "ratio" to "intellectus" in terms of habit specifying a power. Reason and intellect are not two distinct powers in man, he argues, because the intellect functions as a habit specifying the rational power.[11] Philosophy as a function of "intellectus" is a contemplative act; the mind must be receptive. Maritain says "It is difficult to arrive at the degree of intellectual purification at which this act is produced in us, at which we become sufficiently disengaged, sufficiently empty to hear what all things whisper and to listen instead of composing answers."[12]

Thus, as much as Maritain insisted upon a "rational confirmatory analysis" of the intuition of being, he equally insisted that logical analysis alone would not yield the intuition.[13] Philosophy can neither begin nor end with the confirmatory analysis: intellect is related to reason as motion to rest. Analysis by itself lacks insight. Maritain admits that the intuition is beyond technical manipulation. The rational confirmation is a part of a way of judgment, a "via judicii," whose function is to go over the discovered truth and affirm its validity. It does not replace the original intuition or deductions. The explicit rational confirmation, as well as any sophisticated epistemological defense of realism, must finally come to the simple moment of vision. The mystery predominates over the problem. Being remains an object for "enraptured contemplation."[14]

Maritain warns of the two dangers of the average functioning of the intellect in our time, "mental productivism" and the "primacy of verification over truth."[15] Mental productivism elevates the sign over the reality known, as we take more interest in the conceptual apparatus than the real being made manifest by it. Similarly, the mania for an external process of verification and proof could also nullify the vision of being which comes from common experience. Maritain says: "We take more interest in verifying the validity of the signs and symbols we have manufactured than in nourishing ourselves with the truth they reveal." The intuition of being is first and foremost a habit of mind in which the encounter with being is fully appreciated and "suffered." It is a habit of mind rooted in pre-scientific experience. The contemplative moment is a habit alien to a scientific/technological bent of mind. Thus, the intuition of being is an antidote for misplaced abstraction. Whitehead speaks of philosophy as "the critic of abstractions," which completes them "by direct comparison with more concrete intuitions of the universe."[16] As Whitehead appeals to the evidence of pre-scientific experience and poetry, as found for example in Wordsworth, to refute modern subjectivism, Maritain would similarly find in the poet a great support for the recovery of a sense of being.

Maritain is quite adamant in preventing a confusion of poetry and philosophy. In *The Range of Reason* he remarks that, "if one confuses the planes or orders of things, if poetic knowledge claims to become philosophical knowledge," then both are spoiled.[17] On a number of points poetry must be rigorously distinguished from philosophy. First of all, they are entirely different orders of rationality: poetry is ordered to making, not to knowing. Its good is a work produced "ad extra," not a concept or judgment produced within for speculative knowledge. It is axiomatic for Maritain's poetic theory that poetry be held within the genus of making. When freed from this restraint, the poet loses his way. The very object of poetic knowledge is non-conceptualisable.

Thus, poetic intuition is a type of "divination," a knowledge of the heart; the intuition of metaphysics is an "abstractive visualization." Again, the poet engages his subjectivity and emotion as he grasps the world; the philosopher is more purely intellectual. Finally, the poet is engaged more directly with the things of sense, with singularity and particular things. Metaphysics is more universal and abstract. In *Creative Intuition*, Maritain gathers these ideas into a memorable passage:

> Poetry is a divination of the spiritual in the things of the sense—which expresses itself in the things of the sense, and in a delight in sense. Metaphysics also pursues a spiritual prey, but metaphysics is engaged in abstract knowledge, while poetry quickens art. Metaphysics snatches at the spiritual in an idea, by the most abstract intellection; poetry reaches it in the flesh, by the very point of sense sharpened through intelligence. Metaphysics enjoys its possession only in the retreats of eternal regions, while poetry finds its own at every crossroad in the wanderings of the contingent and the singular.[18]

Maritain sharply distinguishes poetry from metaphysics. However, we should not "run the risk of forgetting that though poetry cannot be confounded with metaphysics," Maritain says, "it yet responds to a metaphysical need of the spirit of man, and is metaphysically justified."[19] Poetic knowledge of the world is allied to metaphysics; Maritain says that the poet aims at "being." This is manifest in a number of ways. The poet is existential precisely because he must be directed to the good of the work; a concrete work to be made and "posited in existence." Further, poetic knowledge is existential because it must attend to the sensible particulars; it is less apt to be lost in the cloud of abstraction. By affective connaturality, there resonates "that which is most existent and most concrete in things in that which is most existent and concrete in the subject." Although Maritain's poetic is known most of all for the epistemological notion of the connatural knowing of the self and the world, his theory actually culminates in the metaphysical notion of the superabundance of being. The work of art to open out onto the world of being and presses to infinitude of being itself:

> Poetic intuition does not stop at this given existent; it goes beyond, and infinitely beyond. Precisely because it has no conceptualized object, it tends and extends to the infinite, it tends toward all reality which is engaged in any singular existing thing. . . . As grasped by poetic knowledge, things abound in significance, and swarm with meanings. Things are not only what they are. They ceaselessly pass beyond themselves, and give more than they have, because from all sides they are permeated with the activating influx of the Prime Cause. . . . I would think that this mutual communication in existence and in the spiritual flux from which existence proceeds . . . is perhaps in the last analysis what the poet receives and suffers.[20]

This passage from *Creative Intuition*, similar to a passage contained in *The Situation of Poetry*, corresponds very closely to a section of the *Existence and the Existent*.[21] He explains that the metaphysics of Thomas Aquinas is not essentialist, not centered upon static essences, but rather upon the dynamic reality of existence, grounded in a superabundant divine being. Maritain has discovered here not only the diffusive nature of the good, but also the relevance of process, context, and relation to our understanding of the being of things in the world.[22] Maritain exhibits in his poetic theory a notion that finds some affinity with Whitehead's use of Wordsworth. In *Science and the Modern World* Whitehead points to Wordsworth's awareness of "that mysterious presence of surrounding things, which imposes itself on any separate element that we set up as an individual for its own sake. He always grasps the whole of nature as involved in the tonality of the particular instance."[23] Maritain and Whitehead both see a positive value in sheer self-assertion and endurance of things and the relation of one to another. Granted, the two thinkers conceptualize the insight in very different ways. Whitehead uses the notion of "event" to name the actuality that emerges against the flux; Maritain, of course, retains the perennial notion of "being." But as mentioned above, both would agree that the "poetic rendering of our concrete experience" must not be omitted from a metaphysical account of the real. Time does not permit analysis and judgment as to whose account is truer to the concrete experience.

For its existential mode of knowing and for its grasp of the superabundance of being, poetry is salutary for philosophy given its present state. Although the essence of philosophy is free the poetic mode of knowing, the state of philosophy is another consideration. Maritain says that "to philosophize man must put his whole soul into play, in much the same manner that to run he use his heart and lungs."[24] The poets can enliven the metaphysical habit. The intuition of being may receive a deep confirmation, for example, in the works of Wordsworth, Hopkins, and Eliot; a similar concern may be found in the writers of the American South with whom Maritain was familiar such as Tate, Gordon, and Ransom. These poets are enraptured with being; they recognize that there is indeed ensconced in the humble things of the world "a glory demanding to be recognized." They give it expression through their verses and stories. Maritain remarks in *Preface to Metaphysics* that the metaphysician must be a sensitive man and "keenly and profoundly aware of sensible objects. And he should be plunged into existence, steeped ever more deeply in it by a sensuous and aesthetic perception as acute as possible so that aloft in the third heaven of natural understanding he may feed upon the intelligible substance of things."[25]

I shall end my presentation with a reading from Nathaniel Hawthorne, surveying his garden at the Old Manse:

> Speaking of summer squashes, I must say a word of their beautiful and varied forms. They presented an endless diversity of urns and vases, shallow or deep, scalloped or plain, moulded in patterns which a sculptor would do well to copy, since Art has never invented anything more graceful. A hundred squashes in the garden were worthy—in my eyes, at least—of being rendered indestructible in marble. . . . There was a hearty enjoyment in observing the growth of the crook-necked winter squashes, from the first little bulb, with the withered blossom adhering to it, until they lay strewn upon the soil, big round fellows, hiding their heads beneath the leaves, but turning their great yellow rotundities to the noontide sun. Gazing at them, I felt that, by my agency, something worthwhile living for had been done. A new substance was born into the world. They were real and tangible existences, which the mind could seize hold of and rejoice in.[26]

Hawthorne surely has the germ of Maritain's intuition of being in this appreciation of the squash's "victorious thrust over nothingness." An abstractive step or leap is required to form the terms like the diversity and autonomy of being, the superabundance of being and so forth. But I have learned from the Southern poet and critic, Marion Montgomery, whose work *Why Hawthorne Was Melancholy* I commend to you very highly, that Hawthorne was quite aware of the issue of being and the tragic presumption of men who elevate their mind to a point of denying the givenness of things and the common plight of humanity.[27] Hawthorne faced the specter of Emersonian transcendentalism, a form of idealism or "ideosophy," which seemed to be premised on the denial of the fundamental intuition of being. Emerson viewed nature as a "subjective phenomena," an "apparition" or shadow cast by the knowing mind. "Perhaps there are no objects," Emerson opines. "Once we lived in what we saw; now, the rapaciousness of this power, which threatens to absorb all things, engages us."[28] After witnessing the loss of the world in abstraction, Hawthorne attends to the lowly squash and savors the glory of its being.

Maritain, I think, would be delighted to have these prophetic poets return us to the savor of being as they call forth that intuition. They will strengthen that habit of mind, the habit of being. Ironically, the turn to poetry might bring us around to a more demanding metaphysics of being and a greater appreciation for Thomas' strict logic. The intuition of being—metaphysics or poetry? It is both; but let us distinguish in order to unite.

Notes

Excerpted from "The Intuition of Being: Metaphysics or Poetry," in *Jacques Maritain: The Man and His Metaphysics*, ed. John F. X. Knasas (Mishawaka, Ind.: American Maritain Association, 1988) 71–82.

1. Jacques Maritain, *Existence and the Existent*, trans. Lewis Galantiere and Gerald B. Phelan (New York: Random House, 1966), 12. See *A Preface to Metaphysics* (New York: Sheed and Ward, 1939) "It is this intuition that makes the metaphysician," 44. *The Peasant of the Garonne: An Old Layman Questions Himself about the Present Time*, trans. Michael Cuddihy and Elizabeth Hughes (New York: Holt, Rinehart and Winston, 1968), 110–11. See also, *The Range of Reason* (New York: Charles Scribner's Sons, 1960), 9.

2. *Preface to Metaphysics*, 47–51; *Approaches to God* (New York, 1942), chapter one.

3. *The Peasant of the Garonne*, 111.

4. Maritain, *Existence and the Existent*, 21. See for example, Joseph Owens, *An Interpretation of Existence* (Milwaukee: Bruce Publishing, 1968); John Wippel, "Metaphysics and Separatio in Thomas Aquinas," in *Metaphysical Themes in Thomas Aquinas* (Washington, D.C.: Catholic University of America Press, 1984), 69–104.

5. See, for example, Joseph Owens, *An Interpretation of Existence* (Milwaukee: Bruce Publishing, 1968).

6. *Existence and the Existent*, 17.

7. See John Wippel, "Metaphysics and *Separatio* in Thomas Aquinas," in *Metaphysical Themes in Thomas Aquinas* (Washington, D.C.: Catholic University of America Press, 1984), 69–104.

8. *Preface*, 45.

9. Thomas Aquinas, *De Ver.* XV, 1; In *Boeth. de Trin.*, VI, 1. pt. 3. See J. Peghaire, *Intellectus and Ration selon s. Thomas D'Aquin* (Paris: J. Vinn, 1936) and the author's unpublished M.A. dissertation, "Reason and Intellect in Two Texts of St. Thomas Aquinas," Catholic University of America, 1978.

10. See Aquinas, *De Ver.*, I, 12; In II Sent., d. 9, 1, 8, ad 12.

11. Aquinas, *De Ver.* XV, 1.

12. *Preface to Metaphysics*, 48.

13. See *Preface*, 54–57.

14. *Preface*, 3–7, 56.

15. See *The Range of Reason*, 27.

16. Alfred North Whitehead, *Science and the Modern World* (New York: Macmillan/Free Press, 1967), 87.

17. *Range*, 29.

18. *Creative Intuition in Art and Poetry* (New York: Meridian Press, 1963), 236.

19. *The Situation of Poetry* (New York: Philosophical Library, 1955), 59.

20. *The Situation of Poetry*, 127.

21. *The Situation of Poetry*, 79; *Existence and the Existent*, 42: "Being superabounds everywhere; it scatters its gifts and fruits in profusion. This is the action in which all beings here below communicate with one another and in which, thanks to the divine influx that traverses them, they are at every instant . . . either better or worse than themselves and than the mere fact of their existence at a given moment. By this action they exchange their secrets, influence one another for good or ill, and contribute to or betray in one another the fecundity of being."

22. See for example, Thomas Langan, "Substance, System, and Structure," *New Scholasticism* LXI (1987): 285–306.

23. Alfred North Whitehead, *Science and the Modern World* (New York: Macmillan/Free Press, 1967), 87.

24. On the distinction between nature and state, see Maritain's *An Essay on Christian Philosophy* (New York: Philosophical Press, 1955), 11–33.

25. *Preface to Metaphysics*, 23.

26. Nathaniel Hawthorne, "The Old Manse," in *Tales and Sketches*, The Library of America, ed. Roy Harvey Pearce (New York: Literary Classics of America, 1982), 1132–33.

27. Marion Montgomery, "The Prophetic Poet and the Spirit of the Age," Vol. III *Why Hawthorne Was Melancholy* (LaSalle, Il.: Sherwood, Sugden and Company, 1984). See also *Possum: and Other Receits for the Recovery of "Southern" Being* (Athens, Ga.: University of Georgia Press, 1987).

28. See Emerson's essay "Experience." Irving Howe, in his *American Newness* (Cambridge, Mass.: Harvard University Press, 1986), says "To confront American culture is to feel onself encircled by a thin but strong presence: a mist, a cloud, a climate. I call it Emersonian." In this mist, consciousness becomes "the beginning and end of existence . . . swallowing the very world in its pride."

~

CHAPTER THIRTEEN

Marion Montgomery and the Poet's Recovery of Being

Assessing the Trilogy

Mr. Montgomery's triology, *The Prophetic Poet and the Spirit of the Age*, is difficult to categorize—it is a masterful combination of literary criticism and philosophy; yet it would probably displease many purists in either of the said disciplines. Montgomery admits that his work is not an attempt "to demonstrate or to consider in orderly fashion systems of thought from Descartes and Hegel through Sartre."[1] Moreover, it would displease some contemporary philosophers because of its grand themes; an analytic philosopher has recently said that "no one of any discretion speaks of man, God, or the world."[2] Montgomery's literary interpretations, even though they be textually founded, may upset the literary critic because of the intrusion of philosophical and theological themes and the oblique treatment of literary form and function. But the trilogy derives its power from the fertile combination of disciplines. Montgomery must range outside of traditional disciplines in an attempt to regain a "community of mind" (14). The root of the "civil war of reason and imagination" and the very dissociation of sensibilities is his theme. The poet, as well the philosopher, need the ministration of Montgomery's prophetic poets.

The trilogy shares in the very prophetic function of the poet Montgomery describes; Mr. Wolfe is correct to describe the work as primarily poetic in mode. Thus it shares in the secrets of poetic intuition. Jacques

Maritain's description of poetic intuition is a fitting description of the trilogy:

> For poetic intuition makes things which it grasps diaphanous and alive, and populated with infinite horizons. As grasped by poetic knowledge, things abound in significance, and swarm with meanings.[3]

The trilogy opens up many horizons for inquiry; and his work abounds in philosophical significance. I would like to explore a few of these horizons, such as the intuition of being in Hawthorne and Maritain and the new orientation to the world articulated by John Locke. These are but two of numerous topics that abound in the triology.

After reading the trilogy one has a deep appreciation for the cognitive nature of poetry. As much as the poet and philosopher may have their "ancient quarrel," Montgomery displays their deep kinship. They are both born in wonder and exercise a concern for the first things, for wisdom. Even Socrates, who liked to pick a fight, admitted that the poets say many fine and true things. He complained that they could not ultimately "give an account" and therefore did not possess true knowledge. But for that matter neither did Socrates, by his own ironic admissions of ignorance, claim to possess knowledge or wisdom. A philosophy born of Socratic humility would not be ashamed of turning to the poets. They establish man's first address to the world and they remain in the end when the philosopher understands the limits of his own conceptualizing.

The cognitive nature of poetry may be appreciated in the very titles of the books in Montgomery's trilogy. The titles of the books are quite literally "wonderful": why *did* Flannery O'Connor stay at home? why *did* Poe drink liquor? and why indeed *was* Hawthorne so melancholy? Like the country boys in O'Connor, they bemuse us; but they are in earnest. These questions require answers, but not of the biographical or psychological sort feared by Flannery O'Connor. The questions begin a rational inquiry into the works themselves; we see that the poets do have a logos. In search for answers to these questions the reader is led into the thickets of metaphysics, epistemology, and philosophy of man. Montgomery makes an attempt to "give an account" for the poets. The trilogy is indeed a tantalizing account of American letters in terms of the underlying metaphysical issues.

In order to read the trilogy one need not be overwhelmed by its bulk or the vast number of people and books discussed. This trilogy can be approached through any number of vantage points. Let the reader pick up a copy of Emerson's *Essays* and read some of the key essays discussed by Montgomery in the early chapters of volume three. With the *Tales* of Hawthorne on hand proceed to subsequent chapters. It is true that to accompany Mr. Montgomery on his journey one must be prepared to read and reread many titles in literature, philosophy, and theology. But each step along the way gives a view of many similar themes; in fact the trilogy circles around a few simple themes—man's address to being and God. Montgomery often quotes the lines from Eliot's "Four Quartets":

> We shall not cease from exploration
> And the end of all of our exploring
> Will be to arrive at where we started
> And know the place for the first time.

Surely this could serve as a motto for a reader's venture into the trilogy. In every chapter, each story, novel, or essay discussed brings one around and ever deeper into the mystery of mind and nature. With each encounter with Hawthorne or Emerson, Poe or O'Connor, the reader discovers anew the ever-fresh questions of human existence.

The Intuition of Being

The theme of the trilogy is the deification of consciousness and the subsequent loss of the world. Montgomery refers to the process as "inverted Platonism . . . a relocation of the cause of existence from the transcendent world of Idea to center in the particular temporal consciousness. It is the chief principle of modern gnosticism" (12). The desire to separate mind from nature and thereby exercise control over nature is an essential principle of modern philosophy. The popular spirit now revels in the sensibility forged by modern philosophers and poets. The prophetic poet recalls man to "known but forgotten truths," about the presence of things and their transcendent origin. It is under the aegis of Thomas Aquinas that Montgomery finds the intellectual way out of modern gnosticism and the means for giving an account of the prophetic poets. In the "Introduction" to volume III Montgomery discusses the philosophical key to his work. He explores the distinctions between existence and essence or *esse* and *ens*, vital distinctions drawn from the metaphysics of Thomas Aquinas. From Voeglin, Montgomery has learned the category of gnosticism by which he names the symptoms of the spiritual disease of modernity; but from Etienne Gilson and Jacques Maritain he has his guides to the essential causes.

The distinction between a being and its existence is "crucial," Montgomery says, as a "guard against that pride of intellect which detaches us from the living world" (16). When we conceptualize and objectify the world it is easy to take the abstraction for the thing. The very fact that a thing is, the sheer existence of a thing, escapes our notice because it is so simple but so hard to master. But the existence of the thing, its "*esse*" or "thatness," serves as the anchor in reality. It is a reminder that the thing has an integrity separate from and different from our consciousness. The differences between Hawthorne and Emerson, for example, have much to do with a philosophy of being and truth. Emerson's abstract idealism and Hawthorne's attention to particularity are well explained in terms of the former's abstraction of fact and the latter's recognition of "thatness" or the existence that grounds all being. Montgomery notices that Emerson's description of nature often lacks concrete particulars; he "sees through the most local particular without noticing its presence" (70). He seeks to establish mind's "facts." Hence, the direction of Emerson's thought "obliterates the little nook of the study, the Old Manse, the Concord River; or it desubstantiates them until thought is the only reality" (22). His rejection of the concrete symbols of Christian Eucharist is of a piece with this movement of thought. Hawthorne, on the other hand, is "careful not to speak of abstract flowers. He calls our attention to yellow water lilies on the surface of the Concord River, its roots in mud, among slimy eels and spotted frogs" (73). What is the significance of how two men view the Concord River? In Emerson, fact is detached from the world and thus tempts the knowing consciousness to entertain dreams of its dominion over all that it surveys. In Hawthorne, the mind is returned to existence in things other than consciousness. Finding this anchor in being keeps the finite mind from elevating itself to the cause of being.

Maritain provides an epistemological explanation for this difference in sensibility. He explains how existential judgment returns abstract essence to the concrete matrix of being. The intellect disengages essences and must detach the idea from a material existence at a given point in space and time. But the mind does not stop at contemplation of essence in idea—it restores them to existence through judgment by uttering the simple words "it is." Existential judgment "transposes the mind from the plane of simple essence, of the simple object presented to thought, to the plane of the thing, of the subject possessing existence."[4] Montgomery uses a strikingly similar account of the sensibility of the prophetic poet. He says that in an acknowledgement of being, "we are restored even as we are limited; we are returned out of that land of thought which is its own excuse for being—that is, which takes itself to be its own cause" (17). Existential judgment is a kind of natural piety, an "obeisance" to creation which "leavens our reduction of existence by abstraction" (17). The influence of existential Thomism is quite apparent in Montgomery's accounts of Hawthorne and Emerson.

The poet also helps the philosopher in his account. Philosophers can easily disengage the ideal essences through abstract reasoning. It is precisely the focus upon individual particular existence that makes poetry salutary for philosophy. Given the current state of philosophy, its antimetaphysical bent, the philosopher needs the poet to remind him of the reality of being, to encourage that "intuition of being" so vital to the discipline of metaphysics. If the philosophers ignore it, the poets cannot. They can get us to see again the significance of the problem of essence and existence. Hawthorne's rustic meditation about the old manse provides an opportunity for an intuition of being and the reality of things:

> Speaking of summer squashes, I must say a word of their beautiful and varied forms. They presented an endless diversity of urns and vases, shallow or deep, scalloped or plain, moulded in patterns which a sculptor would do well to copy, since Art has never invented anything more graceful. A hundred squashes in the garden were worthy—in my eyes, at least—of being rendered indestructible in marble. . . . There was a hearty enjoyment in observing the growth of the crook-necked winter squashes, from the first little bulb, with the withered blossom adhering to it, until they lay strewn upon the soil, big round fellows, hiding their heads beneath the leaves, but turning their great yellow rotundities to the noontide sun. Gazing at them, I felt that, by my agency, something worthwhile living for had been done. A new substance was born into the world. They were real and tangible existences, which the mind could seize hold of and rejoice in. A cabbage, too,—especially the early Dutch cabbage, which swells to a monstrous circumference, until its ambitious heart often burst asunder,—is a matter to be proud of, when we can claim a share with the earth and sky in producing it.[5]

Hawthorne possesses some manner of intuition of the being of things and he delights therein. One is reminded of Hopkin's "Pied Beauty" or "Hurrahing in the Harvest." The dynamism of existence is so palpable in the being of the cabbage Hawthorne uses the metaphor of "an ambitious heart" bursting asunder. Maritain would prize such metaphoric descriptions of existence, which he considers "the act of all acts and the perfection of all perfections," taking a formulation of Thomas Aquinas. The simple fact that things are (existence) emerges as a factor over and above what things are (essence). By an existential act, the act of being (*esse*), Maritain says "things surge up against me and triumph over possible disaster, stand there, not merely there, but in themselves, and they shelter in their thickness, in the humble measure meted out to what is perishable, a kind of glory demanding to be recognized."[6] Rational analysis may confirm this insight and conceptualize it in various forms. But the insight is something above deduction and conceptualization. Thus the poetic and philosophic activities have a synergetic effect on each other. The intuition of being is at the root of the intellectual life because it requires a silence before reality and a disposition to attend to what is present in its inexhaustible fullness.

The prophetic poet, according to Montgomery, does not misjudge his or her own conscious mind or will as the ground of being; the old temptation of the human will is to strive for self-sufficiency and to exist by one's own authority and act (20). But existence, in its givenness, "gnaws at any self-willed ground." The contingency of our existence dashes our hopes for sufficiency. And the "anchor of man's peculiar whatness (ens) in thatness (esse) binds man to all creation" (18). Such is the "known but forgotten truth" implicit in the poets and conceptualized by Montgomery through metaphysical distinctions.

Locke: Christian or Secularist?

One source of Hawthorne's melancholy is the inheritance of a Puritan separation from and distrust of the world. The Puritan sensibility turned art to a "spiritually pragmatic" purpose, the salvation of the soul. Montgomery shows how the rhetoric of damnation obscured the goodness of creation and did not allow the poet to delight in the being of things. Things became emblems for the state of soul and its relation to God. Things of the world were not allowed to show forth "in the humble measure meted out to what is perishable, a kind of glory demanding to be recognized," as Maritain so aptly put it. The pragmatic bent of the Puritan address to being, when secularized, became a desire to conquer and master nature for the relief of man's temporal estate. The business of getting to heaven was replaced with the business of commerce. In both cases the world is but an empty stuff to be used for ulterior purpose.

How do Bacon and Descartes, who openly proclaimed the new goal of human mind and will as the conquest of nature, become magically distilled from the essence of American Puritan thought? But the result is not so magical if we understand the intention and achievement of Locke, a disciple of Bacon and Descartes, whom American thinkers adapted for their purposes. For it is clear that Locke had some doing in this transmogrification of American thought. In American letters, Jonathan Edwards brought Locke's influence to bear upon American religious consciousness. Locke's influence on Edwards, and through him to Emerson and American pragmatism, provides a horizon that may help us better understand Locke's philosophical achievement.

Montgomery observes that "Locke contributed to the break with the past and to the intellectual and spiritual fragmentation of our world . . . for Locke reinterprets significantly the old sense of the individual in community and of the community in nature" (129). Yet despite the radical consequences of Locke's thought and its secularizing tendency, Locke appeared to be a friend of the religious man. He was read by many people who decried a Hobbes or Spinoza. Montgomery correctly judges that "Bacon is too robust a creature to supply that empirical thought to the Puritan mind; piety requires the pious Locke" (213). This remark perfectly uncovers the great success of Locke's philosophical rhetoric. The "pious" Locke uses the old terminology, such as virtue, natural law, and even God, but he invests them with a new meaning. Only by the greatest of equivocations can Locke's ethics be called a doctrine of natural law. It departs entirely from the traditional meaning. Yet he uses the ambiguity to its full rhetorical advantage. Although this can be shown in the *Two Treatises of Government* it is fully clear in his *Essay Concerning Human Understanding*. In that massive work we encounter the darker side of Locke's cheerful and Christian surface. Montgomery is to be commended for pursuing this line of inquiry. I would suggest that it be taken further.

The Puritan's were attracted, Montgomery says, to Locke's statement that we should avoid the "vast Ocean of Being" wherein a man has no sure footing. They shared his distrust of the world. In the *Essay* Locke recommends that the mind rest content with its short tether, because if the mind is not suited for metaphysical speculation, it is suited for practical matters: "Our business here is not to know all things, but those which concern our conduct" (1.1.6).[7] Human conduct, Locke says, must be concerned with "convenience" and "virtue"; it is within our reach to discover "the comfortable provision for this life and the way that leads to a better" (1.1.5). Locke combines in his account both the Puritan goal, heaven, and the goal of the "robust Bacon," earthly convenience. In the *Essay* Locke treats of now one goal and then the other; at times he merges the two together. In the final analysis, Locke puts forward a secular Baconian goal and dresses it in Christian garb.

It is the supreme irony of the *Essay* that the divine law is reconstrued in the very attempt to reassure the Christian believer. Locke does not explicitly deny the integrity of faith, or the existence of a life beyond this world. But he makes the conditions for knowledge of divine law so strict reason cannot discover it. For example divine law requires knowledge of divine existence, attributes, and the immortality of the soul. But in the *Essay* Locke admits that reason cannot prove the status of the soul. And the divine attributes are very sketchy. So he allows faith to appropriate the rational morality of earthly peace and convenience. But the "rational morality" is vastly different from the traditional Christian and Aristotelean ethic come to be known as natural law.

The traditional doctrine of natural law appeals to nature as a norm. Within the context of a teleological understanding of nature, the good is defined in terms of human perfection. The good attracts the human agent by its fullness and beauty. The good man performs his functions well and perfects his human faculties of reason and will. Locke constructs a science of ethics that does not depend on a notion of nature with purpose and fulfillment, or depend on any notion of spiritual faculties to be perfected. A notion of "person," as a conscious self, replaces the traditional notion of soul. Consciousness of self has the highest degree of certainty according to Locke. This consciousness is not an abstract or pure mind, however. It is a consciousness of pleasure and pain; it is an agent's awareness of its own ease or uneasiness in the world and is defined in terms of the self's awareness of its own happiness and misery:

> Self is that conscious thinking thing, (whatever Substance, made up of whether Spiritual, or Material, Simple or Compounded, it matters not) which is sensible, or conscious of Pleasure and Pain, capable of Happiness and Misery, and so is concern'd for itself, as far as that consciousness extends. (2.27.17)

The certainty of existence of the entire external world rests upon practical truths connecting the operation of things with the pleasure and pain they produce in the agent. The certainty of things "existing in *rerum Natura*" is as great "as our condition needs" (4.11.8). Human faculties are not suited to a "perfect, clear and comprehensive Knowledge of things" but are suited rather to "the preservation of us, in whom they are; and accommodated to the use of Life: they serve to our purpose well enough, if they will but give us certain notice of those things, which are convenient or inconvenient to us." He goes on to say that the evidence for the external world is as great as we can desire— "as certain to us, as our Pleasure or Pain; i.e., Happiness or Misery; beyond which we have no concernment, either of Knowing or Being" (4.11.8). Locke avoids the "ocean of being" and speculative philosophy because it is not necessary for preservation. Personal convenience dictates Lockean sensibility.

From the perspective of personal consciousness and its own convenience, a rational ordering of choice is possible. The future consequences of an action must be taken into account. And so too must the conditions for continuance of any present good be assured into the future. The fear of loss extends self-consciousness into the future. Ethics is oriented not by a notion of duty or perfection, but by self-advantage and self-interest. Utilitarian calculation harmonizes the interest of the self with the interest of others. But this harmony can be established only by radically restricting the scope of ethics. The content of moral precepts must be pared down to a minimum. It must be made to focus on the civil goods of life, liberty, and property. Without these rules one can be neither safe nor secure. So despite the variability of and the subjectivity of happiness,[8] the precepts of this restricted morality are universal. Everybody requires the protection of their life, liberty, and property whatever their notion of happiness. By lowering the aim of ethics, restricting it scope, Locke can assure its effectiveness. By reorienting ethics to the demands of self-conscious temporal concern he can assure its certainty.

Such is the ethic appropriated by faith: the rational pursuit of happiness, however happiness may be defined, is virtuous conduct. It is really an astounding remark, incorporating as it does, such moral relativism and concern for temporal convenience. The appropriation of the rational laws of utility by faith reorients that faith to the things of this world. The concern for the better world, an afterlife, is superfluous. For if by following the rules for happiness on earth one is de facto virtuous, no other special "religious" concern is called for. In some other passages Locke drops out the aim of finding the way to a better life after this one and speaks only of the aim of using knowledge to increase the stock of conveniences for the advantages of ease and health (4.12.10). And when the two aims are put into juxtaposition the greatest praise by far goes to the inventor as the "greatest benefactor." It does not go to the works of mercy and charity. Nor does it go to contemplation, philosophic or religious.[9] He praises the discoverer of iron and deems him the "Father of Arts and Author of Plenty" (4.12.11). These are striking juxtapositions, that could border on a form of blasphemy. At the very least, the judgment entails an elevation of human power and places God in the background. Technological "know-how" is to be esteemed above the quality of mercy. Technology saves men from the grave, Locke says. But we know that works of mercy may secure men's "eternal estate." Whatever Locke's interest in Christianity, it surely differs from the traditional Christianity in which works of mercy and charity are the stuff of sanctity, and not technological discovery and entrepreneurial ambition. Despite the acknowledgement of God and religious duty, the temporal focus of Locke's practical aim is manifest. Locke has constructed a purely secular ethic.

If faith is superfluous, then why is it even retained? We know that Locke wished to communicate his new ethic to various audiences, including Christian believers. The use of a familiar terminology is retained so that the new ideas are made "easie and intelligible to all sorts of readers," as Locke admits in his "Epistle to the Reader." John Yolton quotes approvingly a statement that "Locke secured for posterity advances by radical and progressive forces." Those who openly professed themselves "antithetical to revealed religion" found in Locke "tools to be exploited." Yolton notes that others of more moderate temperament, aligned to orthodoxy, effected more gradual and long lasting modifications:

> It was in the hands of these men, even more than in those of the Deists who appealed to Locke's epistemology, that the new tendencies within religion were most aided and abetted by the theoretical structure of the *Essay*. The application by the Deists was flashy and superficial; that of the traditionalists much more penetrating, perceptive, and positive.[10]

Locke found a way to enter into the most sacred and guarded of domains—such as theology, morality, and religious belief—and left his philosophic mark. Whereas Bacon, Descartes, and especially Hobbes and Spinoza, stirred up great resistance, Locke was able to introduce modern rationalism and the conquest of nature into the theological heart of the moral and political order. Indeed, Montgomery is right to assign to the "pious Locke," by way of the Puritans in the north and the enlightened statesmen in the south, the most devastating effect on American sensibility. Locke, in his philosophy, was as pious as the Bible salesman in O'Connor's "Good Country Folk." It is no wonder, then, that Hawthorne was melancholy.

Montgomery's account of "Locke North and Locke South" helps us to assess the "popular spirit" in the United States. Since philosophy must proceed in a dialectical fashion, popular opinion must be engaged unless he be resigned to the isolation of pride that Hawthorne so vividly portrays. We cannot simply repeat the old standard truths of Aristotle and Thomas Aquinas. We may be "correct." But we shall be lost to the day. We can no longer assume the natural attitude that makes Aristotelean science or ethics sensible; nor can we assume the aspiration of faith that animates Thomas' theology. We now face a popular spirit that has imbibed modern philosophy, and Lockean philosophy in particular. We can use the terms being, God, good, natural law, and the like. But we may be caught in equivocation of a serious sort. It would be like the sad but humorous situation of Hazel Motes, who says to the lady on the train, "I reckon you think you been redeemed?" To which the lady responded, "Why yes, life is an inspiration ain't it?" The followers of Thomas Aquinas may learn a thing or two from Hazel Motes as they attempt to discourse with the sons of Locke and Emerson.

The "Southern Writer" and the Recovery of Being

Montgomery says of the southern writer that he has a "strong sense of encounter with being in the external world, a sense of presence in the creatures of the world separate from man himself" (139). In those ranks he includes Hawthorne and O'Connor because they share this sense of presence. They feared the spirit of abstraction and separation, the abandonment of *esse*, and used the grotesque to mock the presumption of the will. They also savored the particularity of place and they knew place in "its timeless dimension" (529). The particular time and place where we stand now, "allow our acknowledgement of participation in the created world." Thus Hawthorne muses that a mud puddle, a lily, and a town pump all contain the presence of being. Through particular place Hawthorne found the calling of timeless questions, "questions always besieged by the present moment of our particular being" (110). The prophetic poet, Montgomery states, is led up to but cannot directly grasp "a Presence more abiding than the being of the world itself." We are indebted to the prophetic poets, the southern writers, and Mr. Montgomery for bringing us this far.

To follow the spirit of Hawthorne and Montgomery, perhaps we should conclude with a return to particularities and to acknowledge the significance of Montgomery as a southern writer and the particularities of the south. In an important passage in Volume III, Montgomery reflects upon the two great southern generals, Jackson and Lee; he states:

> Thus the fierce presence of Stonewall Jackson in the valleys of Virginia become a rebuke not only to the presumptuous invader, but as well to the spiritual decay in his own South, and the tragic aura about Robert E Lee in his bearing and in his words, reveals his sacrifice in assuming to himself the intellectual and spiritual failures that cloud the middle South. (136)

This passage provides answers to some questions raised about southern writing. Its primary purpose is not at all for southern partisanship. It is true that Southern agrarianism represents a protest to the consequences of Lockean and Puritan alienation from being and the attempt to dominate nature for temporal convenience. But that failure is universal, it is part of human condition—Montgomery also mentions the decay and failures of the south before the war. At least many in the south have a sense of limitation and the burden of time and place. The "South," according to Montgomery, is found to be not simply a matter of place, a residency, an address on a street; it is an address of the heart and mind to the world, a place in the world, really a habit of being. It is true that "roots" in place may assist one's appreciation of being—but it is no guarantee. So too, the rootless have a hope—because of the very generosity of being. Wherever men live and move and have their being they are capable of that encounter with being and with the timeless presence that surrounds them. Montgomery says that despite the victory of the Gnostic spirit, hope will survive, "whether in the South or East or any region where the celebration of being resists the subjugation of being" (154). Thus, the region is not constituted so much by the Mason Dixon line as it is by the line each one faces everyday as he encounters the wonder of creation and responds to the givenness of being.

The aspects of Southern life celebrated by Mr. Montgomery are further described in his book *Possum: and Other Receits for the Recovery of "Southern" Being*.[11] The Lamar Lectures were founded to provide for "the highest type of scholarship which will aid in the permanent preservation of the values of Southern culture, history, and literature." The first lecture was given in 1956 by Donald Davidson, a Southern Fugitive-Agrarian poet, critic, and contributor to *I'll Take My Stand*. Now thirty years hence Marion Montgomery continues to show the vitality of the Southern literary tradition. Those readers who are daunted by the breadth and scope of *The Prophetic Poet and the Spirit of the Age*, will find in *Possum* a compass and guide to Montgomery's "home truths." Those readers unfamiliar with Marion Montgomery will find a short work which restores to literature its prophetic role in the lives of men.

Ours is an age in which the prophet "borrows the robes of science rather than that of poetry." We find priests and ministers reaching for Toffler's *Future Shock* or Naisbitt's *Megatrends* rather than Augustine's *Confessions* or Dante's *Divine Comedy*. The sociology of Andrew Greely or the latest polls of the *New York Times* are thrown against the voice of Pope John Paul II. The popular spirit easily finds a rationalization for its own fancies and a scout for its desires in the quasi-science of such "prophets." Mr. Montgomery's "prophetic poet" has a more humble, yet more challenging task. The poet calls us "back to known but forgotten things" by appealing to an "older mystical vision anchored in the realities of human nature" and experienced in the "dark wood" of the present.

The Fugitive-Agrarian poets of the South are just such prophetic poets. These writers found themselves in the possession of a vital but inarticulate tradition which provided them a common assumptions about society, man, nature, and God. As Mr. Montgomery puts it, "To have been 'Southern-born' was to have had a laying on of hands by tradition as it were, a touching of both heart and mind." The Agrarians mounted a spirited resistance to the encroachment of a burgeoning secular, industrial order. Mr. Montgomery insists that theirs was neither a sentimental gesture nor a Neo-confederate reaction. Nor was it "a lament for lost Eden." The Agrarian movement was a deliberate and sustained quest for spiritual origins and authentic voice set against the deracinating and dehumanizing acids of modernity. It should be no surprise, therefore, that religion and metaphysics became of overriding concern. In one respect, therefore, Mr. Montgomery's use of Augustine and Aquinas is a continuation and culmination of that Agrarian tradition.

So as to show "the universal in the concrete" (i.e, the nonparochial nature of the quest), Mr. Montgomery discusses a number of other writers such as Eliot, Wordsworth, Pound, Williams, and Solzhenitsyn. They are "Southern" insofar as they too reach back to a more ancient tradition and forms of myth that lead us to see what makes life worth living. As he did in his article "Solzhenitsyn as Southerner,"[12] Mr. Montgomery uses the term "Southerner" to designate qualities and habits of mind and heart; he defends these qualities, "not because they belong to the South," as the Agrarian Stark Young once said, "but because the South belongs to them."

What then is that vision to which the prophetic poets urge us? Simply put, it is a sacramental view of the world. In such a vision, piety toward creation is that by which presumption, pride, and transgression become recognizable. At the heart of the vision lies wonder at the mystery in the everyday. Ultimately the poet encounters God's presence reflected in the created world. Montgomery displays an impressive array of poets in their quest for this visionary moment: Keats, Wordsworth, T. S. Eliot, Hopkins, Flannery O'Connor; and also mystics like Augustine and Julian of Norwich. Each "bears witness to the mystery in the present." At "the still point of the turning world," the timeless intersects with time; the soul is stirred and lifted up to praise. In Flannery O'Connor's novel, The Violent Bear It Away, the character Tarwater tries to resist the importunate presence of mystery: he fears that "If he let his eyes rest for an instant longer than was needed to place something—a spade, a hoe, the mule's hindquarters before his plow, the red furrow under him—that the thing would suddenly stand before him, strange and terrifying. . . . He did all he could to avoid this threatened intimacy of creation." This intimacy of creation demands a love greater than the pragmatic love we manage for the world's improvement.

Such high vision is not an everyday occurrence. Yet Mr. Montgomery argues that our deportment toward the world reflects, or deflects, such a vision. For example, Southern manners show a "warm but unintrusive recognition of personhood." The seemingly trivial acts of graciousness may do much to preserve the dignity of persons. In a recent interview, Saul Bellow bemoans the loss of "the penumbra of private inviolability and mystery that used to surround people." Bellow deplores the violence of the age and the brutality of city life. Indeed, we can appreciate the necessity of violence in the avoidance of that sacramental vision of the world. O'Connor's characters become violent as they negate the existing world to avoid the "intimacy with creation." Mr. Montgomery argues that our age is not materialistic but "abstractionist." That is, people avoid the givenness of things in nature 'and prefer to live in abstract or Gnostic visions of the world. Private consciousness posits itself as "cause of being." Eric Voegelin, T. S. Eliot, and Josef Pieper are among the thinkers summoned to explain the various disassociations of mind and nature, nature and grace, thought and feeling, *intellectus* and *ratio*. The attempts to conquer nature, and to restructure the order of being itself, must come to grief upon the givenness of things.

Perhaps the reader is still wondering what this high-powered critique of modernity has to do with possums. The possum becomes emblematic for the recovery of Southern being because of its lowly stature; it is a "mirror of the lowly ground in which our most presumptuous dreams remained anchored." Mr. Montgomery takes delight in various approaches to "possumness," from a recipe for cooking it to its possible use on a Hallmark greeting card to scientific descriptions of the "*Didelphis marsupialis.*" In so doing he surveys various deportments toward the world such as ironic Southern humor, sentimentality, scientific wonder, and scientific reduction. In the latter case, he remarks that we find no "trace of wonder that possums are, that people eat possums, that being is." From thence Mr. Montgomery turns to another meaning of "possum," as the first person, present tense, singular of "posse," to be able. The words "I am able" and the consciousness of power, leads to eager presumption concerning our gift and potential. The shadow of Adam and Cain falls on us all. "I am able" becomes dominant and its complement "I am enabled" is lost. The givenness of things, a piety toward creation is lost. The recognition and the celebration of being is "absolutely crucial to us if we are to understand a sacramental vision we are witness to from time to time, as poet or scientist or any other possum catcher." He does not mean that each person must become the metaphysician; but rather, a piety toward creation must be reflected in our manners, in our deportment toward the world and in our "practice of the gifts of our calling."

The reader can sense the urgency of Mr. Montgomery's task for the recovery of "Southern being" if it is compared to Emerson's Yankee liberation of self-presumption. Emerson's visage peeps out on occasion from *Possum* in such choice quotes as "The world is nothing; the man is all" and "All that is not me is an apparition." I suggest that readers consult Mr. Montgomery's chapters on Emerson in *Why Hawthorne Was Melancholy* and perhaps Irving Howe's recent book, *American Newness*. Both would admit the triumph of the Emersonian ideal in the popular spirit of our time. Says Mr. Howe: "To confront American culture is to feel onself encircled by a thin but strong presence: a mist, a cloud, a climate. I call it Emersonian." In this mist, consciousness becomes "the beginning and end of existence . . . swallowing the very world in its pride." Mr. Howe cannot quite shake the presence of this Emersonian cloud; his questions and criticisms, often so penetrating, become dispersed in the flow of history or in a feeble and plaintive socialism. Mr. Montgomery, on the other hand, sees symptom, cause, and cure. Taking in hand the story of Adam, as told and retold through Faulkner, Hawthorne, and O'Connor, we cannot but see the folly and sin of human presumption.

Mr. Montgomery's exploration of the Fugitive-Agrarian tradition ends with a call for a new rhetoric in its full spaciousness. Advancing a claim by Tate, he argues that "a figurative language of experience is crucial to men in community if they are to govern their relations with one another in the full light of truth." The decay of public discourse is due in part to the triumph of literal language. Only science and its apparent neutral and literal reading of the world can pass the bar of truth. Of course this quasi-positivist view of science and discourse even makes for a poor philosophy of science. Nevertheless, ever since the Scopes Monkey Trial, the rhetoric of public discourse has disallowed and ridiculed the role of religion in education and public life. Mr. Montgomery points the ironies surrounding this state of affairs. H. L. Mencken, he argues, did more to stir up Fundamentalism into political activity than any preacher. Moreover, science has been pressed into its own form of Fundamentalism. We are subjected to megatrends, opinion polls, and debunking social science, all advancing their claims under the cloak of neutrality and objectivity. As Burke observed over two hundred years ago, the republic must be spared these "sophisters" and restored its robes of moral imagination; we cannot flourish without the poets and critics to rejuvenate the language.

The Southern poets and critics early recognized that language needs a deeper ground than formal correctness and ceremony; it requires an animating "myth." In a fascinating comparison of the Fugitives and T.S. Eliot,

Mr. Montgomery shows how they were always a step ahead of Eliot in their appropriation of tradition and in their appreciation of myth. Eliot at first saw the use of myth as an instrument for private sanity amidst the chaos of modernity. Wallace Steven's "blessed rage for order" and Robert Frost's "momentary stay against confusion" reflected this modernist approach. Such use of myth appeared to lack piety toward the myth's validity. Donald Davidson saw in the modernist use of the myth a spirit similar to the builders of Nashville's Parthenon: "Why do they come? What do they seek?/ Who build but never read their Greek." The Fugitives, on the other hand, anchored myth in creation, in a truth beyond private convenience. Mr. Montgomery's literary criticism is of major importance for the contemporary theological interest in "narrative" and "story." His Southern tradition offers an alternative to the historicist or deconstructionist approaches to myth to which many theologians are fatally attracted. For the latter, "myth and symbol have been reduced to fiction . . . [and accepted] only as the play of fancy on reality and of no visionary authority." For the Southern writer, the work of imagination differs from mere fancy in its "root accommodation of form to reality through the created world." Davidson and Tate, Faulkner and O'Connor, are all too rarely read while we follow Derrida or Rorty after a Nietzschean or Emersonian will'o-the-wisp. Mr. Montgomery would have us open the country boy's Bible.

Mr. Montgomery's recovery of Southern being is nothing less than a recovery of our full human sensibility. It is an important book for our schools, our church, and our polity. We expect to return to the basics in education, but we lack the guidance of vision and the authority of myth; we theologize and dispute our points of doctrine, but we are abstracted from the signs of God in creation; we argue for virtue, but neglect the traditions and ceremonies of our common life. Mr. Montgomery uncovers the still point to which our political and theological clamor must be tuned. His profound and compelling book brings us to a great height of vision, while setting us on the path of common sense and humanity.

Notes

This chapter extracted from "The Poet's Recovery of Being," *Hillsdale Review* VIII, (Spring/Summer 1986): 53–64; and "Review of *Possum and Other Receits for the Recovery of Southern Being*, by Marion Montgomery," in *This World* (Spring 1988).

1. Marion Montgomery, *Why Hawthorne Was Melancholy* (La Salle, Ill.: Sherwood, Sugden & Co., 1984). In all further references the page number from this volume will be placed in parentheses following the quote.

2. Rom Harre, *The Philosophies of Science* (New York: Oxford University Press, 1983).

3. Jacques Maritain, *Creative Intuition in Art and Poetry* (New York: Meridian Books, 1962), 92.

4. Jacques Maritain, *Existence and the Existent* (New York: Random House, 1966), 11, 18.

5. Nathaniel Hawthorne, "The Old Manse," in *Tales and Sketches*, ed. Roy Harvey Pearce (New York: Literary Classics of the United States, 1982), 1132–33.

6. Jacques Maritain, *Peasant of the Garonne* (New York: Holt, Rinehart and Winston, 1968), 111. See also *A Preface to Metaphysics* (New York: Sheed and Ward, 1939), 43–61.

7. All references are to the edition of the *Essay* edited by Peter H. Nidditch, Clarendon Edition (New York: Oxford University Press, 1975). Book, chapter and section numbers are enclosed in parentheses.

8. See Locke's shocking relativism about human happiness: "The Mind has a different relish, as well as the palate; and you will as fruitlessly endeavour to delight all Men with Riches or Glory, (which yet some Men place their Happiness in,) as you would satisfy all Men's Hunger with Cheese or Lobsters; which though very agreeable and delicious fare to some, are to others extremely nauseous and offensive: And many People would Reason prefer the griping of a hungry Belly, to those Dishes, which are a feast to others. Hence, it was, I think, that the Philosophers of old did in vain enquire, whether *Summum bonum* consisted in riches, or bodily Delights, or Virtue, or Contemplation: and they might have as reasonably disputed, whether the best Relish were to be found in Apples, Plumbs, or Nuts; and have divided themselves into Sects upon it. For as pleasant Tastes depend not upon the things themselves, but their agreeableness to this or that particular Palate, wherein there is great variety." (2.21.55)

9. See St. Augustine, *The City of God*, Book 9, chapters 20, 22.

10. John Yolton, *John Locke and the Way of Ideas* (New York: Oxford University Press, 1956), 203–206.

11. Marion Montgomery, *Possum, and Other Receipts for the Recovery of 'Southern' Being/Lamat Memorial Lectures, No 30* (Athens, Ga.: University of Georgia Press, 1987); more recent works by Marion Montgomery include: *The Truth of Things: Liberal Arts and the Recovery of Reality* (Dallas, Tex.: Spence Publications, 1999); *Virtue and Modern Shadows of Turning Preliminary Agitations* (Lanham, Md.: University Press of America, 1990); *Romancing Reality: Homo Viator and the Scandal Called Beauty* (South Bend, Ind.: St. Augustine Press, Inc, 2002); *Romantic Confusions of the Good* (Lanham, Md.: Rowman & Littlefield Publishing, 1997).

12. In *Why the South Will Survive* (Athens, Ga.: University of Georgia Press, 1981).

CHAPTER FOURTEEN

~

Newman, Theology, and the Crisis in Liberal Education

Truth—this was what Newman's university was all about. In our own universities, this idea has become almost as bizarre as a "gentleman" (or "gentlewoman").

—Gertrude Himmelfarb[1]

The priest departs; the divine literatus comes.

—Walt Whitman, *Democratic Vistas*[2]

Newman is customarily invoked at gatherings devoted to the theme of education, not only because of the wonderful quotes that serve to inspire our purpose; he really does explore in depth a variety of important and knotty issues. Even though Newman wrote the lectures constituting the *Idea of a University* in 1852, as Gertrude Himmelfarb notes in a recent review of a new edition of the text "Our debates about multiculturalism and Eurocentrism, religion and morality, professionalism and specialization, teaching and research, the canon and the curriculum—of these leap out of the text to the reader today."[3] A similar point is made by Frank Turner, the editor of the new Yale edition:

The issues that Newman raised—the place of religion and moral values in the university setting, the competing claims of liberal and professional education, the character of the academic community, the cultural role of literature, the relationship of science and religion—continue to be germane, and many are gaining new attention and relevance. Rethinking Newman's major propositions, some of which are explicitly expressed and others implicitly assumed, requires us to rethink our own views of those institutions and the goals of higher education. Coming to grips with Newman's ideas and arguments demands that we make clear to ourselves our own stated and unstated presuppositions about the life of universities.[4]

There are so many topics now to turn too, but I shall choose the issue of the role of theology. Specifically, I wish to retrace Newman's arguments for the role of theology in liberal education. As I see it, it is Newman's case for theology that undergirds his later arguments for liberal education as an end in itself, the ideal I trust that many of us share and from whose demise in higher education today we seek to recover. Further, I hope to suggest how Newman's arguments concerning theology provide very helpful approaches to understanding some of the highs and lows of important trends and discussion in academia today; specifically I shall briefly suggests how we may use Newman to provide some perspective on Wilson's consilience, Rorty's liberalism, Huston Smith's study of religion, and the revival of authentic reading of literary texts.

In this chapter, I shall explore the sense of the crisis due to fragmentation of knowledge and the Newman ideal of knowledge as its own end and knowledge as whole circle, then elaborate on what Newman means by theology. I shall then explore each of Newman's three arguments for theology and consider how each might apply to the contemporary situation. I consider the nature of the university's profession to teach all branches of knowledge; we shall need to understand Newman's understanding of theology and his refutation of the reasons for its exclusion. I hope to show how this helps us understand the Wilson-Rorty debate recently rehearsed in the *Wilson Quarterly*. Then, I shall explore Newman's case for the interdisciplinary value of theology and show its relevance to the study of literature and history. Finally, I shall trace Newman's account of the usurpation of theology and return to the Wilson-Rorty debate.

The Aim of Education

The obvious place to begin with Newman is with his core idea of liberal arts education found in discourses five and six of the book. The crisis of liberal education today is most obviously the fragmentation and the lack of a coherent aim or purpose. Thus, in a recent issue of *The World and I*, N.A.S. president Bradford P. Wilson responds to John Tagg's appraisal of the present crisis in these terms.[5] The editor, in the introduction reviews the standard lament—we cultivate specialized expertise, communicate empirical data over meaning and vision, or we adopt the purpose of destroying belief so that the student must face nothingness with no center to life. John Tagg reviews various assessments of higher education and concludes that the "engine of knowledge is failing." Our institutions of higher education have become "bureaucratized assembly lines for academic credit and have largely ceased to know or care what their students learn" (297). This is reflected in the "instruction paradigm," whereby each department adds to the assembly line of courses one more bolt or fragment of knowledge. In the curriculum, the "parts don't fit together. They don't add up to a coherent whole." The student cannot "transfer methods of analysis" and does not retain much knowledge. As the universities fail, other institutions are moving into education—corporations, business, adult educators, and so on. But Tagg thinks that something will be lost in this transition to new venues of education. "Colleges hold a place in American society that no other institution is likely to fill. They hold the place of liberal education, of education for liberty, of the kind of experience through which children grow into citizens, through which men and women learn the exercise of the freedom that is tempered by choosing responsibility. . . . they remain the institutional focus of the ideal, which survives as an ideal" (305). The young need to develop both heart and mind and we must "set young people on a course that offers not just facility but maturity, not just cleverness but wisdom" (305). Brad Wilson agrees with this diagnosis, and makes some insightful comments about the assessment solution, in part propounded by Tagg. But Wilson digs deeper. He cites Alan Bloom and the "claims to moral and intellectual merit of the twin sources of Western life, Athens and Jerusalem." The return to these sources will assist in the rebirth of higher education. Our first task then is to clarify our purpose and determine what it is that students should learn. The central method should be the ability to identify, to read, and to love beautiful and profound texts (317). Newman continues to be our mentor on this diagnosis and remedy. But as we shall see, the full remedy involves a theological dimension to education, a fact that Brad Wilson implicitly proposes with the inclusion of Jerusalem with Athens.

So let's see how Newman answers Tagg's leading question, "who is the educated person" and see whether he still has something to offer for the "educated person of the new millennium." In the assessment of John Tagg, such a person would know "the reward of learning, the satisfaction of discovery, . . . independence, and the discretion to seek not just information but understanding."

We approach Newman's ideal articulated in Discourse Five, entitled "Knowledge Its Own End." The student should form a "habit of mind" comprised of freedom, equitableness, calmness, moderation, and wisdom, a habit which he calls a "philosophical habit." Of what use is it? Newman observes that particular sciences are the basis for definite arts with tangible fruits—what is the art, what is the fruit of this liberal education? His claim is articulated throughout the discourse—knowledge is capable of beings its own end: "Such is the constitution of the human mind, that any kind of knowledge, if it really be such, is its own reward." Newman cites both Cicero and Aristotle as philosophers who also make this claim: Cicero said "we are all drawn to the pursuit of knowledge; in which to excel we consider excellent, whereas to mistake, to err, to be ignorant, to be deceived is both an evil and a disgrace" (On Duty). This form of knowledge is deemed "liberal" as opposed to servile because there is no ulterior goal or higher end to which such knowledge is subject. He cites Aristotle's Rhetoric: "those are useful which bear fruit; those liberal, which tend to enjoyment. By fruitful I mean which yield revenue; by enjoyable, where nothing accrues of consequence beyond the using." Newman's exposition culminates in section six in which he says that knowledge "prior to being a power is a good; that is, not only an instrument, but an end." Knowledge therefore may be resolved either direction: into "an art, and terminate in mechanical process, and in tangible fruit"; or "it may fall back upon that Reason which informs it, and resolve itself into philosophy." This gives rise to the two modes of education variously labeled useful or liberal, mechanical or philosophical. By philosophical he means " a comprehensive view of truth in all its branches, or the relations of science to science, of their mutual bearings, and their respective values" (V.2).[6] Surely Newman is right to call this "acquired illumination" an "inward endowment." It is a high personal achievement pertaining to the dignity of being human: "Not to know the relative disposition of things is the state of slaves or children; to have mapped out the Universe is the boast or ambition of philosophy." He further explains why "education" is a more appropriate word than "training" or "instruction" for what transpires at a university because of this cultivation of the mind for its own sake. The grand conclusion is that there is a knowledge "which is desirable, though nothing come of it, as being itself a treasure, and a sufficient remuneration of years of labor" (V.6).

It is Discourse Six in which Newman more profoundly explains the real details of the habit of mind cultivated by liberal education. The sixth discourse he entitles "Knowledge Viewed in Relation to Learning." He presents a concrete and dynamic account of the learning process and exhibits just what he means by "philosophy" or "enlargement of mind." He first considers the notion that enlargement of mind means "holding a great deal of knowledge" whereas a narrow mind contains little. He shall urge us to consider that such knowledge is not the germ of philosophy—the mere knowledge or collection of facts does not suffice for liberal education. This is the beginning of education, its matter, but not its form or end. Newman explains the learning of a child where he/she is exposed to many academic courses and develops the habits of reading and studying particular subjects with the end result being primarily the collection of knowledge. Is this collection enough for a person to be educated? How important is the collection of knowledge to our culture— isn't this the way we produce mathematicians, historians, and physicists? A great error of the universities in the nineteenth century was the cramming of knowledge/courses into the students such that the end result was a "shallowness" of mind rather than the enlargement of mind. Newman calls education "the preparation for knowledge." So what is true enlargement of mind? Newman achieves an Aristotelian account, by use of concrete example. It is typical Newman prose—to proceed by way of juxtaposition and layering of examples to attain the insight of definition. That is, Newman in effect proposes the Greek notion that philosophy (enlargement, liberal arts) begins in wonder and is developed through dialectical inquiry using hypothesis of form and an upward ascent toward the One, always illuminated by the good. Here is Newman returning to an Athenian and Socratic source of wisdom.

There is no substitute for the reading of Newman's wonderful prose, but I shall duly provide a synopsis of it. Newman shows that the end of liberal education is not merely possessing mere knowledge, that there is something beyond it that one must possess to truly have enlargement of the mind as follows. He discusses what this "enlargement" might be through a series of experiences—what does one experience the first time he discovers something new—not necessarily through reading alone but through the other senses such as by traveling, looking in a telescope, beholding strange animals, meeting peoples from other cultures, abandoning religious views, acquiring religious views. Newman's prose induces in the reader that primary sense of wonder. Travel from England to the mountains, the Alps perhaps; travel from a quiet village to a bustling metropolis one is "borne forward and find[s] for a time that he has lost his bearings." Or again, viewing the heavens through a telescope may fill the mind and make it "almost whirl around and make it dizzy." Strange animals in their "strangeness and originality" may "throw us out of ourselves into another creation." Physical science in revealing "exuberant riches and resources" elevates, excites, "almost takes away his breath." I think of Newman's contemporary Gerard Manley Hopkins who writes in "Hurrahing in the Harvest" the notion that "these things, these things were there but the beholder wanting; but when eyes meets them, the heart hurls, half hurls itself, under itself." Then surprisingly Newman examines both the loss of religious belief and the acquisition (conversion) of religious belief as experiences of enlargement—wonder at the mystery of the things and the sense of liberation from narrowness and confines of previous settled opinion. Both allow one the opportunity to examine opinion and make an ascent. But the examination, the new seeing, the envisioning of possibility, must be further worked over—"the enlargement consists not merely in passive reception into the mind of a number of ideas hitherto unknown to it, but in the mind's energetic and simultaneous action upon and towards and among those new ideas" (VI.5). Liberal education requires the "action of a formative power, reducing to order and meaning the matter of our acquirements." This means that for enlargement to occur, this knowledge must be made our own. But this is no mere subjective appropriation; its requires that dialectical ascent—there must be "comparison of ideas with another." It is not the "mere addition to our knowledge that is the illumination; but the locomotion, the movement onwards, of that mental energy, to which both what we know, and what we are learning, the accumulating mass of our acquirements, gravitates." We recollect Socrates in *Meno* who says that "all of nature is akin; and that from knowing one thing can come to know all things." True recollection is the drawing out of the implicit, the connecting of the part to the whole. So we come again to that key term for liberal education "wholeness of vision." Newman names the great intellects of mankind (the likes of Aristotle, Aquinas, Newton, Goethe) as having a mind which could take a "connected view of old and new, past and present, far and near, and which has an insight into the influence of all these one on another; without which there is no whole, no centre" (VI.5). Newman criticizes those who merely memorize facts—they are like a dictionary with no grammar; antiquarians, annalists, naturalists—all of whom have fact with no philosophy, or knowledge of relation and connection.

As a concluding note, Newman proposes for our thought a humorous but profound counterpoint—that of seafaring men (with due respect to the navy officer) who

> range from one of the earth to the other; but the multiplicity of external objects, which they have encountered, forms no symmetrical and consistent picture upon their imagination; they see the tapestry of human life, as it were on the wrong side, and it tells no story. They sleep, and they rise up, and they find themselves now in Europe, now in Asia; they see visions of great cities and wild regions; they are in marts of commerce, or amid the islands of the south; they

gaze on Pompey's Pillar, or on the Andes; and nothing which meets them carries them forward or backward, to any idea beyond itself. *Nothing has a drift or relation; nothing has a history or a promise.* Everything stands by itself, and comes and goes in its turn, like the shifting scenes of a show, which leaves the spectator where he was. (VI.5, italics added)

Is this not a parable describing our students in the midst of contemporary higher education, experienced and jaded beyond their years by multiculturalism, gender and gay studies? Reduced to mere spectators at the latest deconstructive sport of their professors? They view the tapestry from the wrong side (reductionism) and have no story. Nothing has history or promise; these are Bloom's souls without longing. They have no formative power; they have no center; they cannot even begin to recollect and trace the lines of the great circle of knowledge, which Newman sees as the great joy of liberal arts education. This in part because Newman thinks theology lies near that center. But more on this below. Let me add more to Newman's salty parable—he goes on to say that you may be near such a man and

expect him to be shocked or perplexed at something which occurs; but one thing is much the same to him as another, or, if he is perplexed, it is as not knowing what to say, whether it be right to admire, or to ridicule, or to disapprove, while conscious that some expression of opinion is expected from him; for in fact he has no standard of judgment at all, and no landmarks to guide him to a conclusion. Such is mere acquisition, and, I repeat, no one would dream of calling it philosophy.

Again can we not see the contemporary educated teacher and student? We have no standards of judgment. We have no capacity to disapprove, no capacity to truly admire. We ridicule everything, and become cynics; or we admire everything and become facile. This explains the anecdotes concerning the students who either cannot or will not judge the Holocaust to be evil. Newman's little parable is worthy of Nietszche's last man and the account of the abuse of history. Newman is no nihilist; he sees a way out. That way out is very much connected to theology.

Here is the positive conclusion to the discourse on knowledge viewed in relation to learning. He elaborates on the "true enlargement of mind which is the power of viewing many things at once as one whole, of referring them severally to their true place in the universal system, of understanding their respective values, and determining their mutual dependence." The philosophic mind always "recollects" that a part is part of the whole and also views things with the "associations which spring from this recollection." "It makes every thing in some sort lead to every thing else; it would communicate the image of the whole to every separate portion [and] all are viewed as one, with correlative functions, and as gradually by successive combinations converging, one and all, to the true centre." Such a philosophical habit affords one a perfection avoiding both dogmatism (fixed on one object, exaggerating its importance) and the skepticism (having no object or principle, thus "thrown out and do not know what to think or say"). Such a mind "cannot be partial, cannot be exclusive, cannot be impetuous, cannot be at a loss, cannot but be patient, collected, and majestically calm, because it discerns the end in every beginning, and the origin in every end . . . because it knows where it stands and how its path lies from one point to another." We thus arrive at Newman's grand finale, perhaps the most quoted portion of the *Idea of a University* in which he encapsulates this great aim of education:

> That perfection of the Intellect, which is the result of Education, and its *beau* ideal, to be imparted to individuals in their respective measures, is the clear, calm, accurate vision and comprehension of all things, as far as the finite mind can embrace them, each in its place, and with its own characteristics upon it. It is almost prophetic from its knowledge of history; it is almost heart-searching from its knowledge of human nature; it has almost supernatural charity from its freedom from littleness and prejudice; it has almost the repose of faith, because nothing can startle it; it has almost the beauty and harmony of heavenly contemplation, so intimate is it with the eternal order of things and the music of the spheres. (VI.6)

So we must press on to consider how Newman accounts for a center, an order, of knowledge that makes liberal education possible. Its origins lie in theology. We may say further, that higher education has become and must become instrumental and not liberal when theology is dropped out.

What Is Theology?

We need to establish a point of reference for Newman's arguments concerning theology in university liberal arts education. We need to understand his definition of theology and we need to consider something of its scope and methods. This should help to establish the urgency of his claim and it should serve as a baseline for considering contemporary issues and problems posed by the Wilson-Rorty debate. For it shall be interesting to note the similar interest both Wilson and Rorty have in promoting Paul Tillich and in trimming the grand notion of theology laid out by Newman. And of course, by appreciating Newman's grand vision, you, the reader, can mark just how far you are willing to go with his enterprise of liberal education.

We should begin with Newman's simple beginning: "Theology, I simply mean the Science of God, or the truths we know about God put into a system; just as we have a science of the stars and call its astronomy, or of the crust of the earth and call it geology" (3.7). His notion he attributes to monotheistic religion, and is common to many of its adherents, Christian, Jewish, and Islam. Thus, he claims that his argument does not depend upon Catholicism per se: "Catholicism has not formally entered into my argument hitherto" (3.7). To appreciate something of its scope and relevance for liberal education I shall quote one of his briefer descriptions:

> With us Catholics, as with the first race of Protestants, as with Mahometans, and all Theists, the word contains, as I have already said, a theology in itself. At the risk of anticipating what I shall have occasion to insist upon in my next Discourse, let me say that, according to the teaching of Monotheism, God is an individual, Self-dependent, All-perfect, Unchangeable Being; intelligent, living, personal, and present; almighty, all seeing, all-remembering; between whom and His creatures there is an infinite gulf; who has no origin, who is all-sufficient for Himself; who created and upholds the universe; who will judge everyone of us, sooner or later, according to the Law of right and wrong which He has written on our hearts. He is One who is sovereign over, operative amidst, independent of, the appointments which He has made; One in whose hands are all things, who has a purpose in every event, and a standard for every deed, and thus has relations of His own towards the subject matter of each particular science which the book of knowledge unfolds; who has with an adorable, never-ceasing energy implicated Himself in all the history of creation, the constitution of nature, the course of the world, the origin of society, the fortunes of nations, the action of the human mind; and who thereby necessarily becomes the subject matter of a science, far wider and more noble than any of those which are included in the circle of secular Education. (II.7)

This passage does contain much that is problematic. Newman in part thinks that we come at the topic already through a tradition[7]; but nevertheless some account of its rationality can be given. He later provides such an account in *Grammar of Assent*.

As for its proper methods, Newman does not elaborate here; although he says enough to include reason and revelation. He does not mean apologetics, catechism instruction, devotional Bible reading, as much as those things may have some relevance to religious knowledge and dispositions toward theological study. Newman is not as much interested in the strict Thomistic categories and distinctions as much as he is interested in the Patristic sources of theology.

It is a method that involves many layers of evidence, many types of study, many lines of approach that grant an inescapable rationality to belief. Suffice it to say that part of the greatness of Newman's work is the power of his prose to enfold the reader in principle and application, general notions and particular cases; and to carry the reader along with an overwhelming stock of items and multiplicity of perspectives to arrive precisely at that real assent to the proposition under consideration; or rather, it is the effect of Newman's prose to make the intellectual and practical decision apparent, and if one has but a small inkling or shred of sympathy with his general drift, then one is drawn into the mounting wave of his arguments. Or again, one has to consistently say no and no again to each phrase of each grand sentence. Newman simply wears down the reader who would resist his argument, and carries aloft that reader who shows the slightest agreement. True of all great writers, it is especially true of Newman that he must be read and is inevitably mangled or diminished by the summations. To return to the main point: theology certainly includes the Bible, creedal formulations, historical developments and perspectives, metaphysics and natural theology, as well as poetry and literature. As we shall see in his argument for theology the sources include virtually all of academic study.

His greatest passage explaining the subject and scope of theology runs for three pages and is found in Discourse Three, section 7. It begins with the statement that "behind the veil of the visible universe, there is an invisible, intelligent Being, acting on and through it, as and when he will." By the end of the passage Newman has us purveying incantations of Balaam, prophesies of the Sibyl, the Greek and Roman drama, and "even the unseemly legends of popular mythology" in which God "casts his shadow and is dimly discerned in the ode or the epic as in troubled waters or in fantastic dreams" (3.7). This reading of nature and history he learned from Patristic writers:

> Some portions of their teaching, magnificent in themselves, came like music to my inward ear, as if in response to ideas, which with the little external to encourage them, I had cherished so long. These were based on the mystical or sacramental principle, and spoke of the various Economies or Dispensations of the Eternal. I understood these passages to mean that the exterior world, physical and historical, was but the manifestation to our senses of realities greater than itself. Nature was a parable: Scripture was an allegory: Pagan literature, philosophy, and mythology, properly understood, were but a preparation for the Gospel. The Greek poets and sages were in a certain sense prophets; for "thoughts beyond their thought to those high bards were given." There had been a directly divine dispensation granted to the Jews; but there had been in some sense dispensation carried on in favor of the Gentiles. He who had taken

the seed of Jacob for his elect people had not therefore cast the rest of mankind out of his sight.[8]

By theology he has in mind a rich and vibrant approach to the supreme being, and not simply the recitation of church formulations. It is a study worthy of the highest aspirations. As that great Greek theologian Aristotle himself had said of his own predecessors, "The world is enclosed by the divine."

In fact, true to Newman's style, all the arguments build and reinforce his central claim on the essential role of theology in university teaching. It is interesting to note that his overall conclusion is phrased as follows: "exclusiveness really attaches, not to those who support that claim, but to those who dispute it" (4.15). Newman is very attuned to practical issues of cooperation, bias, and fair-mindedness. Newman offers three arguments for the role of theology. The arguments each cover one discourse, with the second argument having multiple parts. The first argument is from the nature of the profession of university teaching; it involves a premise concerning the content of theology. But the real force of the argument will devolve to the integrity of what a university claims to be. The second line of argument involves the interdisciplinary value of theology, its influence on other fields, the equilibrium that it helps to maintain. This argument may have the most lasting appeal and relevance to the mission of university teaching. The third argument involves the practical consequences of excluding theology—the usurpation of its role by some other branch.

The Argument for the Integrity of the Profession (Discourse Two: "Theology a Branch of Knowledge")

Newman's conclusion is stunning and provocative: "Theology is knowledge, in as full a sense as Newton's doctrine is knowledge. University teaching without Theology is simply unphilosophical. Theology has at least as good a right to claim a place there as Astronomy" (4.14). The claim is stunning for its boldness; Newman goes right to the core of modern learning, physics and astronomy, not to the periphery. It is provocative because it surely raises an objection or two. But it is just those objections that Newman hopes to take head on and make his demonstration. He will not outline in this work his account of rationality and knowledge. He does produce some account of theology as knowledge. But his main goal is to challenge the profession of the university—what does the university really profess or claim? That is, the university is an institution that must be accountable to the public; in a broad sense of the term "professional," the university is a professional body

which is accountable. Newman engages the university in terms of its profession and practice to show the high degree of inconsistency and bad faith
in casting off theology from the university.

The argument goes something like this: (1) The university professes to
teach universal knowledge. (2) Theology is a branch of knowledge. (3)
Therefore theology belongs in the university. If theology is excluded; then either theology is not knowledge or you do not live up to your profession.

Now obviously the university would not wish to back down in its claim
to teach universal knowledge, so it must base its exclusion upon the denial
of theology as a branch of knowledge. Newman goes through a list of possible reasons for the exclusion and finds them each problematic. Although
many of the positions are in Hume, there is a certain prescience in Newman concerning future uses of empiricist criterion of meaning, Freudian
reduction, materialism, and the like. The first counter argument reveals
the arbitrariness of the exclusion—any criterion produced to exclude theology could be used to exclude some other branch of knowledge. For example, the criterion of sense knowledge excludes ethics; the demand for
intuitive certitude must exclude history; testimony alone, then no metaphysics. And yet theology itself draws upon multiple sources. Newman
says explicitly "Is not the Being of God reported to us by testimony,
handed down by history, inferred by an inductive process, brought home
to us by metaphysical necessity, urged on us by the suggestions of our conscience?" There are many methodological venues for theology. So it cannot be excluded without others also losing their standing. Hence it appears arbitrary to so exclude it. Perhaps, Newman says, we can just divide
the labor and separate off the human from the divine, or the secular from
the sacred; anticipating the next major strand of argument Newman
points out that this is "impossible in fact" if God is God.

If God is God, then we encounter a "fact encompassing, closing in
upon, absorbing, every other fact conceivable. How can we investigate
any part of any order of knowledge and stop short of that which enters into
every order?" So on to the conclusion concerning the university's "profession"—"I do not see how it is possible for a philosophical mind to believe
religious facts to be true; next, consent to ignore them; and thirdly, in
spite of this, to go on to profess to be teaching all the while *de omni scibili*"
(II.3).

It must be excluded for some other reason than the purely methodological, even if methodological reasons are given. It must be because a certain
account of faith and theology have been embraced. Newman traces out the
varieties of subjectivistic accounts of faith and the ultimate collapse of ag-

nosticism, for all practical or pedagogical purposes, into atheism. And this will bring us full circle to issue of "profession."

Here is Newman's account of the nature of faith: "an intellectual act, its object truth, and its result knowledge." As mentioned, Newman's ultimate warrants for this account are given in An Aid to the Grammar of Assent. I might also add that Ms. Himmelfarb also picks up on the importance of this sentence in her short review. Religion is "an external fact and a work of God." So where do we fall away? First Newman examines the view that religion is "but a feeling, an emotion, an affection, an appetency." This view may spring from a sincere religious belief, indeed a view called pietism. Indeed, it is this view to which many contemporary philosophers of religion wish to trace belief, back to Kant and also through William James. If faith is nothing but sentiment, then there is an easy slide down to its vanishing point; that is, from agnosticism to atheism. For if argument has no place, and further, if religion is constituted by "the inward persuasions and consolations" or "sublime fancies," it is but a short step to account for such things in a psychological mode; that is, religion "was nothing beyond a supply of the wants of human nature" and not, as cited above, "an external fact and a work of God." Of course, there should be no chair reserved for theology if faith be but sentiment. Further, Newman anticipates the classification of religion with those personal traits over which one has no control—such as skin color—or perhaps gender and sexual orientation. Ironically, religion is not granted its own chair on this basis as are the other designations. Nor would he anticipate that such a belief would be counted as a negative designation by many. But he did see that on such a view "Religion is not knowledge, has nothing to do with knowledge, and is excluded from the university course of instruction, not simply because the exclusion cannot be helped, from social or political obstacles, but because it has no business there at all" (24). This brings us back to profession. What amazed Newman in 1852 was that the men of letters were not "conscious unbelievers or open scoffers."

So how can they teach everything but theology? The public prayer of an Anglican bishop indicates a view of faith as an external fact and work of God, a position which allows the possibility of "inferring the Divine Being and attributes from the phenomena of nature" (II.6). The public professions do not square with the curricular designs. He says therefore we must be equivocating on the notion of God; one says one thing, but means another; or as he so ironically puts it, a facing of the politically correct before it was so named, "I must be excused if I exercise towards this age, as regards its belief in this doctrine, some portion of that skepticism which it exercises itself towards every received but unscrupulous assertion whatever" (II.7). That is, Newman thinks that the public authorities, magistrates, divines, and professors, have in fact come to embrace Epicurean metaphysics: "If God is more than nature, Theology claims a place among the sciences: but on the other hand, if you are not sure of as much as this, how do you differ from Hume or Epicurus?" (II.8). That is, Newman finds no practical or pedagogical difference in saying there is no God, as to say "nothing definite can be known." When religious education is reduced to sentiment, and belief to "an accidental hue or posture of the mind" then Hume may as well have triumphed, that "acute, but most low-minded of speculators" (II.8). The contemporary reader may say, so Hume has won, face it; go to Kant and we make the best of the situation; or we work out some post-Enlightenment solution. But not so fast. Newman will drive us back to that question of profession.

To recall the basic dilemma: either we must say that theology is not a branch of knowledge, or that we do not teach all that there is to know. To embrace the first side of the dilemma is problematic—in the need for the university of make a profession to the public it serves. Will it then proclaim itself atheistic in principle? Is it not showing its views on all others by its very exclusion of theology from the circle of knowledge. This constitutes a lack of integrity, or at least consistency. Further, society may no longer wish to send its sons and daughters nor to grant its bequests and donations. The universities then would trade for decades, nay centuries, on the equivocation on the term God, without outright denial. I find a parallel to George Grant's account of *English Speaking Justice*; the actual rational account, based on selfishness and this-worldly success alone, could not sustain the dedication and commitment to its institutions; so Protestant faith filled in the void and made our justice attractive.[9] The awe and wonder of religion provided an assumed center to education—a belief in truth and ultimate meaning. But now that this veil is ripped away, we find less love of the polity and less regard for its laws. Newman saw that you cannot have it both ways. Further, the issue of the cultural wars is anticipated here. Newman opens this discourse with the issue of social cooperation. Any social effort, and especially one as large scale as university education, requires the sacrifice of private opinion and dropping of minor differences; indeed "compromise, in the large sense of the term, is the first principle of combination" (II.2). But there are limits on "compromise." Obviously it must be on minor matters; and further there must be no sacrifice of the main object of the combination. Or finally the main object of our cooperation cannot be "compromised or disparaged." Now in founding a university, we cannot compromise the branches of learning, knowledge itself being its very point. So if nothing is professed or taught about the supreme being, we must hold that nothing is known about it. Or to put it most starkly, "such an institution cannot be what it professes to be, if there be a God." Now some may openly embrace the option, there is no God. But the point at stake is, how can you demand cooperation from believers?

One may wish to accept the other side of the dilemma and relinquish the claim to teach all things, that is, to be a university. This would be perhaps an open avowal of disenchantment. Rorty, for example, embraces both sides of the dilemma. It is good to have no center, no unity. On Newman's account one thereby loses the lure of wisdom and the raison d'être for liberal arts education. To break and fracture the circle of knowledge, is to lose the mainspring for education of the whole man, the gentleman, and to lose the opportunity for wonder. As he concludes after his full paragraph on theology and God, the subject matter of theology is "far wider and more noble than any of those which are included in the circle of secular education" (II.7; cf. Aristotle's *Metaphysics* on divine science). And in the next discourse he says that the elimination of theology "unravels the web" and "takes spring from out the year" (III.10). If one now skips ahead to his account of liberal-minded habit, one may better appreciate the example of both the loss of belief and the acquisition of belief to instill that sense of wonder and awe. What would replace this study? One may simply acquiesce in the instrumental view of education; perhaps leave the highest things to private reverie, or other institutions—but then the university has abandoned its noble profession and has surely lost its integrity—its fullness of being at work.

Newman proves to be very helpful for comprehending some contemporary discussion concerning liberal arts and theology. It would be nice if the trend identified and applauded by Alan Wolfe would be the dominant one.[10] In philosophy and literary criticism Wolfe has come to see the importance of a theological conversation. To his peers he argues that religion can "extend the pluralism." And sounding a note direct from Newman, he says that religion can "expand and enrich knowledge." Wolfe does not wish to see religion accepted as a special area like gender or racial studies; this would marginalize it yet again. And he understands that many religious people simply seek "conversation, not conversion." Wolfe is to be applauded for his comments. But his voice is not common; and thus we should examine those contemporary voices that continue to see or recommend its exclusion from the academy.

Perhaps we should appreciate the directness of the argument made by Huston Smith.[11] He reminds us that traditionally when people wanted to know the big picture or ultimate nature of things they referred to sacred texts. But now science is the most revered form of knowing and this has issued in what he calls "scientism." It imposes arbitrary premises, simply asserts that scientific method is the only reliable form of knowledge; and yet it often proceeds by innuendo and surmise, not by honest profession. Smith urges that we must bring this view out into the open. And further, he says, that theology is the custodian of wisdom; it has important things to offer to us, so he says we must seize the day and proceed to discuss theology. He also provides a brief sketch, but this refers to his life's work, an account of the divine that draws on various traditions and can serve as a point of reference for theology today. He understands that science cannot provide the wisdom for the core of liberal arts education, but at the same time he notes: "postmodernism is no better position to compete with theology because it rejects world view in principle."

Now Smith's attempt to get beyond scientism and postmodernism, in a somewhat Newmanesque way, leads to another contemporary issue. It is interesting to approach from Newman's perspective a past issue of the *Wilson Quarterly* in which Edward O. Wilson and Richard Rorty discuss the prospects of consilience.[12] They disagree over the nature of the problem and the solution, but upon deeper examination we shall find some similarities and we shall find Newman a helpful guide in understanding the problems on both sides.

From one point of view, it is Wilson who represents the Newman case for the purpose of liberal education—he strives to overcome fragmentation and discover the unified circle of knowledge. Rorty in typical fashion does clamor against unity and sees no problem with diverse approaches and lack of unity. In fact, his pragmatic approach finds no need to even bring together diverse areas of inquiry. He celebrates the lack of a center, the lack of connection, the lack of order. Wilson proceeds on the basis of a realistic view of science, with an assertion of truth and objectivity; indeed, Wilson praises the ancient Ioanians, the discovers of nature, and it is to a concept of nature (however modified from the authentic Ionian and Greek notion of *physis*) that Wilson appeals. As is well known, Rorty urges the abandonment of the very distinction of *physis/nomos*, or *ad se/in se*,[13] blithely discarded as some worn-out ladder that propelled us to our privileged vantage point. And of course in "Against Unity," Rorty mentions the fact that he and Wilson possess very different notions of truth, the latter believes in correspondence and accurate representation, the former a pragmatic, pluralistic one in which no approach gets any closer to the nature of truth. Rorty intones repeatedly about the sheer instrumental value of scientific education, whereas Wilson speaks of vision, but still for ultimate control and relief of man's estate. Wilson's approach bears a charming freshness and sense of wonder, that very habit of mind so central to Newman's educated gentleman. Rorty's jadedness is all too apparent; his ironic pose may "josh" people out of their serious questions. And indeed, as for religion, Wilson takes a keen interest in religious phenomena, deems the drive for "mystical union" to be an "authentic part of the human spirit." Rorty, as mentioned, cannot hide his disdain for the fanatics of religion, and hopes he may succeed in joshing it away.

Now so as not be overzealous in my praise of Wilson as the Newman, there is one curious reversal. Wilson has high praise for the positivist's project; seeks to renew its quest for a unitary scientific account; and he claims to know why it failed (the lack of scientific data on the brain). Rorty, on the other hand, rejects the positivist's criterion of meaning. Rorty decisively rejects the view that science is coextensive with empirical knowledge; and that nonscientific disciplines should hang their heads in shame. He mentions the value of T. S. Eliot and other writers as providing "new descriptions and evaluative vocabularies" as well as "helpful new tools for reflection and deliberation." And he provides a great statement on his new attitude—"Most of us philosophy professors now look back on logical positivism with some embarrassment, as one looks back on one's own loutishness as a teenager" (32). So will Rorty and former louts let Newman and theology back in the academy? No, a curious bias against religion and theology remain in Rorty, and on the matter he and Wilson are in surprising agreement.

What do Rorty and Wilson have in common? Both of them make frequent references to fundamentalism as the bogey man in the closet who must be ignored. They both simplify and reduce any orthodox belief to that emotive term "fundamentalist." So any trace of the literal, historical, realistic, or creedal religion must be checked at the door of the academy or intellectual responsibility.[14] Surprisingly, Rorty and Wilson both commend Paul Tillich to any thoughtful believer—because Tillich symbolizes religion and makes it vague, abstract, or fuzzy. [15] And yet both also bemoan the fact that such religion will continue to attract and hold the allegiance of many—it is inevitable. Wilson employs the standard Epicurean/Hobbesian account of religion as originating in fear and sustained by a quest for permanence; Rorty also explores James' notion of the desire for the eternal, but adds his own twist. James thought that "coarser religions—revivalistic, orgiastic with blood and miracles and supernatural operations may never be displaced because some need them too much."[16] Rorty adds they will be needed by people placed in circumstances of no wealth, no literacy, no luck. [17]

So Wilson and Rorty both effectively exclude theology from the academic venture. And finally, both seek to be, or hope for, a poet of the vision—a Lucretius for Wilson, a Whitman for Rorty. For this is the other side of the original dilemma posed by Newman. Either admit that you have no regard for theology (it is no branch of knowledge), or cease professing to be a home for universal learning. The latter side of the dilemma would also entail a lack of a center and purpose for liberal learning. So both Wilson and Rorty posit a myth of progress for an unlimited and cheerful human future. Rorty looks to Dewey, transmuted his early religious belief into a "belief in the human future," and a Whitmanesque dream of "plural democratic vistas stretching away into the future;" he approves of James who at times viewed his wider self as "Americanized humanity at furthest reach of the democratic vistas," and who thought of democracy as the "redeemed form of God."[18] Rorty says "Now the things of this world are, for some lucky people, so welcome that they do not have to look beyond nature to the supernatural and beyond life to an afterlife, but only beyond the human past to the human future." And Wilson proposes the poetry of sociobiology which shall replace the highest aspirations of old and even fill the despair of postmodernism: "The true evolutionary epic retold as poetry is intrinsically ennobling as any religious epic. Material reality discovered by science already possesses more content and grandeur than all religious cosmologies combined."[19] Wilson's defender, Paul Gross, in the Wilson Quarterly, seeks to harmonize Rorty and Wilson, by suggesting that Wilson's sociobiology will in fact help to usher in a new age of social justice, and make "life better and more secure" and eventually put an end to cruelty and oppression.[20] Will this serve as a satisfactory substitute for religion and theology?

On the face of it, it seems preposterous just to read either Rorty's or Wilson's views as a new religion, or to think that the so-called impulse to religious belief would be satisfied. The persistence of the traditional belief remains. Effectively both exclude theology; and then they may wonder why there is a crisis in the liberal education. Perhaps it is related to the loss of the theological center, the preserve of mystery and wonder and meaning. It is problematic whether Wilson's sociobiology or Rorty's liberalism would provide a deep enough vision and a sustaining center of meaning. No wonder students clamor for the useful courses—what have the professors offered them by way of meaningful discourse? I believe that it is incorrect to say that the market forces and competition in higher education simply lead students to studies which are relevant to their jobs. Having taught adult students for a number of years, I have found they enjoy and seek further courses in the humanities, especially religious studies and literature.

At his better moments Wilson seeks dialogue and respect from various disciplines in the academy, presumably including theology. He does not seem to have read much besides Tillich and Whitehead. So we can say Newman's suggestions for including theology look even better. Ironically, one point made in favor of theology in the next argument is that theology would help to correct the unrestrained belief in human progress. It is a question of sin. Would that Wilson and Rorty might read Hawthorne's "The Earth's Holocaust," or "Young Goodman Brown," or Marion Montgomery on Hawthorne. They would send us back to the theological question of human perfectibility. Alan Wolfe is on to something when he applauds the influence of religion in the lives of students especially when it brings "a tragic sense of life and a grounding in particular maxims of ethical conduct, and a sense of wonder."[21] Wolfe sees that the humanities at least have much to gain from a religious perspective when discussing themes of "love, evil, envy, meaning, and purpose." But this is to anticipate Newman's second main argument for the inclusion of theology in the curriculum. In sum, theology provides the substaining center to liberal education.

The Argument for the Interdisciplinary Value of Theology (Discourse Three: "The Bearing of Theology on Other Branches of Learning")

Newman's second line of argument explores the interconnection of disciplines, the unity of knowledge, again the fact which gives rise to the very idea of a *university*. It is surely the most enduring, relevant, and irrefutable of the three. The principle is that the various disciplines are each partial and incomplete and therefore each needs to be completed and corrected by the others in order for there to be a whole view of things. More precisely Newman says that the most accurate apprehension of things requires an approximation of the full circle by the breadth of disciplines one has mastered or become acquainted with. One has a defective understanding insofar as one retains a partial and abstract understanding of the subject (III.2). The neglect of the interconnection with other disciplines may occasion the development of "quacks" and "bigots" insofar as a scholar seeks to reduce all things to one specialized cause or abstract schema. Newman elaborates on this principle with many fine examples of interdisciplinary struggle and reduction, not at all theological. An application of the principle to theology would follow as such: theology too helps to make a more accurate apprehension of things, completing and correcting others, as it too must be in some way completed and corrected by the others, a proposition which Newman himself urges. Newman in other words makes the first part of the argument treating theology on par with any discipline of the university—that is all he initially asks. He then proceeds to discuss the great value of theology in terms of its importance, "supreme influence," and broad reception. This makes theology especially necessary for a university education.

Newman regards truth as "facts and their relations." There are an indefinite number of particular facts which have countless relations of every kind one to another, forming a "large system or complex fact."

Knowledge is the apprehension of these facts, whether in themselves, or in their mutual positions and bearings. And, as all taken together form one integral subject for contemplation, so there are no natural or real limits between part and part; one is ever running into another; all, as viewed by the mind, are combined together, and possess a correlative character one with another (III.2).

Newman points out that the complex whole is beyond any simple glance or absolute mastery; it is by "degrees and by circuitous advances does it rise aloft and subject to itself a knowledge of that universe into which it has been born." Each discipline is necessarily partial and abstract. Disciplines may overlap and jostle up against each other. As separate and partial "it follows that on the one hand they need external assistance, one by one, by reason of their incompleteness, and on the other that they are able to afford it to each other by reason, first, of their independence in themselves, and then of their connection in their subject matter." Newman's ideal of learning involves our meager attempts to approximate some grasp of this whole. But it too often happens that one stays with a partial view and exhibits a defect of learning. What he asks provides "an accurate apprehension of man"? The word "only" tends to crop up—man is only—fill in the blank—physiology, sociological, political, economic. So too Newtonian physics makes certain assumptions which may exclude the facts of other disciplines, such a "capillary action." Newman notes that we need to have a "comprehension of the bearings of one science on another, and the use of each to each, and the location and limitation and adjustment and due appreciation of them all, one with another. This belongs "to a sort of science distinct from all of them, and in some sense a science of sciences, which is my own conception of what is meant by philosophy, in the true sense of the word, and of a philosophical habit of mind, and which in these discourses I shall call by that name." He means the liberally educated habit of mind would be able to make such judgments. To lack such a habit he charges leads only to "bigots and quacks" who scorn "all principles and reported facts which do not belong to their own pursuit" (III.3; see also III.6 on "the narrow minded bigot"). He also returns to the theme of "profession"—what university wishes to proclaim to the public that it scoffs "at the action of mind upon matter" or "the claims of mutual justice and charity"? Or is willing to do away with "metaphysical ideas of 'duty,' 'right,' and 'heroism.'" It could not, for "common sense indeed and public opinion set bounds" to such a profession. This line of argument then establishes as its major premise the fact that "the systematic omission of any one science from the catalogue prejudices the accuracy and completeness of our knowledge altogether" (III. 4).

Now the minor premise may be filled in by the previous discourse—theology is a branch of learning, so to exclude it would be to prejudice our general learning. But Newman makes a more complex case. First, he appeals to the analogies of human agency and divine agency—if we do not wish to reduce human agency, then we get some glimmer of the possibility of divine agency. Second, he elaborates on the notion of the subject matter of theology with what may be his finest description of its range and extent, part of which we discuss above (III.7). The prose leaves an overwhelming sense of the grand scale and importance of the theological vision of things. Theology exerts such a "powerful influence" he says that we cannot "blink" the question of its truth. "What science will not find one part or other of its province traversed by its path?" So too is philosophy affected by theological positions. And further he asks "Does it cast no light upon history? Has it no influence on the principles ethics? Is it without any sort of bearing upon physics, metaphysics, political science?" (III.8). Its range is undeniable. The questions are there in every discipline. Important questions are waiting to be searched in the most appropriate terms and with an appropriate method. Finally, Newman turns to what he calls "a prescriptive" case for theology.

The discipline of theology is not the fashion of season, but "has had a place, if not possession, in the intellectual world, since time immemorial." Therefore he says it has "prima facie claims on us." It can be rejected if we can prove it is false; and then we must treat it as astrology or alchemy, a superstition from a bygone age. It must be "distinctly accepted or distinctly reprobated" he says. Again Newman is forcing an honest profession by the university. But even its reprobation is problematic given the deep influence on so many disciplines. He catalogs some English writers—Bacon, Hooker, Taylor, Cudworth, Locke, Newton, Clark, Butler; he mentions Johnson, Shakespeare, and Milton. It is not simply English or Protestant—track it across the continent, to other ages, Greece, Rome, Judea, the East. Theology is quite simply a core discipline for understanding the world, and the various traditions and movements of people within it.

So Newman leads us to his conclusion. "Religious truth is not only a portion, but a condition of general knowledge." Such is a fitting one sentence summary of his position heretofore. I believe that this argument bears the most significance and relevance for the academy today. I shall first examine some negative cases, continuing my analysis of the Wilson-Rorty debate. Then I shall examine some very positive signs of the inclusion of theology and its contributions to the liberal arts in higher education today.

Wilson's ambitious goal, to overcome fragmentation and to take a whole look at nature, is admirable. But his book suffers from the very things Newman wishes to correct in his notion of the mutual illumination and correction of one discipline by another. His project of "consilience" is more of an annexation and reduction than it is mutual support and illumination. Indeed, Wilson's flaw is that Ionian enchantment of the single mode of explanation. In the final chapter of his book, Wilson summarizes his own method as "there is only one class of explanation. It traverses the scales of space, time, and complexity to unite the disparate facts of the disciplines by consilience, the perception of a seamless web of cause and effect."[22] The notion of consilience, both Wilson and Gross acknowledge, is an extrapolation from phenomenon within or across similar disciplines by which the same pattern of cause-effect emerges. Wilson prefers this word to coherence, or one may add convergence, because he envisions, not the overlap or mutual indications, but the reduction of all patterns to the same one. "The central idea of the consilience world view is that all tangible phenomena from the birth of stars to the workings of social institutions are based on material processes that are ultimately reducible, however long and torturous the sequences, to the laws of physics." Wilson has a univocal notion of explanation; and he knows it is a promissory note, yet to be fulfilled. Here again Rorty is right—it is immature and not evident by the cases he presents in his book. In fact, Wilson stumbles through many areas in his attempt to make these connections. He presents an appalling lack of liberal education, try as he might to read his way into the broader view. His book contains errors in history, poor metaphysics, ignorance of theology, faulty logic. One would appreciate some evidence that Wilson had read and seriously considered positions which challenge his own. I will make just a quick list. He says "no compelling reason has ever been offered why the same strategy should not work to unite natural sciences with the social sciences." Has he considered Weber, Nisbet, Taylor? In his enchantment with the Ionian metaphysics, Wilson appears to never have considered Plato's critique in the *Laws*, or Socrates' central problematic stated in *Phaedo*. He characterizes Aquinas' natural law as a function of divine will (not intellect); and sets up a false dilemma of "transcendence" versus "empirical" roots of ethics, a dilemma which natural law is designed to overcome. As for history, Wilson's account of the rise of modern science proceeds without any consideration of Butterfield, Jaki, or others who have shown the connection between science and Christian belief. Finally, when it comes to religion, Wilson is way out of his league. There is no doubt that religious experience has some neurological correlate and that "hypereligiosity" is connected with mental disorder, perhaps the bipolar condition.

But how have religious traditions attempted to discern the difference between a Huxlean brand of chemical mind expansion and authentic mysticism? Wilson just baldly asserts that an ideal condition of omniscience is incompatible with freedom.[23] Theologians have struggled with this issue for centuries—Wilson's account could at least proceed less dogmatically if had taken them into account and argued for his own position. It is curious to note that on the acknowledgment page, listing thirty to forty colleagues whom he consulted, there is but one philosopher and no theologians. This is not a minor quibble; it shows Newman's main point. The disciplines would enrich and correct each other. Wilson's method of consilience admits the findings of another discipline if it is consilient, that is, if it matches the same causal pattern as he is used to plying in his field. If not, it gets a cursory treatment.

The deeper issue however has to do with the notion of a discipline and the type of unity possible and desirable among the branches of learning. As mentioned above, Wilson proceeds with a univocal notion of explanation. He is a Cartesian at heart, as his account readily admits. It is a revival of basic Cartesian project, the method of which excludes the literary, the theological, even the metaphysical from the outset. Newman's vision is fundamentally Aristotelian—the various disciplines each use their different methods and patterns of explanation as appropriate for the subject matter: "For it is the mark of an educated man to look for precision in each class of things just so far as the nature of the subject admits." (*Ethics* 1094b24). The unity of science must proceed on a notion of analogous types of explanation, not the univocal. As Newman urges, the sciences are abstractions, they are partial. Therefore, the interdisciplinary value of each to each is to correct by way of balance and enrichment. For Wilson, there is no sense of abstraction or partiality; correction is by way of redefinition and analysis/reduction to the simple natures as is the Cartesian fashion.[24] Wilson's continuation of the Cartesian project simply invites the postmodern reaction, to celebrate the diversity of things and to assert the independence and even priority of the humanities for studying the human as specifically human.

Rorty sounds much more sensible in this regard. For example on theological matters, despite himself, Rorty rises to a very insightful account of William James and the religious sensibility torn between the Wordsworthian and Whitmanesque vision of things. Here is an interdisciplinary contribution from which a theologian or simple believer could benefit; it is much superior to Wilson's somewhat suggestive but ultimately flat and abstract account of religion in terms of animal hierarchy and the survival value of being a member of the religious community. But Rorty of course goes to the other extreme to assert the utter lack of connections, the purely random play and diverse purposes of human inquiry. He offers us an equivocal notion of knowledge as opposed to Wilson's univocal one. Rorty champions his pragmatic view in which every discipline is a tool in a tool-box and there is no need to ply them at the same trade. This is obviously not the case, as his own interdisciplinary efforts attest. And it surely reveals a central contradiction or inconsistency in his own project. He claims that there is no need to seek order or wholeness or connection among the disciplines. But this means there is no order, no conflict, no priority. His own project establishes just such order and priority. A key article cited above speaks of "the priority of democracy to philosophy." Philosophers must not conflict with the majority's quest for liberty lest they be deemed fanatics and not be a worthy voice to be accounted for. He must urge theology to insulate itself from providing any practical premises or cosmological principle. So Rorty disallows connections. Again we find in Cardinal Newman's vision of liberal education a more accurate and enriching account of what constitutes an academic discipline and how they may fit together for mutual effect.

Now there are positive signs on the academic horizon for the excitement and achievement of Newman's habit of mind. Its stirrings are to be found in literature and political philosophy, and its challenge to be found in the humanities core and historical courses. Alan Wolfe's plea for consideration of the religious point of view was mentioned above. In addition to the enrichment theology adds to social science and humanities in general, he mentions the role of theological perspective in the study of literature. "To study the world's great literary works, many of which were inspired by religious questions, without full appreciation of those questions is like performing *Hamlet* without the Prince." Specifically, Wolfe says that teaching Milton or Tolstoy through the lens of secularism is to "teach them inaccurately."[25] This openness to theological texts and theological issues can be seen in two great literary critics, Alfred Kazin and Roger Shattuck. Kazin's book, *God and the American Writer*, proceeds on a basic assumption which he proves in great detail: "There is a very special connection between religion and literature."[26] Hawthorne, Melville, Frost, and Faulkner—all struggled with the theological issues inherited from Calvinism. "The world they knew from their birth was completely religious." Clearly, then, a student of American literature needs to know the Bible and the theology of John Calvin. Kazin even says that present-day culture is about "decayed Calvinism devoid of transcending belief" and that the lack of interest in religion causes our very language to suffer. Shattuck's marvelous book, *Forbidden Knowledge*, draws on Greek mythology, Hebrew Scripture, as well Milton, Melville, and others. Of course, such openness follows from his return to the author and the text. It is surely part of his meaning in one of his thesis on literature: "Works of literature, through their amalgam of representation and imagination, of clarity and mystery, of the particular and the general, offer revealing evidence about material nature and human nature and whatever may lie beyond. This is why we read and study and discuss literary works."[27] What may lay beyond? Surely theology is a source for consideration. In fact, Shattuck's rationale for the study of great authors contains another opening:

> We can reasonably expect a liberal education in our colleges and universities to serve two principal functions. The first is to present historical basis of our complex culture and the political and moral standards it has evolved. The second is to offer students the intellectual basis for an evaluation of that culture, its ideals and realities. The first explains and even justifies the status quo. The second questions it. Both are essential in a democracy. Those two functions can take place together, almost simultaneously, thanks in great part to a collection of written works that founds our Western tradition and challenges it. . . . They do not pronounce: They probe and reflect. The shared reading of such foundational works gives us a basis for finding the principles and "values" by which we can live together as one country and one culture containing many parts and divisions, many classes and races.

To accomplish the first task, the historical complex, requires theological study. The middle ages, the Renaissance, the Reformation, Counter-Reformation, and Baroque all require sensitivity to the theological dimension of culture. It is a dimension frequently missing from history and humanities surveys, or it is subject to the most extreme deconstruction, debunking, and cynical caricature (Wilson on the Inquisition and Galileo is a case in point). With the controversy surrounding the courses on the Holocaust—the possibility of trivialization, the inability of students to form judgment, and the like, theology would bring a much needed perspective. Indeed, at the end of the day the Holocaust is about theology—the history and identity of the Jewish people, the various sources of anti-Semitism, Christian cooperation and resistance, the totalitarian temptation, and the problem of radical evil, the possibility of redemption and forgiveness, and the presence/absence of God. In my observation of these classes, the materials, the syllabi, the presentations are poor in theology and given over to bias, stereotype, or caricature. While in fact, the profoundest probings of the event directly raise theological issues such as by Weisel or Fackenheim. In short, theology would add a much needed solidity and point of reference for this course and help to fulfill its great potential in the humanities curriculum.

The importance of Jewish theology leads to my final case in point, and that is the importance of the theological issues in contemporary alternatives in political philosophy. The deep influence of Leo Strauss lies in part to his openness to the theological: I have always found it interesting that Strauss ends his chapter on Thucydides in *City and Man* with an assertion that the key question is "quid sit deus." As Brad Wilson said, we must return to the twin sources of Jerusalem and Athens, a clear echo of a Straussian theme. It is not strange to find explorations of Augustine, Maimonides, Aquinas, Luther, and Calvin in discussions of political philosophy in this circle. And beyond this circle, one can think of the importance of a renewed interest in Augustine in thinkers like Glenn Tinder and Jean Beth Elshtain. The ecumenical project initiated by Richard John Neuhaus shows the vitality and relevance of the theological conversation among Jewish, Protestant, and Catholic thinkers and presents a marvelous opportunity for interdisciplinary approaches and courses in the academy today.

The Argument for the Usurpation of Theology (Discourse Four: "The Bearing of Other Branches of Learning on Theology")

Newman's third line of argumentation extends the second. Since the circle of knowledge is constituted as a dynamic unity with delicate equilibrium among the branches of knowledge, it is bound to happen that one science or discipline attempts to encroach upon and displace another. If a discipline is simply ignored or dropped altogether, then the process of encroachment is invited: "If you drop any science out of the circle of knowledge, you cannot keep its place vacant for it; that science is forgotten; the other sciences close up, or rather they exceed their proper bounds, and intrude where they have no right" (IV.2). In typical style, Newman provides many examples. He also explores the habit of mind at work in this encroachment. Finally he applies the abstract principle to the case of theology. He concludes his argument with a biting invocation of the Galileo affair—in reverse, which lends a special urgency to the case in point.

Newman states that "what is unjustly forfeited, others unjustly seize." The result is prejudicial to both the science usurped and to the usurping discipline. The tension amongst the disciplines keeps each honest; as Newman stated in argument two, he repeats for another effect here: "their deductions must be compared with other truths, which must be acknowledged to be truths, in order to verify, complete, and correct them" (IV.12). Without this check, the expansion of one discipline, even in its truth can be made "inordinately, extravagantly, ruinously" and thereby is "sure to become but a great bubble, and to burst." Such often is the case with "the 'large views' of scientific men." Or again, it is easy for any discipline to degenerate into "error and quackery" when carried to excess and have no restraint from other quarters (V.4). Again, theology, as well as any discipline, must play its role in encouraging intellectual responsibility. And because theology has a subject matter the most broad and holistic it is of special importance. The scientists speak truth but not the whole truth (doesn't every science tend to want to speak the whole truth?) So theology is needed to make room for responsible statements about the whole truth.

As a first example Newman ponders the fate of ethics—if it were to be dropped it would be filled in most likely by law, physiology, or political economy. He vastly expands this latter example and ample citations from a disciple of Adam Smith who makes exorbitant claims for political economy, e.g., the pursuit of wealth shall be the great source of moral improvement. He also mentions the physiologist and the treatment of mind and volition, and the secular historian who would reduce the history of the Jews to the most mundane causes.

Newman provides an account about why this inevitably happens, why people allow themselves to go beyond limits of what they know. It is the very dynamic of human understanding to search beyond sense data to find an intelligible pattern and it is the nature of science and philosophy, he says, to be a "habit of viewing the objects which the sense convey to the mind, if throwing them into a system, and uniting and stamping them with one form" (IV.3). It is hard to be restrained in not so stamping all phenomena with this idea or form. The busy mind will ever be viewing, and since "we cannot do without a view, and we put up with an illusion, when we cannot get truth" (IV.3). Newman even brings Lord Bacon to his cause, on idols of the mind.

Theology is often a target for seizure. He shows that religion is regularly a target for seizure—by artists, historians, lawyers, and even geologists—all of whom are impelled to make the grand claims or institute a grand purpose at the expense of theology. Theology needs to be present in the university to hold its own, to defend "its boundaries and to hinder encroachment." If theology is not occupying its proper place, the exorbitant claims of other disciplines will take its place. It needs to be present for responsible thinking about the whole.

Newman ends with the case of Galileo used quite effectively to make his case for theology. Early in the discourse Newman admitted the wrong of the church in imposing scripture on astronomy: he said that Catholics are accused of wanting to make the sun go around the earth in accord with scripture, so here is clear case of usurpation (IV.2). In that section Newman simply wanted to establish the problem of usurpation of one discipline by another. Now in the concluding discourse he turns more forcefully on the "men of science" who would "resist the divine who determined the orbit of Jupiter by the Pentateuch," who may accuse him of "cowardice and illiberality" for defending the role of theology, when he is simply resisting the attempt to theologize by means of astronomy (IV.14).[28] That is, if theology should be kept from determining the orbit of the planets, then science ought not to dictate theology, which needs "its own proper principles for its due formation and disposition." Or to be more to the point: when "Divine Science is ostracized, and La Place, or Buffon, or Humboldt, sits down in its chair, why may not I fairly protest against their exclusiveness, and demand the emancipation of Theology?" (IV.14).

The implicit usurpations by Wilson and Rorty should be apparent from our previous analysis. Their reductionism is a form of usurpation. To claim to give the definitive explanation of religion, as a function of survival, is a form of usurpation. It is a usurpation of theology by biology. It does away with religious belief from the perspective of belief, or other disciplines such as philosophy or literature. Second, the pressure of reduction leads theology to conform itself to science, as Wilson commends Tillich. Theology must not simply adjust or renegotiate its border, but conform entirely to the imperious demands of scientism. Finally, the consilience project seeks to form a new theology, a new myth for the modern age. Wilson claims that science is "religion liberated and writ large." The problem is the latter project simply will not do the job as Wilson hopes; he invites the deconstructionist to seize the ground for human liberation and creativity. The second demand is mere meddling and a fundamental refusal to acknowledge the profound interchange between science and theology that is occurring. And the first, the reduction to biology, fails to account for the distinct intelligibility of the theological enterprise. Wilson is torn by that inevitable appeal of religion. Biology has things to say about human religiosity. But so do literature and the arts; sociology; metaphysics. And so surely do the sacred texts themselves and the mystics, whom Wilson so lavishly praises.

As for Rorty and the liberal vision, we find a usurpation in kind. There is a reduction of religion to the sphere of the private; a demeaning of its practice as fanatical and not worthy of public reason. So too we find a dictation to theology as to its own subject and methods, a dictate to which many liberal theologians are all to ready to conform. And finally, we have seen Rorty's replacement for religion in the unlimited democratic vistas celebrated by Whitman. Part of this vision includes a wish to accelerate the mood of disenchantment so as to make the "world's inhabitants more pragmatic, more tolerant, more liberal, more receptive to the appeal of instrumental rationality."[29] Beginning with this latter point, we may wonder if the increase of disenchantment is what the world's inhabitants need or if this is the way to revive liberal arts education. Also, in fact, we noted Rorty's great confoundment or regret that so many people continue to cling to forms of religious belief. If it is banned from the academy, it shows itself in the overwhelming movement of new age religion. As Huston Smith notes "New age, conservative churches, Asian religions, challenge the naturalistic outlook of mainstream intellectuals." Newman's reflections on the elements of natural religion, infected as they are by fear and superstition, and yet testifying to a divination of moral transgression and hope for communion, stand as a worthy alternative to the liberal dream of progress. As for the second point, the dictation to theology, there is also something wrong with this meddling. Theology to hold its own must renew itself at its own sources. Resourcement, return to sources, and aggiornmento, updating the fundamental truth in contemporary terms, are to be found more in Newman than a theological disciple of Rorty or of the deconstructionists. The first form of usurpation, the demeaning and demoting of religion, has been sufficiently shown by others to be an arbitrary and hypocritical move. I should add, in Newman's terms, it also fails to take into account the positive influence of religion on society as a historical fact.[30] And it fails to consider the internal development within the religions leading to a principled tolerance, authentic ecumenism and dialogue, and support for liberal democracy.

Huston Smith provides a very succinct account of the opportunity and approach for theology today. In the fashion of Newman, he covers a very similar ground. On the point of usurpation, he employs Spinoza's notion of *connatus* to argue that any organism shall expand and dominate until it runs into something to check it. So has science crested into scientism because there has been no sufficient check. He has some choice quotes from Sagan, Hawking, and Dawkins on the pretension of science to account for it all. He says that it is an urgent task to expose scientism as a "paper tiger." He gives us a proof of its limits. If science proceeds on the basis of prediction and control, and if we can only predict and control what is inferior to us; then it follows that science cannot treat anything that is superior, or I might add human in its superiority. Many things are excluded from its purview by definition, such as a deity or an angel. And Smith adds values, meaning, teleology, qualities, or any invisibles not entailed by behavior of visible objects. This is a huge exclusion—our entire "lived world" he says. So it is limited in principle. And he points out the absurdity of conforming theology to these conditions. He says that the mainstream churches are losing ground when they use the word God, but allow its meaning to be "vectored by Darwin, Marx, Nietszche, Freud, and the Big Bang." Smith, like Newman, shows us a way out of the crisis of education, and theology is the key to it.

As a final note, I should also like to mention the work of John Paul II as continuing the work of Newman. His letter on Catholic universities has a very thoughtful agenda that is relevant to all institutions of higher learning. Although the press has focused exclusively on the issue of authority and the teaching of theology, the core of the document contains a restatement of Newman's vision of educating the whole person. It also calls for a search for integration of knowledge, dialogue between faith and reason, an emphasis upon ethics and the dignity of the person, and a theological perspective for achieving these other goals: "it serves other disciplines in their search for meaning . . . and bringing a perspective and an orientation not contained within their own methodologies."[31] Obviously not all institutions of higher education would care to take this vision into account in the same way, if at all. But we can recognize it as a compelling ideal for liberal education, more comprehensive and more magnanimous than either Wilson's or Rorty's ideal. It is Newman's ideal. It can be implemented and instantiated in numerous ways. Perhaps there are limiting conditions that are political and practical. Newman appreciated the fact that not all institutions could embody the vision in the same way. He was aiming his arguments at those who say "Religion is not knowledge, has nothing to do with knowledge, and is excluded from the university course of instruction, not simply because the exclusion cannot be helped, from social or political obstacles, but because it has no business there at all" (II.5). So regardless of obstacles, Newman's principle remains—theology is a branch of knowledge and its exclusion is as arbitrary as it is harmful. Its positive fruit can be seen in John Paul's recent treatment of the Galileo affair; again, although reported in the press in terms similar to Wilson's (it is about the final admission of backward religion and inquisition), the documents in fact reveal a finely nuanced study of relevant intellectual issues concerning proper boundaries of disciplines, epistemological confusions, and the common search for truth. It is a contemporary example of what a full and diverse interdisciplinary approach can reveal. Newman would be proud of this work, so concerned as he was with the full ironies of the reversal of the positions of theology and science usurping the role of each other.

Conclusion: The Emancipation of Theology

Newman was a quiet revolutionary whose arguments carry much force today. We still may wonder about the profession of the university to be a university, yet wonder how to abide the exclusion of theology and the deep hostility toward religion. We still search for the center of that circle of knowledge which points to the mystery at the heart of human existence, and yet must abide one after another such "novel" schemes for reduction and deconstruction. We still yearn to discuss the matters of first principles and absolute being, are told that no one of any discretion will discuss such topics, yet must still abide the quackery of a Carl Sagan, the pontifications of a Richard Rorty, or the imperialism of an Edward Wilson. Does Newman then offer us a still fresh and accurate apprehension of the crisis in liberal education, that being its exclusion of the theological principle? Although Newman himself would forswear a single explanation or cause, I think we can draw a rough sketch of some affinities and correspondences between the contemporary crisis and Newman's case for theology of 1842. Wilson is to be commended for exploring the "frontiers" between science and the humanities, including religion. Perhaps Newman can remind us all of the deepest frontier, the encounter of man with the mystery of the world, which frontier is part and parcel of the human condition and which is intrinsically theological. As one Newman commentator has noted, Newman saw a profound parallel between revelation and reason concerning the centrality of mystery: "It is useless to try to deprive Revelation of its mystery. Rather should we recognize the presence of mystery everywhere. The visible world itself, properly considered, is a mystery so great and of such a nature that it should teach us not to be troubled by mysteries, and in particular by the mystery we encounter in the very core of Revelation."[32] Perhaps the most fruitful consilience is the consilience of the mystery of nature and the mystery of revelation; the consilience of Jerusalem and Athens. The way is fraught with great opportunities as well as risks. Although Newman had a more direct case to make, founding a Catholic University in Ireland, he made the case for all humanity. In the complex secular universities of today and in the context of a deeper theological and philosophical pluralism, there is no simple solution to be found in a single tradition of theology. There are disputes about the very meaning of God. But there are obvious places to begin, following Newman's basic arguments.

First, theology must be revived in its historical context for a proper understanding of great texts and issues in the humanities and the history of science. Second, the very disputes and convergences between religious traditions can be turned to a fruitful educational outcome. Hence, theological disputes can also be a matter for fruitful inquiry. And one becomes a better citizen of the world and the academy by achieving a better and more accurate understanding of the great religions. Third, the openness to mystery and the use of models in science and religion are possible ways to interdisciplinary and liberal learning. Fourth, an exploration of the dynamic interaction of faith and reason can provide an alternative to the postmodern despair of truth. Finally, full theological study of a particular tradition may provide the standard for other explorations, historical and spiritual, enriching all students and learners with a high quality theology that Newman envisioned as the center of liberal education.

Notes

This chapter extracted from "Newman, Theology and Crisis of Liberal Education" *Journal of Interdisciplinary Studies* XI, no. 1/2 (1999): 61–82.

1. Gertrude Himmelfarb, "What It Means to Be Educated," *Wall Street Journal*, 1996.

2. See Alfred Kazin, *God and the American Writer* (New York: Alfred A. Knopf, 1997), 110 and chapter five.

3. Himmelfarb, "What It Means to Be Educated."

4. Frank M. Turner, ed., *The Idea of a University* (New Haven: Yale University Press, 1996), 258.

5. "Issues in Higher Education," *The World and I* June 1998, 297ff.

6. "In default of a recognized term, I have called the perfection or virtue of the intellect by the name of philosophy, philosophical knowledge, enlargement of the mind, or illumination" (VI.1). I am surprised that at least two of the commentators in Turner's new edition insist that the science of sciences is "Roman Catholic theology." This is not at all the case—they confuse the habit of mind with one of its objects; theology itself must be assessed in proper place. So it cannot constitute the judging mind itself.

7. "For Newman, the fundamental truth is henceforth clear—which is not to say that it did not also have its shadowy depth—the truth, namely, that as the God of the Bible is the God of this world, the God who speaks to the soul does so, not by any purely subjective and individual means, but through the great collective consciousness of an historic community, present in the midst of the world we see, in order to make it once again the way of God, which, through sin it had ceased to be. Newman saw too clearly ever again to be in doubt about the matter, that it was by that way, and by

that way alone, that we pass *ex umbris et imaginibut in veritatem.*" Louis Bouyer, *Newman: His Life and Spirituality* (New York: P. J. Kenedy, 1958), 72–73.

8. See Bouyer, *Newman: His Life and Spirituality*, 114–15.

9. While the theoretical foundations of our justice came increasingly to be understood as simply contractual, nevertheless decent legal justice was sustained in our regimes. This can only be comprehended in terms of the intimate and yet ambiguous co-penetration between contractual liberalism and Protestantism in the minds of generations of our people. . . . It is more important to recognize the dependence of secular liberalism for its moral bite upon the strength of Protestantism in English-speaking societies. Most of our history is written by secularists who see the significant happening as the development of secular liberalism. They are therefore likely to interpret the Protestants as passing if useful allies in the realization of our modern regimes. This allows them to patronize Protestant superstitions in a friendly manner, as historically helpful in the development of secularism. . . . This fundamental political vacuum at the heart of contractual liberalism was hidden for many generations by the widespread acceptance of Protestantism. . . . As Protestants accepted the liberalism of autonomous will, they became unable to provide their societies with the public sustenance of uncalculated justice which the contractual account of justice could not provide from itself. . . . Most intellectuals in our societies scorned the fundamental beliefs of the public religion, and yet counted on the continuance of its moral affirmations to serve as the convenient public basis of justice. Clever people generally believed that the foundational principles of justice were chosen conveniences, because of what they had learnt from modern science; nevertheless they could not turn away from a noble content to that justice, because they were enfolded more than they knew in long memories and hopes." George Parkin Grant, *English-Speaking Justice* (Notre Dame, Ind.: Notre Dame Press, 1985), 58–68.

10. Alan Wolfe, "A Welcome Revival of Religion in the Academy," *Chronicle of Higher Education* (19 September 1997): 20–21.

11. Huston Smith, "Scientism: The World's Littlest Religion," *Touchstone* 10, no. 3 (Summer 1997): 12–15. See also, Huston Smith, *Why Religion Matters: The Fate of the Human Spirit in an age of Disbelief* (San Francisco: Harper, 2001).

12. "Is Everything Relative? A Debate on the Unity of Knowledge" in *The Wilson Quarterly* XXII, no. 1 (Winter 1998): 14–57. References will be made to Wilson's book *Consilience* (New York: Knopf, 1998) and selections that appeared in *Atlantic Magazine*, March and April 1998. (See letters to the editor, July 1998.)

13. Richard Rorty "The Priority of Democracy to Philosophy" in *Objectivity, Relativism, and Truth, Philosophical Papers*, Volume 1 (New York: Cambridge University Press, 1991), 193. See Gerald Bradley's essay on Rorty in *Liberalism at the Crossroads*, ed. John Hittinger and Christopher Wolfe (Lanham, Md.: Rowman & Littlefield, 1995).

14. For Wilson, see *Consilience*, chapter 1, passim; Richard Rorty, "Religious Faith, Intellectual Responsibility, and Romance," in *The Cambridge Companion to William James* (New York: Cambridge University Press, 1995), 82–104.

15. On Tillich, see Wilson, *Consilience*, 263; Rorty, "Religious Faith, Intellectual Responsibility, and Romance," 91, 93, 96.

16. "Different indeed, in his views of God and of man, of the claims of God, of man's resources, of the guilt of disobedience, and of the prospect for forgiveness, from those flimsy self-invented notions, which satisfy the reason of the mere man of letters, or the prosperous and self-indulgent philosopher." Newman "On Justice, as a Principle of Divine Governance" in *Fifteen Sermons Preached before the University of Oxford between* A.D. *1826 and 1843*, ed. Mary Katherine Tillman (Notre Dame, Ind.: University of Notre Dame Press, 1997), 99–119; compare with Rorty's statement quoted in the following note.

17. "In past ages of the world, things were so bad that 'a reason to believe' . . was hard to get except by looking to a power not ourselves. In those days, there was little choice but to sacrifice the intellect in order to grasp hold of premises of practical syllogisms—premises concerning the after death consequences of baptism, pilgrimage or participation in holy wars. To be imaginative and to be religious, in those dark times, came to almost the same thing—for the world was too wretched to lift up the heart. But things are different now, because of human beings' gradual success in making their lives, and their world, less wretched. Nonreligious forms of romance have flourished—if only in those lucky parts of the world where wealth, leisure, literacy, and democracy have worked together to prolong our lives and fill our libraries. Now the things of this world are, for some lucky people, so welcome that they do not have to look beyond nature to the supernatural and beyond life to an afterlife, but only beyond the human past to the human future." Rorty, "Religious Faith, Intellectual Responsibility, and Romance," 97; one is reminded of Flannery O'Connor's character, Hazel Motes, who said in *Wiseblood*, "A man with a good car don't need salvation."

18. Rorty, "Religious Faith, Intellectual Responsibility, and Romance," 99.

19. Wilson, *Consilience*, 265; "Once we get over the shock of discovering that the universe was not made with us in mind, all the meaning the brain can master, and all the emotions it can bear, and all the shared adventure we might wish to enjoy, can be found by deciphering the hereditary orderliness that has borne our species through geological time and stamped it with the residues of deep history," 43.

20. Paul Gross, "The Icarian Impulse," *Wilson Quarterly* (Winter 1998): 49.

21. Alan Wolfe, "A Welcome Revival of Religion in the Academy."

22. Wilson, *Consilience*, 266.

23. Wilson, *Consilience*, 119.

24. For Wilson's Cartesianism, see not only his account of Descartes in *Consilience*, but also his account of analysis and synthesis in "Resuming the Enlightenment Quest," *Wilson Quarterly*: 25–27; and we cannot forget that Descartes himself hoped that medical discoveries concerning the brain would improve the moral and psychological dispositions of human beings (*Discourse*, part 6).

25. Wolfe, "Welcome Revival." This truth should be obvious; Jacques Maritain stated this in his Terry Lectures at Yale years ago: "As a matter of fact, theological problems and controversies have permeated the whole development of Western cul-

ture and civilization, and are still at work in its depths, in such a way that the one who would ignore them would be fundamentally unable to grasp his own time and the meaning of its internal conflicts. Thus impaired, he would be like a barbarous and disarmed child walking amidst the queer and incomprehensible trees, fountains statues, gardens, ruins, and building still under construction, of the old park of civilization. The intellectual and political history of the sixteenth, seventeenth and eighteenth centuries, the Reformation and the Counter Reformation, the internal state of British society after the Revolution in England, the achievements of the Pilgrim Fathers, the Rights of Man, and further events in world history have their starting point in the great disputes on nature and grace of our classical age. Neither Dante nor Cervantes nor Rabelais nor Shakespeare nor John Donne nor William Blake, nor even Oscar Wilde or D. H. Lawrence, nor Giotto nor Michelangelo nor El Greco nor Zurbaran, nor Pascal nor Rousseau, nor Madison nor Jefferson nor Edgar Allan Poe nor Baudelaire, nor Goethe nor Nietzsche nor even Karl Marx, nor Tolstoy nor Dostoevski is actually understandable without a serious theological background. Modern philosophy itself, from Descartes to Hegel, remains enigmatic without that, for in actual fact philosophy has burdened itself all through modern times with problems and anxieties taken over from theology, so that the cultural advent of a philosophy purely philosophical is still to be waited for. In the cultural life of the Middle Ages philosophy was subservient to theology or rather wrapped up in it; in that of modern times it was but secularized theology. Thus the considerations I have laid down regarding philosophy are still truer of theology. Nobody can do without theology, at least a concealed and unconscious theology, and the best way of avoiding the inconveniences of an insinuated theology is to deal with theology that is consciously aware of itself. And liberal education cannot complete its task without the knowledge of the specific realm and the concerns of theological wisdom." *Education at the Crossroads.*

26. Alfred Kazin, *God and the American Writer.*

27. Taken from Roger Shattuck, "Standing Up for Literature," *Civilization* (September-October 1995): 70ff.

28. See Newman's sermon entitled "The Usurpations of Reason," in *Fifteen Sermons*, 54–74.

29. Rorty, "The Priority of Democracy to Philosophy," 193.

30. Here is Rorty's take on religion and why it is justly excluded: "moral irresponsibility of religious fundamentalists—the people who burned people at the stake, forbade divorce and dancing, and found others way of making their neighbors miserable for the greater glory of God." Rorty, "Religious Faith, Intellectual Responsibility, and Romance," 92.

31. John Paul II, *Ex Corde Ecclesiae*, Vatican 1990, sections, 7, 15–20.

32. Bouyer, *Cardinal Newman*, 72.

CHAPTER FIFTEEN

~

James V. Schall on Faith, Reason, and Politics

> The church's social doctrine is not a "third way" between liberal capitalism and Marxist collectivism . . . rather it constitutes a category of its own. Nor is it an ideology.
>
> —John Paul II, *Sollicitudo Rei Socialis*

> The neglect of political philosophy seems to have been more harmful to religion than to political philosophy. Religion has sometimes permitted itself to be used as the means to achieve the ends of "modern" political philosophy, ends presupposed to nothing but politics. . . . Thus political philosophy seemingly needs attention on the part of religion in order to save itself from being merely an echo of the modern ideologies.
>
> —James V. Schall

Professor Schall's book, *Reason, Revelation, and the Foundations of Political Philosophy*[1] confirms John Paul II's latest encyclical on social concerns. The pundits in both the Catholic and secular press draw and sharpen their ideological knives. The integrity of Catholic doctrine is shredded left and right. Men attempt to capture the energy of the church within the confines of a modern ideology and to refashion the doctrine to echo their ideology. All the while the Pope forswears ideology and attempts to explain the unique category of Catholic social doctrine as "the accurate formulation of the results of a careful reflection on the complex realities of human existence, in society and in the international order, in the light of faith and of the church's tradition."[2] Why can men not appreciate a truly nonideological proposal concerning human affairs? Why have we this attempt to neutralize religious doctrine and to refuse to let it speak on its own terms? Schall's book addresses itself to just this issue. But he takes us beyond to see the relation of political philosophy to transcendent questions concerning human happiness, friendship, and immortality. When the journalists and pundits have resheathed their knives or turned to another carcass, Schall's book will remain as an enduring work in political philosophy and an important source for understanding the present crisis.

In order to understand the ideological closedness to philosophy and revelation, one must turn to the history of political philosophy; Schall presents a penetrating grasp of the "foundational issues" in political philosophy from Plato to Marx. The great Greek thinkers were neither sophists nor ideologues claiming to provide the definitive ideas or wisdom for a perfect regime on earth. They envisioned limits to the accomplishments of the political order precisely because of their lack of wisdom and their awareness of a higher life beyond the city. Christian revelation, for its part, addresses itself to many philosophical issues; but the proposals of Christianity did not presume to substitute for the political order. Thus, revelation also established moderation in political things because of the transcendent character of the city of God and the fallenness of man. Modern political thought, on the other hand, is inherently immoderate in its proposals because it shifts its focus from reason or revelation to ideological conglomerations that are neither revelational nor philosophical. Modern political philosophy tends to provide a "substitute metaphysics" or a "political ontology" which claims to absorb the higher reality of metaphysics and religion into the substance of the political order. The consequence of this move is the destruction of both politics and religion. In the name of "humanity" or even "charity" the modern ideologue confronts us with the most frightening spectacle of abusive power and intellectual blindness. Modern political thought has abandoned any attempt to proceed by norms of nature or divine law because these are "outside of man"; Schall defines this process as "humanization"—"the active removal by politics of what was not derived from an exclusively human source." Any shred of an appeal to a higher law is seen as a threat to the project. The insecurity of the ideologue can be seen in the intense hatred aimed at those who represent a nonideological position outside of their project. In order to meet this ideological challenge we must reconsider the foundations of political philosophy, a foundation requiring the contribution of both reason and revelation.

This venture into the history of philosophy provides Schall with the opportunity to formulate some very insightful remarks about the relation between reason and revelation; Schall considerably advances the state of present-day discussion on this topic, particularly in his assessment of the position of Leo Strauss. At first sight, Schall may appear to be simply reiterating the call by many contemporary political thinkers such as Hannah Arendt, Leo Strauss, or Eric Voegelin to return to classical political philosophy. Schall does indeed endorse this proposal as an endeavor to "reaffirm the whole of the human being and experience, itself grounded in something more than what man merely chooses, presupposed to nothing but his own autonomous will."[3] But this reaffirmation of wholeness requires the medieval tradition as well. His central thesis is that political philosophy needs the revelational tradition to be what it is in the face of modern ideology and that in turn revelation needs political philosophy to save itself from becoming captured by modern ideology. The classical revival often slights the medievals even though they continued and deepened political philosophy in its own order. Schall argues that moderation "in fact has been philosophically more completely achieved through the challenge of revelation to the city." Thus, the proper direction for political philosophy is to return to the classics and also to develop the Augustinian-Thomistic tradition within Christianity, "if politics as politics is to be preserved."[4]

What is the understanding of reason and revelation that allows Schall to press this bold claim? "Reason and revelation are not two parallel origins of truth, but part of a consistent, noncontradictory whole in which their interrelationship is based on the nature and origin of the whole, man and universe."[5] From the standpoint of faith, reason and revelation cannot be contradictory, for the God who reveals himself is the same God who created the world and its order. Schall, however, advances a solution from the side of reason as well. Classical political theory pursued a number of questions arising from within the experience of political life and philosophical reflection. The Greek philosophers were perplexed about human happiness, immortality, friendship, and the divine. They were unable to resolve many issues in a clear, satisfactory manner.

Christian revelation is an intelligent response to the dilemmas of philosophy: "political philosophy can and must understand what revelation presents as responses to the questions which political philosophy genuinely and constantly proposes to itself from its own sources . . . [and] for which there seem to be no adequate responses in reason itself."[6] The very unresolved tensions within classical philosophy, themselves so salutary and moderating to the Straussians, can also serve as a motive for considering the proposals of revelation. That is, philosophical perplexity can open one to the proposals of revelation. Hannah Arendt observed that Augustine "was the first man of thought who turned to religion because of philosophical perplexities."[7] The very humility of classical philosophy should keep it properly trained on a higher truth. Schall comments that "human reason may be open to, but incomplete before, the reality it does not itself make. Intelligence may thus be broader than reason, so that reason may be more complete in its own order by the facts and challenges of revelation."[8] If revelation can propose a truth which is in principle noncontradictory to the truth of reason and if the proposed truth clarifies the issue at hand in a way that preserves what is best in man, it is worthy of consideration. Schall makes a case for the doctrines of resurrection, creation, Trinity, grace as making more intelligible the problems of immortality and friendship.

In the present day, the serious consideration of Christian revelation allows philosophy "to consider, without lapsing into some Gnostic solution, those higher questions posed to it by the very experience of being and thinking."[9] In short, it may betray despair or a lack of courage to disregard the claims of revelation. The alternatives? Both the Gnostics and the serious student of classical political philosophy must fashion some myth to complete their own being and acting in the world. St. Paul criticized the philosophers for resorting to myths of their own making.

Schall could press his case even harder at this point with Augustine's challenge to the philosophers to distinguish presumption and confession as the true alternative postures to the highest things.[10] But in a similar vein he uses an article by Leo Strauss to a good accord. Strauss and his school reject the Thomistic claim as they maintain that no genuine synthesis is possible between reason and revelation. They do not claim that reason can refute faith; however they do seem to posit a fundamental inconsistency in doctrine and posture. Schall maintains that the fundamental doctrines of Christianity are not excluded in principle by the Greek philosophers for they are not contradicted by the discoveries of reason. It is the posture of philosophy, however, that really seems to keep the Straussians from admitting the possible harmony of reason and revelation. Strauss says that "obedient love" is opposed to "autonomous understanding." Yet Strauss acknowledges that, from the side of faith, knowledge is a good thing if dedicated to the service of God. So from within faith, Schall concludes that human reason can confront the truths of nature and maintain its full autonomy.

Revelation does not and cannot absorb reason and philosophy: faith is not vision. Philosophy is a remainder that we are still on the way to vision. Further, revelation needs the leaven of philosophy to be what it is—intelligible proposals to serious human questions: "revelational answers meant nothing in a philosophic sense unless the questions to which answers were directed were themselves properly discovered and reflected upon as philosophy."[11]

To exemplify this relation of reason and revelation Schall deals with issues of immortality and friendship. To appreciate the uniqueness of his approach one may consider the present-day interest in Aristotle's theory of virtue. Most approaches to Aristotle tend to wrest his account of the virtues out of the context of the Aristotelean philosophy as a whole. It is in the *Ethics* after all that Aristotle says that the moral virtues are instrumental and that the highest happiness is found in contemplation: "We must not follow those who advise us to have human thoughts, since we are only men; on the contrary, we should try to become immortal as far as that is possible."[12] Schall explores the ancient recognition of the two kinds of drives in man, the one that is proper to humans and the one that stretches the human being to something beyond time and the city. The classical tradition was devoted to preserving "the legitimacy of both the city and the highest aims of man as such, so that they will not seem to be in fatal opposition to each other."[13] Plato did not locate the best regime in time; Aristotle posited a higher life, the life of the mind, which belongs to man only indirectly or partially. The proper life of man and the city "did not include, but did not deny the higher happiness."[14] The highest could not be included, because of the limits of time and matter. Yet the highest could not be denied; it would create illusion that full human happiness was not problematic to the extreme. Again we tend to forget that Aristotle's idea of happiness includes as well as virtue, friends, money, health, and good looks, all of which are subject to the "slings of fortune." The obscurities of Aristotle's treatment of happiness are all too easily covered over. The Stoics forced a position on the status of worldly virtue. They absolutized it in a way unthinkable to Aristotle, who held out for a higher life beyond the control of human will. Plato and Aristotle found a balanced position which prevented a "politicizing of the theoretic order" and the "spiritualizing" of the political order.[15] The two lives, politics and contemplation, the properly human and the divine, were kept in uneasy balance. The Epicureans and Stoics all too well understood the irresolvable tensions of the Greek theory.

Yet when the "futility" of these various aspects is "understood the full unity of political philosophy be grasped."[16] The full unity includes reason and revelation. Thus, the claim of revelation can be more readily acknowledged in light of the questions and irresolvable tensions of political philosophy. Augustine and Aquinas made a vital contribution to political philosophy in this regard. By bringing to bear the central doctrines of Christianity on the moral and political order they once again articulated the limits of the city while affirming politics as a legitimate human endeavor. Augustine's "main contribution" was "to free politics itself from ever being the location of this [best] 'polity' or republic."[17] The danger of Augustinianism is the neglect of the city as a legitimate enterprise. Schall sees Aquinas firmly establishing the proper life of man in the natural virtues, while maintaining the transcendent goals of religion. For Schall, the great tradition of the West must include Jerusalem and Athens—and Catholic Rome. For the latter can make a positive contribution "both to the incompleteness of the classic and Old Testament position and to the understanding of and correction of the aberrations of the modern project."[18]

The spirit of modern philosophy with its Gnostic attempts to overcome the limits of the city stands in opposition to the political tradition as outlined above. The "classical and revelational limits of politics were replaced by an anthropological substitute metaphysics."[19] This political metaphysics responds to irresolvable dilemmas of political philosophy. Reaching to the higher things, the modern project offers a parody of them. They appeal to the deep desire in mankind for friendship, beatitude, and immortality—the things that the human city cannot really afford. The Marxist dream of an all-encompassing generic being and a humanized nature is one such attempt. But it is a spurious immortality that cannot preserve the dignity of the individual. The socialist-utopian ideologues are by far the more dangerous; in the democratic-capitalist regimes he sees features of a limited city open to the higher truth in its own order. However, Schall admits that America is not immune from the ideological shifts; he agrees with Strauss that "the modern project, as theoretical endeavor, corrupted this more practical possibility."[20] Thus, while Schall does not dwell on its shortcomings, the American system also offers it versions of pseudo-immortality and pseudo-friendship with consumption of products or sentimental and free love. The American Gnostic dreams may be tied to the rising spirit of Emerson. Marion Montgomery's volume, *Why Hawthorne Was Melancholy* may be consulted in this regard.

Of whatever stripe, East or West, the Gnostic project should not be baptized by religion as if "support of this modern system ought to be its essential tool or goal."[21] Here we have the meeting of minds of Schall and John Paul II as originally seen in the quotations cited at the beginning of this chapter. Christian theology has a vital role to play in the modern world in confronting the Leviathan of the modern state. Schall is surely right to point out that philosophical thought alone is not sufficient to "describe the alternatives to revolutionary and radical humanism."[22] For not only do they deny the very premises of classical thought, they embody an aberrant religious impulse. Only a genuine theology can describe the alternative. Political philosophy, for its part, can remind the theologian of the questions and the limits of political reality. Thus, to understand the appeal and the weakness of modern ideology Schall exhorts us to return to the classics and medieval theory. Reason and revelation together provide the surest means for a return to political moderation and for a safeguard of man's highest aspirations. *Reason, Revelation and the Foundations of Political Philosophy* is not an easy book to work through. As difficult as the task may be, Schall is right to conclude that "this is no mere esoteric exercise or obscure religious contention but an enterprise upon which depends the possibility of a human city."[23] His is a spirited book, as well as philosophical. He speaks of political philosophy as the "first line of defense of a limited city and authentic revelation,"[24] and as standing "guard at the gates of the city to preserve the city and to open individual members to what lies beyond."[25] Professor Schall is a keen sentinel and he deserves our gratitude for this fine book.

Notes

This chapter extracted from "Review of *Reason, Revelation, and Political Philosophy* by James V. Schall," in *Crisis* (April 1988): 52–54.

1. James V. Schall, *Reason, Revelation, and the Foundations of Political Philosophy* (Baton Rouge, La.: Lousiana State University Press, 1990). See more recent works of James Schall, *Reason, Revelation, and Human Affairs: Selected Writings of James V. Schall*, ed. with introduction by Marc Guerra (Lanham, Md.: Lexington Books, 2001); *The Politics of Heaven and Hell: Christian Themes from Classical, Medieval, and Modern Political Philosophy* (Lanham, Md.: University Press of America, 1984); *Jacques Maritain: The Philosopher in Society* (Lanham, Md.: Rowman & Littlefield, 1998).

2. Schall, *Reason, Revelation*, 41.

3. Schall, *Reason, Revelation*, 100.

4. Schall, *Reason, Revelation*, 194.

5. Schall, *Reason, Revelation*, 200.

6. Schall, *Reason, Revelation*, 95.

7. Hannah Arendt, *The Life of the Mind* (New York: Harvest Books, 1989), 84.

8. Schall, *Reason, Revelation*, 104.

9. Schall, *Reason, Revelation*, 194.

10. St. Augustine, *Confessions* VII.20.

11. Schall, *Reason, Revelation*, 202.

12. Aristotle, *Ethics*, 1177b30ff.

13. Schall, *Reason, Revelation*, 13–17.

14. Schall, *Reason, Revelation*, 29.

15. Schall, *Reason, Revelation*, 55.

16. Schall, *Reason, Revelation*, 94.

17. St. Augustine, *Confessions*, 192.

18. Schall, *Reason, Revelation*, 223.

19. Schall, *Reason, Revelation*, 201.
20. Schall, *Reason, Revelation*, 4, 193.
21. Schall, *Reason, Revelation*, 187.
22. Schall, *Reason, Revelation*, 184.
23. Schall, *Reason, Revelation*, 239.
24. Schall, *Reason, Revelation*, 7.
25. Schall, *Reason, Revelation*, 15.

~

CHAPTER SIXTEEN

Maritain on the Cooperation of Church and State

The root requirement for a sound mutual cooperation between Church and the body politic is not the unity of a religio-political body, as the respublica Christiana of the Middle Ages was, but the very unity of the human person, simultaneously a member of the body politic and of the Church, if he freely adheres to her.[1]

On December 8, 1965, the curtain closed on a great religious event of the twentieth century, the Second Vatican Council. Culminating decades of initiatives for renewal, the Council reappropriated and refashioned its fundamental message, or "deposit of faith," in order to bear it more effective witness in the modern world. It was to unleash ferment, doubt, and hesitations within the Catholic Church for decades to come. On that closing day, in the still of a winter afternoon in Rome, perhaps an eye of a storm, a slightly stooped octogenarian approached Pope Paul VI and received from him a message from the Council Fathers to "Men of thought and science." It was a poignant moment for both men, since Paul VI once had referred to Jacques Maritain as his mentor. The message was brief. It offered encouragement and admiration for the great duty and responsibility of intellectual inquiry and its long search. "Our paths could not fail to cross," the Council Fathers wrote to the intellectuals of the world. And indeed Jacques Maritain was just the man at "the crossroads"—a man engaged with many of the great intellectual and practical issues of the century in science and philosophy, politics and ethics, art and religion. But he too was a man of deep faith, whose conversion to

Catholicism was a great story in its own right.[2] So the Council Fathers also offered, "without dazzling brilliance," the light of "our mysterious lamp which is faith." This faith, they said, is a "great friend of intelligence," and they foresaw the possibility of a deep understanding and cooperation between science and faith. They only asked that one does not "stand in the way of this important meeting." Some thirty years later Pope John Paul II would single out Maritain again as an exemplary philosopher whose life and work had exhibited the boldness of reason combined with the illumination of faith.[3]

So too do we find in Maritain's life and work an exemplary account of the relation of church and state. As a citizen of the world, engaged with the United Nations (UNESCO), and as a French ex-patriot in American universities such as Princeton, Notre Dame, and Chicago, Maritain was at the crossroads of new opportunities for church-state relations. Here too did he often argue that the church is a great friend of freedom, calling for a new era of cooperation, and asking that obscurantists not stand in the way of such historic meetings. If faith and science have paths which cannot fail to cross, so too must the church and state. Historically, the relation of church and state is one of the major motifs of history.[4] As early as the 1930s Maritain had begun to unveil his account of the new era for church-state relations that he named "New Christendom." It would involve the recognition of a new historic climate in which the permanent principles would be applied in new creative ways. *Man and the State* reiterates this theme, and often refers back to the groundbreaking work of his previous publications[5] (*The Things That Are Not Caesar's* and *Integral Humanism*). It anticipates the great work of Vatican II in this area, and it finds its fulfillment in Maritain's poorly received book *The Peasant of the Garonne*, published in 1966 but written within a month after that poignant meeting between him and Pope Paul VI.[6]

In this chapter, I wish to sketch Maritain's understanding of church and state as developed in *Man and the State*; then take a brief look at the understanding of Vatican II on the role of the church in the modern world; and finally consider Maritain's attempt in *The Peasant of the Garonne* to interpret the meaning of Vatican II in light of the new relation of church and state that he had previously articulated.

Man and the State and the
Reconciliation of Liberty and Religion

In 1949, Jacques Maritain delivered six lectures at the University of Chicago under the auspices of the Charles R. Walgreen Foundation for the Study of American Institutions. Maritain had high praise for the American Constitution, describing it as "an outstanding lay Christian document tinged with the philosophy of the day."[7] The American political tradition he saw as a viable example of a tradition built upon a sharp distinction between church and state combined with their actual cooperation: "The spirit and inspiration of this great political Christian document is basically repugnant to the idea of making human society stand aloof from God and from any religious faith." He sought to avoid two extremes which had plagued Europe: on the one hand, the practice of a form of civil intolerance which made non-Christians or non-Catholics second-class citizens; on the other hand, the behavior of those who sought to marginalize the church by isolating it from the activities of modern society. The former extreme could take the form of maintaining clerical privilege and keeping up a façade of the Christian state. Maritain saw in this the effect of increased bitterness and misunderstanding, as well the encouragement of Pharisaical citizens. The latter extreme could take the form of indifference to religious affairs, or the historicist claim that the principles of prior ages are irrelevant and religion has no place at all in the modern world. Maritain finds the golden mean through a distinction between the fundamental principles, imperishable principles, and the conditions for application, historic conditions which call for analogous explication and application. That is, he does not merely say that the historic conditions are less than perfect and require a prudential application and approximation, but that the very historic climate of the modern age, different as it is from the sacral age of the medieval time, requires a different analogous understanding of the principles at work. Thus he is neither a historicist on matter of principle nor an absolutist on the question of proper understanding of the relationship between church and state.

Maritain bases his account of church and state on the notion of degrees or orders of human achievement and flourishing. The common good of civil life is "an ultimate end" but in a certain order, that is, the order of temporal achievement. It is an end "worthy in itself." In his first chapter Maritain derives from the Greek sense of the polis an account of the dignity of the political order. The common good of the body politic is constituted by justice and friendship, a form of association that "tends toward a really human and freely achieved communion. It lives on the devotion of human persons and their gift of themselves."[8] The common good includes economic and political infrastructure but most of all "the sociological integration of all the civic conscience, political virtues and sense of law and freedom, of all the activity, material prosperity and spiritual riches of unconsciously operating hereditary wisdom, of moral rectitude, justice, friendship, happiness, virtue and heroism in the individual lives of the members of the body politic." It is important to note that Maritain distinguishes the "state" from the "body politic" the former being the instrument of the body politic to administer justice and good order. Thus the very notion of church and state must recall this distinction during the discussion of their relations and cooperation, for the church finds a place within the notion of the body politic with its various associations and heritage. So the common good of the political society must include "an intrinsic though indirect ordination to something which transcends it." It is subordinate to a higher good because there is in human nature a higher aspiration. The seeds of such transcendence are to be found in natural human aspirations to "spiritual goods" such as truth, justice, and beauty which lead one beyond nation or state. The state can claim no sovereignty over the life of the mind. The political common good cannot be closed in on itself; nor should the state attempt to curb the impulse to truth and beauty, such is the basis for civil liberties for freedom of thought and expression. For the ancients, this aspiration was embodied in the philosopher who existed beyond the city, and who was even beyond that religion which was poetical or civil in nature. But the philosopher embraced a true philosophical religion, a rational or metaphysical religion.

The human person transcends the state and the body politic through "what is supra-temporal." Maritain recognizes a capacity for transcendence in all, not just the few, and that capacity finds an ultimate perfection in religion. From a Christian perspective the absolute ultimate end lies in the supernatural order, union with God through grace. But he is careful to explain each principle and each step of his argument from the standpoint of both the believer and the unbeliever. There will be an "unavoidable mutual misapprehension" between the two,[9] but nevertheless a philosophical case can be made for the notion of "sharp distinction and actual cooperation."

Maritain develops three general principles which he says are "imperishable" or true always and everywhere, but they require historic conditioning in their application. The three general principles are: (1) the freedom of the church to teach and preach and worship; (2) the superiority of the church—that is, of the spiritual—over the body politic and the state; and (3) the necessary cooperation between the church and the body politic and the state. He elaborates and defends each one in turn.

Maritain presents a variety of reasons for freedom of religion. It follows from his overall account of the transcendence of the human person. The perfections of intellect and will which characterize the full development of the human person have a terminus beyond political life in "supra-temporal goods" which "constitute the moral heritage of mankind, the spiritual common good of civilization or the community of minds."[10] We can call this metaphysical ground for freedom of religion. Maritain also gives a more direct political argument. On the basis of freedom of association the freedom of religion or church can be derived. Churches are one of the primary intermediate groups to which the human person is a member and derives much benefit; society as well derives such benefit. So too can we appeal to freedom of conscience, which Maritain calls "the most basic and inalienable of all the human rights." For the believer, on the other hand, there is a more profound basis for freedom of the church. The church is understood to be a superior society by virtue of its supernatural character. It derives from the mandate to preach the Gospel given by Jesus.

The second principle, concerning the superiority of the church, derives from a historical, as well as a theological claim. Prior to the arrival of Christianity the political society would make divine claims for itself or for its ruler. The very distinction between church and state is made possible by Christianity and the admonition to "Render to Caesar what is Caesar's and to God what is God's." As Maritain so eloquently puts it "the terrestrial and national frameworks in which the spiritual was confined have been shattered." The superiority of the spiritual is manifest in the very distinction—God is greater than Caesar.[11] And yet Maritain points out, following Leo XIII, the dedivinizing of the state does not harm the state. The state is "autonomous" within its own order. The church makes no claim for direct rule over temporal affairs on this account.

Finally, for the third principle, perhaps most controversial, is an argument based upon the benefit of the church to society. All the church asks is freedom—in return much will be rendered to the state in terms of moral influence. Of course it is now the very influence on morality that many resent. But the argument from the unity of the human person is brought in precisely at this point. It would be unnatural for the church and state to ignore each other because it would amount to splitting the person in two halves—for the sake of the integrity of the person there must be cooperation between church and state. Determining what kind of cooperation is needed requires us to consider the historic climate in which we now live in contrast to the climate of an earlier era.

Maritain's unique breakthrough on the topic of church and state, and I might add an anticipation of the position adopted by Vatican II, derives from his account of history. Maritain proposes that we approach the issue in light of the "climate or constellation of existential conditions" dealing with juridical, social-political, and intellectual factors that define a given era. The application of the principles in each era calls for a different mode of application. That is, Maritain does not see the historical conditions as so many limits to a prudential application, which in more favorable conditions would allow for a greater achievement. Rather the new era requires an analogous application. The conservatives, if you will, do not grasp the historical climate or opportunities for a new style of Christian witness and a new style of church-state relations. They are abstract absolutists with respect to the principles, but have a univocal grasp of what they mean or entail. For their position would entail a denial of equal civil rights to the nonbeliever and it would ultimately entail a form of violence against them. The liberals, if you will, declare that the principles have now become obsolete and fall into historicism. Their problem stems from an equivocal understanding of the principles. It entails indifferentism and perhaps the aggressive attack on religion in the public square that we witness today. It is part of Maritain's lifelong philosophical and theological project to confront the modern world from the standpoint of the Thomistic tradition and to extend the basic principles to the problems of the day. He wishes to embrace the advances of the modern world but by purifying the errors of its philosophy and first principles.

Maritain's understanding of the modern era centers on a distinction between the "sacral" versus the "lay" state. The distinction is most fully articulated in *Integral Humanism*, and it is the centerpiece of Maritain's understanding of the achievement of Vatican II as explained in *The Peasant of the Garonne*, to be examined below. Maritain describes the medieval era as characterized by a distinction between the two powers, temporal and spiritual, but a unification of the two through the use of faith for the unity of the body politic. Religious creed was used as the basis for unity in the body politic, so a rupture in belief was seen as a rupture in the body politic. The heretic therefore was seen as threat to the political order. The methods of the inquisition served both the church and the state; the state could use it as an instrument for state unity; the church could use the temporal power as a means for its goals. The temporal therefore was subordinated to the spiritual as a means or an instrument for a spiritual end.[12] The medieval era was also characterized by what Maritain calls "fortitude in the service of justice" as its public ideal. The public servant aimed at the embodiment of a noble ideal. With the fragmentation of the religious unity of the state by way of the reformation, the "Baroque era" attempted to refund the unity of the state through the absolutism of the ruler whose faith would guarantee the unity of the spiritual and political order. Maritain views this as a halfway house, unworkable in the long run. The true modern era is described as a lay state whose two guiding principles are the differentiation and autonomy of the temporal sphere, from economics to politics and the public ideal of the conquest of freedom and human dignity. The unity of the state could no longer be grounded in a spiritual and religious unity, so it must be based upon a temporal goal as such. The notion of human dignity and the use of temporal power to empower or liberate human beings from bondage to nature or oppressive rule became the public ideal. The autonomy of the secular affairs Maritain says is a rightful unfolding of the very distinction of the affairs of God and Caesar. The new climate therefore requires the analogous application of the imperishable principles. The entailments are as follows. The state is no longer viewed as the "secular arm" of the church. The state is "autonomous and independent" within its own sphere. [13] Second, the equality of all members of the temporal society is recognized as a fundamental tenant. The holding of office or the enjoyment of the civil rights is the same for all. Third, the church and state both recognize the importance of "inner forces" as a preferred mode over coercion. Faith cannot be imposed by force, but neither can political persuasion or other fundamentals of belief. This leads to the highlighting of conscience as the great key to the new era. Freedom of conscience entails freedom of inquiry and freedom of expression.

In these new conditions Maritain sees a great new era for the relation of church and state, traced back to the unity of the person. There are three aspects to the argument. First, the person is characterized by a unity or integrity—and although living in various orders with various pursuits, he has one conscience. The person is simultaneously a member of the body politic and a member of the church. Hence "he would be cut in two if his temporal membership were cut off from his spiritual membership."[14] The wholeness of the person should incline us toward cooperation rather than antagonism. Second, the religious pursuit is essential to the "pursuit of happiness." Therefore the common good of society, which includes the flourishing of its members, cannot but be favorable toward the religious pursuit. Third, through the influence on conscience "Christian truths and incentives" would pass into the sphere of temporal existence and thereby assist the democratic state in rousing the "inner strength and spiritual stronghold of democracy."[15] The religious beliefs and practices will have a "leavening effect." They should uplift morality and sensitize moral conscience. The civil rights movement of the 1960s would be an example that Maritain has in mind. Maritain anticipates the communitarian critique of liberal philosophy—the attempt to develop a neutral, thin theory of the reason for the political society is impossible or weak. The pluralism of religious belief can be turned to the state's advantage if the various religious traditions can agree on concrete practical principles, but provide a more full-bodied understanding and defense of the principles at a higher level. The educational efforts of the church are very important for the well being of the political society.[16] The students could see "the entire convictions" and personal inspiration behind their principles of government and social practice and embrace them more deeply. For this reason Maritain says that the isolation or separation of church and state would "simply spell suicide."

The very distinction between church and state grants to the church her newfound influence. She stands for universality and for the higher supratemporal good to which the human person aspires. The superiority of the church is therefore not the basis for the use of coercive methods or for the dictation of public policy, but it should operate through the springs of conscience and persuasion. In a poignant passage Maritain says, "A superior agent is not confined or shut up within itself. It radiates. It stimulates the inner forces and energies of other agents—even autonomous in their own peculiar spheres—whose place is less high in the scale of being. Superiority implies a penetrating and vivifying influence. The very token of the superiority of the church is the moral power with which she vitally influence, penetrates and quickens, as a spiritual leaven, temporal existence and the inner energies of nature, so as to carry them to a higher and more perfect level in their own order."[17]

So the autonomy of the temporal sphere is recognized and even celebrated, and the influence of the church is to stimulate within the very political order its own proper excellence and achievement of its own proper end. It requires a distinct metaphysical conception, analogous to the relation of nature and grace—that grace does not destroy but rather builds upon and perfects nature.[18] Maritain's prophetic term for the new relation of church and state, from the standpoint of the church, is called the "sanctification of secular life." The temporal itself bears within itself the mark of the divine, a quid divinum.[19] The church therefore seeks to persuade and to revive the inner energies within the human person, within conscience. It thus forever forswears the use of coercive power. Rather, the church now asks for freedom, the freedom to pursue its spiritual mission. No special privilege is required, just an acknowledgement that the temporal common good of the state is advanced by granting to the church her freedom. It is a temporal good for the reasons mentioned above, the essential component of the pursuit of happiness and the leavening effect of Christian conscience within society at large. This constitutes an in-principled argument against state coercion for religious purposes. In addition there are prudential reasons for limiting even the legitimate secular reasons for morality as mediated through religion. Maritain explains the Thomistic adage that law should be proportionate to the capacity of the people. Thus not every moral standard will be legislated in full force.[20] The actual cooperation should go beyond the negative freedom of the church to be allowed to pursue her mission to preach the gospel. Maritain says that the state should ask the church to do more in domains where she can assist—such as welfare and education. The state can help remove obstacles and "open the doors" for the church to assist the "social and moral work of the nation, to provide people with a leisure worthy of human dignity, and to develop within them the sense of liberty and fraternity."[21] At the end of the day Maritain understands that there will always be an ultimate misapprehension between the believer and the nonbeliever. But he thinks that the task is now clear. The influence of the church on liberty is for the good; she has forsworn the use of coercion for religious purposes. The blind forces, which have attacked religion in the name of freedom and the dignity of the person, must now drop their mask and appear, as they are—opponents of liberty and human dignity. Their antireligious animus, their virulent secularism, now becomes the sole reason for attacking and excluding religion. Maritain has traced our way through the Tocquevillian dilemma: "Where then are we? Men of religion fight against freedom, and lovers of liberty attack religion; noble and generous spirits praise slavery, while low servile minds preach independence; honest and enlightened citizens are the enemies of all progress, while men without patriotism or morals make themselves the apostles of civilization and enlightenment!"[22] And one hundred years later Maritain claims in his *Man and the State*: "Present times, however miserable they are, have the wherewithal to elate those who love the Church and love freedom. . . . The cause of freedom and the cause of the Church are one in the defense of man."[23]

Vatican II on "The Church in the Modern World"

Considered one of the four great documents of Vatican II, "The Church in the Modern World" outlined a new emphasis and new strategy for the role of the church.[24] Seeking to read "the signs of the times" the Council Fathers traced out many positive developments of the modern world, as well as the frustrated aspirations of the modern world. It emphasizes the dignity of the human person and depths of conscience. But one must also notice its Augustinian thread of the dark side, the sinfulness of man, as the ultimate reason for the frustrations and failures of such noble aspirations. Thus it argues that religion, Christianity, the church, have an important role to play in the development of the modern world. Its new emphasis will involve the laity and their special role in the modern world. But throughout, the essential distinction between church and state is recalled and reaffirmed. "The Church and the political community in their own fields are autonomous and independent from each other."[25] And following the position of Maritain the

Council Fathers also emphasize the need for cooperation based upon the unity of the human person; both are devoted to the good of the "same man." Both must therefore foster sounder cooperation between themselves for the good of all. Autonomy therefore does not entail separation or antagonism.

In one of the key sections the council addresses itself to the objection whether "a closer bond between human activity and religion will work against the independence of men, of societies, or of the sciences." In order to properly answer that fear various meanings of autonomy are explored. The proper meaning of autonomy comports with the Christian notion of creation:

> If by the autonomy of earthly affairs we mean that created things and societies themselves enjoy their own laws and values which must be gradually deciphered, put to use, and regulated by men, then it is entirely right to demand that autonomy. Such is not merely required by modern man, but harmonizes also with the will of the Creator. For by the very circumstance of their having been created, all things are endowed with their own stability, truth, goodness, proper laws and order. Man must respect these as he isolates them by the appropriate methods of the individual sciences or arts.[26]

Politics and economics therefore have their own proper autonomy—that is, their own fundamental laws and intelligibility. The political community achieves its proper differentiation from the religious association, the church or any other religious association. Political life has its proper excellence; its own proper dynamism; and its own proper role to play in the development of human beings. But by this same token, the political sphere is not the ultimate; it must not claim the mantle of religion for itself. It is not divine. One manner of claiming divinity or ultimacy for itself would be through self-sufficiency. That is if the state recognizes no power higher than itself, then it will verge toward idolatry of its own proper purpose and thereby distort it. Thus the Council Fathers rightly describe the "false" sense of autonomy:

> But if the expression, the independence of temporal affairs, is taken to mean that created things do not depend on God, and that man can use them without any reference to their Creator, anyone who acknowledges God will see how false such a meaning is. For without the Creator the creature would disappear. For their part, however, all believers of whatever religion always hear His revealing voice in the discourse of creatures. When God is forgotten, however, the creature itself grows unintelligible.[27]

Echoing the Thomistic notion of the *exitus et reditus*, the coming forth from God and the return of creatures to God, the Council Fathers point out that the origin and end of human life transcend the political order, for which a due reverence and respect must be acknowledged.[28] In fact, a great theme of this council is that the denial of this higher origin and destiny leads to the very assault upon human dignity with which the modern world is so concerned. The loss of the Creator entails the loss of the creature. The church is therefore a "sign and safeguard of the transcendent character of the human person."[29] By fostering and elevating all that is true, good and beautiful, the church has a great role to play in developing the modern world and the temporal and political community. It must be said that she uses her own proper methods—"the ways and means proper to the Gospel" which are different from those of the earthly city. In her turn the church asks for freedom "to preach the faith, to teach her social doctrine." In his "Message to Heads of State," Paul VI said, "She asks of you only liberty."[30] The church does not threaten temporal order but rather, "heals everything human of its fatal emptiness, transfigures it and fills it with hope, truth and beauty."[31]

This role becomes especially pronounced in light of the Augustinian theme of human weakness with its need for healing; this theme is taken up into the Thomistic idea of grace perfecting nature and elevating from within. It is the very autonomy of the temporal that is respected here—the ministrations of the church are for the sake of the proper development of the political, the temporal, and the human as such. From the very outset of the document the Council Fathers refer to the problem of evil: the church wishes to help the modern world find the fulfillment of its quest for dignity and freedom. But they must realize that this world is divided by sin.[32] It is an illusion to think that a genuine or total emancipation of mankind will be brought about without an acknowledgement of the deeper root of human failure.[33] It is anthropocentric humanism, premised upon this false sense of autonomy, which thinks that the world can sustain meaning without any reference to the divine, indeed, the modern temptation is to believe that the world lacks meaning only to be filled in by human creativity.[34] But the Council Fathers press the question: "What is this sense of sorrow, of evil, of death, which continues to exist despite so much progress? What purpose have these victories purchased at so high a cost?" Is it not apparent that human beings struggle with evil and find themselves almost unable to deal with it?[35] Sin obscures the very light of conscience.[36] Good human energies are distorted by pride and self love: "constantly imperiled by man's pride and deranged self-love, [they] must be purified and perfected."[37] The purification and perfection of the natural activity and disposition is a task assigned to the lay people. This is a great achievement of the council. The church will fulfill this mission, this benefit to the earthly city, not by assuming temporal power or by using the means proper to the earthly city such as coercion or political power. Rather through the very means proper to the Gospel, through the inspiration of conscience and through a sacramental approach. It is through the lay people because of their unity of life. It is the same person who is a member of the church and who is also a member of the political community. The burden of unity falls upon the individual person, the individual Christian, who is a member of both societies.

Vatican II is known for its lack of anathemas and condemnations, taking a new approach to modernity no longer in terms of a syllabus of errors or condemnation of mistakes, but "to carry forward the work of Christ under the lead of the befriending Spirit."[38] And thus one of the few errors condemned is that on the part of Christians who divorce their own earthly affairs from their religious life: "This split between the faith which many profess and their daily lives deserves to be counted among the more serious errors of our age."[39] A Christian may not claim a warrant to neglect or to shirk their earthly duties because of a concern with the otherworldly. In fact such a Christian "jeopardizes his eternal salvation." The Council Fathers call for Christian laymen to gather into a "vital synthesis with religious values" all their earthly activities—humane, domestic, professional, social, and technical enterprises. Indeed "secularity" is the very mark of the layman—"secular duties and activities belong properly to laymen" and they should work according to the "laws proper to each discipline" and yet seek to inscribe the divine law into the very life of the earthly city—by way of their own conscientious action.[40] The very secular work of the layman accomplishes both a religious mission and a temporal mission, to the benefit of both:

> Even by their secular activity they must aid one another to greater holiness of life, so that the world may be filled with the spirit of Christ and may the more effectively attain its destiny in justice, in love and in peace. The laity enjoys a principle role in the universal fulfillment of this task. Therefore, by their competence in secular disciplines and by their activity, interiorly raised up by grace, let them work earnestly in order that created goods through human labor, technical skill and civil culture may serve the utility of all men according to the plan of the creator and the light of his word . . . Thus, through the members of the Church, will Christ increasingly illuminate the whole of human society with his saving light.[41]

It is part of the universal call to holiness that the layman receives such an important new emphasis according to Vatican II. No longer is the notion of holiness to be reserved for the priests, the religious. And yet the layman is not called to holiness by a secondary imitation of the religious by a flight from the world or by an explicitly ecclesiastical mission; rather it is through unity of life, unity of religious devotion and professional energy, the former illuminating and purifying the latter, that the layman achieves holiness of life. It may be called a sanctification of the world, a sanctification of the temporal order itself, in terms of the proper finalities and autonomy of the temporal order itself. For good reason then did Paul VI remark in his message to rulers that the freedom of the church will first of all benefit "your peoples" since the church "forms for you loyal citizens, friends of social peace and progress." A sharp distinction is drawn between the proper orders of church and state; yet a vital cooperation is recognized, for the benefit of each. Also for good reason, did Paul VI acknowledge Jacques Maritain at the end of the council by presenting him with his "Message to Men of Thought and Science." Paul VI rightly indicated that the Vatican Council was in some ways the fulfillment of the lifelong work of Maritain. Indeed, in his own closing remarks, Paul VI spoke about the religious significance of the Council turning upon a proper understanding of the "whole man."[42] And yet within a few months of that historic occasion, Jacques Maritain published what many took as a bitter attack upon the very work and promise of the council. *The Peasant of the Garonne*, significantly subtitled, "An Old Layman Questions Himself about the Present Time," does not in any way retract or attack his lifelong aspiration and work for a "new Christendom." Indeed this book amplifies it and hones it. It is Maritain's cry of the heart; it is a very personal book for which any careful reader can discern beneath the bitterness of its surface, a rich, a sweet, a highly personal testimony of hope.

The Peasant of the Garonne: Maritain's Last Word, Bitter or Sweet?

The impact of the new council went far beyond what anyone had anticipated. The effects have led some to question whether the council should have been called at all, and others who say that it did not go far enough and further changes are necessary. We still live in the chaos and confusion. But in 1967, Maritain saw the root principle of the excess and wrote this book, *Peasant of the Garonne*, designating a man who would not hesitate to call a "spade a spade." Maritain offers his book as a corrective, a rebuke to both extremes; he attempts to stabilize the core meanings of the council in light of history, spirituality, and philosophy.[43] Maritain wrote *Peasant* less than a year after the close of the council. Its relevance now more than thirty years after is astounding. John Paul II has accomplished the corrections and he has stabilized the core meanings much in the vein traced by Maritain in

Peasant. But much still waits to be discovered. Its call for renewal is still waiting to be discovered. To cover some of the scope of *Peasant*, I plan to explore two themes: first, the achievement of Vatican II, especially the key role of the laity in fulfilling the promise of the new age; second, the difference between the false and true renewal, namely what went wrong after the council and the intellectual and spiritual basis for the true appreciation and fulfillment of the promise of Vatican II.

The Achievement of Vatican II

Maritain opens the book with a chapter entitled "Thanksgiving." He reminds the reader that the council was primarily pastoral and not doctrinal and that it met a historic task requiring "progress in evangelical awareness and attitudes of the heart," rather than the definition of dogma. This pastoral nature has itself been distorted and has become a rationale for abandoning doctrine or changing doctrines. As Maritain wryly notes, the council did in fact devote two documents to dogmatic constitutions; and further, he says that the dogmas have been defined once and for all, and new developments simply make explicit and complete old ones.

He outlines the great achievements—freedom and human dignity, especially freedom of conscience and religion; a new approach to non-Catholics, both Christian and non-Christian, especially the Jewish people; an affirmation of the value, beauty, and dignity of the world; the universal call to holiness, especially of the laity. Each of these great achievements is subject to distortion. Each must be separated from an ideology which preys upon the truth and obscures the great opportunity for a new age. Indeed, the progressive interpretation of these items, both within and outside of the church, conjures up a heady brew of liberalism, ecumenism, secularism, and laicism, the very things which many Catholics have found an enemy, the things that are wrong with modernity. Briefly stated here is what Maritain understands by these achievements: by liberalism, authentic liberalism, as Maritain sought to defend in *Man and the State*, he means the recognition of the "true idea of freedom" and a deeper appreciation of the dignity of the person and human rights. It also mean the recognition of religious freedom and the sanctity of conscience. By ecumenism, he celebrates friendship with non-Catholics, Christian and non-Christian. It especially means the elimination of anti-Semitism. By secularism, Maritain understands the very Thomistic principle of the "value, beauty, and dignity of world" and a corresponding temporal mission of the Christian. And finally, the emphasis upon the laity means that all are called to perfection of charity and the wisdom of the Holy Spirit, all are called to instill the spirit of the Gospel in the temporal order.

These four achievements constitute a massive shift—in church-state relations in particular. It is the end of an era, and the beginning of a new age. The council fulfills the great project which Maritain began with *Integral Humanism* and continued with *Man and the State*. Indeed, it is a fulfillment of a project initiated by his fellow Frenchman Alexis de Tocqueville, to whom we referred above: "Here is accomplished the great reversal of virtue of which it is no longer the human which takes charge of defending the divine, but the divine which offers itself to defend the human." The overarching achievement concerns an epochal change: "every vestige of the Holy Empire is today liquidated; we have definitively emerged from the sacral age and the baroque age." It is an era that requires of the church only freedom—freedom to preach the truth and act with charity. The church's temporal mission is "reaffirmed under the sign of freedom" with a right to intervene not "*ratione peccati*"[44] to repress evil, but "*ratione boni perficiendi*"—"to quicken and prod and assist from above and without trespassing on the autonomy of the temporal."

The great achievements of Vatican II are best brought to focus in the temporal mission of the laity. Maritain elaborates upon the fundamental distinction of the two ends of human history that he made in *Man and the State*. It involves the differentiation of the temporal and the eternal ends of the human person. And this requires a proper understanding of the meaning of the autonomy of the temporal or secular. For as Maritain has long insisted, "we must distinguish in order to unite." The two ends, and their corresponding two missions, are complementary and interactive.

The very distinction between a "relative ultimate end" and an "absolute ultimate end" does present some initial confusions. In *The Peasant of the Garonne* Maritain draws a distinction between the "natural end" or "relatively final end" and a "supernatural end" which is the "absolutely final end." The kingdom of God is beyond history and requires a radical transfiguration of the natural. The natural end engages man in history and constitutes the progress of the temporal or secular order. The Christian engages this secular end in his "temporal mission" as a Christian. The supernatural end engages the Christian in history but as pointing to another world. This constitutes the proper mission of the church, or the "spiritual mission" of the Christian. Now as we shall see, the two are very much interconnected and bound to each other. But the distinctions must be kept.

What is the specific end of secular progress? Maritain combines ancient and modern philosophy in his description of human purpose in this world. He describes it as a "triple and progressive expansion and conquest of man." The triple end comprises, first, the mastery of nature; this means we can affirm "loftiest ambition of modern science" and exercise control over the physical world and aim at elimination of servitude and subjection to another and the "violence of instrumentality." Maritain also speaks of action toward the goal of eliminating hunger, poverty, war, and injustice. The triple end also includes the development of self-perfecting spiritual activities such as knowledge and art and ethical achievement. Finally, it includes the development of the "manifest potentialities of human nature." It is part and parcel of the ontosophic truth to affirm the goodness of the structures and these ends of temporal society. Christians are called to fully participate in these human purposes and help to bring them to perfection.

Although he mentions Descartes, Maritain's position must be distinguished from the modern attempt of mastery of nature for a number of reasons.[45] To begin with, Maritain sets forth a three-point program for this relatively final end, the natural end or purpose of human history. It is not reducible to mastery alone, but is balanced by moral and cultural achievement. In addition, Maritain says that the goal cannot be attained once and for all, it is an unending path to be approached asymptotically. But more can be said—Maritain reminds us of the fact of death. The aspiration of enduring good is rendered futile by death.[46] Maritain in another context speaks about the natural aspiration for immortality and the transnatural aspiration for complete salvation which cannot be a result of natural development.[47] Finally Maritain points to the mystery of evil: the development of evil alongside that of good, and in the practical order the very real futility of individual moral striving. The Thomistic adage concerning grace perfecting nature takes on an additional Augustinian dimension. Society requires "the stimulus and elevation which Christianity naturally brings to the activities of nature in its own sphere."[48] Maritain chastises the modernists because they neglect the role of the cross and asceticism. They forget that we need the life of grace and prayer to make "natural energies more pure and upright in the very order of nature," that is, nature must be healed by grace. Readers of *Gaudium et Spes* often neglect the striking passages on sin in the middle of its description of the Christian's temporal mission, as we noted above. The temporal mission requires a spiritual mission for the reason of sin. Laymen must receive doctrinal and spiritual formation to be ready to go forth in the temporal mission. But so formed, the Christian laity can enter deeply into the struggles and anguish of the modern world and work for the progress in its own order, fully respecting its autonomy.

Toward Authentic Renewal

At Vatican II the Council Fathers acknowledged an opportune time for renewal. Maritain ratified this view and he characterized our era as one of "immense spiritual ferment" and "religious aspiration" and as an era harboring a "nostalgia for the gospel, a passion for the absolute, a fervent presentiment of the liberty, the breadth and variety of the ways of God, a whole hearted longing for the perfection of charity."[49] Catholics, and indeed all Christians, have been presented with a wonderful opportunity for living lives that "bear witness to the love of Jesus for all men and to the generosity of God's spirit." So what has gone wrong? Why are Catholics in such disarray? Why the quibbling and bitter divisions? Indeed why the "immanent apostasy" and desperate forms of witness among contemporary Catholics who thus seem to save but a "dying Christianity for the modern world"? Why the uncertainty and lack of confidence in the "Catholic moment"?[50]

The deepest source of the crisis is a religious one, a spiritual one. It traces back to a pendulum which has swung from a "masked manicheism" characteristic of the church prior to the council to the post-counciliar mistake of "kneeling before the world." The one called forth the other. Both extremes rest upon a fundamental error concerning the value of the world and temporal affairs. It turns on a "misunderstanding with a bitter fruit" concerning the distinction between the "mystical" and the "ontosophic" meaning of the "world." The mystical truth concerning the world is a practical truth, lived out by the saints. The ontosophic truth concerning the world is a speculative truth, affirmed by both theologians and philosophers. The practical truth lived by the saints is a contempt for the world deriving from their boundless love for God. St. Paul refers to the world as a dung hill in comparison with Christ and the knowledge of God. The world is seen as an obstacle to God insofar as the world is in sin and refuses God. The world hates God; it persecutes Christ and his followers. The saints, overwhelmed by their love of God, struggle against the world, exercise self-denial, and show contempt for the world. This is the mystical truth of contempt for the world. The ontosophic truth, a truth of theology and philosophy, reason and revelation, affirms the goodness of the world. The world has natural structures which are intelligible and natural ends which are good. This is the speculative truth. Grace builds upon and perfects but does not destroy nature. The dangerous misunderstanding lies in making the practical truth a speculative one, or vice versa.

Centuries prior to the council the church came to misunderstand the mystical truth. The "dung hill" was extended to the world itself and "a masked Manicheism was thus superimposed on the Christian faith without ruining it."[51] It was a pastoral failure, not a doctrinal one, by which Manicheeism was "spread inwardly, in the form of purely moralistic prohibitions, injunctions to flight, habits of fear, disciplines of denial in which love had no part, and which led the soul to starvation and sickliness, and to a torturing sense of impotence."[52] The moral took precedent over the theological; flight from sin, precedence over charity. Human initiative, and refusal to sin, obscured the divine initiative of love and grace. In addition to this mistaken contempt for the world, Christians prior to the council were well aware of the growing hostility of modern civilization to Christianity and thus formed a defensive reaction and inferiority complex. Further, there was generally poor doctrinal formation. Thus at the time of the council there was present an "enormous weight of frustration and disillusionment and resentment" which burst out into the open on the occasion of *aggiornamento*, or "updating." The pendulum swung from masked manichesim to frenzied modernism. For the theologians it was to mean a love for the latest trends and a love for the ephemeral. The spiritual teaching affirmed the goodness of the world, but failed to mention the other world, the cross, and the demands of sanctity. The temporal mission of the layman was mistaken for the mission of the church as a whole. Such a position of kneeling before the world amounted to a complete temporalization of Christianity, an absorption of the kingdom of God by the temporal mission of the world. The prayer for the kingdom of God was mistaken for a dream of a "glorious parousia of collective man." This describes the present-day activists well enough—either the liberation theologians or the radical feminists, among others, who demand that the church embrace the latest trends of the day. Of course, for the average churchgoer in the West the crisis persists in many confusions about the great achievements of Vatican II: concerning the role of the laity, who must now assume a position in the sacristy; concerning the affirmation of the world which has come to signify middle-class achievement and consumerism; concerning the ecumenical opening of the council which has come to mean little more than religious or doctrinal indifference and the ascendancy of the affective over cognitive religious education; and the hard-won emphasis upon the freedom and dignity of the human person which has come to be the refusal of strict moral demands in the name of free conscience.

The great vision of Christian renewal of temporal structures, the true activation of the temporal mission of the lay Christian, requires a preparation in the order of philosophy and spirituality. It requires "a great and patient work of revitalizing in the order of intelligence and the order of spirituality."[53] We can but briefly outline the tasks ahead which Maritain calls the "true new fire" of renewal: ecumenical dialogue, the liberation of intelligence, and the sources of spiritual renewal in contemplation and liturgy. In these chapters Maritain illustrates and deepens the positions of *Man and the State*; he shows the inner depth behind the formulae. In *Man and the State* Maritain suggested that different points of view on the church-state are often derived from different understandings of "church." For an unbeliever the church is but a sociological or natural phenomenon; for the believer the church is a society representing a reality of a higher order. Misapprehension is inevitable; but if one wishes to do justice to the issue it is incumbent upon both sides to make the best understanding as the other understands itself. Maritain provides a unique opening to the postconciliar understanding of the church and its self-understanding in a new age for church-state relations.

The claim for a new age for church-state relations begins with an inner renewal, according to Maritain. It shall take a new attitude. The new attitude respects the dignity of the person; the Catholic is called to love the person as a person and not simply as a potential convert to the faith. In addition to the theme of a new attitude toward those of a different faith, Maritain returns to a theme found in *Man and the State*: the possibility of practical cooperation in a divided world.[54] Maritain is still confident about the possibility of practical cooperation in a divided world because of a convergence upon the notion of human rights. He always conceded that such an agreement was a minimum one, open to many ambiguities and ultimate differences. But such an agreement upon a "democratic charter" was necessary for political peace. Yet he is now more insistent that we not be led to an opposite extreme of "ignoring the imprescriptible rights of the speculative order—in other words of truth itself, which is superior to every human interest." As we cooperate more frequently on a practical level, truth will be served only if we are willing to actually "strengthen the edges of opposite convictions which divide us." In other words true ecumenical dialogue is vital to secure peace and the deeper understanding of human rights. Maritain cites a marvelous line from Jean Cocteau concerning dialogue: "We must have a tough mind and a tender heart." To which Cocteau adds "the world is full of dried up hearts and flabby minds." Maritain also elaborates the various new approaches opened by Vatican Council II for Christian approaches to non-Catholics and unbelievers. Direct conversion is no longer the only mode nor the first mode of engagement with men and women of diverse creeds. Of particular note is the importance of the sphere of action, all the works of mercy and the efforts to develop social, economic, and cultural advancement for all people. And yet Maritain is not a utopian in his praise for these efforts. He recognizes the limits of achievement in this area. And most of all he says that the renewal requires contemplative love and prayer.

The work of speculative reason is necessary for the proper understanding of the goodness of nature, the "ontosophic" truth of the world which was lost by many prior to the council and confused with a practical truth after the council. Maritain's philosophical efforts must be traced back to his meta-physical approaches to the world, especially his notion of the intuition of be-ing.[55] Maritain fears that the emphasis upon efficacy and pragmatism has ob-scured the fundamental principles of philosophy. In an age of increasing influence of technology, the love of truth, the superior value of truth will have a liberating effect. Men look for substitutes in myths and fables because science itself is unable to answer the deeper personal questions about man, God, and the world. Science will try to extrapolate from science to create fa-bles and myths to answer these questions. Maritain was critical of Teilhard de Chardin because he viewed his efforts as an extrapolation, a poetic myth of science, covering over the deeper yearning for a true philosophical approach to the big issues. Also he criticizes the forms of contemporary philosophy be-cause they bracket the question of being. As forms of epistemological ideal-ism they trap the thinker within his own mind and never experience the rel-ish of true being.

The most important point has to do with faith and reason. The relation of faith and reason is emblematic of the relation between church and state. The issue of faith and reason brings the issue to a very personal dimension, not only a sociological or political one. And the resolution on the level of the person, the concrete thinker, provides clues to the larger political issue. It is as if Maritain would have us reverse the Socratic ploy to see the soul through the city; on this issue of church and state it may be better to view the city through the soul. Maritain's argument for the cooperation of faith and reason proceeds as follows. There is a distinction between philosophy and theology but not a separation. First, a philosopher is a human being with a set of be-liefs about man, God, and the world. These cannot be "locked up in a strong box." It is natural for these beliefs to influence the philosophy of the concrete person. Reason verges into the domain of faith because it has questions to ask of faith. It is not uncommon for the very spark of philosophy to derive from theological considerations, as for example with the ancient Greeks.[56] It also has a desire to discover the internal order of truth and finds an attraction to the higher domain.[57]

Finally, the very quest for wisdom impels us to seek a higher perspective. For its part faith may seek to enter the domain of reason. It is a superior light which elevates reason in its own order. As Maritain said in *Man and the State*—a superior agent is not shut up within itself; it radiates and stimulates from within the very activity of reason or nature. This issue cannot be under-stood without a proper understanding of nature and grace.[58] Faith can assist reason in being more alert to its own internal limits—such as overcoming al-lurements and irrational dreams of ideology.[59] If the person refuses to allow

faith and reason to speak to each other in his own heart and mind then distortions occur in both domains. From the side of faith it is the distortion of
"fideism" to allow faith to become separated from the intellectual life of the
person. Faith would lie "like a stone at the bottom of a pond, no longer vitally
received by a living being."[60] Skepticism and or indifference is bound to occur, undermining faith from within on a popular level. And as for the intellectuals, pastoral values and efficacy become the supreme rule, not truth itself.
But faith is held as mystery of truth, inviting a humble penetration of the
truth. The dynamic of "pastoral" gives rise to historicism and a constant reinterpretation of faith in light of the times. Vatican Council II called for the
reinterpretation of the signs of the times in light of the enduring truths of faith
and philosophy. The distortion from the side of reason concerns its own self-
discipline and a refusal to generate ideology and myths of reason. Modern intellectuals tend to enclose themselves within a rational self-sufficiency which
did not characterize ancient philosophy with its sense of enduring wonder and
the position of the metaxy between beasts and gods. The ever-recurring temptation of science is the one first initiated so well by Lucretius—the poeticiz-
ing of the mechanisms of the world. Edward Wilson consciously invokes this
same muse.[61] The great questions of meaning about man, God, and the world
must lie beyond the scope of science. But science will make its poetic attempt,
often doing bad theology rather than doing none at all. As Maritain says, the
bad money chases out the good. The great hunger of the soul goes unfed.
What is needed is an attention to the very intrinsic order of human intelligence, not the indiscriminate mixing together. Here again is the very rationale for reason's forays into faith—to better appreciate the internal ordering of
truth and to complete its aspiration for wisdom.

This relationship of faith and reason is emblematic of the relationship between church and state. It is the nodal point for the cooperation for church
and state. The elevating influence of faith must primarily come through the
person, in conscience and mind, not through external law.[62] Indeed it may
well be that the different understandings of church and state relations tracks
the fate of faith and theology in higher education.[63] On the basis of the unity
of the person, and the need for a dynamic unity in the cognitive life of the
person, faith will either be engaged or it will become unhinged. Surely it is not
a good thing for the polity to have a proliferation of cults and enthusiasms
smacking of servitude and irrationality. So too does the state exercise its own
self-discipline by refusing ideologies which divinize itself or that make the
fashions of the time the height of wisdom itself. The distinction between the
things of Caesar and the things of God, state and church, rest upon this proper
and salutary relationship between faith and reason.

The final point from the *Peasant* which develops the argument from the unity of the person sketched out in *Man and the State* concerns the very life of the church itself and the new understanding of the role of the laity, the primary agents and the locus for the cooperation between church and state. Maritain celebrates the achievement of Vatican II in putting forward the mystery of the church as a great theme for its reflections. As he said in *Man and the State*, there is an inevitable misapprehension between the believer and the unbeliever because of their different approaches to the reality and nature of the church. If one wishes to understand the agent as he understands himself, then the document *Lumen gentium* is a very important text for all those who are concerned about the relation between church and state. Maritain briefly points out that the council emphasized the mystery of the church; it is more than a sociological phenomenon or a set of external laws and institutions. Perhaps that is all that the unbeliever can see. But there is in addition a historic reality, a unity of being and life across time. There is memory and voice.

The recent statements by John Paul II make sense only within such a context or frame of understanding. He can apologize for what various personnel of the church have done, all the while maintaining the integrity and holiness of the church.[64] In terms resonating with Solzhenitsyn, Maritain quotes his own mentor Cardinal Journet who said that the line of good and evil, of Christ and Belial, passes through the heart of each believer.[65] The emphasis upon the phrase "People of God" adds the historic dimension of the church, its presence in the world as a pilgrim. And it thus follows the emphasis upon the laity to be sent out into the midst of the world. No longer would the church seek separation from the world but be in the midst of the world in service to the world. The cooperation between church and state is actively sought out by the believer, not in the mode of conversion, but as a witness through the very service to the world. As we saw above, Maritain distinguishes the two missions of the believer—a spiritual mission and a temporal mission. The spiritual mission is the work proper of the church—transforming the world spiritually for the ultimate end. But in addition members of the church have a mission to transform the temporal world with a view to the good of the world itself. Here again we face a potential divide with extremes at both ends. There is a divide between the spiritual and the temporal missions, or vocations, of the lay Christian. The separation between the two is an unnatural gash or cleavage which must be remedied first of all. How is this to be done? Maritain outlines the philosophical basis for this. The two vocations are distinct but not separate. It is the unity of the person which must forge their integration. For the concrete person is not a "laborer of the world with a certain portion of his being, and a member of the Church with another portion: it is a member of the Church who is the laborer of the world, sent to the land of the things which are Caesar's."[66] And the unity of the person is achieved as follows: the object of the work is the temporal vocation; the manner or mode in which the work is done is the spiritual vocation. The object of the work is to do the temporal task well—whatever portion of the secular work for which one has responsibility. The effects of the cooperation are salutary for the body politic. "Such a work needs to be vivified, for without the strengthening of Christ's grace our nature is too weak to carry it out."[67]

It is precisely through religious inspiration that we have some hope for overcoming internal weakness and restraint of evil. Justice without love is inhuman; friendship must add to justice. The polity itself needs the ministrations of charity for which the church is a primary agent. The spirit of the work will reflect the Christian's devotion to God and charity of life. The "radiance of the gospel" will shine through the daily task itself. The grace of religion will penetrate and transform the natural activity itself and perfect it within its own order. Maritain thus comes to apply the basic principles of St. Thomas Aquinas, on nature and grace, to the great issue of the day—the vital cooperation of church and state in the new age of freedom.

Conclusion

Maritain prepared the way for a new approach to church and state relations. In the groundwork he laid in earlier works and in *Man and the State* we find a clear mature formulation of the position. In *The Peasant of the Garonne* we find its final elaboration in light of the definitive achievement of Vatican II: "In truth, every vestige of the Holy Empire is today liquidated; we have definitely emerged from the sacral age and the baroque age. After sixteen centuries which it would be shameful to slander or repudiate, but which have completed their death agony and whose grave defects were incontestable, a new age begins."[68] Maritain has given us a fulfillment of Tocqueville's deepest wish. The lover of liberty and the lover of God are one and the same. And with a further echo of Tocqueville, Maritain believes that the new approach will be advanced not by large mass programs or political deals, but through intermediate groups, which Maritain affectionately calls "Little Flocks." Only in the small flocks can the relentless pressures of technology and "massification" be resisted. In the small associations of men and women devoted to the inner tasks of renewal will the promise of the new age be at last fulfilled. As Maritain was fond of saying, the prospects for a "new Christendom" may not be for tomorrow or the day after tomorrow. But it is a concrete historical ideal worth our devotion. And the life of the spirit and efforts of renewal, exemplified by Maritain and his wife, will be a testimony for centuries to come.

Notes

This chapter extracted from "The Cooperation of Church and State: Maritain's Argument from the Unity of the Person," in *Reassessing the Liberal State: Reading Maritain's Man and the State*, ed. John P Hittinger and Timothy Fuller (Washington, D.C.: Catholic University of America, 2001), 179–201.

1. Jacques Maritain, *Man and the State* (Chicago: The University of Chicago Press, 1951), 160.

2. See Raissa Maritain, *We Have Been Friends Together and Adventures in Grace: The Memoirs of Raissa Maritain*, trans. Julie Kernan (Garden City, N.Y.: Image Books, Doubleday, 1961); and ed. Raissa Maritain, *Leon Bloy, Pilgrim of the Absolute* (New York: Pantheon Books, 1947).

3. Pope John Paul II, *Fides et Ratio: On the Relationship between Faith and Reason* (Boston: Daughters of St. Paul, 1998), 74.

4. See Luigi Sturzo, *Church and State*, trans. Barbara Barclay Carter (Notre Dame, Ind.: University of Notre Dame Press, 1962).

5. See Jacques Maritain, *The Things That Are Not Caesar's*, trans. J. F. Scanlan (London: Sheed and Ward, 1939), and Jacques Maritain, *Integral Humanism*, trans. Joseph W. Evans (Notre Dame, Ind.: University of Notre Dame Press, 1973).

6. Jacques Maritain, *The Peasant of the Garonne: An Old Layman Questions Himself about the Present Time* trans. Michael Cuddihy and Elizabeth Hughes (New York: Holt, Rinehart and Winston, 1968).

7. Maritain, *Man and the State*, 183.

8. Maritain, *Man and the State*, 10.

9. Maritain, *Man and the State*, 186.

10. Maritain, *Man and the State*, 150.

11. "The pagan City, which claimed to be the absolute whole of the human being, absorbed the spiritual in the temporal power and at the same time apotheosised the State. Its ultimate worship of the Emperors was the sure consequence of an infallible internal logic." Maritain, *The Things That Are Not Caesar's*, 1.

12. See Maritain, *Integral Humanism*, 142ff.; see also Jacques Maritain, *On the Philosophy of History* (New York: Charles Scribner's Sons, 1957), 111–14.

13. Maritain, *Man and the State*, 161.

14. Maritain, *Man and the State*, 176.

15. Maritain, *Man and the State*, 176.

16. Maritain, *Man and the State*, 121–22.

17. Maritain, *Man and the State*, 164–65.

18. See the book by Maritain's theological mentor, Charles Cardinal Journet, *The Meaning of Grace*, trans. A. V. Littledale (Princeton, NJ.: Scepter Press, 1996).

19. This notion of the *quid divinum* or the divine something that can be discovered at the heart of all secular work was brought to my attention by Fr. Bob Connor, of the Prelature of Opus Dei; he made reference to an important sermon by Mgr. Escrivá entitled "Passionately Loving the World," in Josemaria Escrivá, *Conversations with Mgr Escrivá De Balaguer* (Dublin: Scepter, 1968). Also see his *Friends of God* (Dublin: Scepter, 1981). An elaboration can be found in Jose Luis Illanes, *On the Theology of Work* (Dublin: Four Courts Press, 1982).

20. Maritain, *Man and the State*, 167–71.

21. Maritain, *Man and the State*, 179.

22. Alexis de Tocqueville, *Democracy in America*, trans. George Lawrence, ed. J. P. Mayer (New York: Harper Collins, 1988), 17.

23. Maritain, *Man and the State*, 187; "Here [Vatican II] is accomplished the great reversal of virtue of which it is no longer the human which take charge of defending the divine, but the divine which offers itself to defend the human." Maritain, *The Peasant of the Garonne*, 4.

24. *Pastoral Constitution on the Church in the Modern World (Gaudium et Spes)* (Boston: Daughters of St. Paul, 1965).

25. *Gaudium et Spes*, #76.

26. *Gaudium et Spes*, #36.

27. *Gaudium et Spes*, #36.

28. "Only God is great. God alone is the beginning and end. God alone is the source of your authority and the foundation of your laws." Paul VI, "To the Guardians of Temporal Power: Message to Heads of State." See *Reassessing the Liberal State: Reading Maritain's Man and the State*, ed. Timothy Fuller and John P. Hittinger. (Washington, D.C. Catholic University of America Press, 2001), 246." See *Gaudium et Spes*, #13: "Often refusing to acknowledge God as his beginning, man has disrupted also his proper relationship to his own ultimate goal as well as his whole relationship toward himself and others and all created things."

29. *Gaudium et Spes*, #76.

30. "To the Guardians of Temporal Power: Message to Heads of State," 246.

31. "To the Guardians of Temporal Power: Message to Heads of State," 246.

32. *Gaudium et Spes*, #2.

33. *Gaudium et Spes*, #10.

34. *Gaudium et Spes*, #10.

35. "Human life, whether individual or collective, shows itself to be a dramatic struggle between good and evil, between light and darkness. Indeed, man finds that by himself he is incapable of battling the assaults of evil successfully, so that everyone feels as though he is bound by chains. But the Lord Himself came to free and strengthen man, renewing him inwardly and casting out that prince of this world (John 12:31) who held him in the bondage of sin. For sin has diminished man, blocking his path to fulfillment." *Gaudium et Spes*, #13.

36. *Gaudium et Spes*, #16.

37. *Gaudium et Spes*, #37

38. *Gaudium et Spes*, #3.

39. *Gaudium et Spes*, #43.

40. "Lumen Gentium," in Austin Flannery, ed. *Vatican Council II: The Conciliar and Postconciliar Documents*, Vol. 1 (Northport, New York: Costello, 1998).

41. *Gaudium et Spes*, #36; on the positive meaning of "secularity" for the laity see Pope John Paul II, *The Lay Members of Christ's Faithful People* (Boston: Daughters of St. Paul, 1988) sections 9, 15, 17.41.

42. He said "*Etiam ut nos hominem, hominem verum, hominem integrum penitus noscamus, Deum ipsam antea cognoscamus necesse est.*" Or "In order to know our humanity, true man, the whole man, it is necessary to know God." Emphasis added. See Maritain's use of this term in Maritain, *The Peasant of the Garonne*, 4.

43. Pope Paul VI also made such attempts on the theological front with his post-conciliar writings, especially see Pope Paul VI, *On the Mystery of Faith* (Boston: Daughters of St. Paul, 1966); Pope Paul VI, *On Saints Peter and Paul* (Boston: Daughters of St. Paul, 1967); Pope Paul VI, *The Credo of the People of God* (Boston: Daughters of St. Paul, 1968). See also Candido Pozo, *The Credo of the People of God: A Theological Commentary*, trans. Mark A. Pilon (Chicago: Franciscan Herald Press, 1980).

44. On the notion of the *ratione peccati*, see Maritain's *The Things That Are Not Caesar's*, 128–30.

45. See Richard Kennington, "Descartes and Mastery of Nature" in *Organism, Medicine and Metaphysics: Essays in Honor of Hans Jonas*, ed. S. F. Spicker (Dordrecht: D. Reidel, 1978), 221–33; compare Jacques Maritain, *Three Reformers: Luther, Descartes, Rousseau* (New York: Charles Scribner's Sons, 1929), and Jacques Maritain, *The Dream of Descartes*, trans. Mabelle L. Andison (London: Editions Poetry London, 1946).

46. Maritain, *The Peasant of the Garonne*, 202–03.

47. "The Immortality of the Soul," in *The Range of Reason* (New York: Charles Scribner's Sons, 1968), 51–65.

48. "The Immortality of the Soul," 42.

49. Maritain, *The Peasant of the Garonne* 5.

50. See Ralph McInerny, *What Went Wrong with Vatican II: The Catholic Crisis Explained* (Manchester, N.H.: Sophia Institute Press, 1998), and Ralph M. Wiltgen, *The Rhine Flows into the Tiber: The Unknown Council* (New York: Hawthorne Books, 1967).

51. Maritain, *The Peasant of the Garonne*, 46.

52. Maritain, *The Peasant of the Garonne*, 48.

53. Maritain, *The Peasant of the Garonne*, 53.

54. Maritain, *Man and the State*, 76–80, 108–14; Maritain, *The Peasant of the Garonne*, 64–70. The original speech which Maritain gave to UNESCO on the topic of practical cooperation and the UN Declaration of Human Rights may be found in Jacques Maritain, *The Range of Reason* (New York: Charles Scribner's Sons, 1968), 180ff.

55. See Maritain, *The Peasant of the Garonne*, 99–101, 132–35; see also John P. Hittinger, "The Intuition of Being: Metaphysics or Poetry?" in *Jacques Maritain: The Man and His Metaphysics*, ed. John F. X. Knasas (Notre Dame, Ind.: American Maritain Association/University of Notre Dame Press, 1988), 71–82. Chapter 12 of this volume.

56. See Josef Pieper, *Leisure: The Basis of Culture*, trans. Gerald Malsbary (South Bend, Ind.: Saint Augustine's Press, 1998), 117–34.

57. See Pope John Paul II, *Fides et Ratio*.

58. See Journet, *The Meaning of Grace*.

59. On the need for theology to prevent overall distortions in education, see John P. Hittinger, "Newman, Theology and Crisis of Liberal Education." *Journal of Interdisciplinary Studies* 11, no. 1/2 (1999): 61–82.

60. Maritain, *The Peasant of the Garonne*, 94; also 144–45.

61. Edward O. Wilson, *Consilience—The Unity of Knowledge* (New York: Alfred A. Knopf, 1998), and Edward O. Wilson, "Resuming the Enlightenment Quest," *The Wilson Quarterly* 22, no. 1 (1998): 16–27.

62. See Tocqueville, *Democracy in America*, "On the use which Americans make of associations in civil life," especially 515.

63. See James Tunstead Burtchaell, "The Decline and Fall of the Christian College." *First Things* (April 1991): 16–30.

64. See "The Church, Holy and Penitent," Maritain, *The Peasant of the Garonne*, 185–89; and for a much greater elaboration, see Jacques Maritain, *On the Church of Christ*, trans. Joseph W. Evans (Notre Dame, Ind.: University of Notre Dame Press, 1973).

65. Maritain, *The Peasant of the Garonne*, 188–89; cf. Alexandr Solzhenitsyn, *The Gulag Archipelago: Two*, trans. Thomas P. Whitney (New York: Harper & Row, 1975), 615; see Jacques Maritain, *On the Philosophy of History*, 128–30.

66. Maritain, *The Peasant of the Garonne*, 208.

67. Maritain, *The Peasant of the Garonne*, 204; see also 226.

68. Maritain, *The Peasant of the Garonne*, 4.

Selected Bibliography of Maritain, Pieper, and Simon

Maritain, Jacques. *Three Reformers: Luther, Descartes, Rousseau*. New York: Scribners, 1929.

———. *Religion and Culture*. Translated by J.F. Scanlan. London: Sheed and Ward, 1931.

———. *Freedom in the Modern World*. Translated by Richard O'Sullivan. New York: Scribners, 1936.

———. *The Things That Are Not Caesar's*. Translated by J. F. Scanlan. London: Sheed and Ward, 1939.

———. *A Preface to Metaphysics: Seven Lectures on Being*. New York: Sheed and Ward, 1939.

———. *Ransoming the Time*. New York: Charles Scribner's Sons, 1941.

———. *Saint Thomas and the Problem of Evil*. Milwaukee: Marquette University Press, 1942.

———. *The Rights of Man and Natural Law*. Translated by Doris C. Anson. New York: Scribners, 1943.

———. *Education at the Crossroads*. New Haven: Yale University Press, 1943.

———. *The Dream of Descartes*. Translated by Mabelle L. Andison. London: Editions Poetry London, 1946.

———. *Christianity and Democracy*. Translated by Doris C. Anson. New York: Scribners, 1950.

———. *Man and the State*. Chicago: University of Chicago Press, 1951.

———. *The Range of Reason*. New York: Charles Scribner's Sons, 1952.

———. *Creative Intuition in Art and Poetry*. New York: Pantheon Books, 1953.

———. *Approaches to God*. Translated by Peter O'Reilly. New York: Harper and Brothers, 1954.

———. *The Situation of Poetry*. Translated by Marshall Suther. New York: Philosophical Library, 1955.

———. *An Essay on Christian Philosophy*. Translated by Edward H. Flannery. New York: Philosophical Library, 1955.

———. *On the Philosophy of History*. New York: Scribners, 1957.

———. "On Some Typcial Aspects of Christian Education." In *The Christian Idea of Education*, edited by Edmund Fuller, 173-98. New Haven: Yale University Press, 1957.

———. *Reflections on America*. New York: Scribners, 1958.

———. *St. Thomas Aquinas*. Translated by Peter O'Reilly. New York: Meridian Books, 1958.

———. *The Sin of the Angel*. Translated by William Rossner. Westminster: Newman Press, 1959.

———. *Scholasticism and Politics*. Translated by Mortimer J. Adler. New York: Image Books, 1960.

———. *The Responsibility of the Artist*. New York: Charles Scribner's Sons, 1960.

———. *On the Use of Philosophy*. New York: Atheneum, 1965.

———. *The Person and the Common Good*. Translated by John J. Fitzgerald. Notre Dame: University of Notre Dame Press, 1966.

———. *God and the Permission of Evil*. Translated by Joseph W. Evans. Milwaukee: Bruce Publishing Co, 1966.

———. *The Peasant of the Garonne: An Old Layman Questions Himself About the Present Time*. Translated by Michael Cuddihy and Elizabeth Hughes. New York: Holt, Rinehart and Winston, 1968.

———. *The Range of Reason*. New York: Scribners, 1968.

———. *On the Church of Christ*. Translated by Joseph W. Evans. Notre Dame: University of Notre Dame Press, 1973.

———. *Integral Humanism*. Translated by Joseph W. Evans. Notre Dame: University of Notre Dame Press, 1973.

———. *Notebooks*. Translated by Joseph W. Evans. Albany, N.Y.: Magi Books, 1984.

———. "The Spiritual Mission of the Laity." *Communio*, (Summer 1987): 193-202.

Maritain, Raissa. *We Have Been Friends Together*. Translated by Julie Kernan. New York: Longman's, Green and Co., 1942.

———. *Adventures in Grace*. Translated by Julie Kernan. New York: Longman's, Green and Co., 1945.

———, ed. *Leon Bloy, Pilgrim of the Absolute*. New York: Pantheon Books, 1947.

———. *We Have Been Friends Together and Adventures in Grace: The Memoirs of Raissa Maritain*. Translated by Julie Kernan. Garden City, N.J.: Image Books, Doubleday, 1961.

Pieper, Josef. *About Love*. Chicago: Franciscan Herald Press, 1972.

———. *An Anthology*. San Francisco: Ignatius Press, 1989.

———. *Belief and Faith*. New York: Pantheon Books, 1963.

———. *A Brief Reader on the Virtues of the Human Heart*. San Francisco: Ignatius Press, 1991.

———. *Enthusiasm and Divine Madness on the Platonic Dialogue Phaedrus*. New York: Harcourt, Brace and World, 1964.

——. *Faith, Hope, and Love*. San Francisco: Ignatius Press, 1986.

——. *The Four Cardinal Virtues*. Notre Dame, Ind.: University of Notre Dame, 1966.

——. *Guide to Thomas Aquinas*. San Francisco: Ignatius Press, 1986.

——. *Happiness and Contemplation*. New York: Pantheon Books, 1958.

——. *The Human Wisdom of St. Thomas*. Translated by Drosten Maclaren. Reprint ed. San Francisco: Ignatius Press, 2002.

——. *In Defense of Philosophy*. San Franciso: Ignatius Press, 1992.

——. *In Tune with the World*. Chicago: Franciscan Herald Press, 1965.

——. *Leisure: The Basis of Culture*. Translated by Gerald Malsbary. South Bend: Saint Augustine's Press, 1998.

——. *Leisure the Basis of Culture*. New York: Pantheon Books, 1964.

——. *Scholasticism: Personalities and Problems of Medieval Philosophy*. New York: Mc-Graw-Hill Book, 1964.

——. *The Silence of St. Thomas*. New York: Pantheon Books, 1957.

Simon, Anthony O., ed. *Acquaintance with the Absolute*. New York: Fordham University Press, 1998.

——, ed. *Philosopher At Work*. New York: Rowman and Littlefield Publishers, 1999.

Simon, Yves R. *Critique of Moral Knowledge*. Translated by Ralph McInerny. New York: Fordham University Press, 2002.

——. *The Definition of Moral Virtue*. Edited by Vukan Kuic. New York: Fordham University Press, 1986.

——. "The Doctrinal Issue between the Church and Democracy." In *The Catholic Church in World Affairs*, edited by Gurian and M. Fitzsimons, 87-114. Notre Dame: University of Notre Dame Press, 1954.

——. *Foresight and Knowledge*. Translated by Ralph Nelson and Anthony O. Simon. New York: Fordham University Press, 1995.

——. *Freedom and Community*. Revised ed. New York: Fordham University Press, 2001.

——. *Freedom of Choice*. New York: Fordham University Press, 1969.

——. *A General Theory of Authority*. Notre Dame, Ind.: University of Notre Dame Press, 1962.

——. *The Great Dialogue of Nature and Space*. Edited by Gerard J. Dalcourt. Albany, N.Y.: Magi Books, 1970.

——. *Introduction to Metaphysics of Knowledge*. Translated by Vukan Kuic and Richard J. Thompson. New York: Fordham University Press, 1990.

——. *Nature and Functions of Authority*. Milwaukee: Marquette University Press, 1940.

——. *Philosophy of Democratic Government*. Chicago: University of Chicago Press, 1951.

——. *Practical Knowledge*. Edited by Robert Mulvaney. New York: Fordham University Press, 1991.

——. *The Road to Vichy: 1918-1938*. Translated by James A. Corbett and George J. McMorrow. New York: Sheed and Ward, 1942.

——. *The Tradition of Natural Law*. New York: Fordham University Press, 1967.

Index

~

About the Author

John P. Hittinger was born outside of Indianapolis, Indiana, at Fort Benjamin Harrison on February 8, 1952, the son of Francis Russell Hittinger and Anne Pollard; his father was a career Marine officer, who was killed in action in the Republic of South Vietnam in 1968. John attended Bishop Ireton High School in Alexandria, Virginia, graduating in 1970. He went to the University of Notre Dame; majoring in philosophy he graduated *cum laude* in May 1974. He attended the Catholic University of America graduate program in philosophy from 1974–1976; he worked as a managing editor of the *Review of Metaphysics*; completed a Master's thesis on "Reason and Intellect in Two Texts of Thomas Aquinas." In 1976 he enrolled at the University of Dallas Graduate School and studied philosophy and politics. In 1977 he returned to the Catholic University to finish course work for a Ph.D. He completed a dissertation on "Natural Law in Locke's *Essay Concerning Human Understanding*," in 1986. In 1978 he accepted a faculty position at Benedictine College in Atchison, Kansas. In 1985 he accepted a position at the College of St. Francis in Joliet, Illinois; he served as chairman of the philosophy and theology department from 1987–1991. In 1994 John accepted a position as the first civilian professor in the philosophy department at the United States Air Force Academy. He held rank of full professor and was awarded civilian of the year honor for 1996–1997. In the spring of 2001, John was a sabbatical fellow at the Centre for Philosophy and Public Affairs at St. Andrews University, Scotland, where he worked on a book on the morality of warfare; he presented papers on the philosophy of Maritain in Dublin and Glasgow. In July 2001 he accepted the position of Academic Dean/Provost at St. Mary's College of Ave Maria University in Orchard Lake, Michigan. He is working with the faculty and staff to develop a new Catholic integrated core curriculum and to open a semester abroad program in Krakow, Poland. John has published articles and presented papers on a variety of topics including John Locke, Jacques Maritain, military ethics, liberal education, political philosophy, and the thought of John Paul II. The author has edited two collections of essays: *Liberalism at the Crossroads: An Introduction to Contemporary Liberal Theory and its Critics*, ed. John P. Hittinger and Christopher Wolfe (Lanham, Md: Rowman & Littlefield, 1994); *Reassessing the Liberal State: Reading Maritain's Man and the State*, ed. Timothy Fuller and John P. Hittinger (Washington, D.C.: Catholic University of America Press, 2001). He has two courses on line, Modern Philosophy and Political Philosophy, with the International Catholic University website at http://icu.catholicity.com/. He has been active in the American Maritain Association, the American Catholic Philosophical Association, the Joint Services Conference on Professional Ethics, and the AAUP. John is married to Molly Mulqueen of Council Bluffs, Iowa; he is the father of four children—Jack (1986), Ellie (1988), James (1990), and Joseph (1994).